**FINANCIAL INSTITUTIONS AND SERVICES SERIES**

# LIQUIDITY, INTEREST RATES AND BANKING

# FINANCIAL INSTITUTIONS AND SERVICES SERIES

**Stock Exchanges, IPO's and Mutual funds**
*E. Klein (Editor)*
2004 ISBN: 1-59454-173-6

**Global Banking Issues**
*E. Klein (Editor)*
2005 ISBN: 1-59454-172-8

**Financial Institutions and Development**
*E. Klein (Editor)*
2005 ISBN: 1-59454-177-9

**Capital Formation, Governance and Banking**
*E. Klein (Editor)*
2005 ISBN: 1-59454-191-4

**U. S. Coins: The Price of a Penny**
*Walter M. Carvalho (Editor)*
2009 ISBN: : 978-1-60692-939-1

**Hedge Funds: Regulation and Nonregulation**
*Yeram E. Torrey (Editor)*
2009. ISBN: 978-1-60692-041-1

**Reforming Risk in Financial Markets**
*Melvin R. Turley (Editor)*
2009 ISBN: 978-1-60692-445-7

**Information Sellers and Resellers**
*Shane C. Leger (Editor)*
2009. ISBN: 978-1-60692-228-6

**Econometric Modeling of Value-at-Risk**
*Timotheos Angelidis and Stavros Degiannakis*
2009. ISBN: 978-1-60741-040-9

**Liquidity, Interest Rates and Banking**
*Jeffrey Morrey and Alexander Guyton (Editor)*
2009. ISBN: 978-1-60692-775-5

FINANCIAL INSTITUTIONS AND SERVICES SERIES

# LIQUIDITY, INTEREST RATES AND BANKING

JEFFREY MORREY
AND
ALEXANDER GUYTON
EDITORS

Nova Science Publishers, Inc.
*New York*

Copyright © 2009 by Nova Science Publishers, Inc.

**All rights reserved.** No part of this book may be reproduced, stored in a retrieval system or transmitted in any form or by any means: electronic, electrostatic, magnetic, tape, mechanical photocopying, recording or otherwise without the written permission of the Publisher.

For permission to use material from this book please contact us:
Telephone 631-231-7269; Fax 631-231-8175
Web Site: http://www.novapublishers.com

### NOTICE TO THE READER

The Publisher has taken reasonable care in the preparation of this book, but makes no expressed or implied warranty of any kind and assumes no responsibility for any errors or omissions. No liability is assumed for incidental or consequential damages in connection with or arising out of information contained in this book. The Publisher shall not be liable for any special, consequential, or exemplary damages resulting, in whole or in part, from the readers' use of, or reliance upon, this material. Any parts of this book based on government reports are so indicated and copyright is claimed for those parts to the extent applicable to compilations of such works.

Independent verification should be sought for any data, advice or recommendations contained in this book. In addition, no responsibility is assumed by the publisher for any injury and/or damage to persons or property arising from any methods, products, instructions, ideas or otherwise contained in this publication.

This publication is designed to provide accurate and authoritative information with regard to the subject matter covered herein. It is sold with the clear understanding that the Publisher is not engaged in rendering legal or any other professional services. If legal or any other expert assistance is required, the services of a competent person should be sought. FROM A DECLARATION OF PARTICIPANTS JOINTLY ADOPTED BY A COMMITTEE OF THE AMERICAN BAR ASSOCIATION AND A COMMITTEE OF PUBLISHERS.

**LIBRARY OF CONGRESS CATALOGING-IN-PUBLICATION DATA**
*Available upon request.*

ISBN 978-1-60692-775-5

Published by Nova Science Publishers, Inc. ✦ New York

# CONTENTS

| | | |
|---|---|---|
| **Preface** | | vii |
| **Research and Review Studies** | | 1 |
| **Chapter 1** | The Liquidity Effect: A Survey of the Literature<br>*Mark E. Wohar* | 3 |
| **Chapter 2** | The Ability of the Term Spread to Predict Output Growth, Recessions, and Inflation: A Survey<br>*Mark E. Wohar* | 35 |
| **Chapter 3** | A Latent Variable Approach to Estimating Time-Varying Scale Efficiencies in US Commercial Banking<br>*Dogan Tirtiroglu, Kenneth Daniels and Ercan Tirtiroglu* | 57 |
| **Chapter 4** | Long-Term Real Interest Rates: An Empirical Analysis<br>*Khurshid M. Kiani* | 77 |
| **Chapter 5** | Interest Rate Movements in the Life Insurance Fair Valuation Context<br>*Rosa Cocozza, Emilia Di Lorenzo, Albina Orlando and Marilena Sibillo* | 95 |
| **Chapter 6** | Futures Market Liquidity under Floor and Electronic Trading<br>*Owain ap Gwilym, Ian McManus and Stephen Thomas* | 111 |
| **Chapter 7** | An Analysis of Liquidity across Markets: Execution Costs on the NYSE versus Electronic Markets<br>*Michael A. Goldstein, Gang Hu and J. Ginger Meng* | 139 |
| **Chapter 8** | Payment Systems and Liquidity<br>*Francisco J. Callado Muñoz and Natalia Utrero González* | 169 |
| **Chapter 9** | Optimal Planning, Scheduling and Budgeting with Enterprise-Wide Integration Preserving Liquidity<br>*Mariana Badell* | 189 |

| | | |
|---|---|---|
| **Chapter 10** | Liquidity, Futures Price Dynamics, and Risk Management<br>*Kit Pong Wong* | **213** |
| **Short Communication** | | **233** |
| | Semiparametric Estimation of the Fractional Differencing<br>Parameter in the US Interest Rate<br>*Luis A. Gil-Alana* | **235** |
| **Index** | | **249** |

# PREFACE

Liquidity refers to the degree to which an asset or security can be bought or sold in the market without affecting the asset's price. This book provides important evidence on the changes in market liquidity following the transition to electronic trading, and highlights quite different evidence from that presented in previous studies. Liquidity is also examined across different types of markets by using execution costs as a proxy for liquidity. The links between the concept of liquidity and the role of payment systems in a globalized financial system is investigated as well. Furthermore, a survey of both the theoretical and empirical literature related to the liquidity effect as well as a survey on the ability of the term spread to predict changes in economic activity is examined. The behaviour of long-term interest rates using time-series models is looked as well. Finally, the financial risk in life annuity and pension annuity as influenced by interest rate movements is discussed.

The short-run response of interest rates to changes in the nominal money supply has important implication for macroeconomic theory and policy. The conventional view is that positive money supply shocks, ceteris paribus, have a temporary but persistent negative effects on nominal and real interest rates as economic agents attempt to get rid of money balances through the purchase of bonds. The more inelastic is money demand, the larger is the effect. This "liquidity effect" view is the issue of this paper. Chapter 1 surveys both the theoretical and empirical literature related to the liquidity effect. The liquidity effect is inconsistent with many real business cycle models, which allow money shocks to have a positive effect only on nominal interest rates through the effect of inflationary expectations (the "fisher effect"). If the liquidity effect is found to be empirically relevant, theoretical models of the business cycle must account for this fact (e.g. Lucas 1990; Christiano 1991; Fuerst 1992; and Christiano and Eichenbaum 1992a,b). Leeper (1992) notes that the existence of a liquidity effect can have important consequences for the conduct of monetary policy. The empirical evidence of a liquidity effect is mixed. The pioneering studies of Cagan and Gandofi (1969), Gibson (1970b), Cagan (1972), and Cochrane (1989) support the existence of a liquidity effect. Mishkin (1982), Melvin (1983), Reichenstein (1987), Leeper and Gordon (1992), Pagan and Robertson (1995,1998) and Thornton (2001a,b) fail to find a negative relationship between some measure of money and an interest rate. or find that the effect is not robust across sub-periods. This failure to find evidence of a liquidity effect has been called the "liquidity puzzle". Increases in money supply that leads to an increase in interest rates (a liquidity Puzzle) has been surveyed by Reichenstein (1987) and was re-documented by Leeper and Gordon (1992). Christiano (1991), Christiano and Eichenbaum (1992b), Gali

(1992), Strongin (1995), Gordon and Leeper (1994), Strongin (1995), Lastrapes and Selgin (1995), Christiano, Eichenbaum and Evans (1996a,b), Leeper, Sims and Zha (1996), Hamilton (1997), Bernanke and Mihov (1998a, 1998b), all find a liquidity effect with a number of authors arguing that the liquidity puzzle is the result of problems with econometric identification.

Chapter 2 surveys the literature on the ability of the term spread (i.e. the long-term interest rate minus the short-term interest rate) to predict changes in economic activity. Some studies employ simple regression analysis to forecast changes in output, or dichotomous-choice models to forecast recessions. Other studies use time-varying parameter models, such as Markov Switching models and Smooth Transition Autoregression (STAR) models, to account for structural changes. Studies find that the informational content of the term spread has varied over time, and many conclude that the usefulness of the spread for forecasting changes in economic activity has diminished in recent years. However, most studies using data for the United States and the Euro area find that the term spread predicts output growth up to one year in the future.

Chapter 3 suggests that an estimation of a cost, production or profit function and the resulting performance measures, such as scale efficiency, scale or scope economies, should reflect the dynamic changes happening in the marketplace. Most of these dynamic changes occur latently, making a latent variable approach, as embodied in the Kalman filter, desirable. We implement the proposed latent variable approach by applying it to a cost function and estimating dynamically time-varying scale efficiencies (S-EFF) for the U.S. commercial banking sector for 1934-1991.Using the Federal Deposit Insurance Corporation=s annual aggregated data, we report 1) that S-EFFs varied over time, 2) that the S-EFFs have fluctuated around 80%, and 3) that S-EFFs exhibited high volatility during 1934-1950, slowly increased between 1951-1971 and declined between 1972-1989, implying that commercial banks= substantial investment in the financial systems technologies and production innovations since the 1970s, along with regulatory changes in the U.S., did not lower their average costs, but increased them.

Using data on various United States (US) macroeconomic time series with the models that encompass autoregressive conditional heteroskedasticity and other characteristics dictated by all the data series employed, the present research explores the behavior of the long-term interest rates because of the repeated episodes of large budget deficits in the US economy. The full-sample data for each of the series is split into two sub-sample periods to study the impact of the large budget deficits on long term interest rates within each of these sub-sample periods with reference to the full-sample period for all the series. Additionally, Chapter 4 also investigates if the Fisher hypothesis is in place in each of sample period for all the series studied.

The results show that the repeated episodes of the budget deficits have profound impacts on the long-term interest rates and that the high interest rates are linked to the periods of time wherein large budget deficits were experienced in the economy. Further, the results also reveal that a semi-strong form of Fisher hypotheses is in place when considering cyclically adjusted measure of budget deficits in the models for forecasting long-term interest rates.

The financial risk factor takes up a primary role in the life insurance liability valuations, particularly when referred to life annuity and pension annuity schemes. In this framework a wide literature explains how strong is the influence of the risk connected with the interest rate movements in the life annuity risk mapping, especially if set in the fair value context, as the guidelines given by the international boards engaged in life insurance issues clearly indicate.

The fair behaviour of the discounting process is usually described using a term structure model based on arbitrage assumptions. Chapter 5 focuses on the financial variable for the provision evaluation both in a deterministic and a stochastic perspective. The evaluation risk is approached in a market value assessment with the aim of measuring the interest rate impact on the liability fair value; the study is made through the sensitivity analysis of the net value of the intermediation portfolio to a modification of the interest rate process parameters.

Numerical implementations are illustrated with graphs and tables in life annuity contract cases.

Chapter 6 analyses the impact on liquidity of a transition from open outcry to a fully electronic trading system in the U.K. futures market. The study makes a unique contribution in comparing microstructural characteristics of different trading systems. Particular focus is placed on price clustering and its relationships with bid-ask spreads and trade sizes. Further investigations emphasize the changing relationship between bid-ask spreads, volume and volatility following automation.

Although price clustering is not materially affected by the transition to electronic trading, there is a greatly increased concentration of large trades at more popular prices. Under electronic trading, smaller trades tend to be associated with narrower bid-ask spreads. This is consistent with the anonymous nature of electronic trading and the associated increased problems of asymmetric information and adverse selection compared to floor trading. This appears to offer informed traders a further incentive to conceal their activities by splitting orders into smaller components.

Following automation, there is a modest increase in mean daily volume, while there is a substantial reduction in mean trade size as reduced-depth orders become trades. Consistent with this, the mean daily number of transactions and quotations increases substantially. Bid-ask spreads widen significantly after automation, but this is largely accounted for by the finding that spreads under electronic systems demonstrate an increased sensitivity to price volatility. This effect is accentuated by increased volatility after automation. Cost savings arising from increased operational efficiency of the electronic trading system will be partly offset by this effect.

Overall, the chapter provides important evidence on the changes in market liquidity following the transition to electronic trading, and highlights quite different evidence from that presented in previous studies in this vein.

In Chapter 7 we examine liquidity across different types of markets by using execution costs as a proxy for liquidity. We conduct a thorough analysis of execution costs on the NYSE versus a variety of electronic NASD market centers which also trade NYSE-listed stocks ("Electronic Markets"). We adopt a variety of techniques attempting to correct for the selection bias problem. Unlike current literature, we find that the Electronic Markets offer lower execution costs even after controlling for selection biases. In addition to controlling for selection biases at the sample average level of order difficulty, we also carry out our analysis at different levels of order difficulty, measured by a vector of control variables. Our results are robust under different model specifications. Finally, our what-if analysis shows that the Electronic Markets' (*the NYSE's*) orders would have been worse (*better*) off, had they been executed by the NYSE (*Electronic Markets*). Overall, our results highlight the superiority of the Electronic Markets' liquidity and execution quality.

The purpose of Chapter 8 is to investigate the links between the concept of liquidity and the role of payment systems in a globalized financial system. The actual characteristics of payment systems' design are analyzed, underlining their features and consequences for market and system liquidity. Then, literature on payment systems is reviewed stressing and deepening the understanding of liquidity in this context. Research results are critically analyzed in terms of their relevance for the study of liquidity in payment systems, and some lines of future work are proposed.

In industry the concept behind progress in enterprise systems is the optimization of financial decisions considering the enterprise functionality integration as a cohesive entity including supply chain management and corporate financial management. Acquiescent that every supply chain has a value added chain in parallel (Shapiro 2001), then a value added chain can be seen as the value view of the supply chain. In Chapter 9 we analyze enterprise logics, the value added chain, problems and efforts to improve performance preserving liquidity throughout several modelling / simulation frameworks capable to uphold – with flexibility, simplicity and friendly approach – enterprise-wide financial cross-functional co-ordination links with optimal cash flow management and liquidity control. The results obtainable could reach the optimality of financial and production operations besides the optimal plan, budget and decision making. Integrated solutions models also permit fixed asset investment analysis in an altogether scenario of management. Here we show how different are the investment solutions when transactional objective functions are compared with others that cover the whole functionality as maximum corporate value. In industry the concept behind progress in enterprise systems is the optimization of financial decisions considering the enterprise functionality integration as a cohesive entity (Reklaitis 2005) including supply chain management (Varma et al. 2007) and corporate financial management (Badell et al. 2004). Acquiescent that every supply chain has a value added chain in parallel (Shapiro 2001), then a value added chain can be seen as the value view of the supply chain. Here we analyze enterprise logics, problems and efforts to improve performance preserving liquidity throughout several modeling/simulation frameworks capable to uphold – with flexibility, simplicity and friendly approach – enterprise-wide financial cross-functional co-ordination links with optimal cash flow management and liquidity control. The results obtainable could reach the optimality of financial and production operations besides the optimal plan, budget and decision making. Integrated solutions models also permit fixed asset investment analysis in an altogether scenario of management. Here we show how different are the investment solutions when transactional objective functions are compared with others that cover the whole functionality as maximum corporate value.

Chapter 10 examines the optimal design of a futures hedge program by a competitive firm under output price uncertainty. Due to a capital constraint and the markingto- market procedure of futures contracts, the firm faces endogenous liquidity risk. If the futures prices are sufficiently positively correlated, we show that the capital constraint is non-binding in that the optimal amount of capital earmarked to the futures hedge program is less than the firm's capital endowment. Otherwise, we show that the capital constraint becomes binding in that the firm optimally puts aside all of its capital stock for the futures hedge program. In the case of non-binding capital constraint, we show that the firm's optimal futures position is likely to be an over-hedge for reasonable preferences. In the case of binding capital constraint, the firm's optimal futures position is an under-hedge or an over-hedge, depending on whether the autocorrelation coefficient of the futures price dynamics is below or above a critical positive value, respectively.

The monthly structure of the US interest rate (Federal Funds) is examined in the Short Communication, by means of fractionally integrated techniques. Using several semiparametric methods, we show that the order of integration of the series is smaller than one but close to it, implying that it is nonstationary but with a mean reverting behaviour.

# RESEARCH AND REVIEW STUDIES

In: Liquidity, Interest Rates and Banking
Editors: J. Morrey and A. Guyton, pp. 3-33
ISBN: 978-1-60692-775-5
© 2009 Nova Science Publishers, Inc.

*Chapter 1*

# THE LIQUIDITY EFFECT: A SURVEY OF THE LITERATURE

### *Mark E. Wohar*[*]

Department of Economics, University of Nebraska at Omaha, RH-512K, Omaha, NE, USA

## Abstract

The short-run response of interest rates to changes in the nominal money supply has important implication for macroeconomic theory and policy. The conventional view is that positive money supply shocks, ceteris paribus, have a temporary but persistent negative effects on nominal and real interest rates as economic agents attempt to get rid of money balances through the purchase of bonds. The more inelastic is money demand, the larger is the effect. This "liquidity effect" view is the issue of this paper. This paper surveys both the theoretical and empirical literature related to the liquidity effect. The liquidity effect is inconsistent with many real business cycle models, which allow money shocks to have a positive effect only on nominal interest rates through the effect of inflationary expectations (the "fisher effect"). If the liquidity effect is found to be empirically relevant, theoretical models of the business cycle must account for this fact (e.g. Lucas 1990; Christiano 1991; Fuerst 1992; and Christiano and Eichenbaum 1992a,b). Leeper (1992) notes that the existence of a liquidity effect can have important consequences for the conduct of monetary policy. The empirical evidence of a liquidity effect is mixed. The pioneering studies of Cagan and Gandofi (1969), Gibson (1970b), Cagan (1972), and Cochrane (1989) support the existence of a liquidity effect. Mishkin (1982), Melvin (1983), Reichenstein (1987), Leeper and Gordon (1992), Pagan and Robertson (1995,1998) and Thornton (2001a,b) fail to find a negative relationship between some measure of money and an interest rate. or find that the effect is not robust across sub-periods. This failure to find evidence of a liquidity effect has been called the "liquidity puzzle". Increases in money supply that leads to an increase in interest rates (a liquidity Puzzle) has been surveyed by Reichenstein (1987) and was re-documented by Leeper and Gordon (1992). Christiano (1991), Christiano and Eichenbaum (1992b), Gali (1992), Strongin (1995), Gordon and Leeper (1994), Strongin (1995), Lastrapes and Selgin (1995), Christiano, Eichenbaum and Evans (1996a,b), Leeper, Sims and Zha (1996), Hamilton (1997), Bernanke and Mihov (1998a, 1998b), all find a liquidity effect with a number of authors arguing that the liquidity puzzle is the result of problems with econometric identification.

---

[*] E-mail address: mwohar@unomaha.edu. Phone: 402-554-3712, Fax: 402-554-2853. (Corresponding author.)

# 1. Introduction

The short-run response of interest rates to changes in the nominal money supply has important implication for macroeconomic theory and policy. The conventional view is that positive money supply shocks, ceteris paribus, have a temporary but persistent negative effects on nominal and real interest rates as economic agents attempt to get rid of money balances through the purchase of bonds. The more inelastic is money demand, the larger is the effect. Each morning at the trading desk at the Federal Reserve Bank of New York (Desk) open market operations are conducted to adjust the supply of reserves in the banking system in order to achieve the target Federal Funds Rate set by the Federal Open Market Committee (FOMC). This manipulation of reserves to affect the federal funds rate presupposes the existence of a liquidity effect. This "liquidity effect" view is the issue of this paper. Christiano (1996, p. 3) defines the liquidity effect as "[a]n exogenous, persistent, upward shock in the growth rate of the monetary base engineered by the central bank and not associated with any current or prospective adjustment in distortionary taxes, drives the nominal interest rate down for a significant period of time." This paper surveys both the theoretical and empirical literature related to the liquidity effect. The liquidity effect is inconsistent with many real business cycle models, which allow money shocks to have a positive effect only on nominal interest rates through the effect of inflationary expectations (the "fisher effect"). If the liquidity effect is found to be empirically relevant, theoretical models of the business cycle must account for this fact (e.g. Lucas 1990; Christiano 1991; Fuerst 1992; and Christiano and Eichenbaum 1992a,b). Leeper (1992) notes that the existence of a liquidity effect can have important consequences for the conduct of monetary policy. Limited participation models attracted attention because they replicate the effects of monetary policy on interest rates. Examples include Lucas (1990), Fuerst (1992), and Christiano and Eichenbaum (1992a, 1995).

Although the relation between interest rates and money supply was known for a long time, the first person to use the term liquidity effect was Milton Friedman (1968,1969). Friedman provided a very simple argument to justify the liquidity effect. He noted that when individuals believe that they are going to hold excess money they purchase bonds in an attempt to get rid of excess money balances, which increase bond prices and decrease real and nominal interest rates.

Section 2 of the paper will discuss briefly some of the theoretical literature related to the liquidity effect as a lead into the empirical literature. Section 3 will discuss the extant literature that examines the empirical aspects of the liquidity effect. Section 4 provides a short discussion of the history of Federal Reserve Operating procedures. Section 5 concludes the paper.

# 2. Theoretical Papers

From a theoretical perspective, models that attempt to explain the liquidity effect vary between two polar cases. At one pole are studies of the behavior of money markets focusing on the micro-structure and on interbank relationships (Ho and Saunders 1985; Kopecky and Tucker 1993; Hamilton 1996; and Furfine 2000). At the opposite pole there are the textbook monetary theory models of money markets (Campbell 1987; Coleman, Gilles, Labadie 1996) who have sidestepped the analysis of interbank relationships, the microeconomics of bank's demand for money, and the institutional details that constrain daily Fed operations and banks' liquidity management. Mishkin (1982), Melvin (1983), Reichenstein (1987), Leeper and Gordon (1992), Pagan and Robertson (1995), and Thornton (2001a,b) fail to find any evidence of a liquidity effect--the absence of the negative relationship between monetary base growth (hereafter simply money growth) and nominal interest rates that characterized earlier empirical investigations of the liquidity effect.. About this same time, macroeconomic theory was becoming enamored with dynamic general equilibrium models introduced by Kydland and Prescott (1982) and Long and Plosser (1983). The first of these real business cycle (RBC) models were limited to real economies and did not incorporate money. When money was introduced into the RBC models it was introduced simply by imposing cash-in-advance constraints on agents or by incorporating a transactions demand for money. A generic implication of these models is that, if money growth displays positive persistence then unanticipated shocks to money growth causes interest rates to rise not fall. The reason for this is that in these models, money shocks affect interest rates exclusively through an anticipated inflation effect. This means that in these models money is superneutral in the short run as well as the long run (Cooley and Hansen (1989) and King, et al. (1988)). Superneutrality implies that money growth affects inflation in the long-run and has no affect on the real interest rate. The liquidity effect is inconsistent with many real business cycle models, which allow money shocks to have a positive effect only on nominal interest rates through the effect of inflationary expectations (the "fisher effect"). If the liquidity effect is found to be empirically relevant, theoretical models of the business cycle must account for this fact (Lucas 1990; Christiano 1991; Fuerst 1992; and Christiano and Eichenbaum 1992a,b). Leeper (1992) notes that the existence of a liquidity effect can have important consequences for the conduct of monetary policy. Lucas (1990) and Fuerst (1992) developed general equilibrium models in which purely transitory liquidity effects arise. It wasn't until Fuerst (1992) that a computable dynamic general equilibrium model yielded the negative short-run relationship between money growth and interest rates implied by the liquidity effect. The question then arose, if there is little empirical evidence in favor of a liquidity effect, should macroeconomists build models that generate a liquidity effect? The general equilibrium models of the type developed by Fuerst (1992) could not rationalize persistent liquidity effects. Christiano and Eichenbaum (1992a,b) discusses one way to obtain persistent liquidity effects. However, numerous authors have documented that such models cannot generate liquidity effects ( Christiano, et al. 1997; Kimball, 1995; King and Watson, 1996; and Bernanke and Mihov, 1998a,1998b). Sticky-price monetary models possess a number of characteristics that make them incapable of generating a liquidity effect. The persistence of the money growth process and the sluggish price adjustment process together imply that an expansionary money shock will yield an increase in expected inflation. In addition, the response of real factor prices ( the real rental price of capital) induces an increase in the real interest rate. Both of these effects put upward pressure on the nominal interest rate after the money shock.

Edge (2007) develops a sticky-price monetary business cycle model that is capable of generating a liquidity effect of an empirically plausible duration and magnitude. Models in which nominal shocks have real effects on the economy through sticky prices and/or sticky wages currently is the standard framework for analyzing issues relating to monetary policy. Edge (2007) relaxes a number of assumptions made in a standard sticky-price monetary business cycle model so as to produce a liquidity effect. He allows capital projects time to plan and to build. He allows consumption to be habit persistent. These adjustments to the model's real side allow it to generate a decline in the real interest rate following an expansionary monetary shock that is greater than the expected inflation that also results from the shock, thereby yielding a liquidity effect.

## 3. Empirical Papers

The empirical evidence of a liquidity effect is mixed. The pioneering studies of Cagan and Gandolfi (1969), Gibson (1970), Cagan (1972), and Cochrane (1989) support the existence of a liquidity effect. Mishkin (1982), Melvin (1983), Reichenstein (1987), Leeper and Gordon (1992), Pagan and Robertson (1995,1998), and Thornton (2001a,b) fail to find a negative relationship between some measure of money and an interest rate. or find that the effect is not robust across sub-periods. This failure to find evidence of a liquidity effect has been called the "liquidity puzzle" The above studies employed single equation econometric estimation techniques.

### 3a. Single Equation Studies

The relationship between money supply and the interest rate is straight forward in theory but has some puzzling empirical findings. The extant literature focused on estimating the strength and persistence of the decline in the interest rate in response to the growth in the money supply. The method of estimating the responsiveness interest rates to changes in money stock used by Cagan and Gandolfi (1969), Cagan (1972) and Melvin (1983) is to regress the change in the nominal interest rate on a distributed lag of unanticipated changes in current and past nominal money stock. Cagan and Gandolfi (1969), and Melvin (1983) use changes in the growth rate of money to proxy unanticipated changes in the money supply. Cagan and Gandolfi (1969) found that the interest rate declines for six months following an increase in money growth and then begins to increase. Gibson (1970b) and Stokes and Neuburger (1979) regressed the level of interest rates against the level of the money stock. They found very similar results to Cagan and Gandolfi (1969). Cagan and Gandolfi (1969) finds that a 1% increase in the growth rate of M2 led to a maximum decline in the commercial paper rate of 2.6% when considering the period 1910-1965. Gibson (1970b) estimates a number of different regressions. He regresses interest rates on past levels of money stock. He estimates money stock on past levels of interest rates. He estimates changes in money stock on changes in interest rates. He estimates changes in interest rates on changes in money stock. His estimates show that a change in the money stock produces an immediate negative liquidity effect on interest rates but also produces later a positive effect that later offsets the initial negative effect. He finds that liquidity effects are fully offset by the end of the third month following the month in which M1 is changed and by the end of the fifth month after M2 is changed. It should be noted that the estimation results of Cagan and Gandolfi (1969) and Gibson (1970b) have $R^2$ that are extremely low (below 0.20). Such a poor fit to their equations makes their conclusions suspect.

Melvin (1983) discusses a vanishing liquidity effect and shows that the liquidity effect disappears within a month after the increase in money growth rate in the 1970s due to a dominant anticipated inflation effect. Melvin (1983) regresses first differences of the commercial paper rate on first differences of M2 over the period 1951:01 to 1979:12 and a number of different sub-periods. They find evidence of a pattern of falling interest rates following an increase in money growth followed later by an increase in interest rates. They find interest rates fall for two to five months before starting to rise and would remain below the initial rate for a period of six to twelve months. Their sub-period analysis indicates that the liquidity effect of money on interest rates has become much shorter lived in recent years. Similar to earlier studies, the regressions estimated in their paper have very low $R^2$, in the range of 0.1 to .0.2. When Melvin (1983) focuses on the sub-period 1973:01-1979:12 they find that following an increase in the growth rate of money supply would be offset within a month. In terms of policy implications, the earlier research indicated that the Federal Reserve could induce a decline in interest rates for two or three quarters by increasing the growth rate of the money supply. The results of Melvin (1983) indicate that the short decline in interest rates is not worth the inflationary consequences that accompany higher money growth.

An alternative second methodology, employed by Mishkin (1982), has its roots in the rational expectation/efficient markets literature. This research methodology measures the relationship between unanticipated changes in money (and other demand for money factors) and unanticipated changes in interest rates using autoregressive and multivariate models. Mishkin (1982) estimated the magnitude of the liquidity effect from the structural restriction that only unanticipated money growth can cause a liquidity effect. One of the estimating equations of Mishkin (1982) changes in interest rates regressed on unexpected changes in money supply, unexpected changes in output, and unexpected changes in inflation. Mishkin (1982) finds no evidence for the period 1959:01-1979:04 that unanticipated increases in the quantity of money are associated with unanticipated decreases in short-term or long-term interest rates. In fact he finds that an unanticipated increase in money is associated with an unanticipated increase in short-term rates within the quarter.

All of the above mentioned studies were conducted on data prior to 1979, and thus may suffer from simultaneous-equation bias because the Federal Reserve smoothed interest rate fluctuations. Noting this, Cochrane (1989) concentrated his work on the nonborrowed reserve targeting period October 1979-November 1982, when it is likely there is less feedback from interest rates to money growth in the short-run spectral window he employs. Cochrane (1989) uses a spectral band pass filter technique to re-establish the liquidity effect during the nonborrowed reserve targeting period 1979-1982. He finds evidence of a negative short-run correlation between money and interest rates during this period. Higher money growth was associated with lower interest rates for up to a year. He concludes that the liquidity effect dominates the anticipated inflation effect. He finds that inflation follows money growth with a long lag. He also finds that money growth changes were largely unanticipated. He finds that money growth was a poor predictor of future money growth and that real interest rates did not vary in response to money growth changes. The reduced form negative correlation between money growth and interest rates documented by Cochrane (1989) suggests that there is a liquidity effect, but it does not quantitatively answer the structural question of how much and for how long do interest rates decline when money growth increase?

## 3b. Vector Autoregression Studies

The studies prior to Christiano and Eichenbaum (1992b) were single equation estimation methods. After Christiano and Eichenbaum (1992b) studies began to employ Vector Autoregressions (VAR). Empirical studies such as Christiano, Eichenbaum and Evans (1996a,b) and Leeper, Sims and Zha (1996) find that real output responds persistently to monetary policy shocks. These studies also show that nominal prices respond slowly to monetary policy innovations. Christiano, Eichenbaum, and Evans (1997) argue that a slow response of nominal prices to monetary shocks is an important stylized fact that money models need to replicate.

Increases in money supply that lead to an increase in interest rates (a liquidity Puzzle) has been surveyed by Reichenstein (1987) and was re-documented by Leeper and Gordon (1992). Christiano (1991), Christiano and Eichenbaum (1992b), Gali (1992), Strongin (1995), Gordon and Leeper (1994), Strongin (1995), Lastrapes and Selgin (1995), Christiano, Eichenbaum and Evans (1996a,b), Leeper, Sims and Zha (1996), Hamilton (1997,1998), Bernanke and Mihov (1998a, 1998b), all find a liquidity effect with a number of authors arguing that the liquidity puzzle is the result of problems with econometric identification. Faust and Leeper (1997) and Faust (1998) investigate how reliable are identification restrictions in Vector Autoregression (VAR) models. Bernanke and Blinder (1992), Christiano and Eichenbaum (1992b), Strongin (1995), Eichenbaum (1992), and Sims (1992) all argued that innovations to broad monetary aggregates primarily reflected shocks to money demand rather than shocks to money supply or policy. It was necessary to make alternative identifying assumptions in order to identify money supply shocks. Christiano and Eichenbaum (1992b) argues that the quantity of non-borrowed reserves is the best indicator of monetary policy stance.

The recent search for a way to measure the impact of monetary policy has taken two paths. When monetary aggregates are used to measure monetary policy disturbances, two problems arise. The first problem is that innovations in monetary aggregates seem to be associated with rising, rather than falling interest rates (the liquidity puzzle). The second problem is that while money Granger causes output in VAR models that exclude interest rates, once interest rates are included in the model monetary aggregates no longer Granger-cause output. In VARs that include interest rates and some form of money, innovations in money explain a very small proportion of the variance of output (often 1% or less). In contrast, innovations in interest rates typically explain a very high percentage of the variance of output, often exceeding 40% over a two-year horizon. These results indicate that innovations in policy (as measured by monetary aggregates) have little explanatory power.

The empirical findings are, not surprisingly, quite diverse. At one end of the spectrum are studies that are based on the textbook monetary theory model. At the other end of the spectrum we have studies based on the micro-structure approach. Leeper (1992), Leeper and Gordon (1992) and Lastrapes and Selgin (1995) point out that the main reason for differing results concerning the liquidity effect is that estimates of the liquidity effect are sensitive to the identifying restrictions used to recover economically interpretable shocks from the reduced form representation of the data. As stressed by Leeper (1992) and Leeper and Gordon (1992), the failure to clearly isolate exogenous money supply shocks from endogenous responses of the money stock to other exogenous shocks (such as to real money demand) can lead to misleading measurement and inference about the liquidity effect. Much of the extant literature on the liquidity effect is criticized for improperly identified shocks. Drawing heavily from Lastrapes and Selgin (1995) we note that the bias of studies that assume money exogeneity can be seen from the following simplified example.

$$r_t = \beta M_t + e_{dt},$$

$$M_t = \alpha r_t + e_{st},$$

Where M is money supply, r is the interest rate, $e_{dt}$ is a money demand shock and $e_{st}$ is a money supply stock. Many studies make the identifying restriction that $\alpha = 0$, that is, that $M$ is exogenous, in which case OLS estimates of the first regression are valid estimates of β. The liquidity effect implies that β is negative. However, if there is feedback from $r_t$ to the money supply (that is, $\alpha \neq 0$), then the OLS estimate $b$ from the first regression is given by

$$b = \beta + (1-\alpha\beta)\alpha\sigma_d\left(\alpha^2\sigma_d + \sigma_s\right)^{-1}.$$

If α is positive and β is negative, $b$ will be "more positive" than β, which underestimates the liquidity effect. If money really does feed back on macro variables, this is a likely explanation for not finding a liquidity effect, or finding that it vanishes.

Consider a simply static demand and supply for money of the form[1]

$$m_t^d = \alpha_1 + \alpha_2 r_t + \varepsilon_t^d \qquad (1)$$

$$m_t^d = \beta_1 + \beta_2 r_t + \varepsilon_t^s \qquad (2)$$

$$m_t^d = m_t^s$$

Where d indicates demand, s supply, $m_t$ is the log of nominal money, $r_t$ is the nominal interest rate. The terms $\varepsilon_t^d$ and $\varepsilon_t^s$ are mutually uncorrelated demand and supply shocks. The idea is to identify the liquidity effect (the negative reaction of the interest rate to a rise in money supply). Therefore solving for $r_t$ in the previous system yields

$$r_t = \frac{\beta_1}{\alpha_2 - \beta_2} - \frac{\alpha_1}{\alpha_2 - \beta_2} + \frac{\varepsilon_t^s - \varepsilon_t^d}{\alpha_2 - \beta_2} \qquad (3)$$

The relation $dr_t/d\beta_1 = (\alpha_2 - \beta_2)^{-1}$ indicates that the interest rate decreases when money supply increases, provided $\alpha_2 < 0$ and $\beta_2 \leq -\alpha_2$. Since the money supply (equation 2) has a random variable attached $-\varepsilon_t^s$ — a change in $\beta_1$ can be thought of as a movement in the

---

[1] This section draws heavily from Pagan and Robertson (1995) and Jalil (2004)

expected value of $\beta_1 + \varepsilon_t^s$, and the money supply can be re-labeled $\varepsilon_t^{s'}$. Since, mathematically, a change in the expected value of $\varepsilon_t^{s'}$ is the same as the change in $\varepsilon_t^s$, the standard in the literature has been to concentrate on describing the effects of a change in $\varepsilon_t^s$. With this approach in mind, the liquidity effect can be seen as the response of interest rates to a money supply shock, setting all other shocks to zero.

One commonly used method to analyze the monetary features of the data is to identity and estimate a vector autoregressive (VAR) model. Such a model will help to assess the effects of a monetary policy shock. A sample of the large body of literature employing VAR models includes Leeper and Gordon (1992), Strongin (1995), Leeper, Sims and Zha (1996), Christiano, Eichenbaum, and Evans (1996a,b, 1999), Rotemberg and Woodford (1997), Bernanke and Mihov (1998), and Carpenter and Demiralp (2008). In these models identifying assumptions are needed to isolate the monetary policy shock and to characterize the shocks effect on economic variables in the VAR model. As mentioned above, different identifying assumptions can lead to different conclusions about these effects. Thus, any characterization of the economy's response to a monetary policy shock should be robust over a broad range of identifying assumptions.

Leeper and Gordon (1992) estimates a four variable VAR that includes the monetary base (MB), the federal funds rate (FFR), industrial production, (IP), and the consumer price index (CPI). They find a liquidity puzzle between the MB and the FFR; there is no negative relationship between MB and the FFR. The MB is made up of required reserves, excess reserves, and currency.

Christiano and Eichenbaum (1992b) employ simple cross-correlation analysis between the federal funds rate and different monetary aggregates. Christiano and Eichenbaum (1992b) show that the broad monetary aggregates used in previous studies are inappropriate for identifying the existence of the liquidity effect due to their large endogenous component because changes in broad aggregates reflect both the demand and supply shocks creating the money endogeneity problem. Christiano and Eichenbaum (1992b) argue that the quantity of non-borrowed reserves (NBR) is the best indicator of monetary policy stance. With NBR included in a VAR model instead of broad money supply, the fed funds rate exhibits a sharp persistent decline. Bernanke and Blinder (1992) suggests that the Fed watches the Fed Funds rate closely and concludes that changes in the fed funds rate could be used as a measure of policy shock. Strongin (1995) suggests using the proportion of NBR growth that is orthogonal to total reserves growth as a policy shock measure. Strongin (1995) finds that including this measure in a VAR model, estimated on sub-samples similar to those used by Leeper and Gordon (1992), yields a highly significant and persistent liquidity effect.

Strongin (1995) and Bernanke and Mihov (1998a, 1998b) are interested in the transmission mechanism and model the federal funds market to estimate the liquidity effect. Strongin (1995) argues that the main source of the difficulty in identifying monetary policy from the use of monetary aggregate data is that a significant proportion of the variance in the reserve data is due to the Federal Reserve's accommodation of innovations in the demand for banking reserves rather than policy-induced supply innovations. This leads to a confounding of supply and demand innovations. Strongin (1995) uses a linear representation of the Federal Reserve's operating procedures, which include total reserves and a mix of borrowed and nonborrowed reserves supplied by the Federal Reserve to identify the exogenous disturbances to policy net of accommodation of demand shocks. By using two measures of reserves with different responses to supply and demand innovations it is possible to distinguish between changes in reserves that result from Federal Reserve policy innovations and changes in reserves which result from Federal Reserve's accommodation of demand innovations. Stongin (1995) generalizes a measure of nonborrowed reserves in order to nest different policy regimes. He assumes that the short-run demand for total reserves is inelastic and the open market Desk will provide sufficient reserves to satisfy this demand. Furthermore, he argues that given a policy tightening, the open market Desk contracts nonborrowed reserves, resulting in an increase in borrowed reserves. Thus, the ratio of nonborrowed reserves to total reserves should fall during a policy tightening. He estimates a model of nonborrowed reserves divided by total reserves from the previous month and the federal funds rate. He analyzes the response of these variables to changes in the nonborrowed reserves variable. Strongin (1995) notes that the failure of other studies to find a liquidity effect can be traced, at least in part, to a failure to account for the Federal Reserve's accommodation of the shifts in demand for money or reserves. The findings of Strongin (1995) are quite dramatic when compared to previous work. First, he finds that the liquidity effect holds in all subperiods. Second, his proposed measure of monetary policy disturbances has substantially more explanatory power for interest rates and real output than pure nonborrowed reserves, accounting for 49% of output at the end of two years. Third, the explanatory power of interest rates is substantially reduced when the policy measure is included, accounting for only 2% of the variance of output at the two years horizon. Fourth, nonborrowed reserves Granger-cause output while interest rates do not. Fifth, accommodative policy leads to a permanent and statistically significant increase in the price level.

The above set of results are closely linked to the results in Carpenter and Demiralp (2006) who also find strong evidence of the liquidity effect at the monthly frequency. Their study also highlights the importance of understanding why a liquidity effect may not exist. They note that looking at the contemporaneous correlations, there is a liquidity effect with respect to total reserve balances and the federal funds rate. This relationship does not hold when only non-borrowed reserves are studied. Because reserve requirements are determined by a banks' customers' demand for reservable deposits, which may or may not depend on the federal funds rate in a simple way, there is no reason to expect a liquidity effect between nonborrowed reserves and the federal funds rate in periods when required reserve balances constitute the majority of banks reserve balances.

Lastrapes and Selgin (1995) also estimate a structural VAR. They impose long-run neutrality restrictions on the VAR representation of i) interest rates—3 month T-bill ii) output-industrial production index iii) real money-MB,M1,M2 divided by CPI and iv) nominal money to identify exogenous money supply shocks-MB,M1,M2. They assume that permanent shocks to the level of nominal money (or temporary shocks to the growth rate of money) have no permanent effect on the levels of real variables in the system, and show that these restrictions are sufficient to isolate the liquidity effect. This is a long-run neutrality restriction imposed on nominal shocks. A long-run neutrality restriction used in this study have advantages over other identification schemes in the literature. For example, Melvin (1983) made the assumption that statistical innovations to the money stock represent money supply shocks. That is, money is treated as being weakly exogenous with respect to the parameters that measure the liquidity effect. This assumptions ignores the endogeneity of money that may arise from policy reaction functions. When this endogeneity exists, the response of the interest rate to the money innovation is a combination of money supply and money demand, so that studies that treat money as being exogenous lead to invalid estimates of the liquidity effect. Lastrapes and Selgin (1995) find evidence of the liquidity effect for the post-WW II period. The interest rate responds negatively and persistently to an increase in nominal money supply. They show that the liquidity effect holds up for different measures of money. That is, monetary base, M1, and M2.

In the Lastrapes and Selgin (1995) paper the identification of money supply shocks does not depend on the exogeneity of money. Studies that provide evidence of the liquidity effect within a VAR framework include Leeper and Gordon (1992), Christiano and Eichenbaum (1992b), Gali (1992), Strongin (1995), and Christiano, Eichenbaum, and Evans (1996a,b). As with Lastrapes and Selgin (1995) these studies impose no over-identifying restrictions on the model. Because their long-run restrictions do not over-identify the model, the validity of the restrictions cannot be tested using classical statistical techniques. Their just-identifying restrictions include contemporaneous exclusionary restrictions. Gali (1992) combines long-run neutrality restrictions with zero contemporaneous restrictions and finds evidence of a liquidity effect.

As we have noted above much of the early literature on the liquidity effect was based on single-equation distributed lag models of interest rates using broad measures of money and these studies tended to find little evidence of the liquidity effect (Thornton 1988). As pointed out in Pagan and Robertson (1995) it appears that the finding of a liquidity effect is closely associated with the move towards structural model estimation. A summary of the empirical evidence based on these models can be found in Pagan and Robertson (1995). They find that the results are sensitive to the sample period used for estimation and the measure of money used to identify monetary policy. Pagan and Robertson (1995) estimate a number of different VAR systems in order to determine whether a liquidity effect exists. They estimate models from 1959:01 to 1993:12 as well as shorter time periods; 1982:12-1993:12 and 1974:01-1993:12. Over the 1959-1994 period, a liquidity effect is observed when nonborrwed reserves are used as the money measure in a recursive VAR models. It is argued that innovations to NBR reflect the exogenous policy actions of the Federal Reserve. Christiano, Eichenbaum, and Evans (1996a, p. 18) argues that the evidence of a liquidity effect obtained by their recursive structural VAR stems from the fact that "innovations to NBR primarily reflect exogenous shocks to monetary policy..." But for broader measures of money there is a negligible or positive interest rate response, particularly when money is placed before the interest rate in the recursive ordering. Over the post-1979 period no evidence of a liquidity effect is found.

In contrast to the mixed performance, studies that use nonrecursive simultaneous equation systems seem to have been successful at finding a strong liquidity effect, even for broad measures of money. Christiano and Eichenbaum (1992b) and Pagan and Robertson (1998) find that a significant liquidity effect is only found in strictly recursive systems when nonborrowed reserves are used as the monetary aggregate. However, Gali (1992), Gordon and Leeper (1994) and Lastrapes and Selgin (1995) find strong liquidity effects generated with broad measures of money in nonrecursive structural systems. Pagan and Robertson (1998) attempts to determine the reason for this finding and to examine the robustness of their conclusions to see whether the conclusion reached are empirically fragile.

Pagan and Robertson (1998) examines how robust the conclusions of a number of studies are to various features of the data and the model used. They focus on the econometric issues caused by weak identifying information and also consider different sample periods for estimation. The Gordon and Leeper (1994) model is specified in levels of the series, while Gali (1992) is written in terms of transformations of the series that are assumed to be stationary. Lastrapes and Selgin (1995) assume that the levels of the series are integrated of order 1, I(1),-that is the series need to be first differenced to yield stationary. They assume the variables are I(1) but not cointegrated, allowing them to work with the variables in first differences. Gali (1992) assume that money and prices are I(2)—need to be differenced twice to become stationary, interest rates and output are I(1), and the real interest rate and the growth rate of real balances are stationary. The papers also differ in how they construct confidence intervals. Gordon and Leeper (1994) use the flat-prior Bayesian procedure to obtain confidence intervals for the estimated responses. Lastrapes and Selgin (1995) use a variant of the bootstrap procedure, while Gali (1992) does not report and precision measures for the estimated impact responses but uses the Bayesian procedure to obtain intervals for the dynamic multipliers conditional on the estimated impact responses. They conclude that the evidence for a liquidity effect is much weaker than that found in the original studies. Their results find that the size of the liquidity effect established in Gordon and Leeper (1994) is over estimated due to the effects of weak or invalid instruments. Even after a proper accounting of these features by Pagan and Robertson (1998) find the liquidity effect is still present. The liquidity effect disappears only when the data period is extended back before 1983. Lastrapes and Selgin's (1995) work shows a weak liquidity effect when confidence intervals are constructed to reflect the weak instruments that they use, and the liquidity effect disappears when post-1982 data are used. Gali (1992) makes use of a number of identifying restrictions. Again, Pagan and Robertson (1998) have a concern about the quality of the instruments used. It also seems that the liquidity effect is imprecisely determined. Pagan and Robertson (1998) argue that the more modern structural models do not find any stronger evidence for the liquidity effect than the weal effects found by recursive models.

As mentioned above when NBR are used as the monetary aggregate in structural VAR models it is argued that innovations to NBR reflect the exogenous policy actions of the Federal Reserve. Thornton (2001b) argues that the above statement is wrong. Thornton (2001b) argues just the opposite is true. He shows that the impulse response functions, which the above mentioned authors estimate, reflect the endogenous response of borrowing to the federal funds rate and the Federal Reserves practice of offsetting borrowing and not the liquidity effect. Thornton shows that the Federal Reserve has an incentive to offset bank discount window borrowings when it implements the FOMC policy directive and that this has been going on since the late 1950s. He shows that the evidence of a liquidity effect from the recursive structural VAR models is due to the Federal Reserves' practice of offsetting bank borrowing. This practice has created a negative contemporaneous covariance between NBR and the federal funds rate that has incorrectly been attributed to the liquidity effect. By showing that these models capture the endogenous response of the Federal Reserve to bank borrowing on NBR, rather than the effect of exogenous policy actions. By showing that the estimated liquidity effect is the result of the endogenous response of the Federal Reserve to bank borrowing rather than the exogenous response of the federal funds rate to Federal Reserve policy actions, Thornton (2001b) argues that he has resolved the puzzle of the vanishing liquidity effect noted by Pagan and Robertson

(1995) and Christiano (1995). Thornton argues that the liquidity effect estimated by the recursive structural VAR did not vanish after the early 1980s because of some fundamental change in the Federal Reserve's ability to affect interest rates through open market operations. The response vanished because banks, mainly large banks, decided to stay away from the discount window.

Leeper, Sims, and Zha (1996) examines a 13-variable VAR model that includes consumption and investment (non-residential investment to be exact). They find that after an expansionary monetary policy shock both consumption and investment increase, but the increase in investment is greater than that of consumption. They also find that an expansionary monetary policy shock causes the nominal interest rate to fall (a liquidity effect), output to rise, and the price level to increase slowly.

Christiano, Eichenbaum, and Evans (1996a) estimates a VAR that includes industrial production (IP), the CPI, a commodity price index (CRB), the federal funds rate (FF), nonborrowed reserved (NBR), total reserves (TR) and M1. The authors argue that the liquidity puzzle found in Leeper and Gordon (1992) reflects endogeneity. They argue that fluctuations in the MB reflect both exogenous supply changes as well as endogenous policymaker responses to demand side disturbances. By focusing on NBR, a narrower definition of money, they try to avoid this identification problem. Christiano, Eichenbaum and Evans (1996a,b) find some evidence of the liquidity effect, as total reserves, nonborrowed reserves, and M1 all have a negative and statistically significant liquidity effect.

In their survey article Christiano, Eichenbaum, and Evans (1999) investigate the effects of a monetary policy shock under three of the more popular identification schemes used in the literature for VARs. They consider each set of identifying restriction in a seven-variable VAR model using quarterly data on output (Y=log of RGDP), prices (P=log of implicit GDP price deflator), commodity prices (CRB=smoothed change in the index of sensitive commodity prices), the federal funds rate (FF), total reserves (TR=log of total reserves), nonborrowed reserves (NBR=log of nonborrowed reserves plus extended credit), and money (M=log of M1 or log of M2).

The first identification scheme investigated specifies FF as the policy instrument of the Federal Reserve. Sims (1986) and Bernanke and Blinder (1992) argue the merits of this specification on institutional grounds. The second identification scheme considered assumes that NBR is the policy instrument. Christiano and Eichenbaum (1992b) claim that innovations to NBR are the best measure of exogenous monetary policy shocks. The third identification scheme examined set the policy instrument equal to NBR/TR. This is a scheme adopted in Strongin (1995) who argues that the short-run demand for total reserves is completely inelastic so, the effects of a monetary disturbances are internalized among the components of total reserves (total reserves = nonborrowed reserves plus borrowed reserves). Christiano, Eichenbaum, and Evans (1999) conduct their empirical analysis for each identification scheme separately and find that the results are qualitatively robust to any of the three identification schemes. All three policy measures find that an expansionary monetary policy shock causes the nominal interest rate to fall, output to rise, and the price level to increase slowly.[2]

Hamilton (1997) develops an empirical model of the federal funds market at the daily frequency and attempts to estimate a liquidity effect. The Treasury maintains an account with the Federal Reserve and each day funds are transferred in and out of this account. As funds are transferred in, they are drained from the banking sector, and the federal funds market. Hamilton exploits this relationship and estimates a forecasting equation for the Treasury's Fed account. If the forecasts are unbiased then deviations from the forecasts should, on average, represent exogenous shifts in the supply of reserves, allowing him to identify the liquidity effect. Hamilton's (1997) results suggest that there is a liquidity effect at the daily frequency, however, the effect is only statistically significant on the last two days of the maintenance period. Moreover, the point estimate for the penultimate day of the maintenance period is not economically significant. The liquidity effect found by Hamilton is only for the last day of the maintenance period. The liquidity effect must exist if the demand for reserves is negatively sloped in the funds rate because an exogenous change in the supply of reserves will generate a change in the federal funds rate in the opposite direction. While a negatively sloped demand curve is sufficient for the existence of the liquidity effect, it does not guarantee that it is large and economically meaningful.

Hamilton (1997) notes that most studies that investigate the liquidity effect have used low frequency (monthly or quarterly) data. Hamilton argues that one reason for not being able to isolate the liquidity effect is due to the fact that, low frequency data combines together the effect of policy on economic variables with the effect of economic variables on policy. In an effort to sercomevent this problem Hamilton (1997) develops an alternative measure of the liquidity effect. Rather than attempting to identify the effect of monetary policy over a month or quarter, Hamilton (1997) investigated the effect of an exogenous shock to the supply of reserves on the federal funds rate at daily frequency. The point here is that a reserve supply shock is analogous to an exogenous open market operation. A significant response of the federal funds rate to a reserve supply shock is prema facie evidence that the Fed can generate changes in the federal funds rate through open market operations.

Thorton (2001a) re-examines Hamilton's (1997) results and argues that the liquidity effect cannot be identified. He argues that this is because it is almost impossible to correctly identify the error that the Fed makes in Forecasting the Treasury Balance. Moreover, Thornton (2001a) finds that Hamilton's (1997) result was the consequence of a few days when there were very large changes in the federal funds rate. Thornton (2001a) finds that Hamilton's (1997) settlement-Wednesday effect is due to just six of the sixty nine settlement Wednesdays in his sample period. When these observations are excluded there is no statistically significant liquidity effect on settlement Wednesday or on any other day of the maintenance period. Thornton continues and argues that the liquidity effect can be identified by examining changes in nonborrowed reserves following a change in the target rate. He concludes that the quantities of changes in nonborrowed reserves are relatively small, and thus are likely only signals of a change in target, but not evidence of a liquidity effect itself. Furthermore, using Hamilton's methodology Thornton (2001a) finds no statistically

---

[2] Thornton (2001b) argues that the finding of a liquidity effect in structural VAR models is the result of the Federal Reserves' endogenous response to bank borrowing rather than a response to an exogenous monetary policy shock.

significant negative response of the fed funds rate to reserve supply shocks for the sample periods before and after Hamilton's.

Carpenter and Demiralp (2006) find evidence of a liquidity effect at daily frequency. Moreover, they find that the estimated size of the liquidity effect is economically meaningful. Unlike Hamilton (1997) who used one component of autonomous factors that affect supply and estimated the supply shock (and found a liquidity effect), Carpenter and Demiralp (2006) have all of the autonomous factors that affect reserve supply and have the actual error made by the staff of the Board of Governors in forecasting these factors. They argue that their reserve-supply shock measure is both more comprehensive than Hamilton's (1997) and represents the actual shocks to reserves that occurred in carrying out open market operations.

Judson and Porter (2001) suggests that between one-half and two-thirds of US currency is held abroad. Carpenter and Demiralp (2008) ask why the demand for currency would be linked to the federal funds rate is unclear. The federal funds rate is the interest rate in the market for balances, not the monetary base, and since balances constitute less than 5% of the monetary base, one should not be surprised that there is no statistical relationship. Balances are composed of three components; required reserve balances, contractual clearing balances, and excess balances. Carpenter and Demiralp (2008) argue that total balances is the measure of money that is relevant for studying the liquidity effect relative to the federal funds rate.

Carpenter and Demiralp (2008) argue that reserves are related to "balances" but are not the same thing. They argue that the true liquidity effect is the relationship between balances and the federal funds rate. They argue that the use of nonborrowed reserves is inappropriate. They point out that the open market desk provides balances perfectly elastically at the target rate. As a result balances react endogenously to the federal funds rate and not the opposite. Nonborrowed reserves, which are influenced by changes in balances and banks' demand for vault cash also react endogenously. They argue that it is important to understand that nonborrowed reserves include vault cash and excludes a large fraction of balances (the variable the desk adjusts to maintain the target rate) and shows that the use of noborrowed reserves is an inappropriate measure of money. balances are the preferred variable. Carpenter and Demiralp (2008) estimate a VAR model that includes balances and allows each components of balances to change independently. They do not argue that a single component of balances is the appropriate measure of money to study. They demonstrate that using balances, the federal funds that are actually traded in the federal funds market, one can identify a liquidity effect. They argue that the liquidity puzzle is no puzzle at all, but merely a misspecification. Previous studies that have focused on reserves rather than balances have excluded a crucial component of the federal funds market. They note that Fed Balances can be broken down into three categories; required reserve balances, excess balances, and contractual clearing balances. The last category is not included in the measure of reserves.

Their baseline model includes the effective federal funds rate (FF), reservable deposits (RDEP), required reserve balances (RRB), contractual clearing balances (CCB), and excess reserve balances (ER). The impulse response functions indicate that CCB and ER show a negative reaction to a positive innovation to the federal funds rate, but only the response of CCB is statistically significant. Hence there is no liquidity puzzle. The liquidity effect found here is much larger than that found by Christiano, Eichenbaum and Evans (1996a). If the demand for balances are a function of economic activity then the results of Carpenter and Demiralp (2008) are subject to endogeneity bias. To test endogeneity they include in their

VAR industrial production (IP) and the consumer price index (CPI). They find that the impulse responses for the balances are no different so they continue with their baseline model.

While the VAR literature has clearly examined the impact of a monetary policy shock on the nominal interest rate, an analysis of the components of the nominal interest rate is difficult as we do not have good measures of these components. If agents have rational expectations then the impact of a monetary policy shock on expected inflation is equal to the one period ahead response of the inflation rate to the monetary shock. Hence, the combination of gradually rising prices and falling nominal interest rates causes the real interest rate to decline after an expansionary monetary policy disturbance. With respect to expected inflation the issue is not the direction of the adjustment but the speed and magnitude of the adjustment. In Leeper, Sims, and Zha (1996) and Christiano, Eichenbaum, and Evans (1999) the gradual and protracted rise in the price level after a positive monetary policy shock implies that the inflation rate (and hence the expected inflation rate) response is initially small and peaks several period after the shock. Rotemberg and Woodford (1997), in contrast, examine a three variable VAR model that includes a nominal interest rate (federal funds rate), a measure of inflation (change in log of implicit GDP price deflator) and measure of output (log of RGDP with a linear time trend removed). They find that the peak in expected inflation occurs one period after a monetary disturbance. They also observe that the response of expected inflation to a monetary policy shock cannot be estimated with much precision.

Given the empirical findings of Leeper, Sims and Zha (1996) and Christiano, Eichenbaum and Evans (1999) and others, any plausible model of the monetary transmission mechanism should yield the following results. An expansionary monetary policy shock should result in an increase in output, consumption and investment; a decline in the nominal and real interest rate; and a gradual increase in the price level. The percentage increase in investment should exceed that of consumption. The expansionary monetary policy shock should also result in expected inflation, but it is not clear whether the peak in expected inflation should occur immediately after the shock or as much as several quarters after the shock.

Keen (2004) investigates the effect of a monetary policy shock in a dynamic stochastic general equilibrium model with sticky prices and financial market frictions. His results suggest that their model can account for the following key responses to an expansionary monetary policy shock; a fall in the nominal interest rate (the liquidity effect); an increase in output, investment, and consumption; and a gradual increase in the price level.

Table 1, below, presents a summary of some of the empirical literature that has been discussed above. It is interesting to note that when the liquidity effect is not found, it is, for the most part, within a single equation estimation method (especially the early literature). System based estimation (e.g. VARs) yields results that find evidence of a liquidity effect. Pagan and Robertson (1995) point out four issues concerning these conclusions: i) different definitions of monetary stance, ii) different models, iii) different estimation procedures and restrictions, and iv) different data samples.

**Table 1. Summary of empirical studies of the liquidity effect**[1]

| Author | Sample | Freq | Money Variables | Interest Rate | Other Variables | Model Type | Max Lags | Findings |
|---|---|---|---|---|---|---|---|---|
| Cagan and Gandolfi (1969) | 1910:01-1965:12 | M | DM1,DM2 | DCP | | Single | 38 | Yes |
| Gibson (1970b) | 1947:01-1966:12 | M | M1,M2,DM1,DM2 | TB3,DTB3,TB10,DTB10 | | Single | 11 | Yes |
| Mishkin (1982) | 1959:01-1976:04 | Q | DM2,DM1 | TB6-TB3 | DP,DY | Single | 4 | No |
| Melvin (1983) | 1951:01-1979:12 | M | DM2 | DCP | | Single | 12/36 | No |
| Reichenstein (1987) | 1965:01-1983:03 | M | DM1 | TB3 | DP,DY,U | Single | 4 | No |
| Thornton (1988) | 1959:08-1987:06 | M | DM1,DM0,DNBR | TB3 | DP,DY | Single | 6 | No/Yes |
| Cochrane (1989) | 1979:10-1982:11 | W | NBR,M1 | TB3,TB20 | | Filter | | Yes |
| Christiano and Eichenbaum (1992b) | 1959:01-1990:03 | M/Q | M1,M0,NBR | FF | P,Y | VAR | 14/5 | No/Yes |
| Eichenbaum (1992) | 1965:01-1990:01 | M | M1,M0,NBR | FF | P,Y | VAR | 14 | No/Yes |
| Gali (1992) | 1955:01-1987:02 | Q | DM1 | TB3 | DP,DY | VAR | 4 | Yes |
| Leeper and Gordon (1992) | 1954:07-1990:12 | M | M0,M1,M2 | FF,TB3.CP6 | P,Y | Single/VAR | 36/18 | No |
| Sims (1992) | 1958:04-1991:02 | M | M1 | FF | P,Y,ER,CRB | VAR | 14 | Yes |
| Gordon and Leeper (1994) | 1982:12-1992:04 | M | M2,TR | TB1,FF | TB10,P,Y,U,CRB | VAR | 6 | Yes |
| Pagan and Robertson (1995) | 1959:01-1993:12 | M | M1,NBR,NBRX | FF | P,Y | VAR | 14 | No |

[1] This is an expanded version of a Table in Pagan and Robertson (1995).

## Table 1. Continued

| Author | Sample | Freq | Money Variables | Interest Rate | Other Variables | Model Type | Max Lags | Findings |
|---|---|---|---|---|---|---|---|---|
| Eichenbaum and Evans (1995) | 1974:01-1990:05 | M | NBRX,TR | FF,TB3 | Y,P,RF,RER | VAR | 6 | Yes |
| Lastrapes and Selgin (1995) | 1959:01-1993:12 | M | MB,M1,M1/P | TB3 | Y | VAR | 13 | Yes |
| Strongin (1995) | 1959:01-1992:02 | M | NBR/TR | FF | TR | VAR | 12 | Yes |
| Christiano, Eichenbaum and Evans (1996a) | 1960:01-1992:03 | Q | NBR,M1 | FF | P, Y,CRB,TR | VAR | 4 | Yes |
| Hamilton (1997) | 1986:04-1997:01 | D | NBR | DFF | TRB, Dummies | Single |  | Yes |
| Christiano, Eichenbaum and Evans (1999) | 1965:03-1995:02 | Q | M1,NBR | FF | Y,P,TR,CRB | VAR | 4 | Yes |
| Thornton (2001b) | 1959:01-1996:12 | M | NBR,TR | FF | Y,P,CRB | VAR | 14 | No |
| Bilan (2005) | 1997:01-2003:12 | M | TR | IBR | P,M1 | VAR | 3 | Yes |
| Carpenter and Demiralp (2008) | 1989:02-2005:06 | M | RDEP | FF | RRB,CCB,ER | VAR | 3 | Yes |

Notes: P is price deflator (usually CPI), Y = Real GDP for quarterly data and Industrial production index for monthly data, U = unemployment, ER=excess reserve balances, M0=monetary base, RER=real exchange rate, RF=foreign interest rate, TB6=6-month T-bill rate, TB3=3-month T-bill rte, TB10=10-year Treasury bond rate, TB20=20 year Treasury bond rate, CP=commercial paper rate, CP6=6-month commercial paper rate, CRB = commodity price index, TR=total reserves, TBF=**, TRB=Treasury Balances at the Fed, RDEP=reservable deposits, RRB=required reserve balances, CCB=contractual clearing balances, ER=excess balances, NBRX =NBR/TR, IBR = interbank rate, RRB=required reserve balances, DCP=first difference in commercial paper rate, DM1=first difference in M1. DTB3,DTB10 are the first differences of TB3 and TB10.

The results of Table 1 also indicate that the definitions of money used in different studies determines whether evidence of a liquidity effect is found. Defining money as monetary base or M1 does not usually result in a liquidity effect while such measures as nonborrowed reserves (NBR) or nonborrowed reserves to total reserves (NBRX) do. Thornton (1988) in a single equation analysis, observed that NBR was the only measure of money which displayed evidence of a liquidity effect. After Thorton's publication researchers began using NBR. Thornton's conclusion has been reiterated by Christiano and Eichenbaum (1992b) in a systems context. Subsequently, Strongin (1995) has suggested that the ratio of NBR to total reserves (TR), NBRX, is the best monetary measure, and Eichenbaum and Evans (1995) have adopted NBRX in their work on exchange rates.[1] The most controversial issue related to the use of nonborrowed reserves is whether it constitutes an effective way of measuring exogenous monetary policy. The variable NBRX is highly correlated with borrowed reserves (BR), raising the question about how BR should be treated.

## 4. A Short History of Federal Reserve Operating Procedures[2]

In the empirical studies discussed above, authors often examine various sub-periods to see how their results change over different sample periods. Some of those sample periods correspond to periods of differing Federal Reserve operating procedures. This section describes the history of Federal Reserve operating procedures and develops a set of dates for subsample testing. The section also attempts to give the reader a feel for the evolution of the monetary policy process through time and for some of the subtleties of how the procedures were implemented over time.

Stongin (1995) argues that the period from 1959 to the present can be split into five periods. A large amount of judgment is involved in selecting these subperiods. Where dates have attained a place in the literature, such as the `vanishing liquidity' effect that Melvin (1983) suggests began at the end of 1972. A more complete survey of these issues can be found in Meulendyke (1989). The five periods used as selected by Strongin (1995) are as follows:

1959-1966: Free reserves targeting before the modern Federal funds market
1966-1972: Free reserves targeting and the bank credit proviso
1972-1979: Money growth/Federal funds targeting
1979-1982: Nonborrowed reserves targeting
1982-present: Borrowed reserves/Federal funds targeting

*The 1959-1966 Period*
Though the Federal funds market actually dates back to the early 1950s, it was not until the mid-1960s that the Federal funds market and reserve management began to look like their modern equivalents. As a result, the pre-1966 period may be different than subsequent periods. The reserves market worked in a different way than it does today. This period was characterized by free reserves targeting. Free reserves are equal to excess reserves minus

---
[1] Strongin (1995) actually used NBR divided by $TR_{-1}$.
[2] This discussion draws heavily from Strongin (1995).

borrowed reserves (ER-*BR*). Free reserves targeting is a variant of borrowed reserves targeting with explicit accommodation of excess reserves. The Federal Reserve had no quantitative operating targets during this period and the desk at the New York Federal Reserve bank sought only to stabilize general money market conditions, in line with the FOMC's directives.

*The 1966-1972 Period*

The modern era begins in 1966. The period from 1966 through 1972 was still characterized by a free reserves operating procedure, but the Federal funds market had begun to perform the same function it does today as a major source of bank liquidity. This period was also marked by the introduction of the `proviso' on bank credit into the FOMC's policy directive. The proviso stated that if bank credit growth deviated significantly from target then the desk could adjust the Free Reserve target `modestly'. This shift to a quantitative goal for the operation of monetary policy was a major landmark for Federal Reserve operating procedures, which can be labeled `The Reform of 1966'. As mentioned earlier, before this shift, there were no quantitative objectives. This signaled a substantial increase in the role of monetarist thought within the FOMC. This period ended in the early 1970s as monetary aggregates slowly replaced bank credit as the main focus of long-run policy and the Federal funds rate began to replace free reserves as the main operating focus. In general, the Federal Reserve was still stabilizing general money market conditions and was still accommodating reserve demand shocks through nonborrowed reserves.

*The 1972-1979 Period*

It is interesting to note that the shift from the free reserves targeting of the previous period to the Federal funds targeting of the 1972-1979 period was not viewed as a major event. Borrowing targets and Federal funds rate targets are quite similar in practice, though the dynamics are not quite identical. Stable borrowing levels usually imply stable interest rates. The difference in procedures only becomes evident when there is a shift in the borrowings function. In a free reserves targeting procedure a shift in the borrowing function will cause interest rates to change. In a Federal funds rate targeting procedure the reserve mix will be adjusted to exactly offset the shift in the borrowings function and keep the funds rate steady.

This period is dated as the beginning of 1972, following Melvin (1983). The Federal funds rate targeting procedure was not actually made public in the FOMC's policy directive until 1974, though it could be argued that the switch occurred earlier. One can date the shift to September of 1970. Meulendyke (1989) suggests that while the change began in the early 1970s, its implementation was gradual, lasting until the mid to late 1970s. The ambiguity arises from the fact that the period was characterized by progressively tighter targeting of the Federal funds rate rather than an abrupt shift to strict Federal funds targeting. It was still very much a borrowing reserves targeting type of procedure, except that the operating procedures automatically adjusted for shifts in the borrowings function by stabilizing the Federal funds rates. These operating procedures were in use until 1979 when nonborrowed reserves targeting was introduced. In general, much of the motivation for the 1979 change resulted from a conviction that the preoccupation with keeping interest rates stable, that had developed in the 1972-1979 period, had created an inflationary bias in the application of policy and that only by allowing substantially more interest volatility could inflation be tamed. Similarly, monetary growth regularly exceeding target growth ranges due to an unwillingness to raise interest rates enough.

*The 1979-1982 Period*

During this period the Federal Reserve adopted a nonborrowed reserves operating procedure in order to assert greater control over the money stock. Nonborrowed reserves targeting was the most complicated of the reserve operating procedures that the Federal Reserve has ever used and it lasted the shortest length of time. This operating procedure, in fact, targeted neither nonborrowed reserves nor any other reserve aggregate in any straightforward way. Considerable debate within the Federal Reserve system about how these procedures actually worked is still going on. Despite the avowed intention of controlling money, the Federal Reserve missed its money targets more in this period than in any other before or since. On the other hand, numerous studies, such as Spindt and Tarhan (1987) and Strongin and Tarhan (1990), show that the desire to control money played a large role in the conduct of policy. Financial deregulation and a general increase in economic volatility make it very difficult to sort out exactly what happened during this period. What is clear is that Federal Reserve operating procedures were quite different during this period than in any other, and that little if any effort went into stabilizing either borrowings or interest rates.

The basics of the procedures were quite simple. Short-run money growth targets were established at each FOMC meeting. Nonborrowed reserves targets consistent with these money targets were then derived. The nonborrowed reserves targets were then revised each week in order to bring money back to path. If money growth was above target, the nonborrowed reserves path was lowered. This meant that short-run fluctuations in money and the resulting total reserves movements were being used by the Federal Reserve to determine future nonborrowed reserves targets (i.e., nonborrowed reserves targets changed each week in response to last week's reserve demand shock) and the market used this same information to forecast future Federal Reserve actions and interest rates (see Strongin and Tarhan, 1990). Thus, total reserves movements contained information on future Federal Reserve actions that had contemporaneous effects on interest rates due to Federal Reserve actions that had not yet been taken. This interaction between reserve demand shocks and policy could potentially cause the total reserve variable to absorb more of the policy signal over this period than any other. There are a number other potential problems with this period. First, there is very little data; the operating procedures lasted only three years. Second, the first six months of this period are suspect, in that it took a while to develop and implement the new operating procedures. And third, the last six months are equally suspect, because dissatisfaction with the procedures led the FOMC to accept larger and larger deviations from its short-run money targets during 1982 until borrowed reserves targeting was officially adopted in October of 1982.

*The 1982-present Period*

After October of 1982, the Federal Reserve adopted a borrowed reserves targeting procedure, where the borrowing target changed only by policy action rather than in response to reserve demand shocks. The operating procedures in this period are very similar to the procedures in force in the early 1970s, except that the Federal Reserve has shown much more willingness to change the Federal Funds rate.

*A note on interest rate volatility*

As an additional note, some discussion should be given to the Federal Reserve's attitudes toward interest rate volatility across the above mentioned periods. This is not an easy task in the sense that the Federal Reserve typically does not have a specific policy toward interest rate volatility per se. Nevertheless, the Federal Reserve's attitudes toward interest rate volatility have undergone some large shifts over the years. Beginning in the early 1970s, the Federal Reserve began to look upon interest rate stabilization as an end in itself, and the target ranges for the Federal funds rate became progressively smaller. Earlier periods had emphasized the stability of overall money market conditions. The 1979 shift was in large part a rejection of the interest rate smoothing goal and interest rate volatility was no longer avoided. As the monetary control experiment ended in 1982, dissatisfaction with the large amount of interest rate volatility that nonborrowed reserves targeting had created was one of the strongest factors in the rejection of continued nonborrowed reserves targeting. The 1982-1991 period has once again seen increasingly narrow ranges for Federal funds rates, though the target ranges are moved more often than in the 1972-1979 period. Thus, the 1972-1979 and 1982-1991 periods stand out as having interest rate smoothing as a relatively important Federal Reserve operating goal, especially the 1972-1979 period. The 1979-1982 period stands out as being by far the least concerned with interest rate smoothing. The implications of these changes in attitude are not obvious for reserve management, but it is likely that if a significant percentage of reserve actions were aimed at stabilizing interest rates, it might dampen observed interest rate effects of policy.

By and large one would expect to see differences between periods, but only the 1979-1982 period represents a major shift in operating procedures. Within the literature, Melvin (1983) suggests that 1973-1979 has a diminished liquidity effect, and Cochrane (1989) finds it reappeared in 1979. However, most work finds little or no liquidity effect in any of these periods (see Reichenstein, 1987, for a survey of this work). Further, it is also clear that 1972-1979 is characterized by the greatest desire to smooth interest rates, while 1979-1982 is characterized by the least desire to smooth interest rates.

## 5. Summary

This paper reviews the extant literature (both theoretical and empirical) that examines the liquidity effect. Christiano (1996, p. 3) defines the liquidity effect as "[a]n exogenous, persistent, upward shock in the growth rate of the monetary base engineered by the central bank and not associated with any current or prospective adjustment in distortionary taxes, drives the nominal interest rate down for a significant period of time."

With Respect to the theoretical literature, The liquidity effect is inconsistent with many real business cycle models, which allow money shocks to have a positive effect only on nominal interest rates through the effect of inflationary expectations (the "fisher effect"). A generic implication of RBC models is that, if money growth displays positive persistence then unanticipated shocks to money growth causes interest rates to rise not fall. The reason for this is that in these models, money shocks affect interest rates exclusively through an anticipated inflation effect. This means that in these models money is superneutral in the short run as well as the long run (Cooley and Hansen (1988) and King, et al. (1988)). Superneutrality implies that money growth affects inflation in the long-run and has no affect on the real interest rate.

Edge (2007) develops a sticky-price monetary business cycle model that is capable of generating a liquidity effect of an empirically plausible duration and magnitude. Models in which nominal shocks have real effects on the economy through sticky prices and/or sticky wages currently is the standard framework for analyzing issues relating to monetary policy. Edge (2007) relaxes a number of assumptions made in a standard sticky-price monetary business cycle model so as to produce a liquidity effect.

The empirical evidence of a liquidity effect is mixed. Studies prior to 1992 were single equation studies. Studies post-1992 employed Vector Autoregression (VAR) analysis in which identification issues were crucial to obtaining valid results.

VAR models have been used often to analyze the effects of monetary policy. As noted in the above survey of papers the effect of monetary policy differ across studies. They differ in terms of the variables which make up the model, the sample period for estimation and the and the method of identifying monetary policy shocks. As pointed out above, the identification of these policy shocks (i.e. the determination of exogenous shocks to monetary policy) is an important element in the estimation of the effects of monetary policy shocks. As stressed by Leeper (1992) and Leeper and Gordon (1992), the failure to clearly isolate exogenous money supply shocks from endogenous responses of the money stock to other exogenous shocks (such as to real money demand) can lead to misleading measurement and inference about the liquidity effect. Much of the extant literature on the liquidity effect is criticised for improperly identified shocks. As mentioned above, different identifying assumptions can lead to different conclusions about these effects. Thus, any characterization of the economy's response to a monetary policy shock should be robust over a broad range of identifying assumptions. We will review different identifying schemes.

Two methods have been employed in the VAR literature to identify structural shocks to monetary policy. One approach imposes restrictions on the contemporaneous relations among the variables of the VAR model. A second approach imposes restrictions on the long-run relations among the variables. While institutional and economic arguments are used to rationalize each identifying scheme, there is no consensus as to which approach is the most appropriate. It often depends on the question that the researcher is investigating. Weaknesses of both approaches have been discussed in the literature. Keaton (1992), Lestrapes and Selgin (1995), and McCarthy (1995) look at the limitations of the use of contemporaneous restrictions. Faust and Leeper (1997) discuss potential drawbacks of imposing long-run restrictions.

The effects of different monetary policy shocks for different identification scheme is evaluated by the use of impulse response function analysis. The use of monthly data (as in Bernanke and Mahiv, 1998) is beneficial because it reduces the potential problems that may arise with temporal aggregation (see Christiano and Eichenbaum, 1987). Bernanke and Mihiv (1998) and Christiano, Eichenbaum, and Evans (1999) compared the effects of alternative monetary policy shocks identified employing contemporaneous restrictions, within a common model, and a common sample period, they made no effort to see how their results would differ had they used long-run identifying restrictions. Pagan and Robertson (1995) did not consider the identification schemes of Bernanke and Blinder (1992), Strongin (1995), Bernanke and Mihov (1998a, 1998b), or long-run identifying restrictions. Pagan and Robertson (1995) impose Christiano, Eichenbaum, and Evans (1999) type and Strongin (1995) type restrictions within other modelsthat are a subset of the Christiano, Eichenbaum, and Evans (1999) model. They do not consider long-run identifying restrictions or the

Bernanke and Blinder (1992) or the Bernanke and Mihov (1998a,1998b) schemes. They also compare estimates of the liquidity effect for money supply shocks within a four variable model that includes money, price, output, and an interest rate. They use an identification scheme that imposes long-run restrictions, one that uses only contemporaneous restrictions and one that is a combination of long-run and contemporaneous restrictions.

Pagan and Robertson (1995) estimate a number of different VAR systems in order to determine whether a liquidity effect exists. They estimate models from 1959:01 to 1993:12 as well as shorter time periods; 1982:12-1993:12 and 1974:01-1993:12. Over the 1959-1994 period, a liquidity effect is observed when nonborrwed reserves are used as the money measure in a recursive VAR models. It is argued that innovations to NBR reflect the exogenous policy actions of the Federal Reserve. Christiano, Eichenbaum, and Evans (1996a, p. 18) argues that the evidence of a liquidity effect obtained by their recursive structural VAR stems from the fact that "innovations to NBR primarily reflect exogenous shocks to monetary policy..." But for broader measures of money there is a negligible or positive interest rate response, particularly when money is placed before the interest rate in the recursive ordering. Over the post-1979 period no evidence of a liquidity effect is found.

Pagan and Robertson (1998) compare estimates of the liquidity effect of a shock to a reserve or a monetary aggregate within three different VAR models. One model employed only contemporaneous restrictions to identify a shock to total reserves. One model used only long-run restrictions to identify a shock to either monetary base, M1, or M2. The third model used a combination of contemporaneous and long-run restrictions to identify a money supply (M1) shock. The variables in each model differ and there is not a common sample period used.

Faust and Leeper (1997) and Faust (1998) investigate how reliable are identification restrictions in Vector Autoregression (VAR) models. Bernanke and Blinder (1992), Christiano and Eichenbaum (1992b), Strongin (1995), Eichenbaum (1992), and Sims (1992) all argued that innovations to broad monetary aggregates primarily reflected shocks to money demand rather than shocks to money supply or policy. It was necessary to make alternative identifying assumptions in order to identify money supply shocks. Christiano and Eichenbaum (1992b) argues that the quantity of non-borrowed reserves is the best indicator of monetary policy stance.

Leeper and Gordon (1992) estimates a four variable VAR that includes the monetary base (MB), the federal funds rate (FFR), industrial production, (IP), and the consumer price index (CPI). They find a liquidity puzzle between the MB and the FFR; there is no negative relationship between MB and the FFR. The MB is made up of required reserves, excess reserves, and currency.

Christiano and Eichenbaum (1992b) employ simple cross-correlation analysis between the federal funds rate and different monetary aggregates. Christiano and Eichenbaum (1992b) show that the broad monetary aggregates used in previous studies are inappropriate for identifying the existence of the liquidity effect due to their large endogenous component because changes in broad aggregates reflect both the demand and supply shocks creating the money endogeneity problem. Christiano and Eichenbaum (1992b) argue that the quantity of non-borrowed reserves (NBR) is the best indicator of monetary policy stance. With NBR included in a VAR model instead of broad money supply, the fed funds rate exhibits a sharp persistent decline.

Strongin (1995) suggests using the proportion of NBR growth that is orthogonal to total reserves growth as a policy shock measure. Strongin (1995) finds that including this measure in a VAR model, estimated on sub-samples similar to those used by Leeper and Gordon (1992), yields a highly significant and persistent liquidity effect.

Strongin (1995) and Bernanke and Mihov (1998a,1998b) are interested in the transmission mechanism and model the federal funds market to estimate the liquidity effect. Strongin (1995) argues that the main source of the difficulty in identifying monetary policy from the use of monetary aggregate data is that a significant proportion of the variance in the reserve data is due to the Federal Reserve's accommodation of innovations in the demand for banking reserves rather than policy-induced supply innovations. This leads to a confounding of supply and demand innovations. Strongin (1995) uses a linear representation of the Federal Reserve's operating procedures, which include total reserves and a mix of borrowed and nonborrowed reserves supplied by the Federal Reserve to identify the exogenous disturbances to policy net of accommodation of demand shocks. By using two measures of reserves with different responses to supply and demand innovations it is possible to distinguish between changes in reserves that result from Federal Reserve policy innovations and changes in reserves which result from Federal Reserve's accommodation of demand innovations. Stongin (1995) generalizes a measure of nonborrowed reserves in order to nest different policy regimes. He assumes that the short-run demand for total reserves is inelastic and the open market Desk will provide sufficient reserves to satisfy this demand. Furthermore, he argues that given a policy tightening, the open market Desk contracts nonborrowed reserves, resulting in an increase in borrowed reserves. Thus, the ratio of nonborrowed reserves to total reserves should fall during a policy tightening. He estimates a model of nonborrowed reserves divided by total reserves from the previous month and the federal funds rate. He analyzes the response of these variables to changes in the nonborrowed reserves variable. Strongin (1995) notes that the failure of other studies to find a liquidity effect can be traced, at least in part, to a failure to account for the Federal Reserve's accommodation of the shifts in demand for money or reserves. The findings of Strongin (1995) are quite dramatic when compared to previous work. First, he finds that the liquidity effect holds in all subperiods. Second, his proposed measure of monetary policy disturbances has substantially more explanatory power for interest rates and real output than pure nonborrowed reserves, accounting for 49% of output at the end of two years. Third, the explanatory power of interest rates is substantially reduced when the policy measure is included, accounting for only 2% of the variance of output at the two years horizon. Fourth, nonborrowed reserves Granger-cause output while interest rates do not. Fifth, accommodative policy leads to a permanent and statistically significant increase in the price level.

The above set of results are closely linked to the results in Carpenter and Demiralp (2006) who also find strong evidence of the liquidity effect at the monthly frequency. Their study also highlights the importance of understanding why a liquidity effect may not exist. They note that looking at the contemporaneous correlations, there is a liquidity effect with respect to total reserve balances and the federal funds rate. This relationship does not hold when only non-borrowed reserves are studied. Because reserve requirements are determined by a banks' customers' demand for reservable deposits, which may or may not depend on the federal funds rate in a simple way, there is no reason to expect a liquidity effect between nonborrowed reserves and the federal funds rate in periods when required reserve balances constitute the majority of banks reserve balances.

In contrast to the mixed performance, studies that use nonrecursive simultaneous equation systems seem to have been successful at finding a strong liquidity effect, even for broad measures of money. Christiano and Eichenbaum (1992b) and Pagan and Robertson (1998) find that significant liquidity effect is only found in strictly recursive systems when nonborrowed reserves are used as the monetary aggregate. However, Gali (1992), Gordon and Leeper (1994) and Lastrapes and Selgin (1995) find strong liquidity effects generated with broad measures of money in nonrecursive structural systems. Pagan and Robertson (1998) attempts to determine the reason for this finding and to examine the robustness of their conclusions to see whether the conclusion reached are empirically fragile.

Pagan and Robertson (1998) examines how robust the conclusions of a number of studies are to various features of the data and the model used. They focus on the econometric issues caused by weak identifying information and also consider different sample periods for estimation. The Gordon and Leeper (1994) model is specified in levels of the series, while Lastrapes and Gordon (1995) and Gali (1992) are written in terms of transformations of the series that are assumed to be stationary. Lastrapes and Selgin (1995) assume that the levels of the series are integrated of order 1, I(1),-that is the series need to be first differenced to yield stationary. They assume the variables are I(1) but not cointegrated, allowing them to work with the variables in first differences. Gali (1992) assume that money and prices are I(2)—need to be differenced twice to become stationary, interest rates and output are I(1), and the real interest rate and the growth rate of real balances are stationary. The papers also differ in how they construct confidence intervals. Gordon and Leeper (1994) use the flat-prior Bayesian procedure to obtain confidence intervals for the estimated responses. Lastrapes and Selgin (1995) use a variant of the bootstrap procedure, while Gali (1992) does not report and precision measures for the estimated impact responses but uses the Bayesian procedure to obtain intervals for the dynamic multipliers conditional on the estimated impact responses. They conclude that the evidence for a liquidity effect is much weaker than that found in the original studies.

In their survey article Christiano, Eichenbaum, and Evans (1999) investigate the effects of a monetary policy shock under three of the more popular identification schemes used in the literature for VARs. They consider each set of identifying restriction in a seven-variable VAR model using quarterly data on output (Y=log of RGDP), prices (P=log of implicit GDP price deflator), commodity prices (CRB=smoothed change in the index of sensitive commodity prices), the federal funds rate (FF), total reserves (TR=log of total reserves), nonborrowed reserves (NBR=log of nonborrowed reserves plus extended credit), and money (M=log of M1 or log of M2).

The first identification scheme investigated specifies FF as the policy instrument of the Federal Reserve. Sims (1986) and Bernanke and Blinder (1992) argue the merits of this specification on institutional grounds. The second identification scheme considered assumes that NBR is the policy instrument. Christiano and Eichenbaum (1992b) claim that innovations to NBR are the best measure of exogenous monetary policy shocks. The third identification scheme examined set the policy instrument equal to NBR/TR. This is a scheme adopted in Strongin (1995) who argues that the short-run demand for total reserves is completely inelastic so, the effects of a monetary disturbances are internalized among the components of total reserves (total reserves = nonborrowed reserves plus borrowed reserves). Christiano, Eichenbaum, and Evans (1999) conduct their empirical analysis for each identification scheme separately and find that the results are qualitatively robust to any of the three identification schemes. All three policy measures find that an expansionary monetary policy shock causes the nominal interest rate to fall, output to rise, and the price level to increase slowly.

Carpenter and Demiralp (2008) ask why the demand for currency would be linked to the federal funds rate is unclear. The federal funds rate is the interest rate in the market for balances, not the monetary base, and since balances constitute less than 5% of the monetary base, one should not be surprised that there is no statistical relationship. Balances are composed of three components; required reserve balances, contractual clearing balances, and excess balances. Carpenter and Demiralp (2008) argue that total balances is the measure of money that is relevant for studying the liquidity effect relative to the federal funds rate.

Carpenter and Demiralp (2008) argue that reserves are related to "balances" but are not the same thing. They argue that the true liquidity effect is the relationship between balances and the federal funds rate. They argue that the use of nonborrowed reserves is inappropriate. They point out that the open market desk provides balances perfectly elastically at the target rate. As a result balances react endogenously to the federal funds rate and not the opposite. Nonborrowed reserves, which are influenced by changes in balances and banks' demand for vault cash also react endogenously. They argue that it is important to understand that nonborrowed reserves include vault cash and excludes a large fraction of balances (the variable the desk adjusts to maintain the target rate) and shows that the use of noborrowed reserves is an inappropriate measure of money. balances are the preferred variable. Carpenter and Demiralp (2008) estimate a VAR model that includes balances and allows each components of balances to change independently. They do not argue that a single component of balances is the appropriate measure of money to study. They demonstrate that using balances, the federal funds that are actually traded in the federal funds market, one can identify a liquidity effect. They argue that the liquidity puzzle is no puzzle at all, but merely a misspecification. Previous studies that have focused on reserves rather than balances have excluded a crucial component of the federal funds market. They note that Fed Balances can be broken down into three categories; required reserve balances, excess balances, and contractual clearing balances. The last category is not included in the measure of reserves.

Their baseline model includes the effective federal funds rate (FF), reservable deposits (RDEP), required reserve balances (RRB), contractual clearing balances (CCB), and excess reserve balances (ER). The impulse response functions indicate that CCB and ER show a negative reaction to a positive innovation to the federal funds rate, but only the response of CCB is statistically significant. Hence there is no liquidity puzzle. The liquidity effect found here is much larger than that found by Christiano, Eichenbaum and Evans (1996a). If the demand for balances are a function of economic activity then the results of Carpenter and Demiralp (2008) are subject to endogeneity bias. To test endogeneity they include in their VAR industrial production (IP) and the consumer price index (CPI). They find that the impulse responses for the balances are no different so they continue with their baseline model.

Table 1, below, presents a summary of some of the empirical literature that has been discussed above. It is interesting to note that when the liquidity effect is not found, it is, for the most part, within a single equation estimation method (especially the early literature). System based estimation (e.g. VARs) yield results that find evidence of a liquidity effect. Pagan and Robertson (1995) point out four issues concerning these conclusions: i) different definitions of monetary stance, ii) different models, iii) different estimation procedures and restrictions, and iv) different data samples.

The results of Table 1 also indicate that the definitions of money used in different studies determines whether evidence of a liquidity effect is found. Defining money as monetary base or M1 does not usually result in a liquidity effect while such measures as nonborrowed reserves (NBR) or nonborrowed reserves to total reserves (NBRX) do. Thornton (1988) in a single equation analysis, observed that NBR was the only measure of money which displayed evidence of a liquidity effect. After Thorton's publication researchers began using NBR. Thornton's conclusion has been reiterated by Christiano and Eichenbaum (1992b) in a systems context. Subsequently, Strongin (1995) has suggested that the ratio of NBR to total reserves (TR), NBRX, is the best monetary measure, and Eichenbaum and Evans (1995) have adopted NBRX in their work on exchange rates. The most controversial issue related to the use of nonborrowed reserves is whether it constitutes an effective way of measuring exogenous monetary policy. The variable NBRX is highly correlated with borrowed reserves (BR), raising the question about how BR should be treated.

# References

Bernanke, Ben S. and Alan S. Blinder, "The Federal Funds Rate and the Channels of Monetary Transmission," *American Economic Review*, **82** (1992): 901-921.

Bernanke, Ben S. and LLian Mihov, "Measuring Monetary Policy," *Quarterly Journal of Economics*, **113**(3) (August 1998a): 869-902.

Bernanke, Ben S. and LLian Mihov, "The Liquidity Effect and Long-run Neutrality," *Carnegie-Rochester Conference Series on Public Policy*, **49** (1998b): 149-194.

Bilan, Olena, "In Search of the Liquidity Effect in Ukraine," *Journal of Comparative Economics*, **33** (2005): 500-516

Cagan, Phillip, "Changes in the Cyclical Behavior of Interest Rates," *Review of Economics and Statistics*, **48** (Aug 1966): 219-250.

Cagan, Phillip. The Channels of Monetary Effects on Interest Rates, New York, NBER, 1972

Cagan, Phillip and A. Gandolfi "The Lag in Monetary Policy as Implied by the Time Patter of Monetary Effects on Interest Rates," *American Economic Review*, **2** (May 1969): 277-284.

Campbell, John Y., "Money Announcements, the Demand For Bank Reserves, and the Behavior of the Federal Funds Rate Within the Statement Week," *Journal of Money, Credit and Banking*, **19**(1) (February 1987): 56-67

Carpenter, Seth and Selva Demiralp, "The Liquidity Effect in the Federal Funds Market: Evidence From Daily Open Market Operations," *Journal of Money, Credit and Banking*, **38**(4) (June 2006):901-920.

Carpenter, Seth and Selva Demiralp, "The Liquidity Effect in the Federal Funds Market: Evidence at the Monthly Frequency," *Journal of Money, Credit and Banking*, **40**(1) (February 2008): 1-24.

Christiano, Lawrence J., "Modeling the Liquidity Effect of a Money Shock," *Federal Reserve bank of Minneapolis Quarterly Review*, **15** (Winter 1991): 3-34.

Christiano, Lawrence, "Resolving the Liquidity Effect: Commentary," *Federal Reserve Bank of St. Louis Review*, **77**(3) (1995): 55-61.

Christiano, Lawrence, "Identification and the Liquidity Effect: A Case Study," *Federal Reserve Bank of Chicago Economic Perspectives*, **20**(3) (1996): 2-13.

Christiano, Lawrence J., and Martin Eichenbaum, "Temporal Aggregation and Structural Inference in Macroeconomics," *Carnegie Rochester Conference Series on Public Policy*, **26** (1987): 63-130.

Christiano, Lawrence J., and Martin Eichenbaum, "Liquidity Effects and the Monetary Transmission Mechanism," *American Economic Review*, **82** (1992a): 346-353.

Christiano, Lawrence J., and Martin Eichenbaum, "Identification and the Liquidity Effect of a Monetary Policy Shock," in Alex Cukierman, Zvi Hercowitz, and Leonard Leiderman (eds.) *Business Cycles, Growth and Political Economy*, Cambridge, MA, MIT Press, (1992b), 335-370.

Christiano, Lawrence J., Martin Eichenbaum, "Liquidity Effects, Monetary Policy and the Business Cycle, *Journal of Money, Credit and Banking*, **27** (1995): 1113-1136.

Christiano, Lawrence J., Martin Eichenbaum, and Charles Evans,"The Effects of Monetary Policy Shocks: Some Evidence From the Flow of Funds," *The Review of Economics and Statistics*, **78**(1) (February 1996a): 16-34.

Christiano, Lawrence J., Martin Eichenbaum, and Charles Evans,"Identification and the Effects of Monetary Policy Shocks," In Blejer, M., Eckstein, Z., Hercowitz, Z., Leiderman, L. (eds.). *Financial Factors in Economic Stabilization and Growth*, Cambridge University Press, Cambridge, (1996b): 36-79.

Christiano, Lawrence J., Martin Eichenbaum, and Charles Evans,"Sticky Price and Limited Participation Models of Money: A Comparison," *European Economic Review*, **36** (1997): 1200-1249.

Christiano, Lawrence J., Martin Eichenbaum and Charles Evans, "Monetary Policy Shocks: What Have We Learned and to What End?" in John B. Taylor and Michael Woodford, (eds.) Handbook of Macroeconomics, Vol. 1A, Amsterdam, the Netherlands, *Elsevier Science*, B.V. 1999, Chapter 2, pp. 68-148.

Cochrane, John H., "The Return of the Liquidity Effect: A Study of the Short-run Relation Between Money Growth and Interest Rates," *Journal of Business and Economic Statistics*, .7 (1) (January 1989): 75-83

Coleman, Wilbur John, Christian Giles, and Pamela A. Labadie, "A Model of the Federal Funds Market," *Economic Theory*, 7(2) (March 1996)337-357.

Cooley, Thomas F., and G. Hansen, "The Inflation Tax in a Real Business Cycle Model," *American Economic Review*, (1989): 733-748.

Edge, Rochelle M., "Tim-to-Build, Time-to-Plan, Habit-Persistence, and the Liquidity Effect," *Journal of Monetary Economics*, **54** (2007): 1644-1669.

Eichenbaum, Martin, "Comment on Interpreting the Macroeconomic Time Series Facts: The Effects of Monetary Policy: by Christopher Sims, " *European Economic Review,* **36**(5) (June 1992): 1001-1012.

Eichenbaum, Martin and Charles Evans, "Some Empirical Evidence on the Effects of monetary Policy Shocks on Exchange Rates," *Quarterly Journal of Economics*, **110**(4) (November 1995): 975-1009.

Faust, Jon, "The Robustness of Identified VAR Conclusions About Money," *Carnegie-Rochester Conference Series on Public Policy*, **49** (December 1998): 207-244.

Faust, Jon and Eric M. Leeper, "When do Long-run Identifying Restrictions Give Reliable Results?" *Journal of Business and Economic Statistics*, **15** (July 1997): 345-353.

Friedman, Milton, "The Role of Monetary Policy," *American Economic Review*, **53** (1968): 3-17.

Friedman, Milton, "Factors Affecting the Level of Interest Rates," in Proceedings of the 1968 Conference on Saving and Residential Financing, United States and Loan League Chicago, 1969, pp. 11-27. Reprinted in Current Issues in "Current Issues in Monetary Theory and Policy, Thomas M. Havrilesky and John T. Boorman (eds) Arlington Heights, AHM Publishing Corp. 1976, 362-378.

Fuerst, Timothy, "Liquidity, Loanable Funds, and Real Activity," *Journal of Monetary Economics*, (1992): 3-24/

Furfine, Craig H., "Interbank Payments and the Daily Federal Funds Rate," *Journal of Monetary Economics*, **46**(2) (October 2000): 535-553.

Gali, Jordi, "How Well Does the IS-LM Model Fit Postwar US Data?" *Quarterly Journal of Economics*, **107**(2) (May 1992): 709-738.

Gibson, William E. "The Lag in the Effect of Monetary Policy on Income and Interest Rates," *Quarterly Journal Economics*, **84** (May1970a): 288-300.

Gibson, William E. "Interest Rates and Monetary Policy," *Journal of Political Economy*, (May/June 1970b): 431-455.

Gordon, Donald B., and Eric M. Leeper, "The Dynamic Impacts of Monetary Policy: An Exercise in Tentative Identification," *Journal of Political Economy*, (December 1994): 1228-1247.

Hamilton, James D., "The Daily Market For Fed Funds," *Journal of Political Economy*, **104**(1) (Feburary 1996): 26-56.

Hamilton, James D., "Measuring the Liquidity Effect," *American Economic Review*, **87**(1) (March 1997): 80-97.

Hamilton, James D., "The Supply and Demand For Federal Reserve Deposits," *Carnegie-Rochester Conference Series on Public Policy*, **49** (1998): 1-44.

Ho, Thomas S.Y., and Anthony Saunders, "A Micro Model of the Federal Funds Market," *Journal of Finance*, **40**(3) (December 1985): 977-988.

Jalil, Munir A., In Search of the Liquidity Effect: A Literature Review," *Working Paper* (2004) University of California-San Diego.

Judson, Ruth and Richard Porter, "Overseas Dollar Holdings: What Do We Know?" *Wirtschaftspolitische Blatter*, (2001) 48: 431-440.

Keaton, John W., "Structural Approaches to Vector Autoregressions," *Federal Reserve Bank of St. Louis Review*, **74** (1992): 37-57.

Keen, Benjamin D., "In Search of the Liquidity Effect in a Modern Monetary Model," *Journal of Monetary Economics*, **51** (2004): 1467-1494.

Kydland, Finn E. and Edward C. Prescott, "Time To Build and Aggregate Fluctuations," *Econometrica*, **50** (1982):1345-1370.

Kimball, M.S., "The Quantitative Analytics of the Basic Neomonetarist Model," *Journal of Money, Credit and Banking*, **27** (1995): 1241-1277.

King, R.G., and Mark W. Watson, "Money, Prices, Interest Rates, and the Business Cycle," *Review of Economics and Statistics*, **78** (1996): 35-53.

King, Robert G., Charles I. Plosser, and Sergio T. Rebelo, "Production, Growth in Business Cycles: I. The Basic Neoclassical Model," *Journal of Monetary Economics*, **21** (1988): 195-232.

Kopecky, Kenneth J. and Alan Tucker, "Interest Rate Smoothness and the Nonsettling-Day Behavior of Banks," *Journal of Economics and Business*, **45**(3-4) (August/October 1993)" 297-314.

Lastrapes, William D., and George Selgin, "The Liquidity Effect: Identifying Short-run Interest Rate Dynamics Using Long-run Restrictions," *Journal of Macroeconomics*, **17**(3) (1995): 387-404.

Leeper, Eric M., "Facing Up to Our Ignorance About Measuring Monetary Policy Effects," *Federal Reserve Bank of Atlanta Economic Review*, (May/June 1992): 1-16.

Leeper, Eric M., and David B. Gordon, "In Search of the Liquidity Effect," *Journal of Monetary Economics*, **29** (3) (June 1992): 341-369.

Leeper, Eric M., Christopher Sims, and Tao Zha, "What Does Monetary Policy Do?" *Brookings Papers on Economic Activity*, **2** (1996): 1-63.

Long, John B. Jr, and Charles I. Plosser, "Real Business Cycles," *Journal of Political Economy*, **91** (1983): 39-69.

Lucas, Robert E. Jr. "Liquidity and Interest Rates," *Journal of Economic Theory*," **50** (1990): 237-264.

McCarthy, Jonathan, "VARs and the Identification of Monetary Policy Shocks: A Critique of the Fed Reaction Function," *Unpublished Paper*, Federal Reserve Bank of New York, 1995.

Melvin, Michael, "The Vanishing Liquidity Effect of Money on Interest: Analysis and Implication for Policy," *Economic Inquiry*, **21** (2) (April 1983): 188-202.

Meulendyke, Ann-Marie, "US Monetary Policy and Financial Markets," *Federal Reserve Bank of New York*, New York, 1989.

Mishkin, Frederic S., "Monetary Policy and Short-term Interest Rates: An Efficient Markets-Rational Expectations Approach," *Journal of Finance*, **37**(1) (March 1982): 63-72.

Pagan, Adrian R., and John C. Robertson, "Resolving the Liquidity Effect," Federal Reserve Bank of St. Louis Review, (**77**)3 (May/June 1995): 33-54.

Pagan, Adrian R., and John C. Robertson, "Structural Models of the Liquidity Effect," *The Review of Economics and Statistics*, **80**(2) (May 1998): 202-217.

Reichenstein, William, "The Impact of Money on Short-term Interest Rates," *Economic Inquiry*, **25**(1) (January 1987): 67-82.

Rotemberg, J. and M. Woodford, "An Optimization-Based Econometric Framework for the Evaluation of Monetary Policy," *NBER Macroeconomic Annual*, (1997): 297-345.

Sims, Christopher A., "Are Forecasting Models Usable For Policy Analysis," *Federal Reserve Board of Minneapolis Quarterly Review,* **10** (1986): 2-16.

Sims, Christopher A., "Interpreting the Macroeconomic Time Series Facts: The Effects of Monetary Policy," *European Economic Review*, **36**(5) (June 1992): 975-1000.

Spindt, Paul and Vefa Tarhan, "The Federal Reserve's New Operating Procedures: A Post Mortem," *Journal of Monetary Economics*, **19** (1987): 107-123.

Stokes, H.H., and H. Neuburger, "The Effect of Monetary Changes on Interest Rates: A Box-Jenkins Approach," *Review of Economics and Statistics*, **61** (Nov. 1979): 534-548.

Strongin, Steven, "The Identification of Monetary Policy Disturbances: Explaining the Liquidity Puzzle," *Journal of Monetary Economics*, **25** (1995): 463-497.

Strongin, Steven, and Vefa Tarhan, "Money Supply Announcements and the Market's Perception of Federal Reserve Policy," *Journal of Money, Credit, and Banking*, (May 1990): 135-153.

Thornton, Daniel L., "The Effect of Monetary Policy on Short-term Interest Rates," *Federal Reserve Bank of St. Louis Review*, **70**(3) (June 1988): 53-72

Thornton, Daniel L., "Identifying the Liquidity Effect at the Daily Frequency," *Federal Reserve Bank of St. Louis Review*, **83**(4): (July/August 2001a): 59-78.

Thornton, Daniel L. "The Federal Reserve's Operating Procedures, Nonborrowed Reserves, Borrowed Reserves and the Liquidity Effect," *Journal of Banking and Finance*, **25**(9) (September 2001b): 1717-1739.

In: Liquidity, Interest Rates and Banking
Editors: J. Morrey and A. Guyton, pp. 35-56

ISBN: 978-1-60692-775-5
© 2009 Nova Science Publishers, Inc.

*Chapter 2*

# THE ABILITY OF THE TERM SPREAD TO PREDICT OUTPUT GROWTH, RECESSIONS, AND INFLATION: A SURVEY

## *Mark E. Wohar*[*]

Department of Economics, University of Nebraska at Omaha, RH-512K, Omaha, NE, USA

## Abstract

This article surveys the literature on the ability of the term spread (i.e. the long-term interest rate minus the short-term interest rate) to predict changes in economic activity. Some studies employ simple regression analysis to forecast changes in output, or dichotomous-choice models to forecast recessions. Other studies use time-varying parameter models, such as Markov Switching models and Smooth Transition Autoregression (STAR) models, to account for structural changes. Studies find that the informational content of the term spread has varied over time, and many conclude that the usefulness of the spread for forecasting changes in economic activity has diminished in recent years. However, most studies using data for the United States and the Euro area find that the term spread predicts output growth up to one year in the future.

Information about a country's future economic activity is important to consumers, investors and policymakers. Since Kessel (1965) first discussed how the term structure of interest rates varied with the business cycle, there has been a large amount of research examining whether the term structure is useful for predicting recessions or output growth. Many studies have found that the term spread (e.g., the difference between the yields on 10-Year and 3-month Treasury securities) is useful for forecasting different measures of economic activity, including real GDP growth, inflation, industrial production, consumption,

---

[*] E-mail address: mwohar@mail.unomaha.edu. Phone: 402-554-3712. Fax: 402-554-2853. (Corresponding author)

and recessions. The ability of the spread to predict economic activity has become somewhat of a "stylized fact" among macroeconomists.[1]

This article surveys the literatures on the usefulness of the term spread for forecasting output growth and recessions. We begin with a discussion of theoretical explanations that have been advanced for a relationship between the spread and future economic activity. We then present cross-country data relating the term spread to the business cycle, and survey empirical studies that investigate how well the spread predicts output growth and recessions. Our survey describes the data and methods used in various studies to investigate the predictive power of the term spread, as well as key findings. In summary, the weight of the empirical evidence indicates that the term spread is useful for predicting the growth rate of real GDP and recessions, but that the predictive content of the spread has declined since the mid-1980s.

## Why Might the Term Spread Predict Economic Activity?

Despite a large body of empirical evidence indicating that the term spread is useful for predicting economic activity, there is no standard theory as to why the relationship may exist. To a large extent, the usefulness of the spread for forecasting economic activity is a "stylized fact in search of a theory" (Benati and Goodhart, 2008), and most empirical studies advance only informal explanations for the relationship.

The rational expectations hypothesis of the term structure is the foundation of many explanations for why the term spread is useful in forecasting output growth and recessions. The expectations hypothesis (EH) holds that long-term interest rates are equal to the sum of current and expected future short-term interest rates, plus a term premium. When the public anticipates a recession, expected future short-term interest rates fall (long-term rates fall) and the yield curve flattens or becomes negatively sloped (i.e., long-term rates fall below short-term rates), so that a change in the slope of the yield curve reflects the expected change in economic activity. The simple EH view of the relationship between the term spread and future real economic activity is consistent with explanations that focus on either monetary policy or intertemporal consumption decisions (Benati and Goodhart, 2008).

Many explanations of the relationship between the yield curve and future economic activity focus on monetary policy (e.g., Akhtar, 1995; Bernanke and Blinder, 1992; Estrella and Hardouvelis, 1991; Duecker, 1997; Dotsey, 1998). For example, a monetary policy tightening may cause both short- and long-term interest rates to rise, but short-term rates are likely to rise more than longer-term rates if tighter policy i) is expected to reduce inflation, and therefore expected inflation, and thus, long-term rates will not increase much ii) is likely to result in a slowing of economic activity, and/or iii) is likely to be followed by an easing of monetary policy, and thus a lowering of the short-term interest rate. Hence, a temporary tightening of policy is likely to cause the yield curve to flatten and the term spread to decline. In general, such explanations have been stated without any underlying theory. For example, Estrella and Hardouvelis (1991) and Berk (1998) refer to simple dynamic IS-LM models but do not explicitly derive testable hypotheses from those models.

---

[1] This article uses the words term spread, yield curve, and term structure of interest rates interchangeably.

In contrast to explanations that focus on monetary policy, explanations based on theories of intertemporal consumption derive the relationship between the slope of the yield curve and future economic activity from the structure of the economy (e.g., Harvey, 1988; Hu, 1993; and Plosser and Rouwenhorst 1994). The central assumption in Harvey (1988), for example, is that consumers prefer a stable level of consumption rather than high consumption during economic expansions and low consumption during slowdowns. It follows that when consumers expect a recession in the following year, they will purchase one-year discount bonds to obtain income during the slowdown period. The increased demand for bonds causes the one-year yield to fall. Simultaneously, to finance the purchase of the one-year bonds, consumers will sell short-term financial instruments whose yields will rise. As a result the term structure will become flat or inverted.[2]

One problem with the interpretation of consumption smoothing models is that the theoretical results apply to the *real* term structure, i.e., the term structure adjusted for expected inflation, whereas much of the empirical evidence on the information content of the term structure is based on the *nominal* term structure. Whether the empirical evidence indicating that the yield curve predicts changes in output is consistent with the theoretical relationship depends on the persistence of inflation. If inflation is a random walk, implying that shocks to inflation are permanent, then a shock to inflation has no impact on the slope of the nominal yield curve because expected inflation will change by an identical amount at all horizons. However, if inflation has little persistence, an inflation shock will affect near-term expected inflation more than long-term expected inflation, causing the nominal yield curve to twist. Hence, the extent to which changes in the slope of the nominal yield curve reflect changes in the real yield curve depend on the persistence of inflation which, in turn, reflects the nature of the underlying monetary regime (Benati and Goodhart, 2008).[3]

Estrella (1998; 2005) derives a reduced form relationship between the change in real output and the term spread using a simple linear structural model of the economy of the type presented in Fuhrer and Moore (1995). The model consists of five structural equations: i) an accelerationist Phillips curve; ii) an IS curve relating the long-term interest rate to real output; iii) a monetary policy reaction function relating the short-term interest rate to deviations of the inflation rate from its target; iv) a Fisher equation linking the nominal interest rate to the real interest rate and expected inflation; and v) the expectations form of the term structure linking the long-term interest rate to a weighted average of the current short-term interest rate and the rationally-formed expected future short-term interest rates.

In Estrella's model, the extent to which the yield curve is a good predictor depends on the form of the monetary policy reaction function, which in turn depends on the monetary authority's policy objectives. An important implication of Estrella's model is that the coefficient linking changes in real output growth to the term spread depends on the

---

[2] The work of Rendu de Lint and Stolin (2003) is similar to that of Harvey (1988) in that they study the relationship between the term structure and real output growth in dynamic equilibrium asset pricing model. They find that the term spread predicts future consumption and output growth at long horizons in a stochastic endowment economy model augmented with endogenous production.

[3] Inflation tends to exhibit little persistence under metallic regimes (e.g. Bordo and Schwartz, 1999; Shiller and Siegel, 1977; and Barsky, 1987), or inflation-targeting regimes. Benati (2006) documents the absence of inflation persistence in the United Kingdom under both metallic standards and the current inflation-targeting regime, whereas Benati (2007) shows that inflation persistence is low to non-existent in three other inflation targeting countries – Canada, New Zealand, and Sweden.

coefficients in the monetary policy reaction function. Specifically, the more responsive is the policymaker to deviations of inflation from target inflation, the smaller will be the coefficient linking the spread to future output growth. Put simply, if the central bank is only concerned with stabilizing inflation, then one will find inflation and expected inflation being equal to target inflation, and hence, the expected changes in inflation will be zero. In the Estrella's model when the monetary authority reacts only to output fluctuations and focuses on the change in the interest rate, rather than its level, the yield curve is the optimal predictor of future output growth. The important empirical implication for the aforementioned results is that changes in the monetary policy regime can alter the relationship between the term spread and changes in output growth.[4]

Attempts to discriminate between the theoretical explanations for the ability of the term spread to forecast economic activity have produced mixed results. Harvey (1988) and Rendu de Lint and Stolin (2003) offer support for the consumption-smoothing explanation in that the slope of the yield curve is useful for forecasting both consumption and output growth. Laurent (1988, 1989), however, argues that the yield curve reflects the stance of monetary policy and finds that the term spread predicts changes in the growth rate of real GDP. On the other hand, Estrella and Hardouvelis (1991), Estrella and Mishkin (1997), and Plosser and Rouwenhorst (1994) find that the term spread has significant predictive power for economic growth independent of the information contained in measures of current and future monetary policy. This suggests that monetary policy actions contribute to the observed link between the term spread and economic activity, but cannot explain all of the observed relationship.[5]

Benati and Goodhart (2008) investigate the validity of the monetary policy and consumption-smoothing explanations for the observed correlation between the term spread and future changes in economic activity using Bayesian time-varying parameter vector autoregression models with stochastic volatility. They use data for the United States and the United Kingdom since the gold standard era, and for European countries, Australia and Canada since World War II. Benati and Goodhart (2008) find no clear support for either of the two dominant explanations of why the term spread appears to forecast changes in output. For example, they find that changes in the marginal predictive content of the nominal term spread for output growth since World War II do not match changes in inflation persistence, which is evidence against the consumption-smoothing explanation. On the other hand, similar to Estrella and Hardouvelis (1991) and Plosser and Rouwenhorst (1994), Benati and Goodhart (2008) finds that the term spread helps predict future changes in output even when the short-term interest rate is included in the model, suggesting that monetary policy alone cannot explain the ability of the spread to predict changes in output.

---

[4] Estrella and Mishkin (1997) present empirical evidence supporting a key role for monetary policy in the relationship between the term structure and future economic activity. Also see Feroli (2004).

[5] Estrella (1998) and Hamilton and Kim (2002) address the theoretical question of why the yield spread should forecast real economic activity. Hamilton and Kim (2002) and Ang, Piazzesi, and Wei (2006) show that the contribution of the spread can be decomposed into the effect of expected future changes in short-term interest rates and the effect of the term premium. They find that both factors are relevant for predicting real GDP growth but the respective contributions differ.

## Evidence on the Ability of the Term Spread to Predict Output Growth

Numerous studies have investigated the ability of the term spread to forecast output growth. Although a majority of studies use postwar U.S. data to examine the relationship between the term spread and output or recessions, several recent studies use data for other countries or time periods.

Much of the evidence on the ability of the term spread to forecast output growth comes from the estimation of linear models, such as the following linear regression, or some variant of it:

$$(Y_{t+4} - Y_t) = \alpha + \beta Spread + \gamma(L)\Delta Y_t + \varepsilon_t \qquad (1)$$

where $(Y_{t+4} - Y_t)$ is the growth rate of output (e.g., real GDP) over the next year (the time subscripts assume quarterly data), $\Delta Y_t = (Y_{t+4} - Y_t)$ is the annual growth rate of real GDP, *Spread* is the difference between a long-term interest rate (e.g., the 10-year bond) and a short-term interest rate (e.g., the 3-month Treasury bill yield), $\gamma(L)$ is a lagged polynomial, typically of length four (current and three lags), for example $\gamma(L) = \gamma_1 L^1 + \gamma_2 L^2 + \gamma_3 L^3 + \gamma_4 L^4$, where $L^i \Delta Y_t = \Delta Y_{t-i}$ and $\varepsilon_t$ is an i.i.d. error term.

Among the many studies that examine the predictive content of the yield curve for predicting U.S. output growth are Palash and Radecki (1985), Laurent (1988, 1989), Harvey (1989, 1993), Stock and Watson (1989, 2003), Bernanke (1990), Chen (1991), Estrella and Hardouvelis (1991), Hu (1993), Estrella and Mishkin (1996, 1998), Kozicki (1997), Bonser-Neal and Morley (1997), Dotsey (1998), Filardo (1999), Hamilton and Kim (2002), Estrella et al. (2003), Ang, Piazzesi and Wei (2006), and Bordo and Haubrich (2004, 2008). Studies that examine the relationship using international data include Jorion and Mishkin (1991), Harvey (1991) for the G-7 countries, Cozier and Tkacz (1994) for Canada, Plosser and Rouwenhorst (1994) for US, Canada, and Germany, Davis and Henry (1994) for the United Kingdom and Germany, Bonser-Neal and Morley (1997), Davis and Fagan (1997) for nine European countries, Estella and Mishkin (1997) examines the US, France, Germany, Italy and the UK, Smets and Tsatsaronis (1997), Bernard and Gerlach (1998) for eight countries (Belgium, Canada, France, Germany, Japan, the Netherlands, United Kingdom and United States), Boero, and Torricelli (1998) and Funkle (1997) for Germany, Gonzalez, Spencer and Walz, (2000) for Mexico, and Benati and Goodhart (2008) who examine the US and the UK since the Gold Standard Era and in the eurozone, Canada, and Australia over the post-WW II period.[6]

.Harvey (1988, 1989), Laurent (1988), and Estrella and Hardouvelis (1991) were among the first studies to present empirical evidence on the predictive power of the term spread. Harvey (1989), for example, finds that the spread between the yields on 5-year and 3-month U.S. Treasury securities predicts real GNP growth from 1- to 5-quarters ahead. Similarly, Estrella and Hardouvelis (1991) find that the spread between yields on 10-year and 3-month

---

[6] See Berk (1998) for a more detailed survey of early studies of the information content of the yield curve, and Stock and Watson (2003) for a survey of the literature on the use of asset prices in forecasting output and inflation.

Treasury securities are useful for forecasting U.S. output growth and recessions, as well as consumption and investment, especially at 4- to 6-quarter horizons.

Subsequent research by Plosser and Rouwenhorst (1994), Davis and Fagan (1997), Estrella and Miskin (1997), Berk and van Bergeijk (2001) and others investigate the usefulness of the term spread for forecasting output growth in the US as well as other countries. For example, Plosser and Rouwenhorst (1994) show that term spreads are useful for predicting real GDP growth in the United States, Canada, and Germany, though not in France or the United Kingdom. They also find that foreign term spreads help predict future changes in output in individual countries.

Davis and Fagan (1997) investigate the usefulness of the term spread for forecasting output growth among European Union countries, with an emphasis on out-of-sample forecasting. The authors find that the term spread has statistically significant within-sample explanatory power for output growth for six of nine countries. However, they also find that the spread improves out-of-sample forecasts and satisfies conditions for statistical significance and stability for only three countries (Belgium, Denmark, and the United Kingdom). Finally, Berk and van Bergeijk (2001) found that over the 1970-1998 period, the yield spread contains limited information on future output growth for the euro-area.

Several studies have examined whether the term spread contains information about future economic activity in Japan. Harvey (1991) found that the term spread contains no information about future economic activity in Japan for the period 1970-1989. By contrast, Hu (1993) did find a positive correlation between the terms spread and future economic activity in Japan for the period from January 1957 to April 1991. However, Hu (1993) also found that the lagged changes in stock prices and output growth have more explanatory power than the term spread.

More recently, Kim and Limpaphayom (1997) find that the term spread contains no information about future output in Japan for 1975-1991 as a whole, but that the spread is useful for predicting output growth up to five quarters ahead during 1984-1991. Kim and Limpaphayom (1997) argue that heavy regulation prevented interest rates from reflecting market expectations before 1984, and deregulation explains why the spread is useful for forecasting output growth subsequently. Nakaota (2005) examines whether the relationship between the term spread and output growth in Japan changed over time. The results indicate a break point in the relationship between interest rates and economic activity.

## Is the Term Spread Useful if Other Explanatory Variables Are Included in the Model?

Several studies examine whether the term spread remains useful for predicting output if other explanatory variables are included in the model. As noted previously, both Estrella and Hardouvelis (1991) and Plosser and Rouwenhorst (1994) find that the term spread has significant predictive power for economic growth even when a short-term interest rate is included as an additional explanatory variable. In addition, Stock and Watson (2003) find that including additional explanatory variables does not improve forecasts derived from their bivariate model of the term spread and output growth. However, they note also that the term spread itself has not forecast U.S. output well since the mid-1980s.

Ang, Piazzessi, and Wei (2006) argue that the regressions used in the term spread predictability regressions are unconstrained and do not model regressors endogenously. They build a dynamic model for GDP growth and yields that completely characterize expectations of GDP. Their model does not permit arbitrage. They examine US quarterly data over the period 1952 to 2001 and find, contrary to previous research, that the short-term interest rate predicts real GDP in out-of-sample forecasts better than the term spread, and that including the term spread does not improve forecasts based on the short-term However, Feroli (2004), employing more traditional regression techniques employ quarterly data for the US over the period 1962 to 2004 and adds the short-term interest rate to the right hand side of the output forecasting equation and finds that the yield spread continues to be significant.

Other studies find that the yield spread does contain information on future output growth independent of that contained in other macroeconomic variables. For example, Cozier and Tkacz (1994) find that the spread predicts future changes in real GDP growth even if the output gap is included as an explanatory variable in the forecasting model, suggesting that the predictive power of the term spread does not simply reflect the business cycle.[7]

## Stability of the Relationship between the Term Spread and Output Growth

Most studies of the usefulness of the term spread for forecasting output use post-World War II data for the United States and other developed countries. Kessel (1965) studied the relationship between the yield spread and output over long time periods, but did not explicitly test for structural breaks in the ability of the spread to predict movements in output. Several recent studies find that the spread does not predict output consistently over time and, in particular, that the information contained in the spread for future output has diminished in recent years.

Bordo and Haubrich (2004; 2006; 2008) test whether the term spread predicts movements in real economic activity in the United States throughout the period 1875-1997, and Baltzer and Kling (forthcoming) investigate the German experience over 1870-2003. Bordo and Haubrich (2008) estimate a model of real output growth that includes the term spread and contemporaneous value of real GDP growth and three of its lags as regressors. Bordo and Haubrich (2008) estimate their model over various subperiods distinguished by major changes in the monetary and interest rate environment, including the founding of the Federal Reserve System in 1914, World War II, the Treasury-Fed Accord of 1951, and the closing of the U.S. gold window and collapse of the Bretton Woods System in 1971. Bordo and Haubrich (2008) find that the term spread improves the forecast of output growth, as measured by the mean squared forecast error,[8] in only three of nine subperiods they examine: 1) the period preceding the establishment of the Federal Reserve System (1875-1913), 2) the

---

[7] Hamilton and Kim (2002) investigate the information content of the yield spread for future real GDP, and show that the spread's forecasting contribution can be decomposed into an effect related to expected changes in short-term rates and an effect related to the term premium. They conclude that both factors made statistically important contributions, although the effect of expected short-term rates is more important than the term premium for predicting future GDP.

[8] Judging the ability of the yield spread to predict by looking at the ratio of the two mean squared errors raises a potential problem. How does one know that the difference in the MSEs is due to something more than chance? Some tests have been developed by Diebold and Mariano (1995) and West (1996)\\\ but these tests are not applicable to nested hypotheses and can be particularly misleading in small samples (Clark and West, 2008). For this reason Stock and Watson (2003) do not report tests of forecast equality. Stock and Watson (2003) finds that the short-term interest rate helps to predict real GDP for the period 1971-1994 but not for the period 1985-1999. See Clark and McCracken (2001) for nested models.

first 13 years after the collapse of Bretton Woods (1971-84), and, to a lesser extent, 3) the most recent period (1985-97).[9]

Benati and Goodhart (2008) extend the work of Bordo and Haubrich (2004; 2006; 2008) by examining the marginal predictive content of the term spread for forecasting output growth in a model that also includes a short-term interest rate and inflation, as well as lagged output growth. Benati and Goodhart (2008) also examine whether changes in the marginal predictive content of the spread over time reflect changes in the underlying monetary regime. The study finds that the predictive power of the term spread has changed over time, and that estimates of the marginal predictive content of the spread are sensitive to the inclusion of the short-term interest rate and inflation in the model.[10] For example, from their bivariate model, the authors find that the term spread has a substantially larger predictive content for U.S. output during the 1880s and 1890s than during the first two decades of the 20$^{th}$ century, that the term spread has almost no information about future changes in output during the interwar years, and that the marginal predictive content of the spread during the post-war period is large only during the years of Paul Volcker's Federal Reserve chairmanship (1979-87). However, their four-variable model suggests that the term spread has predictive content only for the last years of the gold standard era before World War I, mixed content for the interwar period, and content only for the years of Volcker's chairmanship and around 2000-01. Benati and Goodhart (2008) also find considerable differences in the marginal predictive content of the term spread over time for other countries and for different forecast horizons.

Several studies find that the predictive content of the yield spread has diminished since the mid-1980s, both for the United States and for other countries (e.g., Haubrich and Dombrosky, 1996; Estrella and Mishkin, 1997; Smets and Tsatsaronis, 1997;and Dotsey, 1998), and researchers have noted that the spread did not clearly forecast the 1990-91 U.S. recession (e.g., Dotsey, 1998; Friedman and Kutner, 1998; Haubrich and Dombrosky, 1996; and Stock and Watson, 2003). Several studies find evidence of structural breaks in the relationship between the slope of the yield curve and output growth, thus calling into question the usefulness of the yield spread as a forecasting tool.

A recent study by Giacomini and Rossi (2006) reexamine the forecasting performance of the yield curve for output growth using forecast breakdown tests developed by Giacomini and (2008). They also perform tests for out-of-sample predictability. Giacomini and Rossi (2006) show the models for output growth are characterized by a predictability breakdown. In particular, they find that the evidence in favor of forecast breakdown at the 1-year horizon is particularly strong for 1974-76 and 1979-1987. Similarly, Estrella and Mishkin (1997) find that the relationship between the yield spread and U.S. economic activity changed in October 1979, when the Federal Reserve instituted monetary aggregate targeting to reduce inflation. As noted previously, Estrella (1998; 2005) and Estrella and Trubin (2006) argues that the usefulness of the term spread for forecasting changes in output growth will vary across monetary policy regimes, and the relationship between the spread and output growth is likely to be weaker, the more tightly the policy authority targets inflation.

---

[9] Bordo and Haubrich (2008) find that the yield spread predicts output less well during the pre-Fed period in rolling regressions with 24 quarter windows. However, their results for the post-Bretton Woods era are robust to the use of rolling regressions.

[10] See Jardet (2004) for a study that examines why the term spread has lost some of its predictive power.

## Evidence from Nonlinear Models

One feature of the literature discussed thus far is that it models the relationship between the term spread and changes in output as a linear framework, without investigation of possible asymmetric effects or nonlinearities in the relationship. However, some recent studies based on data for the United States and Canada have shown that the term spread-output relation might not be linear. Nonlinearity in the relationship between the term spread and changes in output has been modeled explicitly in several recent studies. For example, Galbraith and Tkacz (2000) test for asymmetry in the form of a threshold effect in which the impact of the term spread on future output growth is greater on one side of the threshold than on the other. Galbraith and Tkacz (2000) find evidence of an asymmetric impact of the term spread on the conditional expectations of output growth rates for the United States and Canada, though not for other major developed countries. Specifically, they find that for the United States and Canada, the predictive content of the term spread for output growth depends on past values of the spread.

For example, Tkacz (2001) uses neural network models to study the relationship between the term spread and output growth. Using data for Canada, Tkacz (2001) finds that this class of nonlinear models have smaller forecast errors than linear models. Venetis, Paya, and Peel (2003) use nonlinear smooth transition (STR) models that can accommodate regime-type nonlinear behavior and time-varying parameters to examine the predictive power and stability of the term spread-output relationship. Using data for the United States, United Kingdom, and Canada, Venetis, Paya, and Peel (2003) find that the spread-output growth relationship is stronger when past values of the term spread do not exceed a positive threshold value.[11]

Other studies use Markov-switching models to capture nonlinearities in the relationship between the yield spread and economic activity. Vazquez (2004) employs a Makov-Switching framework to investigate the relationship between the term spread and changes in short-term interest rates. He points out that there is a large body of evidence that finds switch between regimes. Economists have related these interest rates to changes in monetary policy. He argues that one can distinguish between two types of period during US post-war history. There are periods when short-term interest rates behave as a random walk. In the first regime the term spread has no predictive content for changes in the short-rate. This period is also characterized by relatively low and stable interest rates and inflation. The second type of periods are when the short-term interest rates are persistence (short-rate follows a unit root process) but the term spread has some ability to predict changes in short-term interest rates. These periods are characterized by high, volatile interest rates and inflation. It has been argued that the Fed conducts interest rates smoothing of short-term interest rate during low inflation periods and this makes the nominal interest rate appear to be nonstationary. When large shocks occur and inflation and the term spread become higher and more volatile, policymakers can switch to an alternative regime where the short-term interest rate responds positively to large, volatile term spreads in order to fight inflation. Vazquez (2004) finds that i) the short-term rate behaves as a random walk in a regime characterized by low conditional volatility, and the term spread Granger-causes the short-term interest rate characterized by high conditional volatility and ii) the term spread is very persistent, especially in the low

---

[11] For a discussion of STR models, see McMillan (2004, 2007) and McMillan and Spreicht (2007) and the references their in.

volatility regime. Vasguez (2004) shows that all of these features come about when estimating a bivariate Markov Switching VAR model using post-war US interest rate data from the long end of the maturity spectrum.

Anderson and Vahid (2000) employ a bivariate nonlinear model of output and the interest rate spread, and compare its ability for predicting recessions with linear and nonlinear models of output. Their findings support earlier studies in that they find the spread is a better leading indicator for output growth and money supply. They also find that their nonlinear model of output and the spread gives less false warnings of recessions than a linear model. Galvao (2006) develops a model to predict recessions that accounts for nonlinearity and a structural break when the term spread is the leading indicator. The model can estimate and identify time-varying nonlinearity in a Vector Autoregression (VAR) model. Their model with time-varying thresholds predicts better than the timing of recessions that models with constant threshold or with only a break.

Duarte, Venetis, and Paya (2005) use quarterly data for the Euro area over the period 1970:1-2000:4 and apply linear regression as well as nonlinear models to examine the predictive accuracy of the term spread-output growth relationship. They find that the term spread of the Euro area is a useful indicator of future output growth and of future recessions in the Euro area. They find that linear indicator and nonlinear threshold indicator models predict output growth quite well for four quarters ahead (which has been called the 'stylized' fact). The linear models, however, shows signs of instability. They find that there are significant nonlinearities with respect to time and past annual growth. Their nonlinear model outperforms the linear model in out-of-sample forecasts of 1-year ahead annual growth. In addition, they find that probit models that use EMU and US yield spreads are successful in predicting EMU recession. Venetis et al. (2003) employ a Smooth Transition model and find evidence of a strong threshold effect. Specifically, the relationship between the spread and economic growth rates is stronger if past spread values do not exceed a given positive value.

## Evidence on the Usefulness of the Term Spread for Forecasting Recessions

Several studies investigate the usefulness of the yield spread for forecasting recessions. Most of these studies estimate a probit model of the following type, in which the dependent variable is a categorical variable set equal to 1 for recession periods and to 0 otherwise:

$$P(recession_t) = F(\alpha_0 + \alpha_1 S_{t-k}), \qquad (2)$$

where F indicates the normal cumulative distribution function. If the coefficient $\alpha_1$ is statistically significant, then the term spread, $S_{t-k}$, contains information that is useful for forecasting a recession k periods ahead. How well the spread predicts recessions when additional explanatory variables are included in the model can be tested by means of the following regression:

$$P(recession_t) = F(\alpha_0 + \alpha_1 S_{t-k} + \alpha_2 X_{t-k}), \qquad (3)$$

where $X_{t-k}$ is a vector of additional explanatory variables. If $\alpha_1$ is significant in Equation (2) but not in Equation (3), then the ability of the spread to predict recessions is not robust to the inclusion of other variables.

Using probit estimation, Estrella and Hardouvelis (1991) and Estrella and Mishkin (1998) provide evidence that the yield spread significantly outperforms other financial and macroeconomic variables in forecasting U.S. recessions. Estrella and Hardouvelis (1991) document that the spread between the yields on 10-year and 3-month Treasury securities bill rate is a useful predictor of recessions, as well as of future growth of output, consumption, and investment. Estrella and Mishkin (1998) compare the out-of-sample performance of various financial variables, including interest rates, interest rate spreads, stock prices and monetary aggregates, as predictors of U.S. recessions. They find that stock prices are useful for predicting recessions at one-to-three quarter horizon, but that the term spread outperforms all other indicator variables beyond a one quarter forecast horizon. Duecker (2005) confirms the results of Estrella and Mishkin (1998) using a dynamic probit model that includes a lagged dependent variable and also allows for Markov-switching coefficient variation. Finally, Estrella, Rodrigues, and Schich (2003) find that probit models of recession are more stable than models that attempt to estimate the predictive content of the yield spread on continuous variables, such as GDP growth or industrial production.

Evidence on the ability of the term spread to predict recessions in other countries has been mixed. Plosser and Rouwenhorst (1994) find that the spread is useful for forecasting recessions in the United States, Canada, and Germany, but not in France or the United Kingdom. Estrella and Mishkin (1997) examines the US, France, Germany, Italy and the UK to investigate the effect of the term spread on the probability of a recession. They also employ a regression of output growth on the lagged spread. They find that the usefulness of the term spread for forecasting recessions, output growth and inflation varies across countries. By contrast, Bernard and Gerlach (1998) employ a probit model and find that the term spread forecasts recessions up to two years ahead in eight countries (Belgium, Canada, France, Germany, Japan, the Netherlands, United Kingdom and United States) over the period 1972-93. There are notable difference across the countries. While German and US interest rate spreads are significant in the regressions for the other countries, the added information is limited except in Japan and the UK. More recently, Moneta (2005) finds that the spread is useful for predicting recession probabilities for the euro area as a whole, and that the spread appears to contain information beyond that already available in the history of output growth.[12]

Several studies augment a basic probit model (Equation 2) to test whether the usefulness of the term spread for predicting recessions is compromised by including other explanatory variables. For example, Bernard and Gerlach (1998) include both an index of leading indicators and foreign interest rate term spreads in a recession model. While leading indicators contain information beyond that in the term spreads, this information is only useful for forecasting recession, in the immediate future. Bernard and Gerlach (1998) find that the terms spreads of Germany and the United States are particularly useful for forecasting recessions in Japan and the United Kingdom, respectively.

---

[12] Moneta (2005) examines the predictive power of ten yield spreads, representing different segments of the yield curve. Moneta (2005) finds that the spread between the yield on 10-year government bonds and the 3-month interbank rate outperforms all other spreads in predicting recessions in the euro area.

Wright (2006) finds that a probit model that includes the level of the federal funds rate and the yield spread fits better in sample, and provides better out-of-sample prediction of recessions, than a probit model that only includes only the yield spread. Ahrens (2002) augments the standard probit model (Equation 2) with the calculated Markov-switching recession probability as an explanatory variable, and estimates the model using data for eight OECD countries (Canada, France, Germany, Italy, Japan, Netherlands, United Kingdom, and United States). Ahrens (1999, 2002) finds that the term spread is a reliable predictor. For each country analyzed the two estimated regimes are found to be associated with recessions or expansions respectively. They find that business cycle troughs are more difficult to predict than peaks. They find that the estimated recession probabilities are more accurate and less volatile than those probabilities obtained from using a conventional probit approach with unfiltered spread. He also finds that using the Markov-Switching probabilities as the explanatory variable does not significantly improve the predictability of the spread.

Other studies that estimate an augmented probit (or logit) model, or compare results from probit estimation with those obtained using other methods, include Layton and Katsuura (2001), Del Negro (2001), Chauvet and Potter (2002. 2005), and Sensier et al. (2004). Layton and Katsuura (2001) employ three different non-linear models (a probit model, logit model, and a Markov-Switching model) to forecast U.S. business cycles. Their analysis reveals that the Markov Switching models performs the best. Chauvet and Potter (2002) compare recession forecasts obtained using four different probit model specifications: a time-invariant conditionally independent version; a business cycle-specific conditionally independent model; a time-invariant probit model with autocorrelated errors, and a business-cycle specific probit with autocorrelated errors. Chauvet and Potter (2002) find evidence in favor of the business-cycle specific probit with autocorrelated errors, which allows for multiple structural breaks across business cycles and autocorrelation. Duecker (2005) proposes a vector autoregression ("Qual-VAR") model to forecast recessions using data on the term spread, GDP growth, inflation, and the federal funds rate. Duecker (2005) finds that the model fits well in-sample, and accurately forecasted the 2001 recession out of sample. Del Negro (2001) estimates a Bayesian VAR, but it does not perform better than the Estrella and Mishkin (1997) model. Sensier et al. (2004) document that financial and real variables predict recessions in European countries using logit models. They show that international data (specifically, the U.S. leading indicator index, term spread, and short-term interest rate) are useful for predicting European business cycles.

Finally, two other studies that use non-standard methods to estimate the predictive power of the term spread for recessions are Shaaf (2000) and Sephton (2001). Shaff (2000) uses a neural network model employing US data and finds evidence that confirms earlier studies in that a flat or inverted yield curve predicts a recession. His out-of-sample simulation suggests that the forecasts of the artificial net work is more accurate with less error and less variation than those of the regression model. Sephton (2001) uses a nonparametric model called the multivariate adaptive regression splines (MARS), and finds a stronger relationship between the term spread and recessions, especially in-sample, using the MARS approach than with a probit model.

A number of studies have estimated the information content of the Italian term spread along with respect to recession probabilities. For example, Estrella and Mishkin (1997), Moneta (2005), Sensier et al. (2004), Marotta et al. (2006), and Brunetti and Torricelli (2008). Estrella and Mishkin analyze the information content of the term spread on economic activity in Italy at a comparative level with France, Germany, UK and the US. As for the Italian case they report that the term spread has a predictive power with respect to recession probabilities up to one and two years ahead and the result is robust to the inclusion of other monetary indicators. Moneta (2005) tests the predictive power of the spread in Italy, France and Germany to test whether evidence for the whole Euro area, and for single countries is consistent. Even if less strong than in Germany, the author finds a significant predictive power of the term spread also in Italy and shows that the spread is more powerful than the OECD Composite Leading Indicators in forecasting recessions. Sensier et al. (2004) tests the predictive power of the term spread on recession probabilities three months ahead in Italy and Germany, France, and the UK. Even if a logistic rather than a probit model is used, a significant information content of the term spread is reported. He finds that the predictive power of the spread is not maintained when other information variables are added to the model. Marotta et al. (2006) estimates recession probabilities for an application to the Base II capital requirement formula, performing the forecast within a probit model and comparing two different business cycle chonologies, namely ISAE and ECRI ones. He estimates a probit model with both domestic and foreign financial variables. They find that the ISAE chronology are improved if, instead, the ECRI chronology are adopted underlying the importance of a further analysis of the chronology selection issue.

Brunetti and Torricelli (2008) investigates the information content of the Italian term spread as for real output growth rates and recession probabilities and to test the predictive power of the spread. The linkages between the spread and economic growth is modeled as a nonlinear one (specifically, a Logistic Smooth Transition model) while a probit model is implemented to forecast recession probabilities. The study utilizes OECD business cycle chronology. Overall, the evidence supports the information content of the spread in Italy over the entire period (1984-2005) although results are more satisfactory for the period (1992-2005).

## Is the Term Spread Useful in Predicting Output Gap, Inflation or Foreign Yield Curves?

Zagaglia (2006a) provides evidence of a negative long-run relation between yield spread and future output growth. Fluctuations among certain yields and macro variables are becoming increasingly synchronized across countries, in line with increased globalization. An important question related to the yield curve is can information from foreign yield curves help improve domestic yield curve forecasts and vice versa? Diebold, et al. (2006), and Perignon et al. (2007) examine contemporaneous dynamic interdependencies of yield curves across countries and find the existence of common factors which explain a significant part of yield developments in individual countries. Next to the yield curve literature is a related strand of literature that focuses on revealing causality linkages on individual yields across major countries (Frankel et al., 2004; Chinn and Frankel, 2005; Wang et al. 2007). This strand of literature uses a variety of in-sample fit methods including Granger causality tests in an effort to find evidence of strong international dependencies among interest rates, with the direction of causality running from the US to the rest of the world.[13]

---

[13] Wang et al. (2007) performs out-of-sample Granger causality tests for individual rates.

Modugno and Nikolaou (2007) investigate whether international linkages in interest rates help to forecast domestic yield curves out-of-sample. The econometric technique is based on a dynamic factor model. They employ Maximum Likelihood estimation techniques based on the EM algorithm and the Kalman filter (Doz et al. 2006; Coroneo et al. 2007) to estimate and forecast the different model specifications. They identify the factors driving the yield curve as level, slope, and curvature according to the methodology of Diebold and Li (2006). They apply this methodology to three major countries, the US, the UK and Germany. They allow information from foreign yield curves to be a part of domestic yield curves. They compare the forecast accuracy of the international model with the purely domestic model. Each domestic yield curve is summarized by three factors, level, slope, and curvature. Their results suggest that international linkages can help improve yield curve forecasts, especially for countries with lagging dependency patterns. The model works particularly well for the German case. Their results reveal that the German yield curve forecasts are improved by including information from the US and UK, thus suggesting a dynamic dependency of Germany on these two countries. For the US case the relationship appears unidirectional, where the domestic model appears to be the best., thereby confirming its leading role. In the UK, international information from Germany and the US help at the longer forecast horizons, whereas the US appears to be unaffected by yields in Germany and the UK. Germany is found to be particularly dependent on information coming from foreign sources (one way causality with the US and the UK). The UK appears dependent to a smaller degree (two-way causality with Germany and one-way causality with the US). There is an independent role for the US in the international environment (i.e. causality linkages among other countries and the US are unidirectional). The results generalize previous literature results on international linkages in interest rates (Frankel et al., 2004; Chinn and Frankel, 2005; Belke and Gross, 2005), further supporting a loading role for the US and the existence of lagging dependency patterns between US and Germany. (see also Artis 1997, 2004)

It is important to note that first, such linkages are economically significant, (i.e. trading gains can be established based on forecasts). To analyze this the modeling framework would need to include arbitrage opportunities, including trading costs and restrictions to replicate trading strategies. Second, there is no discussion of the causes of such linkages.

Economists are not very good at forecasting recessions. Zarnowitz and Braun (1993) found that economic forecasters made their largest prediction errors during recessions and Diebold and Rudebusch (1989, 1991a, 1991b) provide a pessimistic assessment of the ability of the index of leading indicators to provide useful signals of future recessions. Rudebusch and Williams (2007) provide new evidence by examining the information content of economic forecasts provided by participants in the Survey of Professional Forecasters (SPF). They find that these forecasters have little ability to predict recessions, especially at forecast horizons of a few quarters ahead.

Zagaglia (2006b) examines whether the yield spread predicts the output gap for the US. They find that it does have predictability but only at short horizons of 1 to 3 quarters over the post-WW II sample. When he includes both the federal funds rate and the spread into the output gap equation over the post-1985 sub-sample, he finds that the yield spread continues to predict the output gap. This suggests that monetary policy is statistically irrelevant for prediction of the output gap over the post-1985 sub-sample. For pre-1985 data Zagaglia (2006b) finds that the fed funds rate is statistically significant in the output gap equation (that contains the yield spread). Surprisingly the fed funds rate is insignificantly different from zero during the post-1985 sub-period. Opposite to conventional wisdom, the sign is negative on the federal funds rate.

Tkacz (2004) using interest rate spreads to explain changes in inflation, investigate whether such relationships can be modeled using two-regime threshold models. They find that linearity is rejected in favor of the nonlinear threshold model. He finds that the inflation-yield spread linkage is most pronounced when the yield spread is inverted, which are periods associated with tight monetary policy. He argues that this implies that monetary policy may have an asymmetric effect on inflation.

A few studies have considered the predictive ability of the term spread for inflation but the results are less satisfactory than the prediction of GDP growth. Ivanova, Lahiri and Seitz (2000) examine the ability of yield spreads to forecast future inflation. Other studies include, Mishkin (1990a,b), (1991) who find that the yield curve can predict inflation. Mishkin derives his framework from the fisher equation. Mishkin's results are confirmed by Fama (1990), Jorion and Mishkin (1991), Abken (1993), Frankel and Lown (1994), Gerlach (1997), Estrella and Mishkin (1997), Kozicki (1997), Schich (1999), Nagayasu (2002), Tkacz (2004), and Nielsen (2006).[14]

## Summary

This article surveys the literature on the ability of the term spread (i.e. the long-term interest rate minus the short-term interest rate) to predict output growth, inflation, and recessions. Some studies employ simple regression models to forecast changes in output, or dichotomous-choice models to forecast recessions. Other studies use time-varying parameter models, such as Markov Switching models and Smooth Transition Autoregression (STAR) models, to account for structural changes. In sum studies find that the informational content of the term spread has varied over time, and many studies conclude that the spread generally is able to predict output growth up to 6 quarters in the future. This is true for a number of countries. The spread is also able to predict a recession up to one year in the future. However, the predictability of the spread for these macro variables has diminished in recent years. Studies also find that variables that are added to regression equations in addition to the spread do not improve the forecastability of the dependent variable. It would seem that augmenting the spread with additional macroeconomic variables does not proof to be a useful exercise.

## References

Abken, Peter A., "Inflation and the Yield Curve," *Federal Reserve Bank of Atlanta Economic Review*, **78** (1993): 13-31.
Ahrens, R., "Examining Predictors of U.S. Recessions: A Regime-Switching Approach," *Swiss Journal of Economics and Statistics*, **135** (1): (1999): 97-124.

---

[14] A few studies have considered the predictive ability of the term spread for inflation but the results are less satisfactory than the prediction of GDP growth. Ivanova, Lahiri and Seitz (2000) examine the ability of yield spreads to forecast future inflation. Other studies include, Mishkin (1990), Kozicki (1997), Nagayasu (2002), Tkacz (2004), Nielsen (2006)

Ahrens, R., "Predicting Recessions With Interest Rate Spreads: A Multicountry Regime-Switching Analysis," *Journal of International, Money and Finance*, **21** (2002): 519-537.

Akhtar, M. A., "Monetary Policy and Long-term Interest Rates: A survey of Empirical Literature," *Contemporary Economic Policy*, **XIII**, (1995): 110-130.

Anderson, H.M., and F. Vahid, "Predicting the Probability of a Recession With Nonlinear Autoregressive Leading Indicator," *Macroeconomic Dynamics* **5**:4 (2001): 482-505

Anderson, H.M., and F. Vahid, "Predicting the Probability of a Recession With Nonlinear Autoregressive Leading Indicator," *Monash University Working Paper* (2000-3)

Ang, A. Piazzesi, M., and M. Wei, "What Does the Yield Curve Tell us About GDP Growth?" *Journal of Econometrics*, **131** (2006): 359-403.

Artis, M. J., Kontklemis, Z.G., and D.R. Osborne, "Business Cycles for G-7 and European Countries," *Journal of Business*, **70**:2 (1997): 249-279.

Artis, M.J., Krolzig, H.M., and J. Toro, "The European Business Cycle," *Oxford Economic Papers*, **56**:1 (2004): 1-44.

Bai, j., and P. Perron, "Estimating and Testing Linear Models With Multiple Structural Changes," *Econometrica*, **66** (1998): 47-78.

Baltzer, Markus and Gerhard Kling, "Predictability of Future Economic Growth and the Credibility of Different Monetary Regimes in Germany, 1870-2003," *Applied Economics Letters* (forthcoming),

Barsky R., "The Fisher Hypothesis and the Forecastability and Persistence of Inflation," *Journal of Monetary Economics*, **19**:1 (1987): 3-24.

Belke, A., and D. Gros, "Asymmetries in Trans-Atlantic Monetary Policy Making: Does the ECB Follow the Fed?" *Journal of Common Market Studies*, **43**:5 (2005): 921-946.

Benati, L., "U.K. monetary regimes and macroeconomic stylised facts." Bank of England *Working Paper* No. **290**, 2006.

Benati, L.,"Investigating inflation persistence across monetary regimes." *The Quarterly Journal of Economics*, **123**:3 (2008): 1005-1060.

Benati, L.,"Investigating inflation persistence across monetary regimes." *European Central Bank Working Paper*, forthcoming, (2007).

Benati, L., and C. Goodhart, "Investigating Time Variation in the Marginal Predictive Power of the Yield Spread," *Journal of Economic Dynamics and Control*, **32** (2008): 1236-1272.

Berk, J.M., :"The Information Content of the Yield Curve for Monetary Policy: A Survey," *De Economist*, **146**, (1998): 303-320.

Berk, J.M., and P. van Bergeijk, "Is the Yield Curve a Useful Information Variable for the Eurosystem?" *Kredit and Kapital*, **1**, (2001): 28-47. No. 11 (2000).

Bernanke, B.S., "On the Predictive Power of Interest Rates and Interest Rate Spreads," Federal Reserve Bank of Boston, *New England Economic Review*, (Nov/Dec. 1990): 51-68.

Bernanke, B.S. and A.S., Blinder, "The Federal Funds Rate and the Channels of Monetary Transmission," *American Economic Review*, **82** (1992): 901-921.

Bernard, H.., and S. Gerlach, "Does the Term Structure Predict Recession? The International Evidence," *International Journal of Finance and Economics*, **3** (1998): 195-215.

Bonser-Neal, C., and T. Morley, "Does the Yield Spread Predict Real Economic Activity: A Multicountry Analysis," *Federal Reserve Bank of Kansas City Economic Review*, (1997, 3$^{rd}$ Quarter): 37-53.

Boero G., and C. Torricelli, "The Information in the Term Structure of Germany Interest Rates," *European Journal of Finance*, **8** (1998): 21-45.

Bordo, Michael D, and Joseph G. Haubrich, "The Yield Curve, Recessions, and the Credibility of the Monetary Regime: Long-run Evidence, 1875-1997," *NBER working Paper* no. **10431** (2004)

Bordo, Michael D., and Joseph G. Haubrich, "Forecasting the Yield Curve: Level, Slope and Output: 1875-1997," *Economic Letters,* **99**:1 (2008): 48-50.

Bordo, Michael D., and Joseph G. Haubrich, "The Yield Curve as a Predictor of Growth: Long-run Evidence, 1875-1997," *Review of Economics and Statistics*, **90**:1 (February 2008): 182-185.

Bordo, Michael D., and Anna J. Schwartz, "Monetary Policy Regimes and Economic Performance: The Historical Record," In Taylor, J.B., Woodford, M. (Eds.) *Handbook of Macroeconomics*, North-Holland, Amsterdam (1999).

Bosner, N.C., and T.R., Morley, "Does the Yield Spread Predict Real Economic Activity? A Multicountry Analysis," *Federal Reserve Bank of Kansas City Economic Review*, **82** (1997): 37-53.

Brunetti, Marianna, and Costanza Torricelli, "Economic Activity and Recession Probabilities: Information Content and Predictive Power of the Term Spread in Italy," *Applied Economics*, (2008) Forthcoming

Chauvet, Marcell, and Simon Potter, "Predicting Recessions: Evidence From the Yield Curve in the Presence of Structural Breaks,' *Economics Letters,***77**(2) (2002): 245-253.

Chauvet, Marcelle, and Simon Potter, "Forecasting Recessions Using the Yield Curve," *Journal of Forecasting,* **24** (2) (March 2005): 77-103.

Cecchetti, Stephen G., "Inflation Indicators and Inflation Policy," (pp. 189-219) in B.S. Bernanke and J.J. Rotemberg (Eds.) *NBER Macroeconomic Annuals*, (Cambridge, MIT Press, 1995)

Chen, N., "Financial Investment Opportunities and the Macroeconomy," *Journal of Finance*, **46**: 2 (1991): 529-554.

Chinn, M., and J. Frankel, "The Euro Area and World Interest Rates," Santa Cruz Department of Economics, *Working paper* **1031** (2005)

Clark, Todd E., and Michael W. McCracken, "Tests of Equal Forecast Accuracy and Encompassing for Nested Models," *Journal of Econometrics*, **105** (2001), 85-110.

Clark, Todd E., and Kenneth D. West, "Using Out-of-Sample Mean Squared Prediction Errors to Test the Martingale Difference Hypothesis," *Journal of Econometrics*, in Press (2008)

Coroneo, L., D. Giannone and M. Modugno, "Forecasting the Term Structure of Interest Rates Using a Large Panel of Macroeconomic Data," *Working Paper* (2007)

Cozier, B., and G. Tkacz, , "The Term Structure and Real Activity in Canada " *Bank of Canada Working Paper,* (1994):

Davis, E. P., and G. Fagan, "Are Financial Spreads Useful Indicators of Future Inflation and Output Growth in EU Countries," *Journal of Applied Econometrics*, **12** (1997): 701-714.

Davis, E.Philip, and S.G.B. Henry, "The User of Financial Spreads as Indicator Variables: Evidence for the United Kingdom and Germany," *IMF Staff Papers*, **41** (Sept. 1994): 517-525.

Del Negro, M., "Turn, Turn, Turn: Predicting Turing Points in Economic Activity," *Federal Reserve Bank of Atlanta Economic Review*, (2001, second quarter): 1-12.

Diebold, Francis X., and C. Li, "Forecasting the Term Structure of Government Bond Yields," *Journal of Econometrics*, **130** (2006): 337-364.

Diebold, Francis X., and Robert S. Mariano, "Comparing Predictive Accuracy." *Journal of Business and Economics and Statistics*, **13** (1995): 253-263.

Diebold, Francis X., and Glenn D. Rudebusch, "Scoring the Leading Indicators," *Journal of Business*, **62** (1989): 369-391.

Diebold, Francis X., and Glenn D. Rudebusch, "Forecasting Output With the Composite Leading Index: A Real Time Analysis," *Journal of the American Statistical Association*, **86** (1991a): 603-610.

Diebold, Francis X., and Glenn D. Rudebusch, "Turning Point Prediction With the Composite Leading Index: An Ex-Ante Analysis," in Leading Economic Indicators: New Approaches and Forecasting Records, edited by Lahiri and Moore, Cambridge University Press, (1991b) 231-256.

Diebold, Francis X., Glen D. Rudebusch, and S.B. Aruoba, "The Macroeconomy and the Yield Curve: A Dynamic Latent Factor Approach," *Journal of Econometrics*, **131** (2006): 309-338.

Dotsey, Michael, "The Predictive Content of the Interest Rate Yield spread For Future Economic Growth," *Federal Reserve Bank of Richmond Economic Quarterly*, **84**:3 (1998): 31-51.

Doz, C., D. Giannone and L. Reichlin, "A Quasi Maximum Likelihood Approach for Large Approximate Dynamic Factor Models," *ECB Working Papers* No. **674**. (2006)

Duarte, A., Venetis,, J. and I. Paya, "Predicting Real Growth and the Probability of Recession in the Euro Area Using the Yield Spread, "*International Journal of Forecasting*, **21** (2005): 262-277.

Duecker, Michael J., "Strengthening the Case for the Yield Curve As a Predictor of U.S. Recessions," *Federal Reserve Bank of St. Louis Review*, **79**:2 (1997): 41-51.

Duecker, Michael J., "Dynamic Forecasts of Qualitative Variables: A Qual VAR Model of US Recessions," *Journal of Business and Economics Statistics*, **23** (2005): 96-104.

Estrella, Arturo, "Monetary Policy and the Predictive Power of the Term Structure of Interest Rates,' (November 1998) Federal Reserve Bank of New York

Estrella, Arturo, "Why Does the Yield Curve Predict Output and Inflation," *Economic Journal*, **115**: 505 (2005): 722-744.

Estrella, Arturo, and G.A. Hardouvelis, "The Term Structure as a Predictor of Real Economic Activity," *Journal of Finance*, **46**: 2 (1991): 555-576.

Estrella, Arturo and F.S. Mishkin, "The Yield Curve as a Predictor of U.S. Recessions," *Federal Reserve Bank of New York Current Issues in Economics and Finance*, **2**(7) (1996): 1-6.

Estrella,. Arturo and F..S. Mishkin, "The Predictive Power of the Term Structure of Interest Rates in Europe and the United States: Implications for the European Central Bank," *European Economic Review*, **41**, (1997): 1375-1401.

Estrella, Arturo, and F.S. Mishkin, "Predicting U.S. Recessions: Financial Variables as Leading Indicators," *The Review of Economics and Statistics*, **80** (1998): 45-61.

Estrella, Arturo, and Mary R. Trubin, "The Yield Curve as a Leading Indicator: Some Practical Issues," *Federal Reserve Bank of New York Current Issues in Economics and Finance*, **12** (2006)

Estrella, Arturo, Anthony P. Rodrigues, and Sebastian Schich, "How Stable is the Predictive Power of the Yield Curve? Evidence From Germany and the United States," *Review of Economics and Statistics*, **85**:1 (2003): 629-644.

Fama, Eugene F., "Term Structure Forecasts of Interest Rates, Inflation, and Real Returns," *Journal of Monetary Economics*, **25** (1990): 59-76.

Feroli, Michael, "Monetary Policy and the Information Content of the Yield Spread," *Topics in Macroeconomics*, **4** (1) (2004): Article 13.

Filardo, A. J., "How Reliable are Recession Prediction Models?" *Federal Reserve Bank of Kansas City Economic Review*, (1999, second quarter); 35-55.

Frankel, Jeffrey A., Cara S. Lown, "An Indicator of Future Inflation Extracted From the Steepness of the Interest Rate Yield Curve Along its Entire Length," *Quarterly Journal of Economics*, **109**(2) (May 1994): 517-530.

Frankel, J., S.L. Schmukler, and L. Serven, "Global Transmission of Interest Rates : Monetary Independence and Currency Regimes," *Journal of International Money and Finance*, **23** (2004): 701-733.

Friedman, Benjamin M, and Kenneth M. Kuttner, "Indicator Properties of the Paper-Bill Spread: Less From Recent Experience," *Review of Economics and Statistics*, **80** (1998):34-44.

Fuhrer, J.C., and G.R. Moore, "Monetary Policy Trade-offs and the Correlation Between Nominal Interest Rates and Real Output," *American Economic Review*, **85** (1995): 219-239.

Funkle, N., "Predicting Recessions: Some Evidence For Germany," *Weltwirtschaftliches Archiv*, **133** (1997): 90-102.

Galbraith, J.W., and AG. Tkacz, "Testing For Asymmetry in the link Between the Yield Spread and Output in the G-7 Countries," *Journal of International Money and Finance*, **19** (2000): 657-672.

Galvao, A., "Structural Break Threshold VARs for Predicting US Recessions Using the Spread," *Journal of Applied Econometrics*, **21** (2006): 463-487.

Gerlach, Stefan, "The Information Content of the Term Structure: Evidence For Germany," *Empirical Economics*, **22** (1997): 161-179.

Giacomini, Raffaela, and Barbara Rossi, "Detecting and Predicting Forecast Breakdown," forthcoming in *Review of Economic Studies* (2008)

Giacomini, Raffaella, and Barbara Rossi, "How Stable is the Forecasting Performance of the Yield Curve For Output Growth?" *Oxford Bulletin of Economics and Statistics*, **68**:s1 (2006):783-795.

Gonzalez, Jorge G., Roger W. Spencer, and Daniel T. Walz, "The Term Structure of Interest Rates and the Mexican Economy," *Contemporary Economic Policy*, **18**:3 (2000): 284-294.

Hamilton, J.D., and D.H. Kim, "A Re-examination of the Predictability of the Yield Spread for Real Economic Activity," *Journal of Money, Credit, and Banking*, **34**: (2002): 340-360.

Harvey, Campbell R., "The Real Term Structure and Consumption Growth," *Journal of Financial Economics*, **22** (1988): 305-333.

Harvey, Campbell R., "Forecasts of Economic Growth From the Bond and Stock Markets," *Financial Analysts Journal*, **45** (September/October 1989): 38-45.

Harvey, Campbell R., "The Term Structure and World Economic Growth," *Journal of Fixed Income*, **1** (1991): 26-35.

Harvey, Campbell R., "The Term Structure Forecasts Economic Growth," *Financial Analysts Journal*, **49** (1993): 6-8.

Haubrich, Joseph G, "Does the Yield Curve Signal Recession?" *Federal Reserve Bank of Cleveland Economic Letter*, (2006)

Haubrich, Joseph G., and Ann M. Dombrosky, "Predicting Real Growth Using the Yield Curve," *Federal Reserve Bank of Cleveland Economic Review*, **32**: (First Quarter, 1996): 26-35.

Hu, Z., "The Yield Curve and Real Economic Activity," *IMF Staff Papers*, **40** (December 1993): 781-806.

Ivanova, D., Lahiri, K., and F. Switz, "Interest Rate Spreads as Predictors of German Inflation and Business Cycles," *International Journal of Forecasting*, **16** (2000): 39-58.

Jardet, Caroline, "Why Did the Term Structure of Interest Rates Lose Its Predictive Power?" *Economic Modeling*, **21** (2004): 509-524.

Jorion, P., and F.S. Mishkin, "A Multi-Country Comparison of Term Structure Forecasts at Long Horizons," *Journal of Financial Economics*, **29** (1991): 59-80.

Kessel, Robert A., The Cyclical Behavior of the Term Structure of Interest Rates, *NBER Occasional Paper* **91** (New York, Columbia University Press, 1965).

Kim, K.A., and P. Limpaphayom, "The Effect of Economic Regimes on the Relation Between Term Structure and Real Activity in Japan," *Journal of Economics and Business*, **49** (1997): 379-392.

Kozicki, Sharon, "Predicting Real Growth and Inflation With the Yield Curve," *Federal Reserve Bank of Kansas City Economic Review*, **82** (Quarter Four, 1997): 39-57.

Layton, A.P., and M. Katsuura, "Comparison of Regime Switching, Probit and Logit Models in Dating and Forecasting US Business Cycles," *International Journal of Forecasting*, **17** (2001): 403-417.

Laurent, R.D., "An Interest Rate-Based Indicator of Monetary Policy," *Federal Reserve Bank of Chicago Economic Perspective*, **12**: 1 (1988): 2-14.

Laurent, R.D., "Testing the Spread," *Federal Reserve Bank of Chicago Economic Perspective*, **13** (1989): 22-34.

Marotta, G. Pederzoli, C., and C. Torricelli, "Forward Looking Estimation of Default Probabilities With Italian Data," *Euro-Mediterranean Economics and Finance*, **1** (2006): 6-15.

McMillan, D G, (2004), 'Non-Linear Predictability of Short-Run Deviations in UK Stock Market Returns.' *Economics Letters*, **84**, 149-154.

McMillan, D G, (2007), 'Bubbles in the dividend-price ratio? Evidence from an asymmetric exponential smooth-transition model', *Journal of Banking and Finance*, **31**, 787-804.

McMillan, D G and Speright, A (2007), 'Non-Linear Long Horizon Returns Predictability: Evidence from Six South-East Asian Markets', *Asia-Pacific Financial Markets*, **13**, 95-111.

Mishkin Frederic S., "The Information in the Longer Maturity Term Structure About Future Inflation," *The Quarterly Journal of Economics*, **CV 442** (1990a): 815-828.

Mishkin, F.S., "What Does the Term Structure Tell Us About Future Inflation," *Journal of Monetary Economics*, **25** (1990b): 77-95.

Mishkin, Frederic S., "A Multi-country Study of the Information In the Shorter Maturity Term Structure About Future Inflation," *Journal of International Money and Finance*, **10** (1991): 2-22.

Modugno, Michele, and Kleopatra Nikolaou, "The Forecasting Power of International Yield Curve Linkages," *Working paper*, December 2007.

Moneta, F., "Does the Yield Spread Predict Recession in the Euro Area?" *International Finance*, **8**(2) (2005): 263-301.

Nagayasu, Jun, "On the Term Structure of Interest Rates and Inflation in Japan," *Journal of Economics and Business*, **54** (2002): 505-523.

Nakaota, Hiroshi, "The Term Structure of Interest Rates in Japan: The predictability of Economic Activity," *Japan and the World Economy*, **17** (2005): 311-326.

Nielsen, Christian Mose, "The Information Content of the Term Structure of Interest Rates About Future Inflation—An Illustration of the Importance of Accounting For a Time-Varying Real Interest Rate and Inflation Risk Premium," *The Manchester School*, (2006): 93-115.

Palash, Carl, and Lawrence J. Radecki, "Using Monetary and Financial Variables to Predict Cyclical Downturns," *Federal Reserve Bank Quarterly Review*, **10** (Summer 1985): 36-45.

Perigon, C., D.R. Smith and C. Villa, "Why Common Factors in International Bond Returns are Not So Common," *Journal of International Money and Finance*, **26**:2 (2007): 284-304.

Plosser, C.I., and G. Rouwenhorst, "International Term Structures and Real Economic Growth," *Journal of Monetary Economics*, **33** (1994): 133-155.

Rendu de Lint, Christel and David Stolin, "The Predictive Power of the Yield Curve: A Theoretical Assessment," *Journal of Monetary Economics*, **50** (2003): 1603-1622.

Rudebusch, Glenn D., and John C. Williams, "Forecasting Recessions: The Puzzle of the Enduring Power of the Yield Curve," *Federal Reserve Bank of San Francisco Working paper* 2007-16.

Schich, Sebastian, "The Information Content of the German Term Structure Regarding Inflation," *Applied Financial Economics*, **9** (1999): 385-395.

Sensier, M., Artis, M., Osborn, D., and C. Birchenhall, "Domestic and International Influences On Business Cycle Regimes in Europe," *International Journal of Forecasting*, **20** (2004): 343-357.

Sephton, P., "Forecasting Recessions: Can We Do Better on MARS?" *Federal Reserve Bank of St. Louis Review*, **83**(2) (2001): 39-50.

Shaaf, M., "Predicting Recessions Using the Yield Curve: An Artificial Intelligence and Econometric Comparison," *Eastern Economic Journal*, .**26**(2) (2000): 171-190.

Shiller, R., and J. Siegel, "The Gibson Paradox and Historical Movements in Real Long-term Interest Rates," *Journal of Political Economy*, **85**:1 (1977): 11-30.

Smets, F. and K. Tsatsaronis, "Why Does the Yield Curve Predict Economic Activity? Dissecting the Evidence For Germany and the United States," *Center for Economic Policy Research Discussion Paper* No. **1758**, Bank of International Settlements, December (1997).

Stock, James H. and Mark W. Watson, "Business Cycle Fluctuations in U.S. Macroeconomic Time Series," in Taylor, J., and Woodford, M. (eds.) *Handbook of Macroeconomics*, Vol. 1A, North Holland, Amsterdam New York, Elsevier Science, (1989): 3-64.

Stock, James H.,, and Mark W. Watson, "Forecasting Output and Inflation: The Role of Asset Prices," *Journal of Economic Literature*, **41**:3 (2003): 788-829.

Tkacz, Greg, "Neural Network Forecasting of Canadian GDP Growth," *International Journal of Forecasting*, **17**, (2001): 57-69.

Tkacz, Greg, "Inflation Changes, Yield Spreads, and Threshold Effects," *International Review of Economics and Finance*, **13** (2004): 187-199.

Vazquez, J. "Switching Regimes in the Term Structure of Interest Rates During US Post-war: A Case for the Lucas Proof Equilibrium?" *Studies in Nonlinear Dynamics and Econometrics*, **8** (2004): 1122-1161.

Venetis, I.A., Paya, I., and D.A. Peel, "Re-examination of the predictability of Economic Activity Using the Yield Spread: A Nonlinear Approach," *International Review of Economics and Finance*, **12** (2003): 187-207.

Wang, Z., J. Yang, and Q. Li, "Interest Rate Linkages in the Eurocurrency Market: Contemporaneous and Out-of-Sample Granger Causality Tests," *Journal of International Money and Finance,* **26** (2007): 86-103.

West, Kenneth D., "Asymptotic Inference About Predictive Ability," Econometrica, 64 (1996): 1067-1084.

Wright, Jonathan, "The Yield Curve and Predicting Recessions," *Finance and Economics and Discussion Series*, 2006-07, Federal Reserve Board of Governors.

Zagaglia, Paolo, "Does the Yield Spread Predict The Output Gap in the US?" *Working Paper,* Stockholm University, Research Papers in Economics 2006:5 and University of Bocconi (2006a).

Zagaglia, Paolo, "The Predictive Power of the Yield Spread Under the Veil of Time, *Working Paper,* Stockholm University and University of Bocconi (2006b)

Zarnowitz, Victor and Philip A. Braun, "Twenty-two Years of the NBER-ASA Quarterly Economic Outlook Surveys: Aspects and Comparisons of Forecasting Performance," in *Business Cycles, Indicators, and Forecasting*, Edited by James H. Stock and Mark W. Watson, University Press, 1993.

In: Liquidity, Interest Rates and Banking
Editors: J. Morrey and A. Guyton, pp. 57-75

ISBN: 978-1-60692-775-5
© 2009 Nova Science Publishers, Inc.

*Chapter 3*

# A LATENT VARIABLE APPROACH TO ESTIMATING TIME-VARYING SCALE EFFICIENCIES IN US COMMERCIAL BANKING

*Dogan Tirtiroglu[a], Kenneth Daniels[b] and Ercan Tirtiroglu[c]*

[1]Concordia University, John Molson School of Business, Department of Finance, 1455 de Maisonneuve Blvd. West, Montreal, Quebec H3G 1M8, Canada

[2]Virginia Commonwealth University, School of Business, Department of Finance, Richmond, Virginia 23284-4000, USA

[3]Decision Sciences and Operations Management, University of Massachusetts-Dartmouth, Charlton College of Business, Department of Management, North Dartmouth, MA 02747, USA

## Abstract

This paper suggests that an estimation of a cost, production or profit function and the resulting performance measures, such as scale efficiency, scale or scope economies, should reflect the dynamic changes happening in the marketplace. Most of these dynamic changes occur latently, making a latent variable approach, as embodied in the Kalman filter, desirable. We implement the proposed latent variable approach by applying it to a cost function and estimating dynamically time-varying scale efficiencies (S-EFF) for the U.S. commercial banking sector for 1934-1991.Using the Federal Deposit Insurance Corporation=s annual aggregated data, we report 1) that S-EFFs varied over time, 2) that the S-EFFs have fluctuated around 80%, and 3) that S-EFFs exhibited high volatility during 1934-1950, slowly increased between 1951-1971 and declined between 1972-1989, implying that commercial banks= substantial investment in the financial systems technologies and production innovations since

---

[a] E-mail address: dtirt@jmsb.concordia.ca. Tel: (514) 848-2424 Ext:4119
[b] E-mail address: kdaniels@busnet.bus.vcu.edu. Tel: (804) 828-7127
[c] E-mail address: etirtiroglu@umassd.edu. Tel: (508) 999-8433
We thank Allen Berger, Elizabeth Cooperman and Stephen M. Miller for their constructive suggestions, and A. Sinan Cebenoyan, Loretta Mester, and A. Noulas for clarifying some empirical issues. We are, however, solely responsible for any errors in the paper.
Please send your comments to: Dr. Dogan Tirtiroglu, Concordia University, Department of Finance, 1455 de Maisonneuve Blvd. W., Montreal, Quebec H3G 1M8, Canada.

the 1970s, along with regulatory changes in the U.S., did not lower their average costs, but increased them.

**Journal of Economic Literature Classification:** G21 - Banks; Other Depository Institutions; Mortgages, C32 - Time-Series Models

**Key Words:** Scale efficiencies; Kalman filter; time variation; translog cost function; random coefficients.

# 1. Introduction

Few economists would disagree that the banking environment is quite dynamic and that various factors, such as technological advances, (re)deregulation and production innovations, influence it continuously. Furthermore, processes by which these factors affect the behavior of the banking sector are not immediately known and appear to be latent. Therefore, an econometric measurement of bank performance should be capable of not only enabling researchers or policymakers to observe the dynamic behavior of the banking firms, but also to capture the influence of technological advances, (re)deregulation and production innovations latently. Yet, a brief literature survey reveals that the modeling of bank behavior, to a great extent, has been static and not latent.[1] That is, the existing papers estimate a *single and constant* measure of bank performance of interest, and further policy or evaluate policy issues and the economics of optimal output level, product mix and technological progress on the basis of this constant estimate. Moreover, a great majority of these papers model the *influence of time* on the production process by including a trend (time or technology) index or other proxy variable such as R&D expenditures; in this paper *influence of time* is used generically to indicate the influence of all the factors not explicitly controlled by an econometric model. This approach adopts the view that the *influence of time* is observable and that the trend variable captures all the information arising from it.

There are a number of limitations of this static line of modeling and of the lessons that can be drawn from these empirical results. For example, Saunders (1994, p.231-232) warns that "The real benefits of technological innovation may be long-term and dynamic and that traditional economy of scale and scope studies, which are largely static and ignore the more dynamic aspects of efficiency gains, may not pick up such benefits." In her criticism, Slade (1989, p.36) questions that "Whereas it is obvious that people, machines, and Btus actually enter the production process, it is much less clear that time is an input." She also points out that the *influence of time* will be latent and should be modeled as such. We, too, believe that drawing important conclusions from a single and constant estimate may lead to an incomplete and, sometimes even inaccurate, portrayal of bank behavior. Flaws in policy recommendations and evaluations, and in advising banks about the economics of optimal output level, optimal product mix, regulatory initiatives, and technological progress may follow from such static analyses.

Recent studies by Berger (1993, 1995), Berger and Humphrey (1992), and Bauer et al. (1993) follow a different avenue to model the *influence of time*. They conduct cross-sectional

---

[1]This literature is too extensive to cite here. Examples, which are relevant for our study, include Hunter and Timme (1986, 1991) and Glass and McKillop (1992).

estimations to produce independently time-varying bank performance measures, for each time period, without using time or any other proxy as an input in the cost function. Thus, these papers acknowledge implicitly the latent nature of the *influence of time* on the banks' production process, and obtain temporal measurements by assuming that previous time periods' measurements do not influence the current time period's measurement - contrary to intuition. Certainly, this estimation strategy is a significant advancement; yet, it still falls short of a dynamic modeling of bank behavior.

This paper makes a number of contributions. First, this study is a modest attempt to examine dynamically and latently time-varying cost functions and scale efficiencies (S-EFFs), which measure superior choice of output levels. We use the Federal Deposit Insurance Corporation=s (FDIC) aggregated annual data for the U.S. banking sector for 1934-1991; this is a much longer time period than covered in any existing paper and provides an opportunity to evaluate the long-term performance of the U.S. banking sector with respect to the economics of the optimal output level. At a time when bankers are advancing the argument that mergers will reduce costs and bring higher S-EFFs for the new and giant financial services firms to justify the trend for more merger activities, our historical evidence on S-EFFs in U.S. commercial banking should be useful for policy issues and arguments for or against the benefits and costs of forming giant financial services institutions. Second, we extend the latent variable modeling, as embodied in the Kalman filter (KF), to the estimation of time-varying cost functions and S-EFFs (Kalman, 1960; Kalman and Bucy 1961; Daniels and T2rt2ro lu 1998; T2rt2ro lu, Daniels and T2rt2ro lu 1998).[2] Finally, following in the footsteps of Berger and Humphrey (1992) and Humphrey (1992) and the literature cited therein, we adopt the value-added approach to bank production. This approach incorporates the production of intermediate deposit outputs as well as final loan outputs. Thus, both input and output characteristics of deposits are specified.

Within the limitations of our model and the data, our results indicate that the U.S. commercial banking sector=s S-EFFs have varied over time and that they have fluctuated around 80% for 1934-1991. They were highly volatile between 1934 and1950; had a slowly increasing trend during the period of 1951-1971; and exhibited a declining trend from 1972 to 1989. Commercial banks greatly invested in financial systems technologies and production innovations since the 1970s; our findings for this period indicate that these investments along with regulatory and other external changes did not lower banks' average costs, but actually increased them.

The balance of this paper is organized as follows: Section 2 describes modeling under the KF; Section 3 presents the empirical models and steps in estimating the time-varying cost function and S-EFF; Section 4 describes the data; and Section 5 discusses the empirical results.

---

[2] As far as we can document, Slade's (1989) study in the primary-metal industry, and Daniels and T2rt2ro lu=s (1996) study in U.S. commercial banking are the only ones in the literature modeling the *influence of time* on the cost functions latently.

## 2. Modeling under the Kalman-Filter

We apply the KF, a time-series technique, to a multiproduct/multiple input translog cost function.[3] Meinhold and Singpurwalla (1983) offer two intuitive interpretations for the KF:

1. It is an updating procedure that consists of forming a preliminary guess about the state of nature and then adding a correction guess to it, the correction being how well the guess has performed in predicting the next observation.

2. It is the evolution of a series of regression functions of estimates on the residuals at times 0,1,2,...,t, each having a potentially different intercept and regression coefficient; the evolution stems from a learning process involving all the available data. Under the KF, the parameters of a given empirical model evolve over time stochastically and time-dependently. This, in turn, allows us (**1**) to model the bank behavior dynamically/intertemporarily and latently, without using time as an input in the cost function and (**2**) to estimate dynamically time-varying cost functions and S-EFFs through the evolutions of the parameters and the data.[4] The parameters are assumed to follow random walk processes in this paper. Estimation convenience and parsimony in modeling are the main factors, driving the random walk specification. By imposing the random walk characterization, we model only those changes and innovations that have permanent effects on the cost function over time. The KF is favored over other random coefficients models because it produces consistent estimates of the time-varying parameters. This is achieved because the KF identifies the variance of the observation noise as a part of its optimization process. On the other hand, traditional econometric techniques are forced to make ad hoc assumptions about the variance of the observation noise.

The dynamically estimated time-varying measures of S-EFFs significantly improve on the constant point estimates of previous studies. Moreover, since the information uncovered at time t is fed into the next period's estimation of S-EFFs, this also gives our approach an advantage over cross-sectionally and independently estimated S-EFFs over time.

## 3. Model Development

### 3.1. The Empirical Model

Let $C = f(\mathbf{Q}, \mathbf{P})$ be the dual cost function for a typical bank where C is total costs, that is, interest and noninterest expenses, **Q** is a vector of outputs, and **P** is a vector of input prices. Specifically, we subscribe to a two-output, three-input translog cost function in defining the cost function:

---

[3]The KF can also be applied to a profit or production function. Our choice for a cost function is driven by the data constraints and the consideration for parsimony in demonstrating the methodology.

[4]The KF approach, however, is not suited to model X-efficiency, which measures superior management of resources. A measurement of X-efficiency requires a minimum cost frontier estimated from a cross section of banks. The KF, on the other hand, is to be applied to a time-series data of one banking firm (see Daniels and T2rt2ro lu 1996). Thus, estimation of a minimum cost frontier from a cross-section of banks is not possible under the KF.

$$\ln C = \alpha_0 + \sum_i \beta_i \ln Q_i + \sum_m \alpha_m \ln P_m + 1/2 \sum_m \sum_n \alpha_{mn} \ln P_m \ln P_n$$

$$+ 1/2 \sum_i \sum_j \beta_{ij} \ln Q_i \ln Q_j + \sum_i \sum_m \theta_{im} \ln Q_i \ln P_m + \varepsilon$$

$$i, j = L, D \qquad m, n = W, K, F$$

where outputs are total loans and leases (L) and total produced domestic and foreign deposits (D), and inputs are labor (W), capital (K), and loanable funds (F). More specifically:

C = (Salaries and benefits) + (Occupancy expenses) + [(Total Interest Expenses minus Service Charges)]*[Total Loans/Total Earning Assets],

$Q_L$ = total dollar volume of loans and leases (includes real estate loans, loans to depository institutions, agricultural production, commercial and industrial loans, personal loans, loans to state and government subdivisions, all other loans, lease financing receivables) - (unearned income plus allowance for loans and lease losses),

$Q_D$ = total dollar volume of domestic and foreign deposits (includes deposits by individuals, partnerships, government, corporations, states and political subdivisions, and all other deposits; no purchased deposits are included, though)

where

Total Earning Assets = (Investments + Total Loans + Other Earning Assets)

Price of labor ($P_W$) = Salaries and Benefits/the number of employees

Price of Capital ($P_K$) = Occupancy expenses/bank premises

Price of Loanable Funds ($P_F$) = (Total interest expense - service charges)/total deposits

Following Hunter and Timme (1991), and Mester (1992), we also allocate the interest expenses by the ratio of loans-to-earning assets.[5] Standard symmetry and homogeneity restrictions are imposed on [1].

Virtually all bank studies acknowledge the difficulties with respect to defining output and costs and to aggregating output. A number of studies, including Humphrey (1992), Berger and Humphrey (1992), and Hunter and Timme (1991), subscribed to the criterion of value-added. We also adopt this model of bank production which incorporates the production of

---

[5] We appreciate Loretta Mester's correspondence on the allocation of interest.

intermediate deposit outputs as well as final loan outputs. Thus, both input and output characteristics of deposits are specified simultaneously. (See Humphrey (1992, pp.116-118) for an excellent discussion of the value-added approach.)

We aggregate outputs to minimize the degrees of freedom problem. There is a trade-off between the limited number of observations and the number of parameters to be estimated. Disaggregating outputs increases the number of parameters drastically while the number of observations still remains constant. Moreover, our primary purpose is to examine time-varying S-EFFs dynamically rather than to examine product-specific cost complementarities. We nevertheless believe that equation [1] is a simple and sufficient cost function specification for the purposes of this study. It should also be noted that by aggregating outputs into the two categories above, we implicitly assume that there is only one cost structure underlying the production of each of the following: all classes of loans and all classes of produced deposits.

## 3.2. Modifying the Translog Cost Function under the Kalman-Filter

Under the KF, equation [1] becomes:

$$\ln C_t = \alpha_{0,t} + \sum_i \beta_{i,t} \ln Q_{i,t} + \sum_m \alpha_{m,t} \ln P_{m,t}$$
$$+ 1/2 \sum_m \sum_n \alpha_{mn,t} \ln P_{m,t} \ln P_{n,t} \quad (2.a)$$
$$+ 1/2 \sum_i \sum_j \beta_{ij,t} \ln Q_{i,t} \ln Q_{j,t} + \sum_i \sum_m \theta_{im,t} \ln Q_{i,t} \ln P_{m,t} + \varepsilon_t$$

$$i, j = L, D \quad m, n = W, K, F.$$

and

$$\alpha_{0,t} = \alpha_{0,t-1} + u_{0,t} \quad (2.b)$$

$$\beta_{i,t} = \beta_{i,t-1} + u_{i,t} \quad (2.c)$$

$$\alpha_{m,t} = \alpha_{m,t-1} + u_{m,t} \quad (2.d)$$

$$\alpha_{mn,t} = \alpha_{mn,t-1} + u_{mn,t} \quad (2.e)$$

$$\beta_{ij,t} = \beta_{ij,t-1} + u_{ij,t} \quad (2.f)$$

$$\theta_{im,t} = \theta_{im,t-1} + u_{im,t} \quad (2g)$$

Equations [2.b]-[2.g] specify the evolution of the model's parameter estimates as random walk processes. Equations [2] form a simultaneous equation system and its estimation involves a recursive and complex algorithm. Standard symmetry and homogeneity restrictions are imposed on [2] at all times. An appendix explains the technical aspects of estimating the translog cost function under the KF.[6]

Starting the KF estimation requires initial parameter estimates at time t=0. These values are chosen by the maximum likelihood procedure, a procedure which sweeps the data to determine the most likely initial parameters by maximizing the likelihood function.[7]

## 3.3. Estimating Scale Efficiencies

It is worthwhile to note that the traditional scale economies measure captures only the cost effects of marginal changes in output where the implicit assumption that the distance from the scale-efficient point is negligible is made. Berger (1993), and Evanoff and Israilevich (1991) point out that S-EFFs may differ substantially from scale economies if the point of evaluation is far from the scale-efficient output. Thus, we compute the S-EFFs, not scale economies, to evaluate the entire efficiency loss from not producing at the scale efficient point. This is the point where ray average cost is minimized for an individual bank's product mix and input price vector. Following Berger's (1993, 1995) work, S-EFFs are estimated in two steps:

1. Find the traditional ray scale economy measure (RSCE$_t$) as

$$RSCE_t = \sum_{i=1} \partial \ln C_t / \partial \ln Q_t = \sum_i \beta_{i,t} + \sum_i \text{sumfrom} j\, \beta_{ij,t} \ln Q_{j,t} + \sum_i \sum_m \theta_{im,t} \ln P_{m,t}. \quad (3)$$

The scale efficient point for any given bank occurs where RSCE$_t$=1, i.e., where ray average costs are minimized.

2. Find the scale-efficient point $\mathbf{Q}^{se}_t$ for a bank with output quantity and input price vectors ($\mathbf{Q}_t, \mathbf{P}_t$), by solving the following set of equations:

$$RSCE_t = \sum_i \beta_{i,t} + \sum_i \sum_j \beta_{ij,t} \ln Q^{se}_{j,t} + \text{sumfrom} i \sum_m \theta_{im,t} \ln P_{m,t}, \quad (4.a)$$

$$Q^{se}_{1,t} / Q^{se}_{2,t} = Q_{1,t} / Q_{2,t}, \quad (4.b)$$

where, while the first equation assures that $\mathbf{Q}^{se}_t$ will be scale efficient, the last equation assures that $\mathbf{Q}^{se}_t$ has the same product mix as $\mathbf{Q}_t$. The solution for these equations is given by:

---

[6] We assume that the *influence of time* under the KF is disembodied. In other words, a stable relationship exists between inputs, the cost function, and time. The KF approach is, however, consistent with factor-augmenting technical change where the usage of an input may decrease or increase as a result of learning process or input substitution due to changes in input productivities over time.

[7] The footnote in Table 2 reports the initial values along with the value of the likelihood function.

$$Q_{q,t}^{se} = \exp\left[\left[1 - \left[\sum_i \beta_{i,t} + \sum_i \sum_j \beta_{ij,t}(\ln Q_{j,t} - \ln Q_{2,t}) + \sum_i \sum_m \theta_{im,t} \ln P_{m,t}\right]\right] / \sum_i \sum_j \beta_{ij,t}\right] * (Q_{q,t}/Q_{2,t}), \quad (5)$$

$$q = 1, 2.$$

S-EFFs are given by the ratio of predicted costs for $Q^{se}_t$ to the predicted costs for $Q_t$, multiplied by the ratio of outputs to correct for absolute size differences:

$$S\text{-}EFF_t = \exp\left[\ln\hat{C}(Q_t^{se}, P_t) - \ln\hat{C}(Q_t, P_t)\right] * \left[\left(\sum_i Q_{i,t}\right) / \left(\sum_j Q_{j,t}^{se}\right)\right] \quad (6.a)$$

$$S\text{-}EFF_t = \exp\left[\sum_i \beta_{i,t}(\ln Q_{i,t}^{se} - \ln Q_{i,t}) + 1/2 \sum_i \sum_j \beta_{ij,t}(\ln Q_{i,t}^{se}\ln Q_{j,t}^{se} - \ln Q_{i,t}\ln Q_{j,t}) + \sum_i \sum_m \theta_{im,t}(\ln Q_{i,t}^{se} - \ln Q_{i,t}) \ln P_{m,t}\right] * \left[\left(\sum_i Q_{i,t}\right) / \left(\sum_j Q_{j,t}^{se}\right)\right],$$

(6.b)

where $\ln\hat{C}$ represents predicted costs. This is an estimate of the ratio of predicted average costs along the ray, and ranges over (0,1]. An important difference of S-EFF from other similar performance measures, such as X-efficiency, is that S-EFF is measured relative to the theoretical scale-efficient firm, while X-efficiency is measured relative to the most efficient firm in a sample.[8]

## 4. Data

We use the FDIC's Historical Statistics on Banking 1934-1991. The FDIC adds up the financial data for each bank in the U.S. in a given year and reports this aggregated data set annually. Table 1 provides summary statistics of the cost function variables for 1934-1991. We deflated the 1934-1991 data set by the GNP deflator.

**Table 1. Summary Statistics for the FDIC's Data, 1934-1991.**

|       | MEAN            | STD             |
|-------|-----------------|-----------------|
| TC    | $581,947,758    | $655,543,652    |
| Loan  | $7,452,002,693  | $5,711,757,775  |
| Deposit | $13,823,891,428 | $7,666,111,373 |
| $P_w$ | $206            | $44             |
| $P_k$ | $0.0073         | $0.0030         |
| $P_f$ | 0.0432%         | 0.0290%         |

---

[8] An estimation of S-EFFs allows a distinction between scale economy efficiency for banks that are below efficient scale, and scale diseconomy efficiency for banks that are above efficient scale. See Berger (1995).

We are aware that a use of aggregate data is restrictive and believe that it is not inappropriate for our approach for a number of reasons. First, Jayaratne and Strahan (JS) (1998) point out that the banking deregulations in the 1980s and 1990s enhance the natural tendency of markets to weed out inefficient firms, increasing the likelihood of the selection and survivorship problems that would bias tests based on data from individual banks. They use state-level aggregated banking data to control for these problems. In fact, they document empirically the selection effects, following deregulations, in using firm-level banking data. Second, the FDIC=s aggregate data, to the best of our knowledge, is the *only* U.S. commercial banking data dating back to 1934. The length of the data gives us a unique opportunity to study *dynamically* and *latently* the operating performance over a long period of time, even though the aggregate nature of the data is restrictive. There is currently no evidence on U.S. commercial banks= S-EFF, dating back to 1934 in the literature.[9] Third, we observe that an availability of *only* industry level data has driven many researchers of industrial organization to examine the operating performance of different sectors of an economy using the available aggregate data. For example, Ball and Chambers (1982), Fare et al. (1985), Slade[10] (1989), and Ray and Kim (1995) made use of aggregate data for the U.S. meat product industry, the agricultural industry in Philippines, the U.S. primary-metals industry, and the U.S. steel industry, respectively.[11]

Also, it should be useful to remember that the measurement of S-EFF is relative to the *theoretically* correct level of scale efficiency.[12] Therefore, the relative performance of other banks does not affect S-EFF as much as it does X-efficiency. Finally, we note that the banking sector behaves like a unified entity far more than any other industry does as a result of both this sector=s heavy and closely supervised regulatory structure and the highly interdependent nature of the banking business. Historical evidence on the timing of bank runs, mergers, failures indicates that such events are clustered within a short-period of time, indicating a sector-wide behavior and interdependency, and, therefore, providing motivation for a sector-wide modeling.

## 5. Empirical Results

The banking literature reports empirical evidence that there has been persistent scale and X-efficiencies and that the payoff from technological innovation has been rather low in the U.S. Our overall results are consistent with these reported results. The estimations demonstrate that S-EFFs in U.S. commercial banking have been time-varying and mostly low.

Table 2 reports the parameter estimates of the cost function for 1934, 1963 and 1991. Because of an abundance of estimates under the KF and limited space here, we decided to

---

[9] Glass and McKillop (1992) also use time-series data for an Irish bank in estimating a cost function.
[10] Slade (1989) uses Wills= (1979) aggregate data.
[11] Some other studies use regionally aggregated data to examine various operating performance measures in different industries and countries. See, for example, Denny et al. (1981), Beeson (1987), Domazlicky and Weber (1997).
[12] Chambers (1989) indicates that often data are available only at a relatively high degree of aggregation, requiring an estimation of industry functions on the basis of either cross-sectional or time-series data. He studies the issue of aggregation over firms rigorously and in detail. His work shows that, under a number of aggregation-related considerations, a quasi-homothetic technology arises as a consistent solution.

report the results of three representative time periods; we see that all parameter estimates are highly statistically significant in these periods.

### Table 2. Cost Function Parameter Estimates for Three Different Years.

|  | coeff. | t-stat | coeff. | t-stat | coeff. | t-stat |
|---|---|---|---|---|---|---|
| $''_{0,t}$ | -0.61 | -17.35 | -0.606 | -17.23 | -0.529 | -15.03 |
| $\$_{L,t}$ | 0.164 | 10.12 | 0.136 | 8.41 | 0.132 | 8.15 |
| $\$_{D,t}$ | 0.649 | 53.39 | 0.619 | 50.85 | 0.642 | 52.81 |
| $''_{W,t}$ | 1.003 | 75.01 | 0.986 | 73.74 | 0.998 | 74.63 |
| $''_{F,t}$ | 0.465 | 26.72 | 0.405 | 23.26 | 0.431 | 24.77 |
| $\$_{LL,t}$ | -0.984 | -201.99 | -0.974 | -199.92 | -0.981 | -201.35 |
| $\$_{DD,t}$ | -0.938 | -251.19 | -0.928 | -248.49 | -0.935 | -250.26 |
| $\$_{LD,t}$ | 0.644 | 73.55 | 0.666 | 76.13 | 0.649 | 74.22 |
| $''_{WW,t}$ | -0.742 | -200.17 | -0.74 | -199.65 | -0.736 | -198.74 |
| $''_{FF,t}$ | 0.077 | 7.49 | 0.078 | 7.55 | 0.069 | 6.66 |
| $''_{WF,t}$ | 0.233 | 30.57 | 0.247 | 32.32 | 0.222 | 29.16 |
| $2_{LW,t}$ | -0.431 | -80.69 | -0.419 | -78.56 | -0.428 | -80.28 |
| $2_{LF,t}$ | 0.2 | 14.93 | 0.228 | 17.03 | 0.203 | 15.17 |
| $2_{DW,t}$ | 1.316 | 253.19 | 1.325 | 254.95 | 1.326 | 255.24 |
| $2_{DF,t}$ | -0.203 | -13.17 | -0.163 | -10.58 | -0.195 | -12.66 |
| $2_{LK,t}$ | 0.23 | 13.21 | 0.191 | 10.94 | 0.225 | 12.9 |
| $2_{DK,t}$ | -1.113 | -61.97 | -1.162 | -64.7 | -1.132 | -63 |

**Notes**:
1. The starting values for the Kalman filter were chosen by the maximum likelihood procedure. The maximum of the likelihood was achieved at $-2\ln(1) = -226.80$. The initial values for the respective coefficients were -0.60, 0.16, 0.64, 1.00, 0.47, -0.98, -0.94, 0.64, -0.74, 0.08, 0.23, -0.43, 0.20, 1.32, -0.20.
2. The cost function restrictions are imposed internally.

Time-varying S-EFF estimates are presented in Table 3. A significant majority of these estimates are within the 0.75-0.85 range. The highest S-EFF estimate is 0.94 in 1935 while the lowest is 0.70 in 1940.

**Table 3. Time-Varying Scale Efficiencies, 1934-1991.**

| Time | Year | S. Effic. | Time | Year | S. Effic. |
|---|---|---|---|---|---|
| 1 | 1934 | 0.815648 | 30 | 1963 | 0.827752 |
| 2 | 1935 | 0.941381 | 31 | 1964 | 0.841607 |
| 3 | 1936 | 0.755493 | 32 | 1965 | 0.851897 |
| 4 | 1937 | 0.720571 | 33 | 1966 | 0.853821 |
| 5 | 1938 | 0.721996 | 34 | 1967 | 0.867214 |
| 6 | 1939 | 0.722951 | 35 | 1968 | 0.868855 |
| 7 | 1940 | 0.701877 | 36 | 1969 | 0.852216 |
| 8 | 1941 | 0.717834 | 37 | 1970 | 0.852976 |
| 9 | 1942 | 0.88082 | 38 | 1971 | 0.853046 |
| 10 | 1943 | 0.824133 | 39 | 1972 | 0.861174 |
| 11 | 1944 | 0.843027 | 40 | 1973 | 0.861564 |
| 12 | 1945 | 0.860258 | 41 | 1974 | 0.85844 |
| 13 | 1946 | 0.809284 | 42 | 1975 | 0.850055 |
| 14 | 1947 | 0.802793 | 43 | 1976 | 0.841552 |
| 15 | 1948 | 0.800817 | 44 | 1977 | 0.830553 |
| 16 | 1949 | 0.801703 | 45 | 1978 | 0.818089 |
| 17 | 1950 | 0.78646 | 46 | 1979 | 0.808168 |
| 18 | 1951 | 0.789776 | 47 | 1980 | 0.800529 |
| 19 | 1952 | 0.798803 | 48 | 1981 | 0.790672 |
| 20 | 1953 | 0.799266 | 49 | 1982 | 0.783869 |
| 21 | 1954 | 0.804179 | 50 | 1983 | 0.775617 |
| 22 | 1955 | 0.804237 | 51 | 1984 | 0.765725 |
| 23 | 1956 | 0.804597 | 52 | 1985 | 0.752503 |
| 24 | 1957 | 0.809682 | 53 | 1986 | 0.740118 |
| 25 | 1958 | 0.822536 | 54 | 1987 | 0.73698 |
| 26 | 1959 | 0.818344 | 55 | 1988 | 0.734445 |
| 27 | 1960 | 0.817604 | 56 | 1989 | 0.729059 |
| 28 | 1961 | 0.814579 | 57 | 1990 | 0.731744 |
| 29 | 1962 | 0.822965 | 58 | 1991 | 0.742007 |

Figure 1 graphs time-varying S-EFFs. It shows that S-EFFs during 1934-1950 were volatile with an oscillating pattern; that S-EFFs showed a general, stable and upward trend between 1951-1971; and that, during the 1972-1989 period, S-EFFs completely reversed their upward trend of 1951-1969. We note that we are able to find comparable evidence in the banking literature only for 1972-1989; thus, it seems that the evidence for the first two time periods appears for the first time in the banking literature with this study.

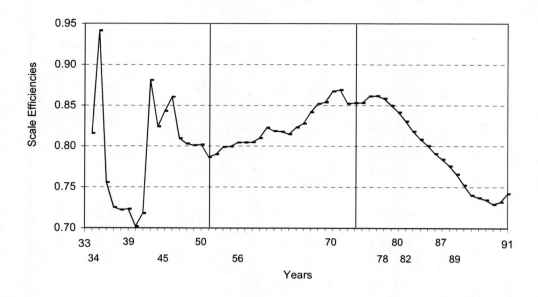

Figure 1. Time-Varying Scale Efficiency Estimates, 1934-1991.

The period of 1934-1950 follows the Great Depression, in which a record number of bank failures occurred. During this period, factors -- too many to count here -- had influenced the banking sector. Among them were the New Deal measures, including the institutionalization of the FDIC and the enactment of the Glass-Steagall Act, to fight off the banking crisis and the residual effects of the Depression; the economic consequences of the Second World War; Regulation Q ceilings; first Britain's (in 1931), followed by other countries' abandonment of the gold standard. S-EFFs volatile behavior during this time period, especially early on, is a clear indication of the U.S. economy's and the banking sector's fragility.

The developments during the period of 1951-1971 were not as drastic and dramatic as they had been during the earlier period. The economic consequences of the Korean and Vietnam Wars, the Treasury's and the Federal Reserve System's Accord to free the Fed from supporting the government securities market at pegged prices, the enactment of the Bank Holding Act, the continued influence of Regulation Q ceilings along with changes in the reserve requirements and significant population gains are among the main factors that potentially have influenced over the commercial banks' S-EFFs, which fluctuated from around 77% to close to 85% during that time period.

It is clear from Figure 1 that S-EFFs exhibited a consistently and smoothly declining trend during the 1972-1989 period. This is consistent with Humphrey's (1992) findings that the total factor productivity growth in the U.S. banking for the 1967-1987 period was low and even slightly negative; with Kwan and Eisenbeis's (1995) findings that significant inefficiencies have persisted in U.S. banking between 1981-1991; with Berger's (1993, 1995) S-EFF results, to the extent that his estimates under the WITHIN estimator reflect the S-EFFs in U.S. banking; and with Boyd and Gertler=s (1993) analyses of the underlying reasons for the decline in U.S. commercial banking during the 1980s and the early 1990s.

A record number of bank failures, since the Great Depression, also took place during the 1980s and early 1990s. Figure 2 shows the Bank Insurance Fund closings and assistance transactions for 1934-1991. A cursory comparison of Figures 1 and 2 suggests that while the number of bank failures per year was increasing during the 1980s and early 1990s, the S-EFF estimates during these years were exhibiting a declining trend, consistent with the problems of this era which haunted the U.S. commercial banking sector. Since our empirical model is for the U.S. commercial banking sector, the output and input amounts will be highly sensitive to changes in the number of banks. This association between the number of bank failures and S-EFFs suggests that an understanding of the reasons underlying the bank failures should be useful information in examining the dynamics of the S-EFF measures.

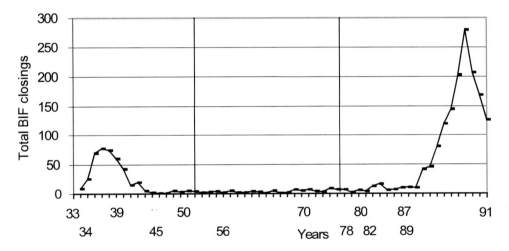

**Source**: FDIC web site (http://www.fdic.gov)

Figure 2. Annual Bank Insurance Fund Closings and Assistance Transactions.

An FDIC report (1997) provides a meticulously detailed study of the banking crises of the 1980s and early 1990s. It points out that the crises resulted from a concurrence of various forces working together to produce a decade of banking crises and that broad economics forces -- such as economic, financial, legislative, and regulatory -- and severe regional and sectoral recessions and finally, some banks= excessive risk-taking, while being insufficiently supervised and ill-equipped to manage the extra risk, all contributed to the rise in the number of bank failures. Two important observations of this study are that the bank failures during the 1980s and early 1990s were highly concentrated in relatively few regions, which included some of the country=s largest markets in terms of number of institutions and dollar resources, and that the bank failures were generally associated with regional recessions that had been preceded by rapid regional expansions. That is, loans that helped a region=s economy to expand rapidly during a boom became a source of problems for banks during the ensuing bust. The report notes that geographically confined crises were translated into a national problems and documents that the incidence of failure was high in states characterized by:

- severe economic downturns related to the collapse in energy prices (Alaska, Louisiana, Oklahoma, Texas, and Wyoming),
- real-estate related downturns (California, the Northeast, and the Southwest),
- the agricultural recession of the early 1980s (Iowa, Kansas, Nebraska, Oklahoma, and Texas),
- an influx of banks chartered in the 1980s (California and Texas) and the parallel phenomenon of mutual-to-stock conversions (Massachusetts),
- prohibitions against branching that limited banks= ability to diversify their loan portfolios geographically and to fund growth through core deposits (Colorado, Illinois, Kansas, Texas, and Wyoming),
- the failure of a single large bank (Illinois) or of a small number of relatively large banks (New York and Pennsylvania).

Our finding that the sector exhibited a trend of decline during the 1970s and 1980s also appears to be consistent with Humphrey=s (1992) work. Humphrey argued that the effective and extended use for corporate cash management in the 1970s and the consumer-based banking deregulation of the 1980s as the main reasons of negative growth in TFP. He points out that the increased use of cash management techniques by corporations in the late 1970s decreased the share of demand deposits from 47% to 24% of total bank liabilities during the 1969-1980 period, making banks rely more on higher-cost purchased funds (a rise from 21% to 47% of total liabilities during the same period).This shift from low-cost to higher-cost funds in the 1970s, Humphrey argues, raised the real average cost per dollar of bank assets even if all input prices were held constant. The deregulatory changes that removed the Regulation Q ceilings permitted the banks to pay higher rates for the use of the same funds. This, in turn, made the share of demand deposits fall further from 24% to 15% over the 1980-1989 period. These low-cost funds, such as zero-interest checking accounts, were replaced by higher-cost time and savings deposits whose share in bank liabilities rose from 29% to 45%, making the aggregate profitability of banks' deposits base fall from $61 billion in constant 1988 dollars in 1980 to $4 billion in 1988.[13]

One of the most important developments during the 1980s (until the present time) has been the U.S. banks' investment in and use of financial systems technology and innovations.[14] The observed trend in the estimates of S-EFF indicates that the investment in technology has not brought the expected reduction in average costs for banks. In fact, the evidence indicates that the investment in technology, along with other factors, led to increased inefficiencies. This finding is consistent with the notion, termed de-engineering, that the remarkably fast evolution of new technology products and technologies and changes in regulation render a given technology obsolete in a relatively short period of time, requiring further and sometimes large investments by banks (see Wysocki, B. Jr., *Wall Street Journal*, April 30,

---

[13] See Figure 5 in Humphrey (1992, p.126) for the dollar amounts of different forms of deposits in the U.S. banking system. See also Saunders (1994, p.68) for the long-term behavior of market to book value. The market-to-book values drop below one after 1973 and continue to remain at below one.

[14] Saunders (1994, p.79) points out that, prior to 1975, almost all transactions in the financial services sector were paper based. The Economist (Oct. 3, 1992, p.21-24) reported that the investment in technology by the U.S. commercial banks went up from about $5.5 billion in 1982 to somewhere about $13 billion in 1991. It appears that almost all year-to-year increases in the investments between 1982 and 1991 were undertaken by the largest 35 banks. Thus, if technology has had any influence on the banks' cost functions, that should be most obvious during the 1972-1991 time period.

1998). Even if banks= return on technology investment has been more than the cost of the technology investment,[15] the margin between the return and the cost has not been large enough to offset other growing bank costs.

## 6. Summary

This study provides an inter-temporal evaluation of the scale efficiency performance of the U.S. commercial banking sector for the 1934-1991 period. We apply the Kalman filter to a multiple input/multiple output translog cost function. Modeling the banking sector=s behavior under the Kalman filter enables us to estimate the scale efficiencies for each sample year, using the FDIC's aggregated data. This modeling approach allows a researcher to observe the influence of all factors evolving latently over time on the production process latently and avoids an arbitrary econometric specification to capture the influence of these time-dependent factors on the production process.

Our evidence demonstrates the inter-temporal variability and relatively low level of scale efficiencies in U.S. commercial banking between 1934 and 1991. Empirical results for the period of 1970s and 1980s show the decline in the U.S. commercial banking sector. One implication we draw from our results is that there is ample room for moving towards the sector=s optimal output level. It appears to us that the historical regulatory structure that defined the U.S. commercial banking sector in this century needs to be reformed to allow banks to exploit the inefficiencies, while bankers should structure their firms to better manage the increasing competition from all facets of the marketplace and the risks introduced by intense competition, financial innovations, changes in the regulations, and advances in information technology and their implications.

## Appendix

### The Kalman-Filter Methodology

This section presents the main features of the Kalman filter. Consider a dynamic system represented by the stochastic linear vector equations:

$$Y_t = B_t X_t + e_t \qquad (A.1)$$

and

$$B_{t+1} = A_t B_t + v_t, \quad t = 0, 1, 2, \ldots, N-1, \qquad (A.2)$$

where
- $X_t$ : an exogenous state vector,
- $Y_t$ : the observation vector,
- $e_t$ : a random noise vector,

---

[15] T2rt2ro lu et al. (1998) report evidence that return on banks= investment in the ATM machines for the early 1970 to the mid-1990s period has been positive, but small.

$v_t$ : a random noise vector,
$B_t$ : a random coefficient vector,
$A_t$ : a given design vector.

The subscript t refers to discrete instants of time.
The following notation will be adopted for this system:

E(.) : the expected value,
cov(.) : the variance-covariance matrix,
$Y^t$ : an ordered sequence of the observation vectors $Y_t$,
superscript T : the transpose of a matrix,
: equality by definition.

The vectors $e_t$ and $v_t$ are assumed to be independent random vectors having the following statistics:

$$E(e_t) = 0, \qquad (A.3)$$

$$E(v_t) = 0, \qquad (A.4)$$

$$cov(e_t e_j^T) = Q_t, \qquad (A.5)$$

$$cov(v_t v_j^T) = R_t, \qquad (A.6)$$

$$cov(e_t v_j^T) = 0, \qquad (A.7)$$

for t, j = 0, 1, 2, . . ., N-1.

The initial state vector $B_0$ is also assumed to be a random vector with a given mean and covariance. An important and interesting feature of the model is that each time-varying coefficient is not observed, or measured directly. However, the stochastic formulation of the model allows an estimate of each time-varying coefficient by the conditional expectation, $E(B_t * Y^t)$, which is the minimum-variance estimator of $B_t$ given $Y^t$. In this sense it is the optimal estimator and the KF allows us to obtain each coefficient and the scale economies recursively.

Now, let

$$B_t^* \cdot E(B_t * Y^t), \qquad (A.8)$$

$$S_t \cdot cov(B_t * Y^t), \qquad (A.9)$$

$$P_t \cdot cov(B_{t+1} * Y^t). \qquad (A.10)$$

Denote the optimal prediction of $B_t$ when $y^k$ is available by $B_{k+1}$.
With these definitions, the KF algorithm consist of the following relationships:

$$P_{k+1} = A_k S_k A_k^T + Q_k, \tag{A.11}$$

$$S_{k+1} = P_k - P_k X_k^T (X_k P_k X_k + R_k)^{-1} X_k P_k, \tag{A.12}$$

$$K_{k+1} = S_{k+1} X_{k+1}^T R^{-1}_{k+1}, \tag{A.13}$$

$$B_{k+1} = A_k B_k^*, \tag{A.14}$$

$$B_{k+1}^* = B_{k+1} + K_{k+1}(Y_{k+1} - B_{k+1} X_{k+1}). \tag{A.15}$$

The KF algorithm begins with the forward recursions in equation [A.14]. This computes the one-step forecast, $B_{k+1}$, which is an update at each interval of the previous estimated value. This update is then used in equation [A.15] to estimate the optimal estimator which is a weighted average of $B_{k+1}$ and the error that one makes in predicting $Y_{k+1}$.

# References

Ball, V.E. and R. Chambers, 1982, An Economic Analysis of Technology in the Meat Product Industry, *American Journal of Agricultural Economics*, **64**, 699-709.

Bauer, P.W., A.N. Berger, and D. Humphrey, 1993, Efficiency and Productivity Growth in U.S. Banking, in: H.O. Fried, C.A.K. Lovell and S.S. Schmidt, eds., *The Measurement of Productive Efficiency: Techniques and Applications* (Oxford University Press), 386-413.

Beeson, P., 1987, Total Factor Productivity Growth and Agglomeration Economies in Manufacturing, 1959-73, *Journal of Regional Science*, **27**:2, 183-199.

Berger, A.N., and D.B. Humphrey, 1992, Measurement and Efficiency Issues in Commercial Banking, in: Zvi Griliches, ed., *Output Measurement in the Service Sectors*, National Bureau of Economic Research, (University of Chicago Press, Chicago, IL), 245-279.

Berger, A.N., 1993, Distribution-Free Estimates of Efficiency in the U.S. Banking Industry and Tests of the Standard Distributional Assumptions, *Journal of Productivity Analysis*, **4**:3, 261-292.

Berger, A.N., 1995, The Profit-Structure Relationship in Banking -- Tests of Market Power and Efficient- Structure Hypotheses, *Journal of Money, Credit, and Banking*, **27**:2, 404-431.

Boyd J.H., and M. Gertler, 1993, U.S. Commercial Banking: Trends, Cycles, and Policy, Working Paper No. 4404, *NBER Working Paper Series*, Cambridge, MA.

Chambers, R.C., 1988, *Applied Production Analysis: A Dual Approach*, Cambridge University Press.

Daniels, K. and D. T2rt2ro lu, April 1998, Total Factor Productivity Growth in US Commercial Banking for 1935-1991: A Latent Variable Approach Using the Kalman-Filter, *Journal of Financial Services Research*, **13**:2, 119-135.

Daniels, K. and D. T2rt2ro lu, Summer 1996, The Temporal Behavior of Scale Economies Within a Banking Firm, *Journal of Economics and Finance*, **33-45**.

Denny, M., M. Fuss, and J.D. May, August 1981, Intertemporal Changes in Regional Productivity in Canadian Manufacturing, *Canadian Journal of Economics*, **14**:3, 390-408.

Domazlicky, B.R. and W.L. Weber, 1997, Total Factor Productivity in the Contiguous United States, 1977-1986, *Journal of Regional Science*, **37**:2, 213-233.

Evanoff, D.D. and P.R. Israilevich, July/August 1991, Productive Efficiency in Banking, *Economic Perspectives*, Federal Reserve Bank of Chicago, 11-32.

Fare, R., R. Graboswki, and S. Grosskopf, April 1985, Technical Efficiency of Philippine Agriculture, *Applied Economics*, **17**:2, 205-215.

Federal Deposit Insurance Corporation, 1997, History of the Eighties and Lessons for the Future: An Examination of the Banking Crises of the 1980s and Early 1990s, (www.fdic.gov).

Friedman, M. and A.J. Schwartz, 1963, *A Monetary History of the United States, 1867-1960*, Princeton University Press, Princeton.

Glass, J.C. and D.G. McKillop, 1992, An Empirical Analysis of Scale and Scope Economies and Technical Change in an Irish Multiproduct Banking Firm, *Journal of Banking and Finance*, **16**, 423-437.

Humphrey, D.B., 1992, Flow versus Stock Indicators of Banking Output: Effects on Productivity and Scale Economy Measurement, *Journal of Financial Services Research*, **6**, 115-135.

Hunter, W.C. and S.G. Timme, 1986, Technical Change, Organizational Form, and the Structure of Bank Production, *Journal of Money, Credit, and Banking*, **18**, 152-166.

Hunter, W.C. and S.G. Timme, 1991, Technological Change in Large U.S. Commercial Banks, *Journal of Business*, **44**:3, 339-362.

Kalman, R.E., 1960, A New Approach to Linear Filtering and Prediction Problem, *Transactions of ASME, Series D: Journal of Basic Engineering*, **82**, 35-45.

Kalman, R.E. and R.S. Bucy, 1961, New Results in Linear Filtering and Prediction Theory, *Journal of Basic Engineering*, **83**, 95-108.

Kwan, H.S. and R.A. Eisenbeis, 1995, *An Analysis of Inefficiencies in Banking: A Stochastic Cost Frontier Approach*, unpublished manuscript, The University of North Carolina, Chapel Hill.

Meinhold, R.J. and N.Z. Singpurwalla, 1983, Understanding Kalman Filter, *American Statistician*, **37**:2, 123-127.

Mester, L.J., 1992, Traditional and Non-traditional Banking: An Information-Theoretic Approach, *Journal of Banking and Finance*, **16**, 545-566.

Saunders, A., 1994, *Financial Institutions Management: A Modern Perspective*, Irwin.

Slade, M.E., 1989, Modeling Stochastic and Cyclical Components of Technical Change: An Application of the Kalman Filter, *Journal of Econometrics*, **41**, 363-383.

Ray, S.C. and H.J. Kim, 1995, Cost efficiency in the U.S steel industry: A Non-parametric Analysis Using Data Envelopment Analysis, *European Journal of Operational Research*, **80**, 654-671.

T2rt2ro lu, D., K. Daniels, and E. T2rt2ro lu, March/April 1998, Total Factor Productivity Growth and Regulation in US Commercial Banking During 1946-1995: An Empirical Investigation, *Journal of Economics and Business*, **50**:2, 171-189.

*The Economist*, Banks and Technology: Cure-all or snake-oil?, October 3, 1992, p.21-25.

The Federal Deposit Insurance Corporation, 1992, *Historical Statistics on Banking* 1934-1991.

The Federal Deposit Insurance Website (http:/www.fdic.gov).

Wills, J., 1979, Technical Change in the U.S. Primary Metals Industry, *Journal of Econometrics*, **10**, 85-98.

Wysocki, B. Jr., Some Firms, Let Down by Costly Computers, Opt to >De-Engineer=, *The Wall Street Journal*, April 30, 1998, p. A1.

In: Liquidity, Interest Rates and Banking
Editors: J. Morrey and A. Guyton, pp. 77-93

ISBN: 978-1-60692-775-5
© 2009 Nova Science Publishers, Inc.

*Chapter 4*

# LONG-TERM REAL INTEREST RATES: AN EMPIRICAL ANALYSIS

### *Khurshid M. Kiani*[*]

Department of Finance, Bang College of Business, Kazakhstan Institute of Management, Economics and Strategic Research
Republic of Kazakhstan

## Abstract

Using data on various United States (US) macroeconomic time series with the models that encompass autoregressive conditional heteroskedasticity and other characteristics dictated by all the data series employed, the present research explores the behavior of the long-term interest rates because of the repeated episodes of large budget deficits in the US economy. The full-sample data for each of the series is split into two sub-sample periods to study the impact of the large budget deficits on long term interest rates within each of these sub-sample periods with reference to the full-sample period for all the series. Additionally, the present work also investigates if the Fisher hypothesis is in place in each of sample period for all the series studied.

The results show that the repeated episodes of the budget deficits have profound impacts on the long-term interest rates and that the high interest rates are linked to the periods of time wherein large budget deficits were experienced in the economy. Further, the results also reveal that a semi-strong form of Fisher hypotheses is in place when considering cyclically adjusted measure of budget deficits in the models for forecasting long-term interest rates.

**Key phrases:** budget deficits; inflation; long-term interest rates; short-term interest rates; yield curve;

**JEL codes:** E34, E43, E62

---

[*] E-mail address: mkkiani@yahoo.com, or kkiani@kimep.kz. Tel: + 7 (727) 270 44 40 Ext. 2320, Fax: + 7 (727) 270 44 63. Address for correspondence: Department of Finance, Bang College of Business, Kazakhstan Institute of Management, Economics and Strategic Research, Room #305, Dostyk Building, 2 Abai Avenue Almaty 050010, Republic of Kazakhstan

## 1. Introduction

A number of empirical studies investigated the impact of budget deficits on short-term and long-term interest rates particularly after inflation rates increased substantially in the United States (US) and other industrialized countries in early 1980s due to oil price shock. However, there appeared no link between budget deficits and long-term interest rates in the US as reported in the studies by Plosser (1982), Hoelscher (1983), Makin (1983), Mascaro and Meltzer (1983), and Evans (1985). Somewhat later, Evans (1987) extended the analysis to Canada, France, Germany, Japan, and the United Kingdom and found no positive association between deficits and interest rates although Barro (1974) provided a theoretical support for the absence of a positive link between large budget deficits and long-term interest rates.

While there appeared no significant literature in this area for over a decade, Reinhart and Sack (2000), using yearly longitudinal data for nineteen industrial nations found that budget deficit changes the slope of yield curve, i.e. raises long-term rates relative to short-term rates. Therefore, it is worthwhile studying the impact of deficit on long-term rather than the short-term rates because the long-term rates are more relevant in terms of the important issue of the crowding out hypothesis. It is because they boost the long-term interest rates and thereby negatively influence the investment expenditures on plant equipment and research and development, which is the reason why larger deficits would adversely affect the long-term growth of living standards. There is another compelling reason not for using short-term interest rates because the Federal Reserve (FED) clearly dominates the short-term interest rates through its interest rates targeting policy. Likewise, while the FED clearly dominates short-term interest rates through its interest rate targeting policies, long-term rates are much less subject to the direct influence by the FED although the long-term rates are dominated by the outlook for inflation and expected rate of return on capital expenditures, and by the outlook for government budgetary conditions. Indeed, the Federal Reserve's principal influence over long-term interest rates is indirect, and comes through its influence on actual and expected inflation.

Studies that include Summers (1984) showed that the interest rates have been more sensitive to inflation in the post World War II era when compared to the earlier times. However, prior to 1946, the US price level behaved in a symmetrical pattern in a sense that the periods of inflations were typically followed by periods of deflation, so the US price level in the early 1940s was not markedly higher than in 1776. Therefore, prices in the pre-World War-II era were much more stable than in the post World War II period, however, after 1945, this long-term stability vanished and persistent upward thrust of the price level emerged.

While Fisher Equation did not show a positive and significant evidence of correlation between inflation and interest rates in the pre World War II period, long-term interest rates in the recent years have been quite sensitive to the outlook of inflation. Therefore, the hypothesis of the present study is that similar conditions may have been responsible for the early findings that the long-term interest rates were not significantly influenced by the deficits before large budget deficits started emerging in the US since early 1980s. This might have been a possible reason for the financial market agent to be sensitized to the budget deficit, who might have behaved differently than the time when both deficits and surpluses were relatively small.

This study employs a slightly modified version of a model of long-term interest rates used by Hoelscher (1986), Cebula and Hung (1992), and Cebula and Rhodd (1993), which in turn was derived in part from earlier models employed by Sargent (1969) and Echols and Elliot (1976), and Kiani (2007) to examine the effect of federal budget deficits on long-term interest rates. The remaining study is organized as follows. Section 2 discusses the model, whereas discussions on hypotheses tests and results are presented in section 3, and finally section 4 incorporates conclusions.

## 2. Model

### 2.1. Theoretical Considerations of the Model

To examine the effect of federal budget deficits on long-term interest rates, and to forecast long-term interest rates in the US, the present research employs an empirical model that was also employed by Kiani (2007). This model was developed from the model employed in the earlier research in this area that includes studies by Hoelscher (1986), Cebula and Hung (1992), Cebula and Rhodd (1992), Sargent (1969) and Echols and Elliot (1976).

First, this model incorporates the budget deficit in supply function (as well as in demand function) to capture the Recardian influence of deficit on private saving behaviour. Secondly for his cyclical variable, Hoelscher employs the change in national income in order to pick up accelerator effects on investment spending (hence on the demand for funds). Hoelscher finds this cyclical measure to be insignificant in most of his regressions. We employ the measure of the cycle rather than the *rate of change* for a couple of reasons. A higher level of economic activity, ceteris peribus is associated with higher capacity utilization rates and with higher expected rates of returns on investments, along with business and consumer confidence, hence greater demand for funds. Thus our framework acknowledges that not only the business borrowing but also household borrowing is likely to vary pro-cyclically. Secondly, by controlling the level of economic activity in the regression equation, we can interpret the coefficient on the deficit variable as the estimated impact of *structural or cyclically adjusted* deficit on long-term interest rates.

It would be advantageous to explain the differences between cyclical budget deficits and structural deficits. The cyclical deficit is the portion of the actual deficit (or surplus), which is attributable to the influence of the business cycle on federal receipts and expenditures. The structural deficit (or surplus) on other hand is the deficit (or surplus) that would hypothetically exist if the economy were at full employment. Contrary to that, many economists would employ a cyclically adjusted deficit or surplus, which calculates the hypothetical deficit or surplus under mid-cycle instead of full employment conditions. The actual deficit or surplus varies with cyclical economic conditions, and in a cyclical downturn, the cyclical and actual deficit increase as tax revenues decline and entitlement expenditures increase. While the interest rates have a tendency to decline in recessions although deficits increase, and since the deficits tend to decline in expansions while interest rates typically increase, it is crucial to incorporate a variable for cyclical conditions in the regression analysis. That is the reason why the variable CYCLE is included in the regression equation since it enables the coefficient on the deficit term to be interpreted as changes in structural or cyclically adjusted budget deficit/surplus on the slope of the yield curve.

The present research employs two classes of models. The first class consists of the models that employ short-term real interest rates that are constructed from GDP deflator ($p_2^e$) henceforth called as $r_2^S$ whereas in the second class of models encompasses short-term real interest rates that are constructed from the Michigan median survey forecast of inflation ($p_1^e$) henceforth called $r_1^S$. Each class of models comprise of four types of models where model1 incorporates DEF1, model2 FEF2, model3 RDEF1, and model4 as RDEF2 as measure of budget deficit. However, because of data limitations, the employed models could not be estimated using short-term rates $r_1^S$ using full-sample as well as sub-sample1 data series, because the Michigan median survey forecast of inflation ($p_1^e$) for this period are unavailable. The models employed in the present research are elaborated in the following Equations:

$$i_{1i}^L = \beta_1 + \beta_2 r_1^S + \beta_3 CYCLE + \beta_4 DEF_i + \varepsilon_1 \qquad (1)$$

where, $r_1^S = tb3 - p_1^e$, where, $p_1^e$ represents Michigan Median Survey forecast of inflation, and $i_1^L$ represents long-term interest rates that are estimated using real short-term interest rates that are calculated from Michigan median survey forecast of inflation for i=1,2,...,4.

$$i_{2i}^L = \beta_1 + \beta_2 r_2^S + \beta_3 CYCLE + \beta_4 DEF_i + \varepsilon_1 \qquad (2)$$

where, $r_2^S = tb3 - p_2^e$, where, $p_2^e = \left(\dfrac{GDPDEF_t}{GDPDEF_{t-4}}\right) X100$, $i_2^L$ represents long-term interest rates that are estimated using real short-term interest rates that are calculated using DGP deflator as a measure of inflation, for i=1,2,...,4.

The variable *CYCLE* in the above model that represents economic activity has an ambiguous sign on it. However, sign on this variable might be positive during the period of higher economic activity when an increase in the demand of funds associated with higher economic activity is likely to surpass the supply. Likewise, considering the fact whether the strict Recardian equivalence conditions are met in reality, the sign on the coefficient of the deficit variable (DEF) is also ambiguous on theoretical grounds although a few studies that include Evans (1985), and Evans (1987) found the counterintuitive finding showing that larger deficits work to reduce interest rates.

## 2.2. Data

Data on 3-month US Treasury bill rates, Michigan median survey of inflation, real GDP, potential GDP, total government budget deficit, federal government budget deficits, GDP deflator, and other series that are employed to construct the exogenous variables for the regression analysis were obtained from the FRED database. These data are divided into two sub-sample periods (sub-sampe1, sub-sample2). Therefore, in addition to employing full-sample period data in the analysis, data on the two sub-sample periods is also employed for studying the impact of large budget deficits on the forecast of long term inflation in the selected sample periods. The first sub-sample spans from the start of the data to the point where the Ragan implemented economic reforms (1960:1-1980:4) to bolster USA economy vis-à-vis Soviet Union. The second data starts from the end of the sub-sample1 to the end of the full-sample data period (2001:4-2007:4). Table 1 shows additional information on all the series employed.

**Table 1. Data on Selected U.S.A. Macroeconomic Time Series**

| Data Series | Series ID | Sample Length | Observations |
|---|---|---|---|
| 10-Year Treasury Constant Maturity Rate | DGS10 | 1953:2- 2007:4 | 219 |
| 3-Month Treasury Bill: Secondary Market Rate | DTB3 | 1953:2- 2007:4 | 219 |
| University of Michigan Inflation Expectation | MICH | 1978:1- 2007:4 | 120 |
| Gross Domestic Product: Implicit Price Deflator | GDPDEF | 1953:1- 2007:4 | 220 |
| Federal Debt Held by Private Investors | FDHBPIN | 1970:1- 2007:4 | 152 |
| Net Federal Government Saving | FGDEF | 1953:1- 2007:4 | 220 |
| Net Government Saving | TGDEF | 1953:1- 2007:4 | 220 |
| Real Gross Domestic Product | GDPC96 | 1953:1- 2007:4 | 220 |
| Real Potential Gross Domestic Product | GDPPOT | 1953:1- 2007:4 | 220 |

**Notes** on Table 1
The table shows selected macroeconomic time series included in the study.
In this table column 1 shows names of macroeconomic time series, column 2 abbreviations used, column 3 sample lengths and column 4 sample periods of each of the data series used.

## 2.3. Construction and Explanations of Variables

Data limitations dictated to use of 10-year bond yield instead of yield on longer maturities. The Federal Reserve's data series for 30-year bond yield commences only in February 1977. Likewise, the 20-year bond yield series is discontinuous during the January 1987-September 1993 interval. However, the use of 10-year bond yield in place of longer maturities makes a little difference in the findings. For the period in which observations are available for both 10-year and 20-year government bond yields, for example, the correlation coefficient between the two series exceeds 0.99. Therefore, for the measure of long-term interest rates, 10-year US government bond yield is employed. Likewise for the ex ante real short-term yield ($r_S$), the difference between the 90-day Treasury bill yield (secondary market) and expected inflation ($p^e$) is employed, although the inflation used is measured in two different ways. Thus, the first measure of expected inflation employed is a purely backward looking, which is known as the annual rate of change of the GDP deflator over the most recent quarters. The second measure of expected inflation employed is the median expected CPI inflation forecast of the Michigan Survey of households[1]. For interpreting cyclical effects in the economy or the business conditions in the model employed that incorporates a relative measure of output gap that is henceforth termed as CYCLE. Specifically, the difference between actual and potential GDP expressed as a percentage of potential GDP[2] is employed.

There is some disagreement in the literature over the appropriate measure of the federal budget deficit for the purpose of economic analysis. In a period in which agent expect inflation to occur, the real value of government bond outstanding is expected to decline. Agents thus expect he real wealth associated with the principal to be transferred from bondholders to the government. Some economists regard this implicit expected transfer of real wealth from bondholder to the government owing to expected inflation essentially as government revenues. In this case, in a period of expected positive inflation, the real deficit (which adjusts the reported deficit for this transfer) will be smaller than the reported national account deficit. Therefore, both the nominal and real measures of deficit are employed in the empirical analysis. The first measure of deficit (DEF) is simply the ratio of the national income accounts deficit to the GDP. The real deficit measure is the ratio of GDP to the difference between national income account deficit and product of inflation rate (using the GDP deflator) and the stock of privately held government debt (the national debt less the portion held by government trust funds and Federal Reserve Funds).

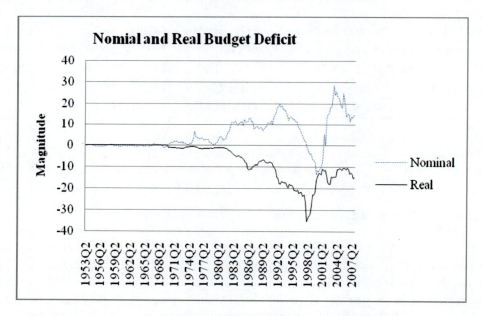

Figure 1. Measures of Nominal (DEF1) and Real Budget Deficit (RDEF1).

---

[1] On the criterion of accuracy, the Michigan median CPI inflation forecast outperformed the Michigan mean, the Livingston mean and median, and survey of professional forecasters' mean CPI inflation forecasts over the 1981:3 –1997:4 period. (See Thomas 1999).

[2] To be precise, the variable CYCLE is defined as [(Actual GDP/Potential GDP)-1]*100. Potential GDP is a measure of trend GDP. In a very strong economy, CYCLE is positive as actual GDP is above the trend GDP. In a weak economy, GDP moves below trend and CYCLE is negative. The potential GDP series employed in the Congressional Budget Office series, available on the Federal Reserve Bank of St. Louis ("FRED") database.

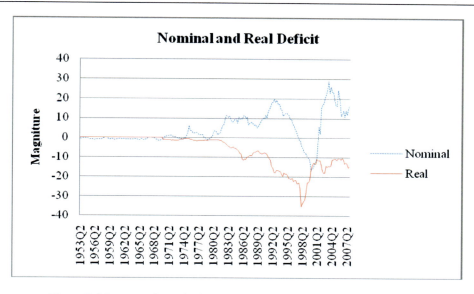

Figure 2. Measure of Nominal (DEF2) and Real Budget Deficit (RDEF2).

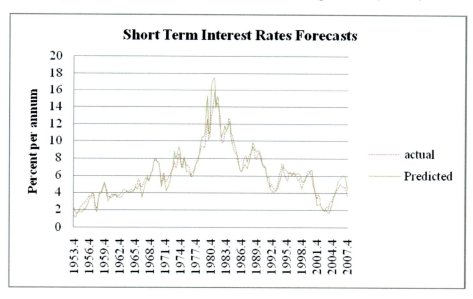

Figure 3. Full-Sample Period Forecast of Short-Term Interest Rates.

Some students of deficit have emphasized potential simultaneity problem in regression analysis when interest rates are regressed on deficit and other variables. Given that higher interest rates result in greater interest expenditures by government, hence larger deficits, a link running from interest rates to deficit is evident. To the extent interest rate rise one for one with expected inflation as postulated by the strong form of the Fisher hypothesis, the use of the real deficit in place of the normal deficit as an independent variable tends to obviate this problem.

The two measures of budget relative to GDP for the 1953:3 – 2007:4 periods are illustrated in Figure 1 and 2 as DEF 1, DEF 2, RDEF 1 and RDEF 2. Because inflation was always positive during this period, RDEF (RDEF1 and RDEF2) is always lower in the Figures. Note that in each of these Figures, the two deficit measures differ appreciably in periods when inflation was relatively severe (1973-1982 and the late 1980s). In periods of mild inflation, the two measures track each other quite closely.

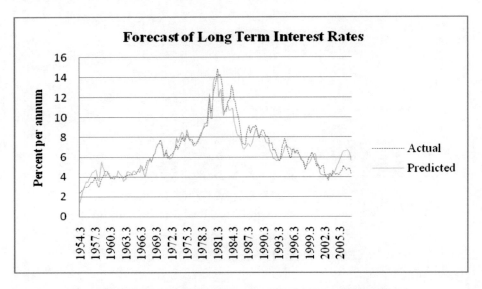

Figure 4. Full-Sample Period Forecast of Long-Term Interest Rates.

## 2.4. Empirical Model

The most general model employed in this study is adopted from the above Equations, which is presented in Equation 3.1 *and* 3.2.

$$i_i^L = \beta_0 + \sum_{i=1}^{t} \beta_{1i} r_{t-i}^S + \sum_{i=1}^{t} \beta_{2i} p_{t-i}^e + \sum_{i=1}^{t} \beta_{3i} CYCLE_{t-i} + \sum_{i=1}^{t} \beta_{4i} DEF_{t-i} + e_t \quad (3.1)$$

$$e_t \sim v_t (h_t)^{1/2}; \quad E(v_t) = 0; \quad and \quad \sigma_v^2 = 1, \text{ and}$$

$$h_t = \alpha_0 + \alpha_i \sum_{i=1}^{p} \varepsilon_{t-i}^2 + \beta_j \sum_{j=1}^{q} h_{t-j} \quad (3.2)$$

w*ehere*, $i = 1,\ldots\ldots\ldots, p$ *and* $j = 1,\ldots\ldots\ldots\ldots,q$

This is an extension to autoregressive conditional heteroskedasticity (ARCH) model (Engle, 1982)[3] wherein in addition to assuming heteroskedasticity in errors an additional term(s) $h_{t-i}$ is included in the model to estimate $h_t$. ARCH is a turning point for time series econometric estimation and is a step away from Box-Jenkins methodology that assumes

---

[3] Engle (1982) estimated UK inflation using ARCH process.

homoskedasticity in errors. GARCH being a step ahead demonstrates that $h_t$ encompasses not only heteroskedastic error term(s) but also consists of lagged $h_{t-i}$ terms. For incorporating independent variables in the model, the variables employed in the model are selected using the model selection criterion due to Schwarz Bayesian Criterion (SBC)[4].

Using Equation 3, spread, and 10-year bond rate is estimated from ex-ante real rate ($r_i^S$), expected inflation ($p_i^e$) GDP deflator, and various deficit measures (i.e. DEF1, DEF2, RDEF1, and RDEF2), and lagged values of independent variables that are selected as per Schwartz Bayesian Criterion (SBC) that resulted in estimating various types of models. In each class of models, the present research estimates four different types of models i.e. model 1, model 2, model 3, and model 4. This division depends on the type of deficit measure used in each model. For example, model 1 uses DEF 1, model 2, DEF2, model 3, RDEF 1, and model 4 employs RDEF 2 as exogenous variable. Moreover, $i_i^L$ represents the long-term interest rate, $r_i^S$ is the ex ante real short-term interest rate, $p_i^e$ represents expected inflation, CYCLE stands for business cycle conditions, and DEF is the budget deficit, for $i = 1,2$.

The purpose of fitting a number of different classes of models is to identify if any of the models employed show different estimates of long-term interest rates using various deficit measures and different measures of ex-ante interest rates and inflation. Similarly, the present work also seeks to explore if different forms of Fisher hypotheses are in place in various sub-sample periods employed in the study.

## 3. Empirical Results

The results on empirical findings are presented in Tables $2-5$. In each of these Tables column 1 shows the names of all the parameters reported in these Tables, column 2 shows parameter estimates for model 1, column 3 for model 2, column 4 for model 3, and column 5 for model 4. Table 2 shows parameter estimates for the four models for the overall period ($1953:2-2007:4$), whereas Table 3 shows the parameter estimates for the sub-sample 1 (1953:2-1980:4), and Table 4 for sub-sample 2 ($1981:1-2007:4$). Likewise, Tables 5 presents parameter estimates for sub-sample 2 with two different measures of inflations i.e. Michigan median measure of inflation forecasts ($p_1^e$) and short-term real interest rates ($r_1^S$) that are employed as independent variables in the models. In the earlier regression models the results from which are presented in Tables $2-4$, GDP deflator ($p_2^e$) is used as a measure of inflation to estimate short-term real interest rates ($r_2^S$).

---

[4] Minimum SBC is model selection criterion.

## Table 2. Parameter Estimates: Sample Period 1953:2 – 2007:4

| Parameters | Model 1 | Model 2 | Model 3 | Model 4 |
|---|---|---|---|---|
| $c$ | 3.1330 | 28595 | 3.4906 | 3.5064 |
|  | (0.000) | (0.0000) | (0.0000) | (0.0000) |
| $RS2$ | -0.6987 | -0.7713 | -0.6879 | -0.6851 |
|  | (0.0000) | (0.0000) | (0.0000) | (0.0000) |
| $PD2$ | 0.6845 | 0.7585 | 0.6668 | 0.6639 |
|  | (0.0000) | (0.0000) | (0.0000) | (0.0000) |
| $GAP$ | 0.0146 | 0.0103 | 0.0069 | 0.0011 |
|  | (0.7074) | (0.8434) | (0.8387) | (0.9747) |
| $GAP_{-1}$ | -0.1063 | -0.1026 | -0.0990 | -0.0943 |
|  | (0.0407) | (0.1539) | (0.0278) | (0.0354) |
| $GAP_{-2}$ | -0.1251 | -0.1219 | -0.1234 | -0.1106 |
|  | (0.0005) | (0.0551) | (0.0073) | (0.0130) |
| $GAP_{-3}$ |  | -0.0381 | -0.0111 | -0.0269 |
|  |  | (0.5936) | (0.8278) | (0.0130) |
| $GAP_{-4}$ |  | -0.0044 | -0.0198 | -0.0193 |
|  |  | (0.9193) | (0.6599) | (0.6456) |
| $GAP_{-5}$ |  |  | -0.0355 | -0.0305 |
|  |  |  | (0.2657) | (0.3195) |
| $DEF1$ | 0.0722 |  |  |  |
|  | (0.0000) |  |  |  |
| $DEF2$ |  | 0.0265 |  |  |
|  |  | (0.0000) |  |  |
| $RDEF1$ |  |  | -0.0267 |  |
|  |  |  | (0.0000) |  |
| $RDEF2$ |  |  |  | -0.0267 |
|  |  |  |  | (0.0000) |
| Variance Equation ||||
| A | 0.0571 | 0.0755 | 0.0765 | 0.0745 |
|  | (0.0006) | (0.0004) | (0.0000) | (0.0000) |
| B | 0.9462 | 0.7018 | 1.0870 | 1.0983 |
|  | (0.0000) | (0.0010) | (0.0000) | (0.0000) |
| C | 0.0967 | 0.2224 | -0.0649 | -0.0614 |
|  | (0.1791) | (0.0279) | (0.0009) | (0.1668) |

**Notes** on Tables 2

The most general model is of the form, $i_i^L = \beta_0 + \beta_1 r_i^S + \beta_2 p_i^e + \beta_3 CYCLE + \beta_4 DEF_i + u_t$ encompassing GARCH specification as shown in Equations 3.1 *and* 3.2. However, all models differ only in one explanatory variable. Model1 incorporates DEF1, Model2 DEF2, Model3 RDEF1, and Model4 RDEF2.

$p_2^e = [\frac{GDPDEF(t)}{GDPDEF(t-4)}] * 100$; Where $GDPDEF = GDP\ DEFLATOR$

CYCLE=$[\frac{GDP}{GDPOT} - 1] * 100$; where $GDPOT = POTENTIAL\ GDP$

$DEF1 = [\frac{FGDEF}{GDP}]*100$; Where $FGDEG = FEDERAL\ GOVERNMENT\ DEFICIT$

$DEF1 = [\frac{TGDEF}{GDP}]*100$; Where $TGDEG = TOTAL\ GOVERNMENT\ DEFICIT$

$RDEF1 = [\frac{FGDEF - PD2(FBHBNPIN)}{GDP}]*100$;

where $FBHBPIN = Federal\ Bond\ Holding\ between\ Private\ Investors$

$RDEF2 = [\frac{TGDEF - PD2(FBHBNPIN)}{GDP}]*100$

$r_2^S = tb3 - p_2^e$

$gs3 = three - year\ bond\ yield$

$gs10 = 10 - year\ bond\ yield$

$p_1^2 = Michigan\ Median\ Inflation\ Forecast$

$r_1^S = tb3 - p_1^e$

tb3=3-month treasury bill rates

$i_1^L = long - term\ interest\ rates\ estimate\ using\ real\ short - term\ rates\ r_1^s$

$i_2^L = long - term\ interest\ rates\ estimated\ using\ real\ short - term\ rates\ r_2^s$

**Table 3. Parameter Estimates: Sample Period 1953:2 – 1980:4**

| Parameters | Model 1 | Model 2 | Model 3 | Model 4 |
|---|---|---|---|---|
| C | 2.0424 (0.0000) | 2.4364 (0.0000) | 2.3608 (0.0000) | 2.3386 (0.0000) |
| RS2 | -0.7096 (0.0000) | -0.7409 (0.0000) | -0.6804 (0.0000) | -0.6825 (0.0000) |
| PD2 | 0.7076 (0.0000) | 0.7347 (0.0000) | 0.6751 (0.0000) | 0.6774 (0.0000) |
| CYCLE | -0.0384 (0.1724) | -0.0114 (0.7021) | -0.0011 (0.9074) | 0.0135 (0.3446) |
| $CYCLE_{-1}$ | -0.0034 (0.9503) | -0.1128 (0.0002) | -0.1045 (0.0000) | -0.1074 (0.0000) |
| $CYCLE_{-2}$ | -0.0640 (0.0069) | | | |
| DEF1 | 0.2665 (0.0000) | | | |
| DEF2 | | -0.0116 (0.7582) | | |

## Table 3. Continued

| Parameters | Model 1 | Model 2 | Model 3 | Model 4 |
|---|---|---|---|---|
| $DEF2_{-1}$ | | 0.0823 (0.2975) | | |
| $DEF2_{-2}$ | | 0.2968 (0.0009) | | |
| $DEF2_{-3}$ | | 0.0529 (0.4633) | | |
| $RDEF1$ | | | -0.8067 (0.0000) | |
| $RDEF2$ | | | | -0.8063 (0.0000) |
| Variance Equation ||||
| $\alpha$ | 0.0006 (0.8736) | 0.0059 (0.2209) | 0.0208 (0.0058) | 0.0209 (0.0105) |
| $\beta$ | 0.3639 (0.0727) | 0.9380 (0.0017) | 1.4328 (0.0000) | 1.4333 (0.0001) |
| $\zeta$ | 0.7226 (0.0000) | 0.3237 (0.0002) | -0.0858 (0.0038) | -0.0861 (0.0502) |

**Notes** on Tables 3
See notes in Table 2.

## Table 4. Parameter Estimates: Sample Period 1981:1 – 2007:4

| Parameters | Model 1 | Model 2 | Model 3 | Model 4 |
|---|---|---|---|---|
| $c$ | 3.8614 (0.0000) | 3.6001 (0.0000) | 3.5215 (0.0000) | 3.5217 (0.0000) |
| $RS2$ | -0.7660 (0.0000) | -0.7628 (0.0000) | -0.7893 (0.0000) | -0.7893 (0.0000) |
| $PD2$ | 0.7458 (0.0000) | 0.7456 (0.0000) | 0.7997 (0.0000) | 0.7997 (0.0000) |
| $PD2_{-1}$ | | | | |
| $PD2_{-2}$ | | | | |
| $CYCLE$ | 0.1077 (0.2127) | 0.1640 (0.0007) | 0.1993 (0.0063) | 0.1996 (0.0037) |
| $GAP_{-1}$ | -0.0147 (0.1624) | | -0.1989 (0.1042) | -0.1991 (0.1000) |
| $CYCLE_{-2}$ | -0.1549 (0.1786) | | -0.3079 (0.0000) | -0.3079 (0.0000) |
| $CYCLE_{-3}$ | -0.1868 (0.0447) | | | |
| $DEF1$ | -0.0145 (0.1624) | | | |

## Table 4. Continued

| Parameters | Model 1 | Model 2 | Model 3 | Model 4 |
|---|---|---|---|---|
| $DEF2$ | | 0.0031<br>(0.6067) | | |
| $DEF2_{-1}$ | | | | |
| $RDEF1$ | | | 0.0798<br>(0.0006) | |
| $RDEF2$ | | | | 0.0799<br>(0.0008) |
| **Variance Equation** | | | | |
| a | 0.12573<br>(0.1175) | 0.0707<br>(0.0255) | 0.1231<br>(0.0605) | 0.1229<br>(0.0650) |
| b | 1.1292<br>(0.0129) | 1.3541<br>(0.0001) | 0.9973<br>(0.0143) | 0.9979<br>(0.0022) |
| c | -0.1441<br>(0.4267) | -0.0787<br>(0.0872) | -0.2121<br>(0.3338) | -0.2120<br>(0.2427) |

**Notes** on Tables 4
See notes in Table 2.

## Table 5. Parameter Estimates: Sample Period 1981:1 – 2007:4

| Parameters | Model 1 | Model 2 | Model 3 | Model 4 |
|---|---|---|---|---|
| $C$ | 2.1328<br>(0.0000) | 2.2840<br>(0.0000) | 3.5913<br>(0.0000) | 3.5973<br>(0.0000) |
| $RS1$ | -0.7419<br>(0.0000) | -0.6923<br>(0.0000) | -0.5815<br>(0.0000) | -0.5817<br>(0.0000) |
| $RS1_{-1}$ | | | -0.1864<br>(0.0065) | -0.1885<br>(0.0087) |
| $PD1$ | 1.10383<br>(0.0000) | 0.8701<br>(0.0000) | 0.7342<br>(0.0000) | 0.7338<br>(0.0000) |
| $PD1_{-1}$ | | | | |
| $CYCLE$ | 0.02719<br>(0.7280) | 0.1113<br>(0.0676) | 0.2235<br>(0.0192) | 0.2239<br>(0.0074) |
| $CYCLE_{-1}$ | -0.2464<br>(0.0107) | | -0.5013<br>(0.0000) | -0.5019<br>(0.0000) |
| $CYCLE_{-2}$ | -0.1891<br>(0.0328) | | | |
| $DEF1$ | -0.0068<br>(0.4639) | | | |
| $DEF2$ | | 0.0134<br>(0.0676) | | |
| $RDEF1$ | | | 0.0446<br>(0.0001) | |

**Table 5. Continued**

| Parameters | Model 1 | Model 2 | Model 3 | Model 4 |
|---|---|---|---|---|
| RDEF2 | | | | 0.0428 |
| | | | | (0.0001) |
| **Variance Equation** | | | | |
| a | 0.1832 | 0.1278 | 0.1214 | 0.1138 |
|   | (0.0005) | (0.0014) | (0.0125) | (0.0315) |
| b | 0.9682 | 1.1003 | 1.0112 | 1.0319 |
|   | (0.0024) | (0.0034) | (0.0034) | (0.0000) |
| c | -0.2749 | -0.1211 | -0.1116 | -0.1134 |
|   | (0.0002) | (0.1229) | (0.0002) | (0.2910) |

**Notes** on Tables 5
See notes in Table 2.

The results show that for the full-sample period (1953:2-2007:4) all the nominal (DEF1 and DEF2) and real measures of deficit variables (RDEF1 and RDEF2) are significant at all levels (1, 5, and 10 percent) of significance, however, the coefficients on the nominal deficits variable take on positive signs whereas the coefficients on real deficit variables take on negative signs. For sub-sample1, the nominal measure DEF1 and both the real measure of the budget deficit are statistically significant at all level of significance. However, the results for the sub-sample2 reveal that both the real measures of the budget deficits are statistically significant at all levels but the coefficients on both the nominal measures of deficits are insignificant. Further, the results that are shown in Table 5 do not change much when a different measure of inflation (Michigan median measure of inflation forecasts) and the related measures of short-term interest rates is employed as an independent variable in the regression models used in the present study.

While data limitations hampered our ability to analyze full-sample data with inflation measure pertaining to the Michigan median survey of inflation forecasts and short-term interest rates constructed from it, there appears some disparity in the results obtained using these two different measures of forecast of inflation in the empirical analysis. However, the study results reveal that there appears statistically significant relationship between budget deficits and long-term interest rates in the US.

### 3.1. Budget Deficit and Long-term Rates

The principal hypothesis of this study is that market agent become sensitive to the outlook for budget deficits after large structural deficits appeared in the early 1980s. In the two decades encompassing the 1960s and 1970s, the deficit/GNP ratio in the United States averaged 3.4 percent, an increase in nearly 400 percent. In the 1980s presidential campaign, Ronald Ragan complained in a platform that included large across-the-board personal and corporate income tax as well as the need to bolster the nation's national defence capability in order to strengthen America's hegemony in international affairs vis-a-vis the Soviet Union. With the election of president Reagan in November 1980 and the passage of economic recovery Tax Act in 1981, coupled with the ensuing rapid build up of national defence expenditures, perspective agents soon become aware that large structural deficits were unfolding that the deficits were therefore not likely to be transitionary phenomenon. Agents likely became increasingly sensitized to the outlook for budget deficits, just as they became increasingly sensitized to inflation after the mid-1960s as US inflation accelerated as a result of the military build up associated with the Vietnam War, Federal Reserve Policies, and the oil shocks of the 1970s.

In order to test this hypothesis the overall sample period that spans from 1953:4 to 2007:4 is divided into two sub periods. The dividing line is determined by the inauguration date of the first Reagan Administration (January 1981). Hence, the two sub-sample periods include 1960:1 – 1980:4, and 1981:1 – 2007:4.

According to the results presented in Tables 2 – 4, and 5 the evidence for the role of deficits in long-term interest rate determination is significant. The level of significance for the nominal variables of budget deficits change from sample to sample but there appears no significant change in the overall significance of the impact of the real budget deficit on long-term interest rates within the samples as well across the samples. This indicates that the economic agent seems more focused on the budget cuts to anticipate long-term yield curve.

## 3.2. Inflation and the Long-Term Rates

The second hypothesis of the study is to know which form of Fisher hypothesis hold for the present study. According to strong form Fisher hypothesis there is one-on-one relationship between inflation and the nominal interest rates.

For the full-sample period under study, the coefficients of inflation are statistically significant at all levels of significance. Likewise, results for each of the sub-sample periods show that each of the measures of inflation is statistically significant at all level of significance. However, from the magnitude of the coefficients of various measures of inflation forecasts for each of the models estimated it transpires that there is less than one-on-one relationship between inflation and nominal interest rates in the US.

Thus, the general findings are robust with respect to the measure of expected inflation as well as the use of nominal and real deficits. These findings confirm the intuitive notion that changes in the outlook for the fiscal posture of the Federal government in the US is reflected in changes in the slope of the yield curve.

# 4. Conclusions

In this research a number of macroeconomic time series are employed to construct variables that are used to estimate long-term interest rates in the US using time series models encompassing generalized autoregressive conditional heteroskedasdiecty and other attributes dictated by the data series. Moreover, the present work also forecasts short as well as real long-term rates in addition to testing the hypothesis if the Fisher hypothesis is in place in the US economy. Thus, the basic hypothesis of this study is that just as emergence of high rates of inflation after 1965 caused financial market agents to become more sensitive to the outlook for inflation, the emergence of large and persistent federal budget deficits after 1980 caused agents to focus more intensively than previously on the outlook for the fiscal stance of government. This may help account for the predominant early findings (using pre- 1980s data) in the literature of no significant link between budget deficits and interest rates in the era in which deficits were relatively small and/or non-persistent.

The finding reported in this study suggest that, over the past 20 years, each one percentage point change in ratio of the cyclically adjusted budget deficit to GDP changed the difference between 10-year and 3-month US government security (Spread) yields by approximately 50 basis points using sub-sample1, and 99 basis points using sub-sample period2 which clearly indicates that economic agents became sensitized to the outlook of the large budget deficits and in turn the long-term interest rates after 1980s when large budget deficits emerged. However, when Michigan median inflation forecasts, and short-term real interest rates were incorporated in the models to forecast the long-term interest rates, using cyclically adjusted real budget deficits to GDP in the US showed one percentage point change in cyclically adjusted budget deficit to GDP that changed the spread to 40 basis points only. Alternately, using full-sample period data series, the change in the spread appeared to be about 60 basis points which also confirms that the agent became sensitized to the outlook of the slope of the yield curve when large budget deficits appeared in the US after 1980s. Therefore, if this hypothesis about increased financial market sensitivity to the outlook for the federal budgetary posture is correct, it is important that the long-term fiscal policies be designed with a view towards avoiding large structural deficits in future.

The study results based on both the sub-samples (sub-sample1 and sub-sample2) that are estimated using short-term real interest rates that are constructed from the backward looking measure of inflation forecasts (GDP deflator) show that there is less than one on one correspondence between inflation and short-term rates. These results are in conformance with those obtained from the models that employ short-tem real rates constructed from Michigan median survey forecast of inflation. Finally, the results obtained from the full-sample period do confirm these results, therefore, based on the present study results a semi strong Fisher hypothesis appears to be in place in the US economy.

# References

Barro, Robert J., "Are Government Bonds New Wealth?" *Journal of political Economy* **82** (November/December 1974), 1095-1117.

Cebula, Richard J, and Chao-shun Hung, "Government Budget Deficits and Interest Rates: An Empirical Analysis for United States and Canada," *Revista Internazionale e di Scienze Economiche e Commerciali* **39** (1992), pp. 917-928.

Cebula, Richard J. and Rupert G. Rhodd, "A Note on Budget Deficits, Debt Service Payments and Interest Rates," *The Quarterly journal of Economics and Finance* **4**, Winter 1993, pp. 439-445.

Echols, Michael E., and Jane Walter Elliot, "Rational Expectations in a Disequilibrium Model of the Term Structure," *American Economic Review* **66** (March 1976), 28-44.

Engle, R. F, "Autoregressive Conditional Heteroscedasticity With Estimates of the Variance of United Kingdom Inflation", *Econometrica,* **50** (1982), 987-1007.

Evans, Paul, "Do Large Deficits Produce High Interest Rates?" *American Economic Review* **75** (March 1985), 68-87.

Evans, Paul, "Do Budget Deficits Raise nominal Interest Rates?" *Journal of Monetary Economics* **20** (May 1987), pp. 281-300.

Fledstein, Martin S., "Budget Deficits, Tax Rules and Real Interest Rates," Working Paper Number 1970 (July 1986), National Bureau of Economic Research, Cambridge, Mass.

Hoelscher, Gregory. "New Evidence on Deficits and Interest Rates," *Southern Economic Journal* **50**, (October 1983), 319-333.

Hoelscher, Gregory. "New Evidence on Deficits and interest Rates," *Journal of Money Credit and Banking* **18** (Feburary 1986), 1-17.

Kiani, Khurshid. "Federal Budget Deficits and Long Term Interest Rates in USA," *The Quarterly Review of Economics and Finance* **49** (July 2009), 74-84.

Makin, John, "Real Interest Rates, Money Surprises, Anticipated Inflation, and Fiscal Deficits," *Review of Economics and Statistics* **65** (August 1983), 374-384.

Mascaro, Angelo and Allen H. Meltzer, "Long and Short Term Interest Rates in a Risky World," *Journal of Monetary Economics* **12** (November 1983), 485-518.

Plosser, Charles I., "Government Financing Decisions and Asset Returns, "*Journal of Monetary Economics* **9** (May 1982), 325-352.

Reinhard, Vincent and Brain Sack, "The Economic Consequences of Disappearing Government Debt," *Brooking Papers of Economic Activity,* 2000:2, 163-209.

Sargent, Thomas J., "Commodity Price Expectations and the Interest Rates," *Quartely journal of Economics* **83** (Feburary 1969), 127-140.

Summers, Laurence, "The Nonadjustment of Nominal Interest Rates: A Study of Fisher Effect, in *Macroeonomics*: Prices and Quantities, edited by James Tobin (Washington: The Brooking Institution, 1983).

Thomas, Lloyd B., "Survey Measures of Expected U.S. Inflation," *Journal of Economic Perspectives* **13** (Fall 1999), 124-144.

In: Liquidity, Interest Rates and Banking
Editors: J. Morrey and A. Guyton, pp. 95-110

ISBN 978-1-60692-775-5
© 2009 Nova Science Publishers, Inc.

*Chapter 5*

# INTEREST RATE MOVEMENTS IN THE LIFE INSURANCE FAIR VALUATION CONTEXT[*]

*Rosa Cocozza*[1,†] *Emilia Di Lorenzo*[2,‡] *Albina Orlando*[3,§] *and Marilena Sibillo*[4,¶]
[1]Dipartimento di Economia Aziendale,
Facolta' di Economia Universita' degli Studi di Napoli "Federico II",
via Cintia, Complesso Monte S.Angelo 80126 Napoli Italy
[2]Dipartimento di Matematica e Statistica,
Facolta' di Economia Universita' degli Studi di Napoli "Federico II",
via Cintia, Complesso Monte S.Angelo 80126 Napoli Italy
[3]Consiglio Nazionale delle Ricerche,
Istituto per le Applicazioni del Calcolo Mauro Picone,
via P. Castellino 80131 Napoli Italy
[4]Dipartimento di Scienze Economiche e Statistiche,
Facolta' di Economia Universita' degli Studi di Salerno,
via Ponte Don Melillo 84084 Fisciano (SA) Italy

### Abstract

The financial risk factor takes up a primary role in the life insurance liability valuations, particularly when referred to life annuity and pension annuity schemes. In this framework a wide literature explains how strong is the influence of the risk connected with the interest rate movements in the life annuity risk mapping, especially if set in the fair value context, as the guidelines given by the international boards engaged in life insurance issues clearly indicate.

The fair behaviour of the discounting process is usually described using a term structure model based on arbitrage assumptions. The paper focuses on the financial variable for the provision evaluation both in a deterministic and a stochastic perspective. The evaluation risk is approached in a market value assessment with the aim of

---

[*]Although the paper is the result of a joint effort, sections 1 and 2 are due exclusively to R. Cocozza whilst section 3 is due to E. Di Lorenzo, A. Orlando and M. Sibillo.
[†]E-mail address: rosa.cocozza@unina.it
[‡]E-mail address: diloremi@unina.it. tel.: 0039081675102.
[§]E-mail address: a.orlando@na.iac.cnr.it. tel.: 00390816132395.
[¶]E-mail address: msibillo@unisa.it. tel.: 0039089962001.

measuring the interest rate impact on the liability fair value; the study is made through the sensitivity analysis of the net value of the intermediation portfolio to a modification of the interest rate process parameters.

Numerical implementations are illustrated with graphs and tables in life annuity contract cases.

**Key words and phrases:** *Life insurance, financial risk, mathematical provisions, financial regulation*

**JEL classification: G22, G28, G13**

## 1. Introduction

Life insurance business is traditionally characterised by a complex system of risks that can be essentially split into two main type of drivers: actuarial and financial; within the pricing process, they refer to the insurance company aptitude to select the "right" mortality table, and to apply the "right" discounting process, where accuracy covers forecasting prociency. Both the aspects can be regarded at the same time as risk drivers and value drivers, since they can give rise to a loss or a profit if the ex ante expected values prove to be higher or lower than the ex post actual realizations. With special reference to the intermediation portfolio (contingent claims versus corresponding assets), these effects can be enhanced by the specific accounting standard applied for the financial statement; in other words a fair valuation system can substantially modify the disclosure of the economic result and the solvency appraisal in time and space.

At the end of March 2004, the International Accounting Standards Board issued the International Financial Reporting Standard 4 Insurance Contracts. For the first time, it provides guidance on accounting for insurance contracts, and marks the first step in the IASB's project to achieve the convergence of widely varying insurance industry accounting practices around the world. More specifically, the IFRS *permits an insurer to change its accounting policies for insurance contracts only if, as a result, its nancial statements present information that is more relevant and no less reliable, or more reliable and no less relevant. Moreover, it permits the introduction of an accounting policy that involves remeasuring designated insurance liabilities consistently in each period to reect current market interest rates (and, if the insurer so elects, other current estimates and assumptions)* , thus giving rise to a potential reclassication of some or all financial assets as *at fair value through prot or loss*. On the one hand, the compromising solution derives from the recognition of a fair value disclosure requirement, also to comply with a more general tendency concerning financial statements. On the other hand, it stems from the equally widespread and deep worries concerning the lack of agreement upon a definition of fair value as well as of any guidance from the Board on how the fair value has to be calculated. According to the majority of commentators including the National Association of Insurance Commissioners, the International Association of Insurance Supervisors, and the Basle Committee on Banking Supervision, this uncertainty may lead to fair value disclosures that are unreliable and inconsistently measured among insurance entities. As also the American Academy of Actuaries (2003) clearly states, market valuations do not exist for many items on the insurance balance sheet and this would lead to the reliance on entity specic measurement for determining insurance contract and asset fair values. However, such values would be unreasonably subject to wide ranges of judgment, subject to signicant abuse, and may provide information that is not at all comparable among companies. The cause for this concern is the risk margin component of the fair value. Risk margins are clearly a part of market values of uncertain assets and liabilities, but with respect to many insurance contracts, their value cannot be reliably calibrated to the market.

This statement gives rise to a wider trouble. If there is an amendment in the evaluation criteria for the reserve from one year to another according to current market yields or even to current mortality tables there is a possible change in the value of the reserve according to the application of a more stringent or, at the opposite, a more flexible criterion. This may turn into a proper *fair valuation risk*.

In the accounting perspective, the introduction of an accounting policy involving remeasuring designated insurance liabilities consistently in each period to reflect current market interest rates (and, if the insurer so elects, other current estimates and assumptions) implies that the fair value of the mathematical provision is properly a current value or a net present value. Consistently, the fair value of the mathematical provision could be properly defined as the net present value of the residual debt towards the policyholders evaluated at current interest rates and, eventually, at current mortality rates. In a sense, this is marking to market. However, this is the crucial point. From the accounting perspective a fair value is not necessarily an equilibrium price, but merely a market price.

In a mathematical perspective, marking to market implies the discovery of a price and more specifically of an equilibrium price, while in the accounting perspective the current value is not necessarily an equilibrium price, but merely a market price. Many problems and misunderstanding arise from this cultural discrepancy: the majority of the actuarial models are very difficult to implement on a large scale in a fair value accounting and give rise to a high space/time variability, while the issue is the comparability of the results across different companies. In a sense, there is a proper fair valuation risk, which can be defined as the change in the economic results due to a change in the evaluation criteria adopted for insurance liabilities. This evaluation risk will produce a twofold impact on the portfolio performance: a current earning impact, that can be measured trough the variability of the net income from year to year according to changes in relevant variables ([Cocozza et al., 2004a]), and a market value impact, that can be measured trough the sensitivity of the net value of the intermediation portfolio to a modification of specific risk drivers ([Cocozza et al., 2004b]). As a consequence, there is a need for a measure of variability. The paper focuses on such aspect and tries to model the effect of such variations in the case of a life annuity portfolio. Therefore, it focuses on financial variables for the provision evaluation and tries to address to question of the sensitivity of the fair valuation to interest rates parameters, in both a deterministic and stochastic scenario, using a proper term structure of interest rates estimated by means of a Cox-Ingersoll-Ross model.

To this end, the paper starts with a complete balance-sheet modelling of the insurance business, which consents to identify all the variable (risk and value drivers). A special attention is devoted to the fair valuation risk, defined as the change in the economic results due to a change in the evaluation criteria adopted for insurance liabilities, which proves to be proportional to the value and the duration of the portfolio reserve (section 2). The specific question of the current value of the reserve is subsequently put into a stochastic context (section 3) by means of a cash flow analysis, where relevant reserve risk drivers are randomly treated. The appraisal of the mathematical reserve at current interest rates is prospected, where the fair valuation of the mathematical provisions is focused on the financial driver while the actuarial components are appreciated by means of an opportunely projected mortality table. In this section the reader will find the details of the term structure, the current values in a continuous approach with a closed form for the analytical solution to the current valuation of the mathematical provision.

## 2. The Basic Model within a Deterministic Environment

As showed elsewhere ([Cocozza et al., 2004a]), the net value of the intermediation portfolio in any $t$-year ($K_t$) can essentially be represented as the algebraic sum of: insurer capital at the end of preceding year (plus); premiums written during the year (plus); return accrued on the final reserve of preceding year and on the initial capital (plus/minus); the claims paid during the year (minus); the provision at the end of the year (minus).

For an immediate unitary annuity the following relation holds:

$$K_t = \left[ K_{t-1} + N^x(t-1) \sum_{r=1}^{n-t-1} {}_rp_{x+t-1} e^{-r\delta_{L_{t-1}}} \right] e^{\delta_{A_{t-1}}} - N^x(t) \left[ 1 + \sum_{r=1}^{n-t} {}_rp_{x+t} e^{-r\delta_{L_t}} \right] \tag{1}$$

where
$n$ = duration of the policy
$x$ = initial age of the insured
$c$ = number of policies sold (cohort constituents)
$N^x(r)$ = actual number of survivors at age $x + r$
${}_rp_x$ = mortality table applied in the reserve evaluation at the end of the $r$-year
$\delta_{L_r}$ = instantaneous interest rate applied in the reserve evaluation at the end of the $r$-year
$\delta_{A_r}$ = instantaneous rate of return on assets earned during the $r$-year

Similarly, using the same symbols, for a deferred unitary annuity with periodical premiums ($P$) the following formulas hold respectively before and after the maturity of the deferral period ($d$):

$$K_{t|t<d} = \left[ K_{t-1} + N^x(t-1) \left( \sum_{r=d-t-1}^{n-t-1} {}_rp_{x+t-1} e^{-r\delta_{L_{t-1}}} - P \sum_{r=0}^{d-t-1} {}_rp_{x+t} e^{-r\delta_{L_{t-1}}} \right) \right] e^{\delta_{A_{t-1}}} + \tag{2}$$

$$- N^x(t) \left[ \sum_{r=d-t}^{n-t} {}_rp_{x+t} e^{-r\delta_{L_t}} - P \sum_{r=0}^{d-t} {}_rp_{x+t} e^{-r\delta_{L_t}} \right]$$

$$K_{t|t \geq d} = \left[ K_{t-1} + N^x(t-1) \left( \sum_{r=0}^{n-t-1} {}_rp_{x+t-1} e^{-r\delta_{L_{t-1}}} - 1 \right) \right] e^{\delta_{A_{t-1}}} + \tag{3}$$

$$- N^x(t) \left[ \sum_{r=0}^{n-t} {}_rp_{x+t} e^{-r\delta_{L_t}} \right]$$

It can be easily inferred that the net value of the intermediation portfolio depends not only on the insurer initial capital $K_{t-1}$, on the actual number of contracts existing at the end of the $t$-year $(N^x(t))$ and on the return on assets earned in the year $(\delta_{A_t})$, but also on the table adopted for provision evaluation $(_rp_{x+t})$, as well as on the rate selected for the evaluation $\delta_{L_r}$. The net value, in all cases, is a growing function of the two interest rates while is inversely affected by an increase in the actual number of survivors at the end of the year. Consistently, the choice at the end of the year of a mortality table different from that applied in any previous evaluation (both for pricing and reserving) produces a difference of the net value which is opposite with respect to the "sign" to the variant of the table itself. As a matter of fact, the choice for example of a more prudential table, showing higher probability of surviving, will give rise to an increase in the present value of future net outflows and therefore a decrease in the net value, while the selection of a table showing lower probability will end up in an increase in the same value. As far as the intensity of this impact is concerned, it is easy to verify that is filtered by the size of the portfolio under observation and by its implicit financial discounting process.

This modelling gives the opportunity to measure directly the impact of a change in the evaluation rate (evaluation rate risk). In this context, the measurement can be easily obtained through the first derivative with respect to the rate applied for the evaluation of the mathematical provision $(R_t)$, that is

$$R_t = N^x(t) \sum_{r=1}^{n-t} {}_rp_{x+t} e^{-r\delta_{L_t}} \tag{4}$$

$$\frac{\partial R_t}{\partial \delta_{L_t}} = -N^x(t) \sum_{r=1}^{n-t} r \cdot {}_rp_{x+t} e^{-r\delta_{L_t}} \tag{5}$$

$$R_{t|t<d} = N^x(t) \left[ \sum_{r=d-t}^{n-t} {}_rp_{x+t} e^{-r\delta_{L_t}} - P \sum_{r=0}^{d-t} {}_rp_{x+t} e^{-r\delta_{L_t}} \right] \tag{6}$$

$$\frac{\partial R_{t|t<d}}{\partial \delta_{L_t}} = -N^x(t) \left[ \sum_{r=d-t}^{n-t} r \cdot {}_rp_{x+t} e^{-r\delta_{L_t}} + P \sum_{r=0}^{d-t} r \cdot {}_rp_{x+t} e^{-r\delta_{L_t}} \right] \tag{7}$$

$$R_{t|t\geq d} = N^x(t) \sum_{r=0}^{n-t} {}_rp_{x+t} e^{-r\delta_{L_t}} \tag{8}$$

$$\frac{\partial R_{t|t\geq d}}{\partial \delta_{L_t}} = -N^x(t) \sum_{r=0}^{n-t} r \cdot {}_rp_{x+t} e^{-r\delta_{L_t}} \tag{9}$$

It is easy to demonstrate that the dollar change in the value of the reserve is directly proportional to the Macaulay duration of the mathematical provision $D_{R_t}$ since

$$\frac{\partial R_t}{\partial \delta_{L_t}} \frac{1}{R_t} = -\frac{N^x(t) \sum_{r=1}^{n-t} r \cdot {}_rp_{x+t} e^{-r\delta_{L_t}}}{N^x(t) \sum_{r=1}^{n-t} {}_rp_{x+t} e^{-r\delta_{L_t}}} = -D_{R_t} \quad \Rightarrow \quad \Delta R_t \simeq -R_t D_{R_t} \Delta \delta_{L_t} \tag{10}$$

Likewise, the impact of a change in the evaluation rate for a mix of provisions, that can be also a non homogeneous, can be measured through weighted average of the duration of the single portfolio components. For example, in the case of a portfolio with two homogeneous components, the reserve for the whole portfolio $(PR)$ will exhibit the following sensitivity

$$\frac{\partial PR_t}{\partial \delta_{L_t}}\frac{1}{PR_t} = -\left(D_{R_t}\frac{R_t}{PR_t} + D_{R_t|t<d}\frac{R_{t|t<d}}{PR_t}\right) \Rightarrow \qquad (11)$$

$$\Rightarrow \quad \Delta PR_t \simeq -(R_t D_{R_t} + R_{t|t<d}D_{R_t|t<d})\Delta\delta_{L_t}$$

Formulations (10) and (11) give the opportunity to state that the evaluation rate risk can be effectively indexed to the Macaulay duration of the reserve and to the value of the reserve. Moreover, it can be measured through the value-at-risk of the reserve, after the selection of a measure of interest rates volatility.

Therefore, any change in the interest rates parameters is able to alter more steadily those reserve which exhibit higher absolute values and higher duration values (sensitivity indexes).

## 2.1. Numerical Evidence for the Basic Model

We consider two different kinds of life annuity portfolios, each contract with maturity 10 years: the first one consisting in immediate unitary annuities and the other consisting in deferred unitary annuities with deferment period of 3 years, periodical premiums and anticipated payments. For the sake of clarity it is supposed that all premiums are earned exactly at the beginning of the year as well as the payments concerning the deferred annuity, while the claims on the immediate annuity are paid exactly al the end of the period. Calculations have been performed with both a fixed 4% rate and with a term structure (CIR Model Table 1) The survival probabilities are deduced by the Italian Mortality Table IPS55.

**Table 1. Interest rates scenario and parameters**

| | | t=1, 2, ... 10 |
|---|---|---|
| $r(0;t)$ | Risk-free Spot Rate for the horizon (0,t) | [4.41%; 4.62%; 4.75%; 4.84%; 4.90%; 4.95%; 4.98%; 5.01%; 5.03%; 5.04%] |
| $\delta_{(0,t)}$ | Interest Rates Intensity | [4.31%; 4.52%; 4.64%; 4.73%; 4.79%; 4.83%; 4.86%; 4.89%; 4.90%; 4.92%] |
| $r_0$ | Starting value of the spot rate | 3.91% |
| $\mu_r$ | Long term mean | 4.88% |
| $\sigma_r$ | Volatility of the instantaneous rate | 5.68% |
| $\alpha$ | Mean reversion coefficient | 0.8 |

In Table 1 we report the data describing the financial scenario we suppose formalized with completely deterministic assumptions. Here the values chosen for the process parameters are listed. In Table 2 the fair values of the reserve of a portfolio of 1000 contracts in the two cases of 10 years immediate life annuity and of a 3- years deferred life annuity with duration 7 years, both issued on an insured aged 40, are illustrated. The values are obtained supposing to evaluate at the fixed interest rate 4%. It is evident the strictly decreasing behaviour of the reserve values in the case of the immediate annuities. In the case

**Table 2. Value of the reserve (policy rates)**

| Fixed 4% year | 10 years annuity Value | Deferred annuity Value |
|---|---|---|
| 0 | 8,060.80 | 1,911.26 |
| 1 | 7,384.15 | 1,987.71 |
| 2 | 6,681.41 | 3,302.22 |
| 3 | 5,951.64 | 5,417.07 |
| 4 | 5,193.85 | 5,408.95 |
| 5 | 4,407.04 | 4,589.53 |
| 6 | 3,590.17 | 3,738.67 |
| 7 | 2,742.20 | 2,855.29 |
| 8 | 1,862.00 | 988.13 |
| 9 | 948.35 | 722.01 |
| 10 | 0.00 | 0.00 |

of the deferred annuities the trend is initially increasing, during the deferment period of 3 years, and then decreasing during the 7 years of the annuitization period. Table 3 concerns the same results reported in Table 2 supposing in this case the evaluation carried out by means of the CIR process for the term structure of the interest rates, modelled with the data reported in Table 1, The hypotheses made on the long term mean value with respect to the previous 4% applied in Table 2 justifies the lower values of Table 3 with respect to the corresponding ones of Table 2. In Table 4 the non homogeneous portfolio made up by both the preceding two is considered. The fair values of its reserve are reported when valued at 4% and with the CIR as modelled in Table 1. Finally in Table 5 the movements of the reserves at different years of valuations and for different values for the drift coefficient are listed. When the drift increases, for each time of valuation the fair values strictly decrease. This means that a stronger force attracting the process toward the long term mean produces higher values of the interest rates applied in the evaluations.

## 3. The Cash-Flow Model within a Stochastic Environment

The fair valuation context involves a risk-based appraisal, where the most relevant risk drivers lye in the demographic and financial factors. In our analysis the last one refers to the unsystematic phenomenon of mortality, that is the random deviations of the mortality rates from their anticipated values.

As usually done in literature, we assume the mortality randomness independent on the interest rate stochastic fluctuations; let us introduce the probability space $(\Omega, \mathfrak{F}, P)$ in which $\mathfrak{F}$ contains the information flow about mortality and financial history (cf. [Ballotta et al., 2006]).

In the *fair valuation* perspective, the market is assumed to be frictionless, with continuous trading and no restrictions on borrowing or short-sales, and in which the zero-bonds

**Table 3. Fair Value of the reserve (market rates)**

| CIR IPS55 year | 10years annuity Value | Deferred annuity Value |
|---|---|---|
| 0 | 7,700.39 | 1,021.36 |
| 1 | 7,040.89 | 1,729.74 |
| 2 | 6,382.89 | 3,119.67 |
| 3 | 5,705.68 | 5,278.02 |
| 4 | 5,001.41 | 5,267.26 |
| 5 | 4,263.94 | 4,490.9 |
| 6 | 3,492.53 | 3,678.08 |
| 7 | 2,685.41 | 2,826.64 |
| 8 | 1,837.78 | 988.13 |
| 9 | 938.16 | 663.34 |
| 10 | 0.00 | 0.00 |

**Table 4. Fair Value of the portfolio reserve**

| year | 4% | CIR |
|---|---|---|
| 0 | 9,972.06 | 8,721.75 |
| 1 | 9,371.86 | 8,770.63 |
| 2 | 9,983.63 | 9,502.56 |
| 3 | 11,368.71 | 10,983.70 |
| 4 | 10,602.80 | 10,268.67 |
| 5 | 8,996.57 | 8,754.83 |
| 6 | 7,328.85 | 7,170.60 |
| 7 | 5,597.49 | 5,512.05 |
| 8 | 2,850.13 | 2,825.91 |
| 9 | 1,670.37 | 1,601.50 |
| 10 | 0.00 | 0.00 |

and the stocks are both infinitely divisible.

Let us consider a portfolio of $c$ policies; indicating by $\{X_j\}$ the cash-flow referred to time $j$, in a risk-neutral valuation, we can write the fair value at time $t$ as follows

$$\mathfrak{V}_t = \mathbb{E}\left[\sum_{j>t} c\mathbf{1}_{\{K_{x,t}>j\}} X_j v(t,j) | \mathfrak{F}_t\right] \qquad (12)$$

where $\mathbb{E}$ is the expectation under the risk-neutral probability measure and the indicator function $\mathbf{1}_{\{K_{x,t}>j\}}$ assumes values 1 or 0, according to the considered contract (i.e. for a life annuity contract it takes the value 1 if the curtate future lifetime of the insured, aged

## Table 5. Immediate life annuity: reserve fair value and drift coefficient

| t/k | 0 | 0.5 | 0.8 | 1.6 | 2.4 | 3 |
|-----|---|-----|-----|-----|-----|---|
| 1 | 7409.48486 | 7148.18066 | 7114.58056 | 7081.84326 | 7081.84100 | 7081.71337 |
| 2 | 6710.80175 | 6476.26855 | 6453.30859 | 6440.43457 | 6439.24169 | 6439.16406 |
| 3 | 5983.74902 | 5785.94921 | 5771.85791 | 5766.40429 | 5766.12402 | 5766.10644 |
| 4 | 5227.35351 | 5069.55517 | 5061.55419 | 5060.6742 | 5059.50048 | 5058.84742 |
| 5 | 4440.47216 | 4321.97998 | 4317.72998 | 4316.77099 | 4316.68505 | 4316.65380 |
| 6 | 3621.77954 | 3539.31811 | 3537.22924 | 3536.88598 | 3536.85522 | 3536.83764 |
| 7 | 2769.82568 | 2718.40209 | 2717.52978 | 2717.50463 | 2717.48749 | 2717.47635 |
| 8 | 1883.25354 | 1856.60205 | 1856.25061 | 1856.17785 | 1856.14514 | 1856.12878 |
| 9 | 960.51702 | 951.31610 | 951.22412 | 951.21179 | 951.21032 | 951.20788 |

$x$ at issue, takes values greater than $t + j$ ($j = 1, 2, \ldots$), that is if the insured aged $x + t$ survives up to the time $t + j$, 0 otherwise. On the contrary, it takes the complementary values in the case of life insurance, such as whole life and term insurance).

In the case of a portfolio of identical immediate life annuities, formula (12) becomes (cf. [Cocozza et al., 2005])

$$\mathfrak{V}_t = \sum_{j>t} c X_j \, {}_tp_x \, {}_jp_{x+t} \mathbb{E}[v(t,j)|\mathfrak{F}_t] \qquad (13)$$

In the general case of portfolio constituted by non-homogeneous life annuities, we develop a system of homogeneous sub-portfolios, say $m$ their number, identified by common characteristics, such as age at issue, policy duration, and so on. Following the basic notations of [Cocozza et al., 2005]), we assume:

- $n_i$ = policy duration for the $i$-th group

- $c_i$ = number of policies in the $i$-th group ($\sum_{i=1}^{n} c_i = c$)

- $x_i$ = age at issue of the insureds of the $i$-th group

- $T_i$ = deferment period of the annuities in the $i$-th group ($0 \leq T_i < n_i$)

- $B_{i,s}$ = benefit payable to each insured of the $i$-th group at time $s$,

- $P_{i,s}$ = premium payable by each insured of the $i$-th group at time $s$,

- $n = \max_i n_i$

- $X_{i,s}$ = the flow at time $s$ related to each insured of the $i$-th group, with

$$X_{i,s} = \begin{cases} -P_{i,s} & \text{if } s < T_i \\ B_{i,s} & \text{if } s \geq T_i \end{cases}$$

It holds:

$$\mathfrak{V}_t = \mathbb{E}\left[\sum_{i=1}^{m}\sum_{j>t} X_{i,j} c_i \mathbf{1}_{\{K_{x_i,t}>j\}} v(t,j)|\mathfrak{F}_t\right] = \\ = \sum_{i=1}^{m}\sum_{j>t} c_i X_{i,j}\ {}_tp_{x_i}\ {}_jp_{x_i+t}\mathbb{E}[v(t,j)|\mathfrak{F}_t]. \quad (14)$$

## 3.1. Basic Assumptions for the Fair Valuation

Now we summarize the financial and demographic scenarios chosen for the numerical application.

*The financial framework: notation and calculus basis*

The term structure we will use in the following, in order to frame the fair valuation, is expressed by means of the Cox-Ingersoll-Ross square root model; it is possible to estimate its parameters on the basis of a simple discretisation (cf. [Chan *et al.*, 1992]) in which the continuous interest rate involves the stochastic differential equation

$$dr_t = -k(r_t - \gamma)dt + \sigma\sqrt{r_t}dB_t \quad (15)$$

with $k$, the drift coefficient, and $\sigma$, the diffusion coefficient, positive constants, $\gamma$ the long term mean and $B_t$ the Brownian motion.

The parameter estimation is obtained by the classical Brown and Dybvig procedure, estimating the risk adjusted parameter vector $\theta = \{\hat{k}, \hat{\gamma}, \hat{\sigma}\}$ with $\hat{k} = k - \pi$ and $\hat{\gamma} = k\gamma$, where $k$ and $\gamma$ are referred to the objective measure dynamics of the model, and $\pi$ is the risk premium such that the market price of risk is $q(r(t), t) = \frac{\pi\sqrt{r(t)}}{\sigma}$.

We briefly recall the basic guidelines of the estimation procedure due to Brown and Dybvig (for a deeper understanding see [Brown it et al., 1986]).

As well known, the CIR model provides an explicit formula for the price of a zero coupon bond with a given maturity:

$$v(t,s) = A(t,s)e^{r(t)B(t,s)}$$

with:

$$A(t,s) = \left(\frac{de^{d_1(s-t)}}{d_1(e^{d_1(s-t)} - 1) + d}\right)^v$$

$$B(t,s) = \frac{e^{d(s-t)} - 1}{d_1(e^{d_1(s-t)} - 1) + d}$$

where

$$d = \sqrt{(k-\pi)^2 + 2\sigma^2}$$

$$d_1 = \frac{k - \pi + d}{2}$$

and

$$v = \frac{2k\gamma}{\sigma^2}$$

By means of a non linear regression technique applied to bonds with different maturities priced in $t$, the Brown and Dybvig calibration procedure allows to estimate the risk adjusted parameter vector $\theta$ which gives the best fitting between model prices and observed ones.

*The demographic framework*

In order to take into account the longevity phenomenon, that is the increasing of the survival probabilities due to the betterment of the mortality trend in the industrialized countries, we choose the Lee-Carter model to describe the survival phenomenon.

Such model is expressed by the following formula (cf. [Lee and Carter,1992]):

$$m_{x,t} = e^{a_x + k_t b_x + e_{x,t}} \qquad (16)$$

where $m_{x,t}$ describes the age specific death rate and $ln m_{x,t}$ is given by the sum of $a_x$, an age specific parameter independent of time, a component given by the product of $k_t$, a time-varying parameter reflecting the general level of mortality, and $b_x$, representing how rapidly or slowly the mortality at each age changes as the general level of mortality changes. $e_{x,t}$ represents that part of the mortality which is not caught by the model, with mean equal to zero and finite variance. In the numerical application we construct the Lee-Carter survival probabilities for the male Italian population.

## 3.2. The Reserve Fair Value Sensitivity: Numerical Applications

The hypotheses of modelling the term structure of interest rates by means of a Cox, Ingersoll and Ross model is often set in literature, particularly when the aim is the evaluation of future obligations. Referring to the equation (15), the characteristic parameters are well defined by the following expressions: the first one describes the deterministic component of the process while the second describes the random component:

$$\lim_{h \to 0} \frac{E_t[r(t+h) - r(t)]}{h} = k[\gamma - r(t)]$$

$$\lim_{h \to 0} \frac{[E_t[r(t+h) - r(t)]]^2}{h} = \sigma^2 r(t)$$

They consist respectively in the infinitesimal mean and variance of the process and give a clear message on the parameter meanings. In particular, stopping briefly on the deterministic part, we recall the mean value of the process:

$$[E_t[r(s)] = \gamma - [\gamma - r(t)]e^{-k(s-t)}, \qquad t \leq s$$

from which immediately one obtains:

$$E_\infty[r(t)] = \gamma$$

$\gamma$ plainly means the long term rate toward which the process moves elastically pushed by the action of the drift k; this parameter determines the speed of adjustment (cf. [Cox et al. 1985]) holding the role of reporting the process itself to the long term mean.

In what follows we deepen the sensitivity of the fair valuation treated in the paper to the parameters characterizing the deterministic component of the Cox, Ingersoll and Ross stochastic process.

We consider a portfolio of 1000 unitary life annuities, both in the immediate case and in the deferred case; each policy is issued on a male aged 40. For the deferred annuities we assume a constant premium payed during the whole deferment period.

The time series related to the interest rates has been extracted from Bank of Italy official statistics and consists of annualised net interest rate of Government 3-month T-Bill rate covering the period from January 1996 until January 2004.

We obtain $r_0 = 0.0391, \sigma = 0.0568, k = 0.8, \gamma = 0.0488$.

Aim of this application is to illustrate the behavior of the reserve fair values of the above portfolios, when the interest rate process parameters vary. As first step we analyze the influence of the drift coefficient $k$ on the reserve fair values in the case of the immediate life annuities.

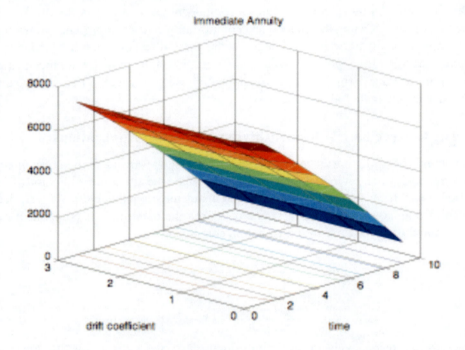

Figure 1. Immediate life annuity portfolio: reserve fair value and drift coefficient.

In Figure 1 and in Table 5 the reserve fair value is represented as function of the valuation time $t$ and the drift parameter $k$. For every fixed value of $t$, the fair value generally decreases when $k$ increases, since for high value of $k$ the interest rate is forced towards the long term mean $\gamma$, so that the present values of the future cash-flows decrease and tend to a sort of steady fair value for each valuation time and high values of the drift. In general we can say that it does not seem the drift variation has a strong influence on the reserve fair values for high value of $t$.

In Figure 2 and in Table 6 the reserve fair value is represented as function of the valuation time $t$ and the long term mean $\gamma$. For every fixed value of $t$, we observe a strictly decreasing behavior of the fair values when the long term mean increases. In particular this is more evident for low values of $t$.

**Table 6. Immediate life annuity portfolio: reserve fair value and long term mean**

| t/γ | 0.01 | 0.02 | 0.0391 | 0.0488 | 0.10 | 0.15 |
|---|---|---|---|---|---|---|
| 1 | 8399.26660 | 8040.19824 | 7409.47998 | 7114.58056 | 5797.54785 | 4819.81201 |
| 2 | 7568.18261 | 7258.27099 | 6710.78564 | 6453.30859 | 5290.54296 | 4412.03222 |
| 3 | 6682.05175 | 6430.92333 | 5983.75781 | 5771.85791 | 4800.69873 | 4049.23754 |
| 4 | 5767.42138 | 5574.26806 | 5227.35937 | 5061.55419 | 4288.82666 | 3674.49291 |
| 5 | 4835.441894 | 4695.01855 | 4440.47558 | 4317.72998 | 3735.45996 | 3258.81420 |
| 6 | 3890.46118 | 3795.50439 | 3621.77832 | 3537.22924 | 3128.71411 | 2784.02246 |
| 7 | 2876.33935 | 2769.02197 | 2717.52978 | 2594.83422 | 2459.81884 | 2235.52172 |
| 8 | 1966.80163 | 1937.67736 | 1883.26354 | 1856.25061 | 1720.85583 | 1599.13562 |
| 9 | 988.88922 | 979.01971 | 960.51470 | 951.22412 | 903.81817 | 859.74572 |

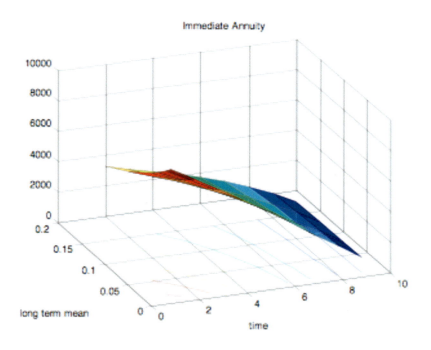

Figure 2. Immediate life annuity portfolio: reserve fair value and long term mean.

The same analysis is given for the 3-years deferred case, with a deferment period of 3 years. In Figures 3 and 4 and Tables 7 and 8, all the trends observed in the immediate case are confirmed, as well as it is evident the change of the reserve pattern in correspondence of the end of the deferment period.

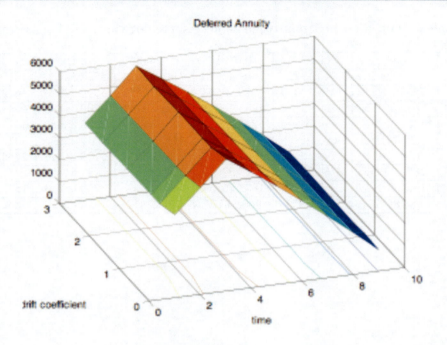

Figure 3. Deferred life annuity portfolio: reserve fair value and drift coefficient.

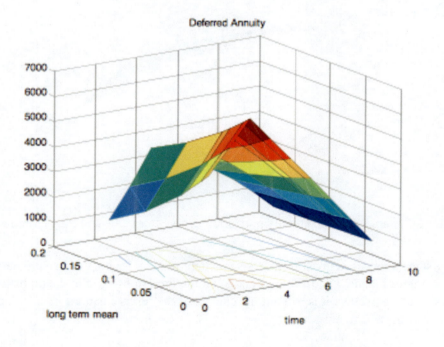

Figure 4. Deferred life annuity portfolio: reserve fair value and long term mean.

**Table 7. Deferred life annuity portfolio: reserve fair value and drift coefficient**

| t/k | 0 | 0.5 | 0.8 | 1.6 | 2.4 | 3 |
|---|---|---|---|---|---|---|
| 1 | 3793.61547 | 3552.238037 | 3524.44116 | 3504.26708 | 3500.20483 | 3499.27685 |
| 2 | 4866.83984 | 4638.86230 | 4617.31005 | 4605.55419 | 4604.30126 | 4604.15917 |
| 3 | 5983.74902 | 5785.94921 | 5771.85791 | 5766.40429 | 5766.12402 | 5766.10644 |
| 4 | 5227.35351 | 5069.55517 | 5061.55419 | 5059.51374 | 5059.50048 | 5059.49492 |
| 5 | 4440.47216 | 4321.97998 | 4317.72998 | 4316.77099 | 4316.68505 | 4316.65380 |
| 6 | 3621.77954 | 3539.31811 | 3537.22924 | 3536.88598 | 3536.855226 | 3536.83764 |
| 7 | 2769.82568 | 2718.40209 | 2717.52978 | 2717.50463 | 2717.45957 | 2717.37934 |
| 8 | 1883.25354 | 1856.60205 | 1856.25061 | 1856.17785 | 1856.14514 | 1856.12878 |
| 9 | 960.51702 | 951.31610 | 951.22412 | 951.21179 | 951.21032 | 951.20788 |

**Table 8. Deferred life annuity portfolio: reserve fair value and long term mean**

| t/$\gamma$ | 0.01 | 0.02 | 0.0391 | 0.0488 | 0.10 | 0.15 |
|---|---|---|---|---|---|---|
| 1 | 4704.56103 | 4372.88867 | 3793.61669 | 3524.44116 | 2338.46997 | 1481.60742 |
| 2 | 5699.96582 | 5398.49414 | 4866.83789 | 4617.31005 | 3495.44165 | 2655.19018 |
| 3 | 6682.05175 | 6430.92333 | 5983.75781 | 5771.85791 | 4800.69873 | 4049.23754 |
| 4 | 5767.42138 | 5574.26806 | 5227.359375 | 5061.55419 | 4288.82660 | 3674.49291 |
| 5 | 4835.44189 | 4695.01855 | 4440.47558 | 4317.72998 | 3735.45996 | 3258.81420 |
| 6 | 3890.46118 | 3795.50439 | 3621.77832 | 3537.22924 | 3128.71411 | 2784.02246 |
| 7 | 2934.02197 | 2876.33935 | 2769.02197 | 2717.52978 | 2459.81884 | 2235.52172 |
| 8 | 1966.80163 | 1937.67736 | 1883.26354 | 1856.25061 | 1720.85583 | 1599.13562 |
| 9 | 988.88922 | 979.01971 | 960.514470 | 951.22412 | 903.81817 | 859.74572 |

# References

[American Academy of Actuaries, 2003]American Academy of Actuaries.

*Comment Letter on Exposure Draft 5 Insurance Contracts* .

http://www.iasb.org/docs/ed05/ed5-cl92.pdf, 2003.

[Ballotta et al., 2006] L. Ballotta, S. Haberman. The fair valuation problem of guaranteed annuity options: the stochastic mortality environment case. Insurance: Mathematics and Economics 38, 195-214.

[Brown et al., 1986] S. J. Brown, P. H. Dybvig. The Empirical Implications of the Cox, Ingersoll, Ross Theory of the Term Structure of Interest Rates, Journal of Finance, American Finance Association, vol. 41(3), pages 617-30, July.

[Chan et al., 1992]K.C. Chan, A.G. Karolyi, F.A. Longstaff and A.B. Sanders. An Empirical Comparison of Alternative Models of the Short- Term Interest Rate. *The Journal of Finance*, 47, pages 1209-1227, 1992.

[Cocozza et al., 2004] R. Cocozza, E. Di Lorenzo and M. Sibillo. Methodological problems in solvency assessment of an insurance company. *Investment management and financial innovation*, Issue 2, 2004.

[Cocozza et al., 2005] R. Cocozza, D. De Feo, E. Di Lorenzo and M. Sibillo. On the financial risk factors in fair valuation of the mathematical provision. Proceedings of The 36th International Astin Colloquium, September 4-7, 2005, ETH, Zurich *http://papers.ssrn.com/sol3/papers.cfm?abstract_id=997202*, 2005.

[Cocozza et al., 2008] R. Cocozza, E. Di Lorenzo, A. Orlando e M. Sibillo. 16) The VaR of the mathematical provision: Critical issues. *Journal of Risk Management in Financial Institutions*, vol 1/3, (2008), to appear.

[Cox et al., 1985] J. C. Cox, J. E. Ingersoll and S. A. Ross, A theory of the term structure of interest rates, *Econometrica*, Vol. 53, No.2 (March 1985).

[IAIS, 2000] IAIS Solvency & Actuarial Issues Subcommittee. *On solvency, solvency assessments and actuarial issues*. IAIS, March, 2000.

[IAIS, 2002] IAIS Solvency & Actuarial Issues Subcommittee. *Principles on capital adequacy and solvency*, IAIS, January, 2002.

[IAIS, 2004] International Accounting Standards Board, *International Financial Reporting Standard 4 Insurance Contracts*, IAIS, January, 2004

[IASB, 2003] International Accounting Standards Board. *Exposure Draft 5 Insurance Contracts*. International Accounting Standards Board Committee Foundation, London, 2003.

[Lee and Carter, 1992] R. Lee, L. Carter. Modelling and forecasting U.S. mortality. *Journal of the Statistical Association*, vol. 87, No. 419, 1992.

In: Liquidity, Interest Rates and Banking
Editors: J. Morrey and A. Guyton, pp. 111-138

ISBN: 978-1-60692-775-5
© 2009 Nova Science Publishers, Inc.

*Chapter 6*

# FUTURES MARKET LIQUIDITY UNDER FLOOR AND ELECTRONIC TRADING

## *Owain ap Gwilym[1,*], Ian McManus[2] and Stephen Thomas[3]*

[1]Bangor Business School, Bangor University, Wales, UK. SY23 3DD.
[2]School of Management, University of Southampton, UK. SO17 1BJ.
[3]Cass Business School, City University, 106 Bunhill Row, London, UK. EC1Y 8TZ.

## Abstract

This chapter analyses the impact on liquidity of a transition from open outcry to a fully electronic trading system in the U.K. futures market. The study makes a unique contribution in comparing microstructural characteristics of different trading systems. Particular focus is placed on price clustering and its relationships with bid-ask spreads and trade sizes. Further investigations emphasize the changing relationship between bid-ask spreads, volume and volatility following automation.

Although price clustering is not materially affected by the transition to electronic trading, there is a greatly increased concentration of large trades at more popular prices. Under electronic trading, smaller trades tend to be associated with narrower bid-ask spreads. This is consistent with the anonymous nature of electronic trading and the associated increased problems of asymmetric information and adverse selection compared to floor trading. This appears to offer informed traders a further incentive to conceal their activities by splitting orders into smaller components.

Following automation, there is a modest increase in mean daily volume, while there is a substantial reduction in mean trade size as reduced-depth orders become trades. Consistent with this, the mean daily number of transactions and quotations increases substantially. Bid-ask spreads widen significantly after automation, but this is largely accounted for by the finding that spreads under electronic systems demonstrate an increased sensitivity to price volatility. This effect is accentuated by increased volatility after automation. Cost savings arising from increased operational efficiency of the electronic trading system will be partly offset by this effect.

Overall, the chapter provides important evidence on the changes in market liquidity following the transition to electronic trading, and highlights quite different evidence from that presented in previous studies in this vein.

---

[*] E-mail address: owain.apgwilym@bangor.ac.uk. (Corresponding author)

## Introduction

The trend towards automated trading in financial markets and its associated perceived economic benefits has attracted considerable recent attention. A number of international derivatives exchanges have converted from open outcry to electronic trading, e.g. the London International Financial Futures and Options Exchange (LIFFE) during 1998-2000, France's MATIF in June 1998, and the Sydney Futures Exchange in 1999. Another pertinent example is the success of Eurex (and formerly Deutsche Termin Borse, DTB) in securing a dominant role in the trading of German Bund futures via electronic trading while competing with LIFFE's open outcry system.

Transitions from floor based to electronic trading offer opportunities for the investigation of various aspects of market microstructure under the two systems. Evidence of differing market behavior under electronic trading is of potential interest to exchanges and regulators with regard to liquidity, transaction costs, tick sizes, and the design of trading systems, and offers practical insights for investors. Much previous work has compared screen based trading of a given instrument on one exchange with floor trading on another. A heavily researched example of this is German Bund futures which were traded in both London and Frankfurt (see Martens [1998], Frino et al [1998] and references therein). Others compare execution costs for similar stocks traded on different exchanges under floor and electronic trading (e.g. Venkataraman [2001]). Further studies have compared screen trading of the same instrument on different exchanges (e.g. Kappi and Siivonen [2000]). Another avenue has involved comparison of floor trading with after-hours screen trading of the same instrument (e.g. Chow et al [1998]; Wang [1999]).

Madhavan [2001] notes the pitfalls involved in comparing "apples to oranges" in studies of floor versus electronic trading. The current study examines the liquidity of a futures contract on the same exchange before and after a migration to electronic trading. In contrast to some of the previous literature, it therefore offers a clean and direct test of the relative merits of screen and floor trading since identical contracts were traded under the two systems at the same exchange before and after automation. Similar studies in this vein include Blennerhassett and Bowman [1998], Ferris et al [1997], Griffiths et al [1998], Jiang et al [2001], Naidu and Rozeff [1994] and Tse and Zabotina [2001]. In anticipation of our results, we report some key differences compared with the earlier work from futures markets, especially relating to liquidity and the role of price clustering.

This chapter extends the literature in this area by investigating the impact of automation of trading of U.K. long term government bond futures at LIFFE upon various aspects of liquidity. For the 10 year contract known as the Long Gilt, with effect from 12th April 1999, the futures contract was traded on the electronic platform known as LIFFE CONNECT™. Previously trading was conducted by open outcry during normal business hours, followed by an evening Automated Pit Trading (APT) session. We can thus compare three different trading systems within the same framework. Specifically, we compare floor versus electronic for daytime trading and APT versus electronic for evening trading. Particular attention is placed here on price clustering and bid-ask spread behavior. A number of theoretical predictions are formulated and tested relating to the impact of automation on price clustering, bid-ask spreads, trading volume, trade sizes, trading frequency and price volatility.

The chapter is structured as follows. The next section reviews the relevant theoretical and empirical literature on floor versus electronic trading systems. The section headed "Data, Research Methods and Hypotheses" outlines the change in market structure and discusses the data and methodology employed in the empirical study. The empirical results are then presented, followed by the concluding section.

## Literature Review

Electronic trading systems are increasingly viewed by exchanges as a means of competing more effectively and boosting trading volumes. There has been widespread recent debate in the financial press and among regulators and policy-makers regarding the relative merits of screen and floor trading. The fixed costs of running an electronic traded market are lower than for floor trading, which in a competitive environment should translate into lower trading costs. These developments hastened the introduction of electronic trading at LIFFE and other exchanges.

Beyond the cost arguments in favor of electronic trading, the theoretical literature highlights advantages in both floor and screen based trading systems. A key advantage of floor based trading is cited as being a high level of liquidity, especially in active periods. This can be attributed to various factors, e.g. the greater willingness of locals trading on their own accounts to provide liquidity (e.g. Massimb and Phelps [1994]), and the ability of dealers to distinguish more accurately between informed and liquidity traders (Benveniste et al [1992]). With regard to the former, Khan and Ireland [1994] suggest that there is less activity by locals in screen based markets because of the high setup costs, an inability to get in and out of positions quickly, and an inability to see orders coming as they would on the floor. Benveniste et al [1992] demonstrate that, under certain conditions, floor trading is superior to anonymous screen trading because it is easier to distinguish between informed and uninformed traders. A market maker obtains this knowledge through interaction in an open outcry environment, and can use this to offer better prices to liquidity traders. This should imply that the open outcry market is more liquid, and although bid-ask spreads will be narrower, the market maker is compensated by higher volume.

The advantages of screen based trading include low trading costs, fast order execution, fast information dissemination, anonymity, and the possibility of trading remotely and thus possibly in several markets simultaneously. These factors should lead to greater liquidity. Kempf and Korn [1998] note that it could be argued that screen based exchanges perform well under normal market conditions but not so well in periods of high volatility. One explanation is tied to the fact that most electronic systems ensure anonymity of the trader. Theoretical models suggest that if screen based trading is less transparent than floor trading, there will be a disproportionate concentration of informed trading, thus increasing the adverse selection component of the bid-ask spread. This problem could be more acute during periods of high volatility when knowledge of the counterparty may be more important. An alternative explanation may be that posting limit orders in an electronic order book provides a free option to other traders, which is especially valuable in volatile periods.

The existence of a limit order book in electronic markets provides depth even in quiet periods. However, in very busy periods, the limit order book can have the disadvantage of delays in the replacement of old quotes with new. In contrast, under open outcry, a simple hand signal is sufficient to change quotes, thus providing this system with an advantage in price discovery during fast moving markets. This is empirically supported by Martens [1998] and others.

Particularly since the publication of findings of alleged collusion on Nasdaq by Christie and Schultz [1994] and Christie et al [1994], regulators and policy makers have placed increasing emphasis on questions of market transparency and the possibilities for collusive behavior by market participants under different trading systems. Henker [1999] suggests that there is little potential for collusion among market makers on an electronic trading system with anonymously posted prices because it is difficult to identify any agent who cheats on the colluding group. In contrast, under floor trading, the long-standing professional and personal relationships that evolve on a trading floor could induce cooperation among traders. Game theory shows that cooperation is a dominant strategy in a repeated game. There is ample opportunity for reciprocity among colluding traders and punishment for defecting ones.

Overall, there is no clear consensus in the above literature relating to the merits of floor versus screen trading and the relationship between trading technology and market performance. However, in practice there has been an increasing trend towards market participants favoring electronic trading (see first section). Due to the lack of conclusive theoretical arguments, it is especially important to consider the empirical evidence on the performance of screen versus floor based systems. However, the existing evidence is also found to be mixed.

Studies of the relative bid-ask spreads on the German Bund futures contract which was traded on the floor at LIFFE and electronically at the DTB during the 1990s have been inconclusive. Kofman and Moser [1997] report that spreads are equal on both markets, while Pirrong [1996] reports narrower spreads on the DTB and Shyy and Lee [1995] report narrower spreads at LIFFE. Fremault and Sandmann [1995] compare spreads on the Nikkei Stock Average futures contract traded on the Singapore International Monetary Exchange (SIMEX) under open outcry and at the Osaka Securities Exchange (OSE) under a screen based system. They find that the automated trading system attracts less frequent but larger orders than the open outcry system, and that bid-ask spreads are wider on the automated trading system.

Blennerhassett and Bowman [1998] investigate the impact of the switch from open outcry to electronic trading at the New Zealand Stock Exchange in 1991, and conclude that transaction costs declined as a result. There was an increase in the supply of liquidity as measured by the increased availability of bid and ask quotes. Naidu and Rozeff [1994] examine the automation of the Singapore Stock Exchange in 1989, and find that this resulted in a substantial increase in trading volume for individual stocks but bid-ask spreads and their variability increased slightly. Griffiths et al [1998] examine data from the Toronto Stock Exchange (TSE closed its trading floor in April 1997), finding that effective bid-ask spreads, trading volume and average trade size are generally unchanged following the introduction of electronic trading.

Ferris et al [1997] examine the automation of trading on the Vancouver Stock Exchange and find that liquidity was not reduced relative to a comparable set of firms listed on US exchanges. Mean daily traded volume rose slightly in the post-automation period. For Hong Kong stock index futures, Jiang et al [2001] find that bid-ask spreads are narrower under electronic trading, after controlling for price volatility and trading volume. However, they also suggest that the automated system may not perform as well at times of heavy volumes. In the most closely related previous study, Tse and Zabotina [2001] report that the median daily time-weighted spreads are lower following automation of the FTSE100 stock index futures market at LIFFE. However, they suggest that market quality and pricing efficiency were superior under the previous open outcry setting.

## Data, Research Methods and Hypotheses

### Market Structure and Data

In June 1998, an overwhelming majority of LIFFE members voted in favor of a move to electronic trading and subsequently LIFFE established the electronic trading platform known as LIFFE CONNECT$^{TM}$, with access points available in all major financial centers. The aim of the transition was to reduce trading costs and thus to enhance competitiveness in the European market. MATIF in Paris had opened the first 24 hour trading system, while Frankfurt had introduced longer trading hours and was already using screen based trading. LIFFE was losing market share to these European competitors; for example, it lost dominance in German Bund futures trading to Eurex. The electronic trading system was introduced in phases to ensure a smooth transition, with each new release focusing on a particular market segment.

Prior to automation, the Long Gilt contract traded by floor based open outcry from 0800-1615 GMT, and by Automated Pit Trading (APT) from 1622-1800 GMT. Separate results are presented in the chapter for comparing floor trading and APT with electronic trading. Under the electronic trading system, the trading day can open earlier and close later, allowing for continuous trading from 0800-1800 GMT. For comparability with the previous regime, separate results are presented for the periods 0800-1621 GMT and 1622-1800 GMT. Commencing with the contract for September 1998 delivery, the unit of trading was £100,000 nominal. Prices are quoted per £100 nominal value. Subsequent to conversion from fractional to decimal pricing in May 1998, the minimum price movement is £0.01, which has a value of £10.[1]

Delivery months are March, June, September and December, with the nearest three delivery months trading at any given time. Trading is heavily concentrated in the front month contract. Rollover of volume and open interest to the second nearest contract will typically occur before a counterparty is exposed to the obligation to receive a delivered gilt. Under the terms of the futures contract, delivery can be made of any Gilts on LIFFE's List of Deliverable Gilts and such delivery can occur on any business day in the delivery month (at the seller's discretion). The possibility of delivery at the seller's discretion is likely to deter speculative trading during the delivery month. In practice, rollover is driven by the first notice day, which is two trading days prior to the first day of the delivery month. Open interest tends to rollover on the first notice day but rollover of trading volume is at the beginning of the delivery month. Following from this, the analysis in this chapter employs the front month contract only, with rollover to the next contract at the beginning of each delivery month.

---

[1] An empirical investigation of the decimalization of the Long Gilt futures contract appears in ap Gwilym et al [2005].

The data sample consists of all quotes and trades for the period 24th October 1998 to 4th October 1999, which provides approximately six months of data either side of the move to electronic trading on 12th April 1999. During this period, there are 114 trading days prior to the conversion and 123 trading days afterwards.[2] The data source is the LIFFE Time and Sales data on CD-ROM, which contains information on the time to the nearest second, an identifier for floor/APT/electronic trading, delivery month, price, transaction code (bid, ask or trade), and traded volume. There is volume data associated with all trades, and with all quotes for the electronic trading period. For front month contracts, the dataset contains a total of 349,305 valid floor trading observations, 54,413 valid APT observations, 1,339,985 valid daytime electronic trading observations, and 76,884 valid after-hours electronic trading observations.

## Methods and Hypotheses

Empirical evidence suggests a link between trading costs and price clustering, e.g. Christie and Schultz [1994] and ap Gwilym et al [1998a]. A number of theories attempting to explain price clustering are reviewed in the latter[3]. The initial investigation in this chapter analyses price clustering in this futures contract before and after the move to electronic trading. Standardized ranges between observed and expected proportions occurring at each final digit of price are employed as a metric for the level of price clustering (see Grossman et al [1997]).

Harris [1991] suggests that negotiation costs are higher in high volume markets, and in periods of higher price volatility. An important prediction in the current context is that traders would use larger increments when trading face-to-face as opposed to anonymously. This leads to the conjecture that the level of price clustering will reduce following the move to electronic trading. With further reference to the negotiation hypothesis, we examine the link between trading volume and price clustering, and investigate the distribution of mean trade sizes across the final digit of price.

Following from the analysis in the previous section, assuming that there is a greater adverse selection problem due to informed trading and a reduced level of activity by locals in the automated environment, we postulate that bid-ask spreads will be wider (reduced liquidity) following the move to electronic trading. We analyze the distribution of the values taken by the bid-ask spread before and after the automation of trading, and postulate that there will be a smaller proportion of quoted spreads at one tick. The analysis then proceeds to consider more directly the impact on quoted and effective spreads, and we postulate larger mean values under electronic trading.

Three measures of quoted spreads are employed in the empirical investigation. The 'quote based' method calculates a new spread for each new bid or ask observation. A restriction is placed to include only quoted bid-ask pairs which are time-stamped within three

---

[2] There is no data for APT sessions on four days where floor trading did occur. Three of these days are during the 1998 Christmas period (24th December when the market closed at 1223 GMT, 29th and 30th December when the market closed at 1615 GMT), while the other appears to be an omission in the data source (on 22nd January 1999 where the data stops at 1615 GMT). Additionally, there are two days where no data appears for after-hours electronic trading (the data stops at 1558 GMT on 9th September 1999, and at 1402 GMT on 15th September 1999). These are most likely to have been caused by technical problems.

[3] Clustering implies 'de facto' use of wider intervals; the effect is that of engendering a framework in which bid-ask spreads are generally wider. In turn, this leads to decreased liquidity, which motivates our focus on clustering.

seconds of each other. This is motivated by a rule that quotes during floor trading at LIFFE were valid "as long as the breath is warm" (see ap Gwilym and Thomas [2002]).[4] The 'trade based' method calculates a new spread at each new trade observation, thus employs the most recent bid-ask pair occurring immediately prior to a trade. A time constraint of seven seconds is imposed in order to produce an equivalent proportion of valid observations as that for the 'quote based' method.[5] The volume-weighted 'trade based' method extends this by weighting each quoted spread by the volume traded in the subsequent trade.

The quoted spread may overstate trading costs since trades can occur at prices within this spread, and this motivates calculation of the effective spread where transactions data is available.[6] Petersen and Fialkowski [1994] calculate the effective spread for stocks based on the notion of price improvement, which is the reduction in trading costs compared to the posted quotes. The price improvement is calculated as:

Ask price - Transaction price for buy orders, and
Transaction price - Bid price for sell orders.

As for most futures markets datasets, it is not known from the LIFFE data whether a trade is buyer- or seller-initiated. However, an appropriate assumption is that transactions at prices exceeding the prevailing quote midpoint are buyer initiated and those below the midpoint are seller initiated. Petersen and Fialkowski [1994] note that a trader may receive price improvement both buying and selling, and thus:

$$\text{Effective spread} = \text{Quoted spread} - 2 \times \text{Price improvement} \qquad (1)$$

The above equation assumes that the same price improvement is received on both the buy and the sell side. If this is not true, the estimated effective spread will be incorrect for individual observations. However, Petersen and Fialkowski [1994] show that the average estimated effective spread will still be correct.

We then examine whether trading volume has changed following automation. Increased efficiency of trading may lead to enhanced levels of volume but a wider bid-ask spread may counteract this. We therefore hypothesize no significant change in the daily mean traded volume. We investigate changes in the components of volume following automation, namely trade sizes and the number of transactions. We anticipate splitting of large orders under

---

[4] We empirically investigate the validity of applying this rule through a frequency plot of the time between bid and ask quotes against the number of observations. In the case of floor and APT trading, the frequency of observations declines rapidly as the time between bid and ask quotes increases beyond three seconds. This implies a high level of activity in the domain of these (rapidly occurring) quotes. The rate of decline in the frequency of occurrences at longer values of the time between bid and ask quotes is clearly lower, with a distinct structural break at the 3 second value, which we conjecture is evidence of the onset of 'staleness' of bids and asks. By this, we imply an increasing dilution in the coupling / relationship between successive quotes. No such structural break is in evidence in the case of electronic trading, but we apply the same rule to ensure consistent comparisons. The proportion of data excluded by the application of all of these screens in combination is approximately 3%.

[5] The seven second interval is that which begins with the first of the quotes in the bid-ask (or ask-bid) pair, and ends with the subsequent trade.

[6] Campbell et al [1997] suggest that transactions may occur within the bid-ask spread due to one or more of the following aspects of market maker behavior: failure to update quotes in a timely fashion; desire to rebalance inventory resulting in willingness to temporarily offer more favorable quotes in order to achieve this; willingness to provide discounts to customers that are trading for reasons other than private information.

automated trading in order to achieve priority in the order book and thus a more favorable average trade price. Therefore, we hypothesize a lower mean trade size. As a result of the above hypotheses, we then conjecture that the daily mean number of transactions and quotes will increase. Finally, we investigate price volatility before and after automation.

Tests are conducted for overall changes in the above aspects of market behavior, i.e. quoted spread, effective spread, total volume traded, total number of quoted prices, total number of traded prices, mean trade size, and the standard deviation of the midpoint price. Statistical significance is based primarily on standard Group t-tests, comparing Means across the Floor Trading / Electronic Trading dimension; these are predicated upon the Normal distribution of the means, a fact assured (for the large sample sizes here) by the Central Limit Theorem (see Johnson [1995]). However, distribution-free U-Mann-Whitney tests, which are sensitive to differences in the distributions of these variables, are also carried out over the pre- and post-automation periods[7].

To summarize the above, the empirical investigation tests the following null hypotheses:

1. The negotiation hypothesis implies that price clustering will decrease following the move to electronic trading, because traders will be more inclined to use finer increments when trading anonymously.

2. Volume-weighted price clustering will be less than equally-weighted price clustering, both before and after automation. Under the negotiation hypothesis, larger trades will tend to use more of the available price grid in order to arrive at the most appropriate price, with any additional negotiation cost becoming worthwhile given the larger trade size.

3. The most popular final digits of price will have lower mean trade sizes, both before and after automation. Relatively small trades will tend to concentrate at the more 'popular' prices, thus lowering the mean trade size at these final digits of price.

A reduced presence of locals and an increased adverse selection problem after automation lead to the next two hypotheses:

4. There will be a smaller proportion of quoted spreads observed at one tick after automation.

5. Mean quoted and effective spreads will increase following the move to electronic trading.

6. There will be no significant difference between mean daily traded volume before and after automation, because of the trade-off between increased efficiency (resulting from lower operational costs) and wider bid-ask spreads.

7. Mean trade size will be smaller after automation as reduced-depth orders become trades.

---

[7] Inferences from the two sets of tests are virtually identical; the results of the Mann Whitney tests are therefore not shown here, but are available on request from the authors.

8. Following from the above two hypotheses, the mean daily number of transactions will increase after automation, and associated with this, the mean daily number of quotes will also increase.

9. After automation, there will be no significant change in price volatility, as measured by the standard deviation of the mid-point price.

In order to further investigate whether any change in liquidity (as measured by bid-ask spreads) can be attributed to the automation of trading, we estimate the model in equation (2) below. This is similar to Jiang et al [2001], but we use a higher data frequency and different estimation methods. Separate estimations are conducted for (a) the main part of the trading day where the variables are calculated based on hourly intervals between 0800-1600 GMT; and (b) evening trading, where the variables are based on a single interval (1622-1800 GMT) each day. The model controls for changes in the determinants of the spread, specifically trading volume and price volatility, between the different trading systems.

The model is specified as follows:

$$S_i = \alpha + \beta_1 D_i + \beta_2 V_i + \beta_3 \sigma_i + \beta_4 D_i V_i + \beta_5 D_i \sigma_i + \varepsilon_i \qquad (2)$$

where $S_i$ is the mean quoted spread (measured in ticks) during the interval, i indexes intervals in the dataset (either hourly or one per day). $D_i$ is a dummy variable taking the value one during electronic trading and zero otherwise. $V_i$ is the square root of the trading volume during the interval. The volatility during each interval, $\sigma_i$, is calculated as the standard deviation of the midpoint quoted prices (using the 'trade based' method discussed above) during that interval. The interactive variables are included in the model to capture any systematic changes in the relationship between spreads and volume, and between spreads and volatility, after automation.

The hypothesized signs of the coefficients (with dummy variable polarity as in the first case above) are as follows:

$\beta_1$ : Positive due to wider spreads during electronic trading (as discussed above);

$\beta_2$ : Negative due to narrower spreads in heavier trading. When trading is more active, participants are able to change their positions faster, thus reducing risk and capital requirements;

$\beta_3$ : Positive due to wider spreads at more volatile times. Higher volatility increases risk for participants, and is regarded as an indirect measure of informed trading;

$\beta_4$ and $\beta_5$ : Positive due to an enhanced sensitivity of the spread to volatility and volume following automation (e.g. see Kempf and Korn [1998]; Jiang et al [2001]; Wang [1999]).

## Empirical Results

This section presents empirical results in relation to the above prior hypotheses.

## Exhibit 1. Sample sizes and even versus odd final price digits
### Front month contract only

| Trading System | Floor(0800-1615) | | | | APT(1622-1800) | | | | Electronic(0800-1621) | | | | Electronic(1622-1800) | | | |
|---|---|---|---|---|---|---|---|---|---|---|---|---|---|---|---|---|
| Weighting | Equal | | Volume | | Equal | | Volume | | Equal | | Volume | | Equal | | Volume | |
| Case No.* | 1 | 5 | | 11 | 2 | 6 | | 12 | 3 | 7 | 9 | 13 | 4 | 8 | 10 | 14 |
| Type | Quotes | Trades | | Trades | Quotes | Trades | | Trades | Quotes | Trades | Quotes | Trades | Quotes | Trades | Quotes | Trades |
| Observations | 227,930 | 121,375 | | | 41,227 | 13,186 | | | 906,069 | 433,916 | 906,069 | 433,916 | 54,451 | 22,433 | 54,451 | 22,433 |
| % Even | 53.27 | 53.79 | | 54.09 | 53.61 | 55.40 | | 55.92 | 51.91 | 52.88 | 54.87 | 54.97 | 51.88 | 53.06 | 53.64 | 54.15 |
| % Odd | 46.73 | 46.21 | | 45.91 | 46.39 | 44.60 | | 44.08 | 48.09 | 47.12 | 45.13 | 45.03 | 48.12 | 46.94 | 46.36 | 45.85 |

* Case numbers identify the intersections of Floor vs. Electronic trading, Normal vs. 'After Hours' trading and Quotes vs. Trades; they are referred to in the text (see description of empirical results) and additionally in Exhibits 2 & 4 - 9.

## Price Clustering and the Attraction Hypothesis

Exhibit 1 presents the sample sizes under investigation and documents the proportion of trade and quote observations occurring at even and odd prices. It is clear that the number of quote and trade observations is around four times greater under daytime electronic trading (despite there being only 8% more days in our post-automation sample). There is a more modest increase in after-hours trading activity. Prices with even final digits are more popular than odd prices in all cases. On a volume-weighted basis, there is a greater tendency for quotes and trades to fall on even prices, i.e. relatively larger trades tend to fall more frequently on even prices. These initial conclusions are now discussed in more detail, incorporating tests of statistical significance.

## 'Even vs. Odd Digit' Clustering

Exhibit 1 implicitly defines fourteen cases (denoted 1-14) representing all possible combinations of trading system (Floor/Electronic); trading session (Normal/After Hours); Quotes vs. Trades; and Equal vs. Volume-weighted treatment of Quotes[1] and Trades.

**Exhibit 2. Proportion of Even Prices (with Confidence Intervals).**

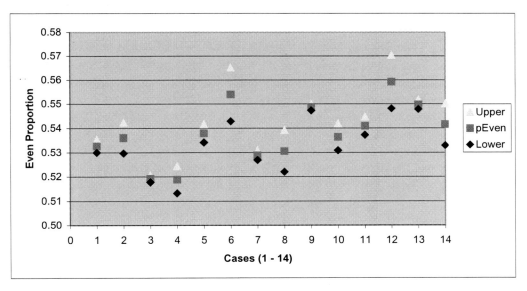

Evaluation of clustering behavior is considered by an examination of the proportion, in each of the cases, of Quotes or Trades which correspond to Even final price digits; these being considered initially against a null hypothesis of $p= 0.5$ (i.e. an equal proportion of Even and Odd final digits). Exhibit 2 plots proportions by case, each proportion being bracketed by its associated confidence interval[2] at the 1% level of significance (this level considered appropriate in the context of the large sample sizes involved here).

---

[1] Note, however, that volume data is absent in the case of Quotes under the Floor trading regime. This reduces the number of cases from 16 to 14.
[2] Confidence intervals are computed based upon a standard error given by the square root of the product of the proportions (of Even and Odd final digits) divided by the sample size.

None of the confidence intervals in the fourteen cases spans the level p= 0.5, rejecting the null hypothesis and thus indicating the presence of clustering (in favor of even digits) in all cases. Exhibit 2 also provides a convenient means of considering pair-wise cross-comparisons between cases.

Considering firstly the comparison between normal and after-hours trading (Case 1 {Normal Hours} vs. Case 2 {APT} for Floor Quotes, Case 3 vs. Case 4 (similarly, for Electronic Quotes) and cases 5 – 8 for the corresponding Trades, it is evident that in three of the four equal-weighted cross comparisons between Normal Hours and APT, the narrower interval corresponding to normal-hours trading is encompassed by the wider after-hours interval[3]. This provides evidence of 'no significant difference' between the proportions. The exception is case 6 (Floor trades, after hours), where the higher proportion, coupled with non-overlapping confidence intervals, is indicative of a significantly greater degree of (Even) clustering relative to the normal hours case (5). The same is true of case 12 relative to case 11, where the corresponding volume-weighted comparison is drawn. It is however evident that there is no significant difference in proportion between case 11 and case 5, and between case 12 and case 6; this suggests that the change to volume-weighted measures has no significant impact in the case of floor trading.

The change to the volume-weighted measure *is* influential, however, in the case of (normal hours) electronic trading; higher proportions, again coupled with non-overlapping confidence intervals, being indicative of a significantly greater degree of clustering relative to the corresponding equally-weighted cases (e.g. compare case 3 with case 9, case 7 with case 13 for Quotes and Trades respectively). The inference to be drawn from this evidence is that, for electronic trading, clustering increases with increasing volume, on average and *ceteris paribus*.

In respect of direct comparisons between floor trading cases and electronic trading cases, the effect of the volume-weighted measure is again influential; thus, comparing case 1 with case 3 (normal hours quotes); and case 5 with case 7 (normal hours trades), the proportions *reduce* (less clustering) with the move from floor to electronic trading (under equal weighting); the converse is true under volume-weighting (see case 11 compared to case 13), where the proportion *increases*. All of these comparisons are statistically significant (at the 1% level). The inference to be drawn here seems to be that for low volumes, clustering is *less* in the case of electronic trading; however, the 'volume effect' (which applies to electronic trading but not floor trading, as discussed above) then dominates in the case of high volumes. We conclude from this evidence that large (small) trades exhibit greater (less) clustering in favor of Even digits.

Finally, comparing across the dimension of Quotes – Trades, (cases 1-5, 3-7, 9-13 in respect of normal hours activity), proportions (and therefore clustering) are/is generally higher in the case of Trades; though only the comparison between 3-7 (electronic, equal weighting) achieves significance (at 1%).

The attraction hypothesis of price clustering predicts that the distribution of prices across the available final digits will follow the ranking: 0, 5, (7=3), (8=2), (4=6), (1=9). Rounding to prices which are multiples of 5 will be most popular, and thus adjacent prices with final digits of 1, 4, 6, and 9 will be least popular. Further, traders will be more likely to round, say 98.79 or 98.81 to 98.80 than to round 98.84 or 98.86 to 98.85.

---

[3] The wider confidence interval in the case of after-hours trading arises primarily because of the smaller sample sizes involved, relative to those in the case of normal-hours trading.

## Exhibit 3. The distribution of the final digit of price

Front month contract only. The Exhibit presents the observed proportion at each final digit, with expected values of one absent clustering. StDev is the standard deviation of the frequencies; StR is the standardized range between the highest and lowest percentages for final digits.

| Trading System | Floor(0800-1615) | | | | APT(1622-1800) | | | | Electronic(0800-1621) | | | | Electronic(1622-1800) | | | |
|---|---|---|---|---|---|---|---|---|---|---|---|---|---|---|---|---|
| Weighting | Equal | | Volume | | Equal | | Volume | | Equal | | Volume | | Equal | | Volume | |
| Type | Quotes | Trades | Quotes | Trades | Quotes | Trades | Quotes | Trades | Quotes | Trades | Quotes | Trades | Quotes | Trades | Quotes | Trades |
| 0 | 1.299 | 1.432 | | 1.518 | 1.542 | 1.808 | | 1.797 | 1.314 | 1.492 | 1.908 | 1.918 | 1.367 | 1.607 | 1.855 | 2.068 |
| 1 | 0.815 | 0.783 | | 0.752 | 0.765 | 0.692 | | 0.653 | 0.881 | 0.840 | 0.708 | 0.734 | 0.857 | 0.837 | 0.689 | 0.736 |
| 2 | 1.077 | 1.048 | | 1.032 | 0.883 | 0.813 | | 0.779 | 0.996 | 0.977 | 0.934 | 0.940 | 0.967 | 0.928 | 0.906 | 0.895 |
| 3 | 0.965 | 0.946 | | 0.964 | 0.884 | 0.772 | | 0.729 | 0.954 | 0.908 | 0.827 | 0.813 | 0.944 | 0.874 | 0.814 | 0.828 |
| 4 | 0.923 | 0.905 | | 0.910 | 0.882 | 0.840 | | 0.788 | 0.949 | 0.927 | 0.845 | 0.852 | 0.923 | 0.877 | 0.772 | 0.712 |
| 5 | 1.146 | 1.173 | | 1.170 | 1.289 | 1.389 | | 1.379 | 1.121 | 1.208 | 1.418 | 1.409 | 1.159 | 1.259 | 1.483 | 1.369 |
| 6 | 0.923 | 0.895 | | 0.884 | 0.933 | 0.953 | | 1.037 | 0.929 | 0.900 | 0.824 | 0.815 | 0.907 | 0.873 | 0.747 | 0.744 |
| 7 | 0.956 | 0.941 | | 0.924 | 0.893 | 0.865 | | 0.949 | 0.948 | 0.902 | 0.822 | 0.809 | 0.935 | 0.870 | 0.834 | 0.797 |
| 8 | 1.104 | 1.098 | | 1.065 | 1.121 | 1.126 | | 1.192 | 1.004 | 0.992 | 0.976 | 0.972 | 1.023 | 1.021 | 1.084 | 0.995 |
| 9 | 0.792 | 0.778 | | 0.781 | 0.809 | 0.743 | | 0.698 | 0.905 | 0.853 | 0.739 | 0.737 | 0.918 | 0.855 | 0.816 | 0.854 |
| StDev | 0.148 | 0.187 | | 0.210 | 0.233 | 0.334 | | 0.346 | 0.122 | 0.191 | 0.357 | 0.358 | 0.145 | 0.235 | 0.359 | 0.400 |
| StR | 0.507 | 0.654 | | 0.765 | 0.777 | 1.116 | | 1.144 | 0.433 | 0.652 | 1.200 | 1.184 | 0.511 | 0.770 | 1.166 | 1.356 |

Exhibit 3 presents the results on price clustering in relation to trading prior to and after automation. We focus primarily on the equal-weighted case in this section and analyze the volume-weighted case further in the next section. The evidence conforms to a large extent with the attraction hypothesis. Under all trading systems, for both trades and quotes, 0 is the most popular final digit, followed by 5 and then 8. Further, 1 and 9 are the least popular final digits except for the volume-weighted cases for after-hours electronic trading where 9 becomes relatively more popular.

**Exhibit 4. Case #1, Floor Quotes (Normal Hours)**

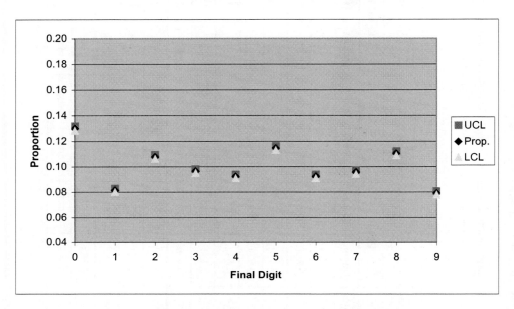

**Exhibit 5. Case #5, Floor Trades (Normal Hours)**

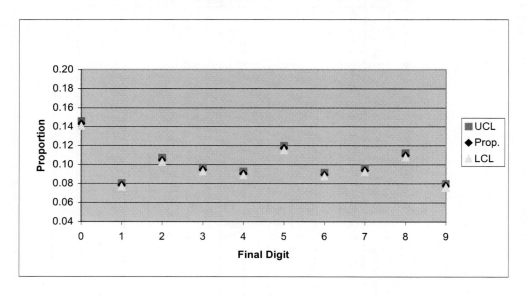

**Exhibit 6. Case #11, Floor Trades (Normal Hours, Vol. weighted)**

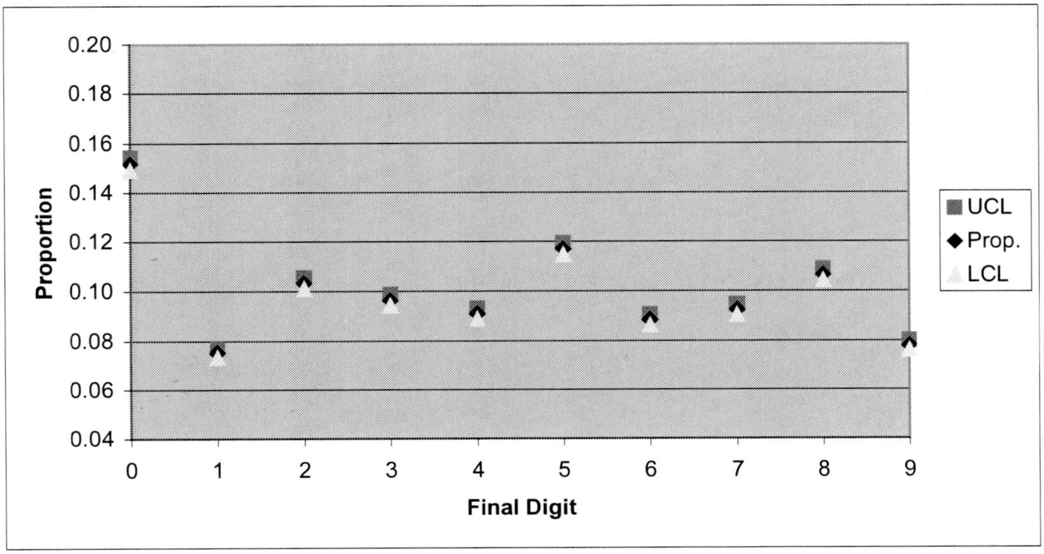

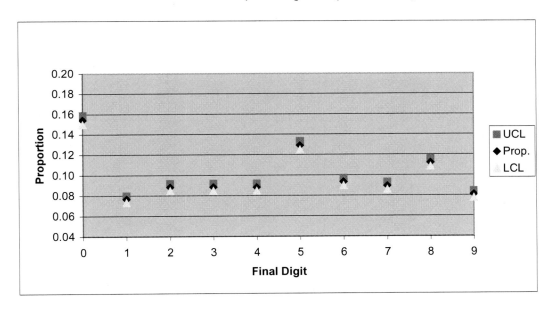

**Exhibit 7. Case #2, Floor Quotes (After Hours)**

These preliminary findings are also subjected to further tests of statistical significance. The distribution of the final digit of price is also shown in the (graphical) Exhibits (4 – 9) associated with (tabular) Exhibit 3[1]. We again perform confidence interval determinations based upon the data, but before doing so, perform two preliminary (Chi-squared) tests upon

---

[1] Exhibit 3 and its associated Exhibits (4 – 9) are derived from a common set of data.

the proportions calculated in the various cases[2]. The first of these indicates that (in every case) the null hypothesis (that each final digit of price (0-9) is equally likely to occur with a proportion of 0.1) is overwhelmingly rejected at meaningful levels of significance (degrees of freedom = 9). The second test focuses, in turn, upon individual final digits occurring versus any other digit occurring (degrees of freedom = 1). Here again, the null hypothesis is similarly overwhelmingly rejected.

**Exhibit 8. Case #6, Floor Trades (After Hours)**

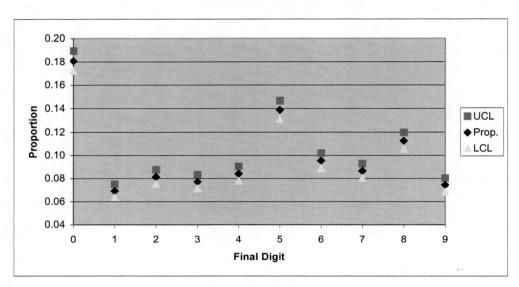

**Exhibit 9. Case #12, Floor Trades (After Hours, Vol. weighted)**

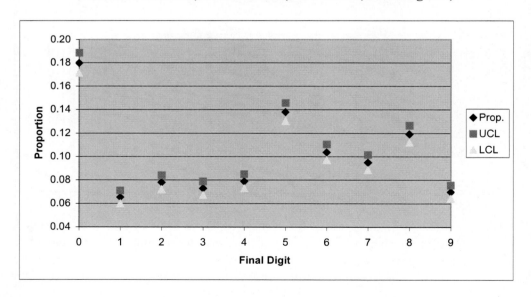

---

[2] Because we focus primarily here upon tests based on confidence intervals, the preliminary Chi-squared tests are not reported in detail here; but are available (on request) from the authors.

Referring to (Case 1) Normal Hours Quotes in the case of Floor trading (see Exhibit 3's associated Exhibit 4) we see that clustering is associated with (in descending order) digits 0, 5, 8, 2. These all have proportions which are statistically significantly greater than the null hypothesis would suggest (0.1), ranging from 0.1299 down to 0.1077. All other digits feature less often than is suggested by the null, with the least popular being 1 and 9, both close to 0.08. (In all of the latter cases, digit proportions are significantly below 0.1[3]

Case 5, Normal Hours Trades exhibit a pattern almost identical to the above, albeit with a slightly increased dispersion away from the null (Exhibit 5). Only the increased tilt toward the digit '0' is significantly different, at 0.1432. This trend (of increasing dispersion) continues into the corresponding volume-weighted case (Exhibit 6), where digit '0' is again statistically significantly different, at 0.1518. Again, in all cases, digit proportions are significantly different to 0.1.

The trend for increasing dispersion continues into After Hours trading, with digits 0, 5 and 8 being popular; trades again show an increased dispersion relative to quotes, but the application of volume-weighting now has little effect (see Exhibits 7, 8 & 9). For Trades, only digit 6 (6 and 7 in the volume-weighted case) fail to reject the null hypothesis (due to the generally wider confidence intervals in the case of After-Hours trading).

Grossman et al [1997] proposes using the range between the highest and lowest frequencies of the final digit as a measure of the level of price clustering. They also show that a standardized range can be used to compare clustering in different markets, and this is calculated by dividing the range of frequencies by the expected quotation frequency per unit without clustering. Higher values represent a greater degree of clustering. Using this metric, we find that (equal weighted) clustering of traded prices is more severe than for quotes (consistent with ap Gwilym et al [1998a].

When comparing floor trading with the after-hours APT system, it is clear that there was a greater degree of clustering under APT. The same is true for the day versus after-hours comparison of electronic trading except for the case of volume-weighted quoted prices. When comparing daytime trading for floor versus electronic systems, there is slightly less clustering of quoted prices under the electronic system, but the clustering levels of traded prices are almost identical. For after-hours trading, there is less clustering on the electronic system than on APT for the equal weighted case but vice versa on a volume weighted basis. Indeed, it is the comparison between the equally-weighted and volume-weighted cases which (in the cases of Electronic trading) is the most marked (see the section below which discusses volume-weighted price clustering).

Grossman et al [1997] calculated standardized ranges of 2.4 for dollar/yen foreign exchange quotes, 2.0 for dollar/mark foreign exchange quotes, 1.4 for London gold market clearing prices, 1.36 for Nasdaq quotes, 0.8 for yen/mark foreign exchange quotes, 0.7 for ISE quotes, and 0.24 for quotes at NYSE/AMEX. Exhibit 3 presents values for standardized range for daytime floor and electronic trading (equal weighted case) which are lower than all the above except NYSE/AMEX. Price clustering during after-hours trading is somewhat higher, particularly for trades on APT. Generally, the clustering levels compare favorably with the international evidence in Grossman et al [1997].

In summary, hypothesis 1 is not supported by the evidence, and price clustering levels and patterns (in the equally-weighted comparison) are not substantially altered after automation.

---

[3] None of the 1% confidence intervals spans the expected level of 0.1

## Volume-Weighted Price Clustering, Mean Trade Sizes and the Negotiation Hypothesis

If the negotiation hypothesis holds, one would expect the most popular integers to have lower mean trade sizes, since the benefits of negotiating prices (resulting in higher price resolution) are greater for large trades. Also, Brown et al [1991] discuss a model of equilibrium tick size which predicts that larger trade size should increase price resolution, and present evidence from silver futures to support this assertion. For Nasdaq stocks whose market makers rarely use odd-eighths, Christie and Schultz [1994] find that large trades are far more likely to occur on the (less popular) odd eighths than are small trades. For stock index futures at LIFFE, ap Gwilym et al [1998b] find that the mean size of trades occurring at half index points is three times larger than that of trades occurring at full index points. In contrast, Aitken et al [1996] find that clustering increases with trade size on the Australian Stock Exchange.

**Exhibit 10. Mean trade size for each final digit of price**

Front month contract only. Standard Errors ( ) accompany each of the Mean Volume values.

| Trading system | Floor (0800-1615) | APT (1622-1800) | Electronic (0800-1621) | | Electronic (1622-1800) | |
|---|---|---|---|---|---|---|
| | Trades | Trades | Quotes | Trades | Quotes | Trades |
| Observations | 121,375 | 13,186 | 906,069 | 433,916 | 54,451 | 22,433 |
| Final digit | | | | | | |
| 0 | 24.83 (0.27) | 11.20 (0.34) | 26.00 (0.12) | 9.28 (0.08) | 22.09 (0.37) | 10.18 (0.80) |
| 1 | 22.51 (0.20) | 10.64 (0.61) | 14.37 (0.08) | 6.31 (0.08) | 13.10 (0.34) | 6.96 (0.40) |
| 2 | 23.08 (0.23) | 10.80 (0.67) | 16.79 (0.10) | 6.95 (0.08) | 15.25 (0.36) | 7.63 (0.77) |
| 3 | 23.88 (0.83) | 10.64 (0.60) | 15.52 (0.09) | 6.47 (0.08) | 14.04 (0.47) | 7.50 (0.93) |
| 4 | 23.56 (0.33) | 10.57 (0.52) | 15.94 (0.09) | 6.64 (0.09) | 13.63 (0.31) | 6.43 (0.26) |
| 5 | 23.36 (0.23) | 11.19 (0.37) | 22.64 (0.13) | 8.43 (0.09) | 20.83 (0.43) | 8.60 (0.29) |
| 6 | 23.14 (0.36) | 12.27 (0.58) | 15.88 (0.10) | 6.54 (0.08) | 13.40 (0.32) | 6.75 (0.26) |
| 7 | 23.02 (0.33) | 12.37 (0.73) | 15.52 (0.09) | 6.48 (0.10) | 14.53 (0.32) | 7.25 (0.29) |
| 8 | 22.73 (0.22) | 11.93 (1.06) | 17.40 (0.09) | 7.07 (0.07) | 17.25 (0.46) | 7.71 (0.47) |
| 9 | 23.51 (0.34) | 10.59 (0.45) | 14.61 (0.11) | 6.24 (0.08) | 14.48 (0.48) | 7.91 (0.94) |

We now test hypotheses 2 and 3 by examining whether certain prices tend to attract systematically larger or smaller trades. Initially, we consider the results on volume-weighted price clustering in Exhibit 3. For each case, the standardized range is higher for the volume-weighted basis. However, the comparison is more dramatic for the electronic cases where the standardized range more than doubles for the quoted prices. Here, clustering behavior is encapsulated in the very distinct behavior of the two most popular digits, 0 and 5. It is these digits which account almost entirely for proportions which exceed the expected value.[4] Clustering increases markedly between the equal- and volume weighted cases, such that in the

---

[4] In the case of Electronic trading, the 3rd and 4th most popular digits (2 and 8) are (in all cases except one) either insignificantly different to, or less than, the expected proportion (0.1). The single minor exception is that of digit 8 in the case of after-hours Quotes (Volume weighted). Clustering therefore largely manifests itself as a concentration in digits 0 and 5, with at or below-expected proportions shared among the remaining digits (none of these particularly dominant in terms of the magnitude of the departure from the expectation).

extreme case of after-hours trades, the proportion of traded volume at final digit zero is over twice the level expected. Overall, this might suggest that the more popular digits also attract relatively larger trades, but closer inspection through comparison of values at each final digit for equal versus volume weighting reveals this not to be precisely the case.

This can be viewed more directly in Exhibit 10, by considering the mean trade size[5] for each final digit of price. Here, there is a clear difference demonstrated between trading systems. For electronic trading, the ranking of final digits is similar to that in Exhibit 3 and the most popular final digits (0 then 5) attract relatively larger trades. In contrast, for floor trading (and even more so for APT), the mean trade sizes do not follow the same ranking as the popularity of final digits of price. Relatively large trades occur for less popular digits e.g. prices ending in 6 and 7 for APT.

The evidence indicates rejection of hypothesis 2 because volume-weighted clustering is more severe than equal weighted clustering. In relation to hypothesis 3, we find support for the negotiation hypothesis through the evidence that many larger trades occur at less popular prices under floor trading and APT. However, under electronic trading, the evidence is opposite to this conjecture, and large trades tend to occur at the most popular prices (multiples of 5).

In summary, the presence of clustering implies the de facto use, by market participants, of wider intervals; whatever the reason for this, whether it be due (in extremis) to any form of collusion such as that suggested by Christie and Schultz [1994]; or for any other reason which fails to utilize the availability of the finer grid, then the effect is the same – spreads are likely to be wider, and liquidity is reduced as a consequence.

## The Distribution of Bid-Ask Spreads

Exhibit 11 presents the distribution of values taken by the bid-ask spread, in ticks, prior to and following automation; figures in brackets represent +/- confidence intervals (at the 1% confidence level). The 'quote based' measure of quoted spreads produces a more dispersed distribution with fewer observations at the minimum value compared to the 'trade based' measure in each case. Due to the construction of these methods, this result is consistent with the intuitive increased likelihood of a trade occurring when the currently quoted spread is relatively narrow. For electronic trading (where the comparison is possible), the weighted 'quote based' method displays greater dispersion across values than the weighted 'trade based' method.

---

[5] Each Mean Trade Size is accompanied (in Exhibit 10) by its associated Standard Error, to assist interpretation/ inference of the values.

## Exhibit 11. Distribution of values of the bid-ask spread

Front month contract only. The Exhibit presents the percentage of quoted spread observations occurring at each value in ticks. Figures in brackets() represent the +/- range (%) corresponding to the 1% confidence interval surrounding the 'percentage of quoted spread' figure above. These are shown for spreads in the range 1 – 4.

| Trading System | Floor (0800-1615) | | | APT (1622-1800) | | | Electronic (0800-1621) | | | | Electronic (1622-1800) | | | |
|---|---|---|---|---|---|---|---|---|---|---|---|---|---|---|
| Method | Quote based | Trade based | Weighted trade based | Quote based | Trade based | Weighted trade based | Quote based | Trade based | Weighted quote based | Weighted trade based | Quote based | Trade based | Weighted quote based | Weighted trade based |
| | | | | | | Spread, in ticks | | | | | | | | |
| 1 | 55.14 (0.52) | 67.78 (0.78) | 68.10 (0.78) | 23.25 (0.89) | 42.77 (2.46) | 39.22 (2.43) | 44.10 (0.19) | 63.39 (0.25) | 42.01 (0.18) | 59.95 (0.25) | 38.29 (0.98) | 58.76 (1.50) | 39.83 (1.04) | 54.50 (1.52) |
| 2 | 35.97 (0.51) | 26.63 (0.74) | 26.59 (0.74) | 22.98 (0.88) | 23.66 (2.12) | 21.12 (2.03) | 29.63 (0.18) | 23.99 (0.22) | 31.80 (0.17) | 25.99 (0.22) | 25.27 (0.88) | 22.50 (1.28) | 25.49 (0.93) | 23.52 (1.30) |
| 3 | 6.77 (0.26) | 4.29 (0.34) | 4.12 (0.33) | 16.86 (0.79) | 13.23 (1.69) | 14.91 (1.77) | 14.74 (0.14) | 7.68 (0.14) | 14.98 (0.13) | 8.61 (0.14) | 16.31 (0.75) | 9.63 (0.90) | 15.43 (0.77) | 11.33 (0.97) |
| 4 | 1.45 (0.13) | 0.85 (0.15) | 0.75 (0.14) | 12.29 (0.69) | 7.10 (1.28) | 8.99 (1.42) | 6.24 (0.09) | 2.61 (0.08) | 6.03 (0.09) | 2.87 (0.08) | 8.91 (0.58) | 4.05 (0.60) | 8.67 (0.60) | 4.53 (0.64) |
| 5 | 0.54 | 0.40 | 0.36 | 8.95 | 6.17 | 7.16 | 2.65 | 1.14 | 2.62 | 1.25 | 5.07 | 2.50 | 5.05 | 2.91 |
| 6 | 0.06 | 0.02 | 0.02 | 4.63 | 1.53 | 3.37 | 1.16 | 0.47 | 1.03 | 0.48 | 2.47 | 0.98 | 1.92 | 1.34 |
| 7 | 0.01 | 0.02 | 0.02 | 3.18 | 1.79 | 1.91 | 0.59 | 0.25 | 0.56 | 0.30 | 1.32 | 0.42 | 1.58 | 0.42 |
| 8 | 0.04 | 0.00 | 0.00 | 2.23 | 0.86 | 0.59 | 0.32 | 0.16 | 0.30 | 0.17 | 0.74 | 0.37 | 0.91 | 0.29 |
| 9 | 0.00 | 0.00 | 0.00 | 1.46 | 0.60 | 0.40 | 0.19 | 0.08 | 0.20 | 0.09 | 0.44 | 0.15 | 0.31 | 0.26 |
| 10 | 0.02 | 0.02 | 0.03 | 1.46 | 1.27 | 1.02 | 0.11 | 0.06 | 0.13 | 0.07 | 0.38 | 0.30 | 0.27 | 0.38 |
| >10 | 0.00 | 0.00 | 0.00 | 2.70 | 1.01 | 1.30 | 0.28 | 0.17 | 0.33 | 0.23 | 0.81 | 0.34 | 0.55 | 0.51 |

**Note** (to Exhibit 11): The 'quote based' method includes all quoted bid-ask pairs which are time-stamped within three seconds of each other. This is motivated by a rule that quotes are valid 'as long as the breath is warm' (see ap Gwilym and Thomas [2002]). The 'trade based' method employs all bid-ask pairs occurring immediately prior to a trade. A time constraint of seven seconds is imposed to produce an equivalent proportion of valid observations as that for the 'quote based' method. The volume-weighted 'trade based' method extends this by weighting each spread by the volume traded in the subsequent trade.

Comparing floor trading against APT, it is clear that the distribution of spread values is shifted upwards under the latter system. A similar observation applies to the daytime versus after-hours comparison under electronic trading, but the difference is far less pronounced. Following automation, there is an upward shift in the distribution of spreads during daytime trading but the opposite is true for the after-hours comparison. This is consistent across calculation methods.

Comparing (for the 'trade based' method) the equally weighted and the volume weighted equivalent, the floor trading case demonstrates a slightly greater concentration at low values of the spread for the weighted method. This suggests a slight tendency for narrower spreads for relatively larger trades. The opposite is generally found for APT and for electronic trading (with the exception of the after-hours electronic 'quote based' case). Therefore, under electronic trading, the tendency is for narrower spreads to be associated with relatively smaller trades (see discussion in next section).

Overall, the conjecture in hypothesis 4 is supported by these results.

## Bid-Ask Spreads, Trade Size and Market Activity

Exhibit 12 presents results on bid-ask spreads, trade size and market activity. The first aspect of interest is liquidity in the form of quoted and effective bid-ask spreads. It is clear that quoted spreads are far wider during the APT evening trading session compared to floor trading. The daytime versus after-hours electronic trading comparison also reveals an increase for the latter, but at a much more modest level. Quoted spreads during daytime electronic trading are significantly wider than for floor trading but spreads during after-hours trading are significantly narrower than for APT. For floor trading, the mean 'trade based' spread is narrower than the mean 'quote based' spread, and wider than the mean weighted trade based spread. For APT and electronic trading, the mean 'trade based' spread is narrower than both its volume weighted equivalent and the mean 'quote based' spread. These findings are entirely consistent with the discussion of Exhibit 11 in the previous section.

Exhibit 12 presents mean values for equally-weighted and volume-weighted effective spreads.[1] Broadly, the pattern is similar to that for quoted spreads. The electronic system produces spreads which are significantly wider than the floor system but significantly narrower than APT. On a volume weighted basis, the mean effective spread is slightly narrower than the equal weighted equivalent for the floor system but noticeably wider for APT and the electronic system. In the latter case, the impact of volume weighting is much greater than was reported for the quoted spread.

Under electronic trading, there is a clear tendency for narrower spreads to be associated with relatively smaller trades. These findings are consistent with the anonymous nature of automated trading and the greater problems of asymmetric information and adverse selection.[2] This appears to offer informed traders a further incentive to conceal their activities by splitting orders into smaller components. Our prior hypothesis 5 is supported by this

---

[1] Since cases where the effective spread is zero or negative are omitted from the sample, the mean effective spread is based on a slightly different sample to the mean quoted spread. This explains why the former is not smaller than the latter in every pair-wise comparison.

[2] However, this does not explain the APT results since trading was not anonymous on this system.

evidence, but further insights are offered in the next section, where we control for sensitivity to volume and volatility.

### Exhibit 12. Bid-ask spreads, trade size and market activity

Front month contract only. Figures in parentheses are absolute values of test statistics to indicate the statistical significance of the difference between the mean value of each characteristic for floor or APT versus electronic trading. These are based on standard t-tests.

| Trading system | Floor (0800-1615) | APT (1622-1800) | Electronic (0800-1621) | Electronic (1622-1800) |
|---|---|---|---|---|
| Number of trading days | 114 | 110 | 123 | 121 |
| Mean quoted spread (Quote based) | 1.569 | 3.475 | 2.064 (128.71)[a] | 2.491 (34.48)[a] |
| Mean quoted spread (Trade based) | 1.397 | 2.492 | 1.603 (41.81)[a] | 1.829 (14.55)[a] |
| Mean quoted spread (Weighted trade based) | 1.390 | 2.665 | 1.667 (55.69)[a] | 1.967 (14.83)[a] |
| Mean effective spread (Trade based) | 1.442 | 2.490 | 1.822 (61.30)[a] | 2.028 (9.78)[a] |
| Mean effective spread (Weighted trade based) | 1.433 | 2.672 | 2.382 (97.07)[a] | 2.425 (4.86)[a] |
| Mean daily traded volume | 24948.3 | 1351.2 | 25475.8 (0.45) | 1466.4 (0.98) |
| Mean trade size | 23.43 | 11.27 | 7.22 (135.41)[a] | 7.91 (11.97)[a] |
| Mean daily number of recorded trades | 1064.7 | 119.9 | 3527.8 (18.19)[a] | 185.4 (5.26)[a] |
| Mean daily number of recorded quotes | 1999.4 | 374.8 | 7366.4 (19.88)[a] | 450.0 (2.34)[b] |
| Avg. Standard deviation of midpoint prices (Trades) | 4.877 | 4.533 | 5.479 (4.01)[a] | 5.173 (1.18) |

[a] denotes statistical significance at the 1% level, and [b] at the 5% level.

The 'quote based' method includes all quoted bid-ask pairs which are time-stamped within three seconds of each other. This is motivated by a rule that quotes are valid 'as long as the breath is warm' (see ap Gwilym and Thomas [2002]). The 'trade based' method employs all bid-ask pairs occurring immediately prior to a trade. A time constraint of seven seconds is imposed to produce an equivalent proportion of valid observations as that for the 'quote based' method. The volume-weighted 'trade based' method extends this by weighting each spread by the volume traded in the subsequent trade.

The standard deviation of midpoint prices is based on hourly observations for the daytime comparison and daily observations for the after-hours comparison.

Exhibit 12 shows evidence that mean daily traded volume increases by a small, but not statistically significant, amount after automation. Hypothesis 6 is supported by this evidence, suggesting that the impact of wider bid-ask spreads counteracts any volume increases that might accrue from the greater operational efficiency of the electronic system. Both before and after automation, after-hours volumes are very low in comparison with daytime trading, as would be expected. The average traded volume per minute is 50.4, 13.8, 50.8 and 15.0 for floor trading, APT, daytime electronic, and after-hours electronic, respectively.

Consistent with Exhibit 10, mean trade sizes are significantly lower for electronic trading than for both the floor and APT systems, though the decrease is much more modest in the after-hours case. This supports hypothesis 7 and reflects reduced-depth orders. Whereas the mean trade size for APT is approximately half the size of that for floor trading, the mean trade size for after-hours electronic trading is larger than that for daytime electronic trading.

For daytime trading, the mean daily number of transactions increases by a statistically significant three-fold amount after automation. This is entirely consistent with the prior discussion of slightly increased volume and substantially decreased mean trade size. Associated with this, the mean daily number of quotes also increases by a substantial, statistically significant amount. For after-hours trading, the mean daily number of transactions increased by a statistically significant factor of 1.5. This reflects a slight increase in volume and a more modest reduction in mean trade size. The average number of trades per minute is 2.2, 1.2, 7.0 and 1.9 for floor trading, APT, daytime electronic, and after-hours electronic, respectively. The mean daily number of quotes during after-hours trading increases by a more modest amount than for daytime trading, but the increase is still statistically significant at the 5% level. This evidence clearly supports hypothesis 8.

The final row of Exhibit 12 investigates pre- and post-automation levels of price volatility. Volatility is measured by the standard deviation of midpoint prices within each hourly interval (for daytime trading) or within each daily trading session (for after-hours trading). For daytime trading, the increase in price volatility after automation is statistically significant at the 1% level, while for after-hours trading the statistical significance of the increase is not significant.

**Exhibit 13. A comparison of price volatility by contract maturity**

In price comparisons, we analyze each contract maturity as a separate instrument.

| Method | Standard deviation of midpoint of quoted spread (quote based) | | | | Standard deviation of midpoint of quoted spread (trade based) | | | |
| --- | --- | --- | --- | --- | --- | --- | --- | --- |
| Trading System | Floor (0800-1615) | APT (1622-1800) | Electronic (0800-1621) | Electronic (1622-1800) | Floor (0800-1615) | APT (1622-1800) | Electronic (0800-1621) | Electronic (1622-1800) |
| Dec 1998 | 91.71 | 83.76 | n.a. | n.a. | 84.59 | 85.85 | n.a. | n.a. |
| March 1999 | 105.51 | 108.71 | n.a. | n.a. | 105.13 | 113.53 | n.a. | n.a. |
| June 1999 | 75.76 | 83.65 | 123.67 (0.0000[a]) | 122.65 (0.0000[a]) | 78.83 | 87.02 | 106.60 (0.0000[a]) | 98.81 (0.0001[a]) |
| Sept 1999 | n.a. | n.a. | 126.10 | 119.01 | n.a. | n.a. | 116.14 | 109.21 |
| Dec 1999 | n.a. | n.a. | 93.47 | 88.85 | n.a. | n.a. | 88.10 | 80.46 |

The 'quote based' method includes all quoted bid-ask pairs which are time-stamped within three seconds of each other. This is motivated by a rule that quotes are valid 'as long as the breath is warm' (see ap Gwilym and Thomas [2002]). The 'trade based' method employs all bid-ask pairs occurring immediately prior to a trade. A time constraint of seven seconds is imposed to produce an equivalent proportion of valid observations as that for the 'quote based' method.

The June 1999 contract provides a direct means of comparing the volatilities of the midpoint of quoted spread. Figures in brackets ( ) indicate (to four decimal places) the p- values related to F-tests on the ratio of the variances, using the appropriate degrees of freedom associated with the numbers of observations in each case.

Exhibit 13 presents a contract-by-contract comparison of the levels of price volatility in this market prior to and following automation. The standard deviation of midpoint prices is employed as a measure of price variability, and we analyze each contract maturity as a separate instrument in order to avoid economically meaningless price jumps at contract rollover. Exhibit 13 shows little difference between volatility levels for daytime versus after-hours trading for each contract. The June 1999 contract presents the clearest basis for comparing price volatility prior to and after automation, since this contract straddles both trading systems. The evidence from this contract suggests a statistically highly significant 30-50% increase in volatility after automation. However, the later contract maturities offer mixed evidence.

Overall, hypothesis 9 is not supported by the evidence, which indicates a higher level of price volatility after automation.

## Regression Model of Spreads

This section presents the results from estimation of the model in equation (2). The initial estimation was by OLS but diagnostic tests of the residuals revealed serial correlation and heteroscedasticity. The results are based on a robust maximum likelihood estimation with lagged error terms introduced to account for serial correlation. Eight lags are included in the daytime analysis due to the eight hourly intervals per day, and five lags are included in the after-hours analysis to account for days of the week. Exhibit 14 displays the coefficients and t-ratios. The full model results are presented together with reduced models formed by stepwise removal of regressors according to significance levels until adjusted $R^2$ values are maximized.[3]

In Exhibit 14, considering daytime trading firstly, we find that the dummy coefficient for the change of system is not significantly different from zero, and hence the wider mean bid-ask spread following automation (documented in Exhibit 12) is accounted for by the other explanatory variables in the model. We find a significant negative relationship between the bid-ask spread and volume (coefficient of -0.0024 in the reduced model), in line with prior expectations. The sensitivity of the spread to volume is not significantly different following automation. There is a strongly positive and significant relationship between the bid-ask spread and volatility. The sensitivity of the spread to volatility is significantly greater under the electronic system, with coefficients of 0.026 under floor trading and 0.058 under electronic trading (in the reduced models). The first four, the seventh and the eighth lagged error terms are statistically significant at the 2% level. For the reduced model, the likelihood ratio test indicates that restricting the other coefficients to zero is valid.

For the after-hours comparison, we again find that the dummy coefficient for the change of system is not significantly different from zero, thus the narrower bid-ask spreads following automation (documented in Exhibit 12) are accounted for by the other explanatory variables. The negative relationship between spread and volume is repeated in the case of electronic trading, but the sensitivity is greater (coefficient of -0.016 in the reduced model). No significant relationship between spread and volume exists for APT trading and the differential

---

[3] In the case of daytime trading, a very slight reduction from the maximum possible value of adjusted $R^2$ was tolerated in order to eliminate regressors which were not significant at the 10% level (with the validity of the zero restrictions evaluated by likelihood ratio tests).

in sensitivity (0.019) is significant at the 10% level. Compared to daytime trading, the bid-ask spread is more sensitive to volatility, with coefficients of 0.08 for after-hours electronic and 0.12 for APT. The differential between these is not statistically significant at the 10% level. The fifth lagged term (which corresponds to one week in this case) is statistically significant. For the reduced model, the likelihood ratio test indicates that restricting the other coefficients to zero is valid.

### Exhibit 14. Determinants of bid-ask spread

The Exhibit presents results from estimation of the following model:

$$S_i = \alpha + \beta_1 D_i + \beta_2 V_i + \beta_3 \sigma_i + \beta_4 D_i V_i + \beta_5 D_i \sigma_i + \varepsilon_i$$

where $S_i$ is the mean quoted spread, $i$ indexes intervals in the dataset (either hourly or daily). $D_i$ is a dummy variable taking the value one during automated trading and zero otherwise. $V_i$ is the square root of trading volume during the interval and $\sigma_i$ is the standard deviation of the midpoint quoted prices during that interval. $\gamma(N)$ denote coefficients on lagged error terms (of order N). Absolute values of t-ratios are in parentheses.

|  | Floor versus Electronic (0800-1600) |  | APT versus Electronic (1622-1800) |  |
|---|---|---|---|---|
|  | Full | Reduced | Full | Reduced |
| $\alpha$ | 1.3065 (34.13) | 1.3094 (53.46) | 1.7240 (9.83) | 1.7397 (17.15) |
| $\beta_1$ | 0.0102 (0.20) |  | -0.0322 (0.13) |  |
| $\beta_2$ | -0.0035 (2.27) | -0.0024 (3.15) | 0.0031 (0.25) |  |
| $\beta_3$ | 0.0292 (6.66) | 0.0264 (7.56) | 0.1179 (4.54) | 0.1215 (6.48) |
| $\beta_4$ | 0.0016 (0.91) |  | -0.0172 (1.16) | -0.0157 (2.16) |
| $\beta_5$ | 0.0255 (4.19) | 0.0312 (7.58) | -0.0349 (1.08) | -0.0407 (1.64) |
| $\gamma(1)$ | 0.1224 (5.24) | 0.1250 (5.36) | 0.0479 (0.69) |  |
| $\gamma(2)$ | 0.1150 (4.89) | 0.1187 (5.07) | -0.0172 (0.25) |  |
| $\gamma(3)$ | 0.0734 (3.11) | 0.0797 (3.40) | 0.0397 (0.57) |  |
| $\gamma(4)$ | 0.0533 (2.25) | 0.0594 (2.54) | 0.0049 (0.07) |  |
| $\gamma(5)$ | 0.0282 (1.19) |  | 0.1196 (1.75) | 0.1177 (1.75) |
| $\gamma(6)$ | 0.0372 (1.57) |  |  |  |
| $\gamma(7)$ | 0.0505 (2.15) | 0.0570 (2.46) |  |  |
| $\gamma(8)$ | 0.0603 (2.58) | 0.0651 (2.82) |  |  |
| Adj $R^2$ | 0.24 | 0.24 | 0.20 | 0.22 |
| LR |  | 5.349 (0.253) |  | 1.053 (0.984) |

Overall, the models demonstrate that wider bid-ask spreads following automation can largely be explained by an increased sensitivity to volatility under electronic trading. In this sense, the increase can be attributed to the nature of the trading system. This effect is accentuated by the increased volatility levels after automation.

# Conclusion

This chapter analyses the impact on liquidity of a move from daytime open outcry and evening screen trading to a fully electronic system in the U.K. Long Gilt futures market. The study makes a unique contribution in comparing microstructural characteristics of these three trading systems. Particular focus is placed on price clustering and its relationships with bid-ask spreads and trade sizes. Further investigations emphasize the changing relationship between bid-ask spreads, volume and volatility following automation.

Although price clustering is not materially affected by the transition to electronic trading, there is a greatly increased concentration of large trades at more popular prices. Under electronic trading, narrower bid-ask spreads tend to be associated with relatively smaller trades. This is consistent with the anonymous nature of electronic trading and the associated increased problems of asymmetric information and adverse selection compared to floor trading. This appears to offer informed traders a further incentive to conceal their activities by splitting orders into smaller components.

Following automation, mean daily volume increases by a small, but not statistically significant amount, while there is a substantial reduction in mean trade size as reduced-depth orders become trades. Consistent with this, the mean daily number of transactions and quotations increases substantially. Bid-ask spreads widen significantly after automation, but this is largely accounted for by the finding that spreads under electronic systems demonstrate an increased sensitivity to price volatility. This effect is accentuated by increased volatility after automation. Cost savings arising from increased operational efficiency of the electronic trading system will be partly offset by this effect.

Overall, the chapter provides important evidence on the changes in market liquidity following the transition to electronic trading, and highlights different evidence from that presented in previous studies in this vein. In contrast to our findings, the most closely related previous study (Tse and Zabotina [2001]) report narrower bid-ask spreads in the FTSE100 stock index futures contract following the transition to electronic trading at LIFFE. A key factor in their results is the dramatic reduction in price clustering in this contract (see ap Gwilym and Alibo [2003]) as a result of automated trading. No such changes in price clustering were identified in the current chapter and bid-ask spreads responded very differently following automation.

## References

Aitken, M., P. Brown, C. Buckland, H.Y. Izan, and T. Walter, 1996, "Price clustering on the Australian Stock Exchange", *Pacific Basin Finance Journal*, **4**, 297-314.

ap Gwilym, O. and E. Alibo, 2003, "Decreased price clustering in FTSE100 futures contracts following a transfer from floor to electronic trading", *Journal of Futures Markets*, **23**, 647-659.

ap Gwilym, O., A.D. Clare and S.H. Thomas, 1998a, "Price clustering and bid-ask spreads in international bond futures", *Journal of International Financial Markets, Institutions and Money*, **8**, 377-391.

ap Gwilym, O., A.D. Clare, and S.H. Thomas, 1998b, "Extreme price clustering in the London equity index futures and options markets", *Journal of Banking and Finance*, **22**, 1193-1206.

ap Gwilym, O., I.D. McManus and S.H. Thomas, 2005, "Fractional versus decimal pricing: Evidence from the U.K. Long Gilt futures market", *Journal of Futures Markets*, **25**, 419-514.

ap Gwilym, O. and S.H. Thomas, 2002, "An empirical comparison of quoted and implied bid-ask spreads on futures contracts", *Journal of International Financial Markets, Institutions and Money*, **12**, 81-99.

Benveniste, L.M., A.J. Marcus and W.J. Wilhelm, 1992, "What's special about the specialist? Floor exchange versus computerized market mechanisms", *Journal of Financial Economics*, **32**, 61-86.

Blennerhassett, M. and R.G. Bowman, 1998, "A change in market microstructure: The switch to electronic screen trading on the New Zealand stock exchange", *Journal of International Financial Markets, Institutions and Money*, **8**, 261-276.

Brown, S., P. Laux, and B. Schachter, 1991, "On the existence of an optimal tick size", *Review of Futures Markets*, **10**, 50-72.

Campbell, J. Y., A. W. Lo and A. C. MacKinlay, 1997, "The econometrics of financial markets", Princeton University Press, Princeton, New Jersey.

Chow, E.H., J.-H. Lee and G. Shyy, 1996, "Trading mechanisms and trading preferences on a 24hour futures market: A case study of the Floor/Globex switch on MATIF", *Journal of Banking and Finance*, **20**, 1695-1713.

Christie, W.G. and P.H. Schultz, 1994, "Why do Nasdaq market makers avoid odd-eighth quotes?", *Journal of Finance*, **49**, 1813-1840.

Christie, W.G., J.H. Harris and P.H. Schultz, 1994, "Why did Nasdaq market makers stop avoiding odd-eighth quotes?", *Journal of Finance*, **49**, 1841-1860.

Ferris, A.P., T.H. McInish and R.A. Wood, 1997, "Automated trade execution and trading activity: The case of the Vancouver Stock Exchange", *Journal of International Financial Markets, Institutions and Money*, **7**, 61-72.

Fremault, A., and G. Sandmann, 1995, "Floor trading versus electronic screen trading: An empirical analysis of market liquidity in the Nikkei stock index futures contract", London School of Economics, Financial Markets Group Discussion Paper 218.

Frino, A., T.H. McInish and M. Toner, 1998, "The liquidity of automated exchanges: New evidence from German Bund futures", *Journal of International Financial Markets, Institutions and Money*, **8**, 225-241.

Griffiths, M.D., B.F. Smith, D.A.S. Turnbull and R.W. White, 1998, "Information flows and open outcry: Evidence of imitation trading", *Journal of International Financial Markets, Institutions and Money*, **8**, 101-116.

Grossman, S.J., M.H. Miller, D.R. Fischel, K.R. Cone and D.J. Ross, 1997, "Clustering and competition in asset markets", *Journal of Law and Economics*, **40**, 23-60.

Harris, L.E., 1991, "Stock price clustering and discreteness", *Review of Financial Studies*, **4**, 389-415.

Henker, T., 1999, "An academic perspective on the trading platform debate", *Working paper*, School of Management, University of Massachusetts.

Jiang, G., N. Tang and E. Law, 2001, "Electronic trading in Hong Kong and its impact on market functioning", *Working paper*, Hong Kong Monetary Authority. Presented at Central Bank Economists' meeting, Basel, Autumn.

Johnson D.H., 1995, "Statistical Sirens: The Allure of Nonparametrics", *Ecology*, Vol. 76, No. 6. (September), 1998-2000.

Kappi, J. and R. Siivonen, 2000, "Market liquidity and depth on two different electronic trading systems: A comparison of Bund futures trading on the APT and DTB", *Journal of Financial Markets*, **3**, 389-402.

Kempf, A. and O. Korn, 1998, "Trading system and market integration", *Journal of Financial Intermediation*, **7**, 220-239.

Khan, B. and J. Ireland, 1993, "The use of technology for competitive advantage: A study of screen versus floor trading", City Research Project paper, London Business School.

Kofman, P. and J. Moser, 1997, "Spreads, information flows and transparency across trading systems", *Applied Financial Economics*, **7**, 281-294.

Madhavan, A., 2001, "Discussion of Venkataraman (2001)", *Journal of Finance*, **56**, 1485-1488.

Martens, M., 1998, "Price discovery in high and low volatility periods: Open outcry versus electronic trading", *Journal of International Financial Markets, Institutions and Money*, **8**, 243-260.

Massimb, M.N. and B.D. Phelps, 1994, "Electronic trading, market structure and liquidity", *Financial Analysts Journal*, Jan-Feb, 39-50.

Naidu, G.N. and M.S. Rozeff, 1994, "Volume, volatility, liquidity and efficiency of the Singapore Stock Exchange before and after automation", *Pacific-Basin Finance Journal*, **2**, 23-42.

Petersen, M. A. and D. Fialkowski, 1994, "Posted versus effective spreads: Good prices or bad quotes?", *Journal of Financial Economics*, **35**, 269-292.

Pirrong, C., 1996, "Market liquidity and depth on computerized and open outcry trading systems: A comparison of DTB and LIFFE Bund contracts", *Journal of Futures Markets*, **16**, 519-543.

Shyy, G. and J.H. Lee, 1995, "Price transmission and information asymmetry in Bund futures markets: LIFFE vs. DTB", *Journal of Futures Markets*, **15**, 87-99.

Tse, Y. and T.V. Zabotina, 2001, "Transaction costs and market quality: Open outcry versus electronic trading", *Journal of Futures Markets*, **21**, 713-736.

Venkataraman, K., 2001, "Automated versus floor trading: An analysis of execution costs on the Paris and New York exchanges", *Journal of Finance*, **56**, 1445-1485.

Wang, J., 1999, "Asymmetric information and the bid-ask spread: An empirical comparison between automated order execution and open outcry auction", *Journal of International Financial Markets, Institutions and Money*, **9**, 115-128.

In: Liquidity, Interest Rates and Banking
Editors: J. Morrey and A. Guyton, pp. 139-167

ISBN: 978-1-60692-775-5
© 2009 Nova Science Publishers, Inc.

*Chapter 7*

# AN ANALYSIS OF LIQUIDITY ACROSS MARKETS: EXECUTION COSTS ON THE NYSE VERSUS ELECTRONIC MARKETS

### *Michael A. Goldstein[1,a], Gang Hu[1,b] and J. Ginger Meng[2,c]*
[1]Babson College, Babson Park, MA, USA
[2]Stonehill College, Easton, MA, USA

## Abstract

We examine liquidity across different types of markets by using execution costs as a proxy for liquidity. We conduct a thorough analysis of execution costs on the NYSE versus a variety of electronic NASD market centers which also trade NYSE-listed stocks ("Electronic Markets"). We adopt a variety of techniques attempting to correct for the selection bias problem. Unlike current literature, we find that the Electronic Markets offer lower execution costs even after controlling for selection biases. In addition to controlling for selection biases at the sample average level of order difficulty, we also carry out our analysis at different levels of order difficulty, measured by a vector of control variables. Our results are robust under different model specifications. Finally, our what-if analysis shows that the Electronic Markets' (*the NYSE's*) orders would have been worse (*better*) off, had they been executed by the NYSE (*Electronic Markets*). Overall, our results highlight the superiority of the Electronic Markets' liquidity and execution quality.

---

[a] E-mail address: goldstein@babson.edu. Professor of Finance, Babson College, 223 Tomasso Hall, Babson Park, MA 02457. Phone: 781-239-4402. Fax: 781-239-5004.
[b] E-mail address: ghu@babson.edu. Phone: 781-239-4946. Fax: 781-239-5004. Assistant Professor of Finance, Babson College, 121 Tomasso Hall, Babson Park, MA 02457.
[c] E-mail address: gmeng@stonehill.edu. Phone: 508-565-1986. Assistant Professor of Finance, Department of Business Administration, Stonehill College, 320 Washington Street, Easton, MA 02357.
For helpful comments and discussions, we thank Thomas Chemmanur, Ani Chitaley, Arthur Lewbel, Eric Roiter, Erik Sirri, Zhijie Xiao, and seminar participants at Boston College. Meng acknowledges support from a Fidelity Investments research grant. All remaining errors and omissions are our own.

# 1. Introduction

It is a world-wide trend that the stock exchanges are changing their traditional trading mechanisms, largely attributed to the competition among exchanges. For example, the modernization of European stock markets since the mid-eighties, including the switch to continuous trading and electronic markets, was spurred by the competitive pressure of London. Electronic markets continue to evolve and improve. Pagano and Schwartz (2003) provide a detailed analysis of one of such improvements: the introduction of electronic closing call auctions at Euronext Paris that lowered execution costs for individual participants and sharpened price discovery for the broad market. In the United States, liquidity in NYSE stocks is moving away from the floor of the NYSE towards electronic markets. From the second half of 2003 until the end of 2005, in the 18 months, the percentage of NYSE-listed shares executed electronically increased from 2.4% to almost 10%. As Regulation NMS is implemented, this percentage will likely increase substantially. In the literature, evidence on the relative advantage of the NYSE versus electronic markets is mixed. For example, Kalay and Portniaguina (2001) document the first voluntary switch of a NYSE firm (Aeroflex) to NASDAQ, and find that the switch announcement resulted in a significantly positive abnormal return, subsequent narrowing of the daily bid-ask spread, and significant increase of the daily volume. In contrast, Pruitt, Van Ness, and Van Ness (2002) find that Aeroflex's switch resulted in economically and statistically significant degradations in key trading metrics such as the bid-ask spread and the number of equity trades. Pruitt, Van Ness, and Van Ness (2002) did not find any observed improvements in trading or quoting behavior as a result of the switch. On December 20, 2005, Charles Schwab (SCHW) effectively dropped its dual listing and decided to list only on the NASDAQ. At the same time, the NYSE is taking a series of actions to move fast from flooring trading to electronic trading, for example, its IPO through the merger with the ARCA Exchange (an electronic exchange that used to be an ECN), and the new Hybrid Market system.[1]

Trading costs and listing fees are the main determinants for the exchanges to attract firms interested in listing and for investors. NASDAQ offers lower fees; however, many previous studies find that the NYSE offers lower execution costs over the years. Researchers such as Christie and Schultz (1994) and Chung, Van Ness, and Van Ness (2001) attribute "implicit collusion" among NASDAQ dealers as the cause. On the other hand, there is another strand of literature showing that electronic markets' execution costs have been declining over the years.[2] Van Ness, Van Ness, and Warr (2005) document that NASDAQ spreads steadily declined from 1993 to 2002. Bessembinder (2003) find that the execution costs on electronic markets are actually lower than the NYSE for market orders. However, researchers attribute this difference to order difficulty differences, i.e., the NYSE have been receiving more difficult orders to execute.

In this paper, we conduct a thorough analysis comparing execution costs between the NYSE and electronic NASD market centers which also trade NYSE-listed stocks ("Electronic

---

[1] See Davis, Pagano, and Schwartz (2006) for a description and discussion of the new NYSE Hybrid Market.
[2] The term "Electronic Markets" or "Electronic Market Center" refers to the combination of NASDAQ book available to brokers and market makers who are members of NASD, the ECN books available to all brokers, market makers and investors sponsored by brokers. All these electronic markets are voluntarily interconnected. See Goldstein, Shkilko, Van Ness, and Van Ness (2008) for a recent study on competition in these markets during a similar period across market makers and three major ECNs in NASDAQ stocks.

Markets"), adopting a variety of techniques attempting to correct for the selection bias problem. Conventionally, the point comparison of execution costs is conducted at each market's own average, which is widely criticized because of the selection bias problem, i.e., the difficulties of the orders routed to the two markets could be different. Several recent papers attempt to account for the selection bias problem. For example, Lipson (2005) finds that "once we account for the difference in order flow difficulty, the NYSE is no more costly than other exchanges and much less costly than many." Unlike current literature, we find that after controlling for the selection bias problem, the Electronic Markets still offer lower execution costs. We also shed light on what impact different factors have on execution costs. The results are robust under different model specifications.

We make use of a sample of 1,138 NYSE-listed stocks which are traded on both the NYSE and the Electronic Markets. We start with the conventional simple mean comparison as well as share-weighted mean comparison of execution costs, measured by effective spreads. The univariate results show that the effective spreads on the Electronic Markets are lower than those on the NYSE.

We then proceed to OLS regression analysis controlling for order difficulty. We study a wide range of potential explanatory variables and eventually reach a model with a set of significant explanatory variables explaining effective spreads. The model is cross-sectional and is set up with two dummy variables indicating whether the order is executed on the NYSE or the Electronic Markets. The explanatory variables are all constructed as the deviation from the in-sample mean, so that the coefficients of the two dummy indicators may be interpreted as the conditional mean effective spreads at the mean of the explanatory variables vector. The results confirm that execution costs are lower on the Electronic Markets than on the NYSE.

Next we adopted the two-stage procedure advocated by Heckman (1979) and Maddala (1983). This method involves first estimating a Probit model for the choice of venues, generating two new variables from the Probit estimation, and then including these two new variables in an OLS regression model as controls for selection bias. Our results based on this two-stage procedure confirm the superiority of the Electronic Markets' execution.

We conduct several robustness checks of our results. Since the above OLS and two-stage analysis is effectively a point comparison at the sample mean of control variables, it is worthwhile to check whether the results hold at other locations of the sample domain. To do that, we split our sample into two sub-samples according to the fitted values, which is a measure of order difficulty, and repeat our OLS and two-stage selection analysis in both difficulty sub-samples. The results are similar.

As another extension and robustness check, we try to answer the following question: if the NYSE executed the Electronic Markets' orders, will these orders receive better or worse execution? Similarly, what if the Electronic Markets executed the NYSE's orders? In order to answer the former question, we first estimate a model for the NYSE's orders alone. Then we plug in explanatory variables of the Electronic Markets' orders into the NYSE model. The fitted values represent "as-if" NYSE execution costs of the Electronic Markets' orders. The latter question is similarly answered by first estimating the Electronic Markets model, and then plugging in explanatory variables of the NYSE's orders. Results of the above what-if analysis suggest that the Electronic Markets' (*the NYSE's*) orders would have been worse (*better*) off, had they been executed by the NYSE (*Electronic Markets*). Therefore, our results clearly show that the Electronic Markets offer better execution quality than the NYSE.

Given our results of lower execution costs on the Electronic Markets, one might find it puzzling that the NYSE is still dominant in the market place even though it is not fully electronic. We note that although execution costs and listing fees are important considerations in a firm's listing decision, they are by no means the only factors a firm might consider. Chemmanur and Fulghieri (2006) develop a theoretical model of firms' listing decisions in an environment of competition and co-operation among exchanges with endogenous listing standards. In their model, reputation, asymmetric information, and investors' ability to produce information are the main concerns in a firm's listing decision making process. Our results are thus consistent with their theoretical analysis: execution costs alone do not drive a firm's listing decision.

The rest of the paper is organized as follows. Section 2 describes the data and sample selection procedures. Section 3 presents univariate analysis. Section 4 presents OLS and two-stage selection model analysis. Section 5 presents difficulty sub-sample analysis. Section 6 contains an extension answering the what-if question. Section 7 concludes.

## 2. Data and Sample Selection

### 2.1. Data

Execution costs are often computed based on trade level data such as Trade and Quote database (TAQ), disseminated by the NYSE. The drawback is that order direction, order size, and order arrival time are not observable and must be estimated using approximation methods. On November 17, 2000, the SEC adopted Exchange Act Rule 11Ac1-5 (the "Dash-5 reports"). Regarding the purpose of compiling Dash-5 reports, the SEC states *"one of the primary objectives of the Rule is to generate statistical measures of execution quality that provides a fair and useful basis for comparisons among different market centers."* The main advantages of the Dash-5 reports are that the order direction is known, the benchmark price is the best quote at order receipt time, the time between order receipt and execution is reported, and they provide order volume and execution quality for all market centers individually. Dash-5 reports have drawbacks as well. For example, they only report aggregate monthly averages. Due to the advantages of Dash-5 reports, several recent academic studies use Dash-5 data to answer related research questions (see, e.g., Bessembinder (2003), Lipson (2005), and Nguyen, Van Ness, and Van Ness (2005)). The Dash-5 reports provide the most relevant publicly available data for our analysis. Our Dash-5 data are from Transaction Audit Group, Inc (www.tagaudit.com).

Exchange Act Rule 11Ac1-5 mandates that all markets in the United States report order data and regular-way execution data received for all stock orders of less than 10,000 shares from both individual and institutional investors. Dash-5 reports do not include any order for which the customer requests special handling, such as orders to be executed at the market opening price or closing price, orders submitted with stop prices, orders to be executed only at their full size, orders to be executed on a particular type of tick or bid, orders submitted on a "not held" basis, orders for other than regular settlement, and orders to be executed at prices unrelated to the market price of the security at the time of execution. Dash-5 reports provide data by order size/order type/security/market center/month/participant. The orders are divided into four size categories: 100 to 499 shares, 500 to 1999 shares, 2000 to 4999 shares, and

5000 or greater shares. Order size can be viewed as a measure of order difficulty. Executions for large orders are generally expected to be more costly than for small orders.

Dash 5 reports include market orders and marketable limit orders. We follow Boehmer (2005) and focus on market orders only. As pointed out by Boehmer (2005), results for marketable limit orders based on Dash-5 reports are hard to interpret for at least the following four reasons. "First, because Dash 5 reports do not include information on the opportunity cost of non-execution, ex post execution costs for marketable limits understate their true cost. Consequently, estimates for marketable limits would not be comparable to those in SEC (2001), which uses an ex post adjustment for unfilled marketable limits. This analysis cannot be replicated using Dash 5 data, because they include only monthly aggregates. Second, the time-to-execution for this order type is censored, because cancelled and expired orders are not considered in the computation. Third, summary statistics on speed are dominated by orders that happen to be submitted as the market moves away and, therefore, do not execute immediately. Finally, usage of marketable limit orders differs systematically across markets. All NYSE specialists accept market orders, but some Nasdaq market centers do not. For example, some marketable limits reported by Island, which does not accept market orders, are probably functionally equivalent to market orders." See Peterson and Sirri (2002) for an analysis of the two order types.

## 2.2. Sample Selection

The Center for Research in Security Prices (CRSP) database is used to construct the sample of stocks and several control variables based on stock characteristics, such as price, volume, shares outstanding, and return. We select NYSE-listed stocks from the CRSP database. The sample selection criteria are similar to those used in SEC (2001). Our Dash-5 data are from January to December 2003. We start with all the 2,557 NYSE listed securities as of December 31, 2002. From this list, we eliminated dual classes, foreign-incorporated securities, ADRS, REITS, Certificates, SNIs, Units, Closed End Funds, etc., leaving us with 1,329 NYSE common stocks. This list was further reduced to 1,138 NYSE securities after removing securities whose daily trading volume was less than $20,000, whose average closing price was less than $3, which switched exchanges, or which had missing data, or for which data was not available in Dash-5 reports. The detailed sample selection procedure is shown in the Appendix, Table A1. The sample was then merged with Dash-5 reports data. We further apply a filter to exclude outliers: we exclude orders where the effective spread or the quoted spread is equal to or larger than half of the trading price. In our data, there are 7 NYSE specialist firms and 32 electronic market centers. The list of market centers are in the Appendix, Table A2.

## 3. Univariate Analysis

### 3.1. Measures of Execution Costs

The *quoted spread* is defined as the bid ask difference, which reflects market and order flow conditions at the time of order arrival. The *effective spread,* first developed by Blume and

Goldstein (1992) and Petersen and Fialkowski (1994), is defined, for buy orders, as double the amount of the difference between the execution price and the midpoint of the consolidated best bid and offer at the time of order receipt and, for sell orders, as double the amount of difference between the midpoint of the consolidated best bid and offer at the time of order receipt and the execution price. Dash-5 data calculate at a record level, the share-weighted average of effective spreads for order executions in the month. The *realized spread* is defined, for buy orders, as double the amount of difference between the execution price and the midpoint of the consolidated best bid and offer five minutes after the time of order execution and, for sell orders, and double the amount of difference between the midpoint of the consolidated best bid and offer five minutes after the time of order execution and the execution price.

As noted in Blume and Goldstein (1992) and Petersen and Fialkowski (1994), effective spreads are a better measure of execution costs than quoted spreads, because orders do not always execute exactly at the bid or offer price. The effective spread takes this into account by incorporating any price improvement or dis-improvement that an order may receive. The effective spread calculates how much above the midpoint price you paid on a buy order and how much below the midpoint price you received on a sell order. While price improvement is a good tool for measuring execution quality, effective spread captures both how often, and also by how much, a broker-dealer price improves trades. Therefore, the effective spread can be interpreted as the total price impact of the trade, a measure of the non-commission, out-of-pocket cost of a trader.

Effective spreads can be decomposed into two parts: realized spread and the information component or price impact, which is the difference of the bid-ask midpoint five minutes later and that at the time of order receipt. The information component can measure the extent to which "informed" and "uninformed" orders are routed to different market centers. Informed orders are those submitted by persons with better information than is generally available in the market. They therefore represent a substantial risk to liquidity providers that take the other side of these informed trades. In contrast, order submitted by persons without an information advantage (often small orders) present less risk to liquidity providers and in theory should receive the most favorable effective spreads available in the market.

The smaller the average realized spread, the more market prices have moved adversely to the market cent's liquidity providers after the order was executed, which shrinks the spread "realized" by the liquidity providers. In other words, a low average realized spread indicates that the market center was providing liquidity even though prices where moving against it for reasons such as news or market volatility. Spreads are not the perfect measure of trading costs. However, they are simple to measure, readily available, and are usually reasonable indicators of actual trading costs.

## 3.2. Univariate Results

Table 1 presents summary statistics of execution quality measures in the two markets, the NYSE and the Electronic Markets. It reports the median, simple average, as well as share-weighted average (aggregated across all stocks traded at each market over the 12 month period) of the effective spread, quoted spread, realized spread, information component (effective spread less realized spread), and execution speed.

## Table 1. Summary Statistics

This table presents summary statistics from Dash-5 database for the 1,138 selected securities. Summary statistics are computed separately for the NYSE and the Electronic Markets (EM), and are further divided into four size categories: very small (100~499 shares), small (500~1,999 shares), medium (2,000~4,999 shares), and large (5,000~9,999 shares). Monthly shares ordered, monthly shares executed, and monthly number of orders are reported in millions. Average effective spread (AES), average quoted spread (AQS), average realized spread (ARS), and average information component (INFO, the difference of AES and ARS) are reported in cents. Average speed (SPEED) is also reported, in seconds. Median, mean, and share-weighted mean are reported for the above variables.

| | | NYSE | | | | | Electronic Markets (EM) | | | | |
|---|---|---|---|---|---|---|---|---|---|---|---|
| | | All | Very Small | Small | Medium | Large | All | Very Small | Small | Medium | Large |
| Shares Ordered (M) | | 5,517.10 | 1,620.73 | 2,188.51 | 1,150.60 | 557.27 | 769.94 | 185.81 | 332.42 | 171.74 | 79.97 |
| Shares Executed(M) | | 5,455.13 | 1,602.38 | 2,161.68 | 1,139.94 | 551.13 | 743.28 | 181.71 | 324.45 | 163.37 | 73.74 |
| Number of Orders (M) | | 11.98 | 8.83 | 2.63 | 0.42 | 0.09 | 1.43 | 0.95 | 0.40 | 0.07 | 0.01 |
| AES (cents) | Median | 3.53 | 2.39 | 3.36 | 6.12 | 8.76 | 2.33 | 1.84 | 2.33 | 3.41 | 2.39 |
| | Mean | 5.95 | 2.80 | 4.70 | 8.31 | 11.63 | 3.94 | 2.30 | 3.36 | 6.13 | 2.80 |
| | Wtd. Mean | 3.03 | 2.38 | 2.83 | 3.58 | 4.59 | 2.16 | 1.47 | 1.85 | 2.80 | 2.38 |
| | Median | 8.04 | 6.62 | 7.57 | 10.33 | 13.03 | 5.04 | 4.59 | 5.00 | 5.98 | 6.20 |
| AQS (cents) | Mean | 10.81 | 8.02 | 9.51 | 12.96 | 16.18 | 9.47 | 8.31 | 8.76 | 11.54 | 12.39 |
| | Wtd. Mean | 7.28 | 6.70 | 7.16 | 7.65 | 8.65 | 5.88 | 4.78 | 5.63 | 6.74 | 7.81 |
| | Median | 1.00 | 0.40 | 0.79 | 2.04 | 3.49 | 1.27 | 1.20 | 1.15 | 1.56 | 1.95 |
| ARS (cents) | Mean | 2.52 | 1.09 | 2.52 | 2.84 | 5.11 | 1.69 | 1.23 | 1.25 | 2.59 | 3.18 |
| | Wtd. Mean | 10.40 | 6.53 | 20.40 | 1.07 | 1.76 | 1.07 | 0.97 | 0.85 | 1.33 | 1.73 |
| | Median | 2.71 | 1.97 | 2.68 | 3.92 | 4.57 | 1.00 | 0.51 | 1.11 | 2.00 | 2.18 |
| INFO (cents) | Mean | 3.43 | 1.72 | 2.18 | 5.46 | 6.51 | 2.25 | 1.07 | 2.11 | 3.54 | 4.72 |
| | Wtd. Mean | -7.37 | -4.14 | -17.58 | 2.51 | 2.82 | 1.09 | 0.50 | 1.00 | 1.47 | 2.07 |
| | Median | 17.05 | 14.33 | 15.51 | 19.33 | 23.80 | 13.21 | 7.91 | 12.00 | 19.70 | 28.80 |
| SPEED | Mean | 19.43 | 16.40 | 17.33 | 21.41 | 27.26 | 31.07 | 21.73 | 24.26 | 38.55 | 76.50 |
| | Wtd. Mean | 17.14 | 16.03 | 16.61 | 18.02 | 20.66 | 14.37 | 5.51 | 9.92 | 22.88 | 36.96 |

Statistics are averaged across all categories and aggregated up to the markets level (either the NYSE or the Electronic Markets (*EM*)). This method, while simple, may be distorted by variations in executed volume among market centers. Share-weighted average statistics are also provide to account for share volume differences. We also report monthly shares ordered, shares executed, and number of orders. We further examine the above variables in four order size categories: very small (100~499 shares), small (500~1,999 shares), medium (2,000~4,999 shares) and large (5,000~9,999 shares).

NYSE orders seem to have higher average effective and quoted spreads. The overall effective spread reported by the Electronic Markets has a simple mean of 3.94 cents versus 5.95 cents for the NYSE, and a share-weighted mean of 2.16 cents versus 3.03 cents. In addition, the Electronic Markets' effective spread is lower across all four size categories.

One explanation for why the Electronic Markets can offer lower effective spreads than the NYSE for the same NYSE stocks is that the Electronic Markets compete and attract "easy orders." This selection bias could cause the difference in effective spreads. Before formally accounting for this selection bias in a multivariate selection model framework, we first sort the data on quoted spread, an important variable since it reflects the market condition at the time of the order. We segment the data into 8 ranges of quoted spread. Then we calculate the share-weighted effective spread for all the NYSE records in each of the 8 quoted spread ranges. We do the same for all records in the Electronic Markets. The results are shown in Table 2. The Electronic Markets offer lower average effective spreads in 7 out of the 8 ranges of quoted spreads. The NYSE only offers marginally lower effective spreads in the lowest quoted spread range (0~4 cents), 1.17 cent for the NYSE versus 1.23 for the Electronic Markets. Note that this range also contains relatively less number of symbols and shares executed. In summary, results in Table 2 suggest that the Electronic Markets seem to be able to offer lower effective spreads than the NYSE even after controlling for the differences in quoted spreads across these two markets.

## Table 2. Quoted Spread Bins

This table presents results by splitting the data according to quoted spread bins. The number of symbols, shares executed in millions, and share-weighted effective spreads in each range for the NYSE versus the Electronic Markets (EM) are reported.

| Quoted Spread | Number of Symbols NYSE | Number of Symbols EM | Shares Executed (M) NYSE | Shares Executed (M) EM | AES (cents) NYSE | AES (cents) EM |
|---|---|---|---|---|---|---|
| 0~4 cents | 16 | 39 | 4,800 | 2,695 | 1.17 | 1.23 |
| 4~6 cents | 130 | 212 | 17,053 | 3,318 | 1.94 | 1.74 |
| 6~8 cents | 276 | 228 | 23,871 | 1,556 | 2.82 | 2.53 |
| 8~10 cents | 260 | 204 | 10,850 | 701 | 3.90 | 3.69 |
| 10~12 cents | 181 | 126 | 5,642 | 220 | 4.91 | 4.73 |
| 12~14 cents | 114 | 108 | 2,221 | 180 | 6.14 | 5.09 |
| 14~16 cents | 59 | 80 | 614 | 130 | 7.29 | 5.54 |
| >= 16 cents | 102 | 141 | 423 | 132 | 10.07 | 7.72 |

# 4. Regression and Selection Model Analysis

## 4.1. Factors Affecting Execution Costs

We consider a wide range of variables explaining execution costs based on related microstructure literature. Many of these variables have been used in one or more of previous studies, such as Bessembinder (2003), Boehmer (2005), Lipson (2005), and Nguyen, Van Ness, and Van Ness (2005). Some of these variables are cost-based, while others are only reflective. For example, the quoted spread directly represents the financial loss a trader incurs from a particular transaction. On the other hand, though the trading volume indicates whether a particular stock is liquid or not, it does not show us how costly it is to actually trade the stock. The explanatory variables can be classified into two groups: order-specific measures and stock-specific measures. Order-specific measures capture the nature and difficulty of different orders, while stock-specific measures capture the characteristics of stocks traded and are the same across different orders within the same stock. We further divide the stock-specific measures into liquidity measures and volatility measures. The detailed definitions of these variables are as follows:

Order-specific Measures:

*Log(num.ord)*: The natural logarithm of the number of orders.

*AQS*: Average quoted spread. This variable is included as a measure of market conditions at order time. It can be viewed as a cost-based liquidity measure because it examines the financial loss a trader incurs from a particular transaction. It is highly correlated with the average effective spread.

*INFO*: It is defined as the difference between the effective spread and the realized spread. Therefore it is the mirror image of realized spread. The smaller the average realized spread, the more market prices have moved adversely to the market center's liquidity providers after the order was executed, which shrinks the spread "realized" by the liquidity providers. In other words, a low average realized spread indicates that the market center was providing liquidity even though prices were moving against it for reasons such as news or market volatility.

*SPEED*: Another dimension of execution quality measures beyond trading costs. There is a trade-off between the urgency and the absolute cost. Therefore one would expect that the faster the speed, the higher the cost. SEC (2001) used a five-day period in June and found that for smaller orders (orders below 5,000 shares), the NYSE execution costs are below NASDAQ costs, but NASDAQ orders generally execute faster. Boehmer (2005) extended this part of study and found that small orders (below 2,000 shares) execute at lower cost on the NYSE, but substantially faster on NASDAQ. However this results reverses for larger orders (between 2,000 and 9,999 shares). These execute more cheaply on NASDAQ, but faster on the NYSE.

*Log(Ord.Sz) and Ord.Sz/Vol*: Ord.Sz/Vol is the standardized order size, calculated as the order size for the security at the specific markets, versus its total trading volume in the last month of 2002. It is intuitive that larger orders should be more difficult to execute (due to pure liquidity reasons, regardless of information content) and also should contain more information. We expect both reasons to cause a positive relationship between order size and the effective spread. Boehmer (2005) describes a specific example for why larger NYSE orders should contain more information. He reasons that traders who have either no private information or whose information is sufficiently long-lived often use floor brokers to work large orders. This involves delegating control over the actual trading decisions to a floor broker, who then seeks favorable (partial) executions until the order is filled. An informed trader with short-lived information cannot afford to use this option because it is slow, and the trader risks that others discover the same information before the orders are filled. For the same reason, small NYSE orders are not useful for informed traders because they are executed sequentially. One would thus expect informed traders (or their agents) to submit large orders directly to the specialist.

Stock-specific Measures:

Liquidity measures: Illiquidity reflects the impact of order flow on price: the discount that a seller concedes or the premium that a buyer pays when executing a market order, which results from adverse selection costs and inventory costs.

*MCAP and MCAP Rank*: MCAP is the market capitalization, calculated as the product of price and shares outstanding. MCAP Rank is the market capitalization rank (1~20) based on Fama-French NYSE Breakpoints. They are common proxies for liquidity since a larger stock issue has smaller price impact for a given order flow and a smaller bid–ask spread: large firms are more liquid.

*1/PRC*: The inverse of price. The higher this factor, the more liquid the order.

*Turnover*: The volume in the stock divided by the number of shares outstanding.

*ADV*: Average dollar volume (price times share volume) in the fourth quarter of 2002. High volume levels may indicate that a particular security is very liquid. However, it does not tell us how costly it is to actually trade the security.

*CBMA*: Gibbs estimate of transaction cost, *c*, from Basic Market-Adjusted Model from Hasbrouck (2006). It is a daily liquidity proxy.

$$CBMA = \begin{cases} \sqrt{-\text{cov}(r_t, r_{t-1})} & \text{if } \text{cov}(r_t, r_{t-1}) < 0 \\ 0 & \text{otherwise} \end{cases}. \quad (1)$$

*I1*: Amihud's (2002) illiquidity measure, calculated as the average daily ratio over year of the absolute value of daily return divided by the daily trading volume in millions of dollars.

$$I1 = 1,000,000 \times \frac{abs(ret)}{prc \times vol}. \quad (2)$$

As can be seen from the above definition, Amihud's illiquidity measure can be interpreted as the daily price response (sensitivity) associated with one dollar of trading volume, thus serving as a rough measure of price impact. Amihud (2002) shows that illiquid stocks are more difficult to trade. We expect orders in more illiquid stocks more likely to be submitted to NYSE rather than the Electronic markets.

*PSGAMMA:* Pastor-Stambaugh (2003) gamma. However, the authors caution against its use as a liquidity measure for individual securities, noting the large sample error in the individual estimates.

Volatility Measures:

*VOLA*: The standard deviation of daily returns in the fourth quarter of 2002. The specification of this variable is slightly different in other papers. For example, Lipson (2005) defines it as the standard deviation of daily trade-weighted prices.

*RR*: The average daily relative price range during the fourth quarter of 2002. Daily relative price range is defined as the daily range divided by the closing price. This is an intra-day measure. Compare to the other volatility measure *VOLA*, *RR* does not rely on stationary assumptions over the period of time needed to calculation *VOLA*.

## 4.2. OLS Regressions

The OLS regression method is specified in the following model, across different stocks:

$$AES_{ip} = \alpha_1 NYSE_{ip} + \alpha_2 NON.NYSE_{ip} + \alpha_3 X_{ip} + e_{ip}, \qquad (3)$$

where $AES_{ip}$ is the mean effective spread for stocks $i$ at market $p$, $p \in (N, EM)$. $NYSE_{ip}$ is a dummy variable which equals one if the market is $N$, zero if the market is $EM$. $NON.NYSE_{ip}$ is another dummy variable which equals zero if the market is $N$, and one if the market is $EM$. $X_{ip}$ is a vector of explanatory variables selected from the list of variables discussed previously. All $X_{ip}$ are measured as deviations from their own sample cross-sectional mean. This way, when the $X_{ip}$ are excluded from the regression, the coefficients estimates $\alpha_1$ and $\alpha_2$ produce the simple cross-sectional mean effective spreads of the two markets. When the control variables $X_{ip}$ are included in the regression, the coefficient estimates on the two dummy variables reveal conditional mean execution costs on the NYSE versus the Electronic Markets, evaluated at the mean of the variables that comprise the $X_{ip}$ vector.

We start our OLS regression analysis with specifications similar to Bessembinder (2003), and then add other potentially related factors discussed previously. The results are shown in Table 3. We run different specifications of the following regression model:

$$AES_{ip} = \alpha_1 NYSE_{ip} + \alpha_2 EM_{ip} + \alpha_3 \log(NUM.ORD_i) + \alpha_4 INFO_{ip}$$
$$+ \alpha_5 \frac{1}{PRC_i} + \alpha_6 \frac{ORD.SZ_{ip}}{VOL_i} + \alpha_7 SPEED_{ip} + \alpha_8 ADV_i + \alpha_9 TURNOVER_i \qquad (4)$$
$$+ \alpha_{10} MCAP.RANK_i + \alpha_{11} VOLA_i + \alpha_{12} RR_i + e_{ip}$$

We start by running an OLS regression on the two dummy variables: one for the NYSE and one for the Electronic Markets (therefore there is no intercept term). The coefficients on the two dummy variables represent the unconditional cross-sectional simple averages for these two markets. Specifically, the effective spread is 7.65 cents for the NYSE and 4.92 cents for the Electronic Markets. In other words, the effective spread for the Electronic Markets is 2.73 cents (or 36%) lower than the NYSE.

## Table 3. OLS Regressions

This table presents OLS regression results. The dependent variable is average effective spread (AES). NYSE is a dummy variable that equals 1 for orders executed by the NYSE and 0 otherwise. EM is a dummy variable that equals 1 for orders executed by the Electronic Markets and 0 otherwise. There is no intercept term since both NYSE and EM are included in the regression.

|  | NYSE | EM | Log(NUM.ORD) | INFO | 1/PRC | ORD.SZ/VOL | SPEED | ADV | TURNOVER | MCAP.RANK | VOLA | RR | $R^2$ |
|---|---|---|---|---|---|---|---|---|---|---|---|---|---|
|  | $\alpha_1$ | $\alpha_2$ | $\alpha_3$ | $\alpha_4$ | $\alpha_5$ | $\alpha_6$ | $\alpha_7$ | $\alpha_8$ | $\alpha_9$ | $\alpha_{10}$ | $\alpha_{11}$ | $\alpha_{12}$ |  |
| Model 1 | 7.65 | 4.92 |  |  |  |  |  |  |  |  |  |  | 70.45% |
| (t-stat) | 59.20*** | 37.26*** |  |  |  |  |  |  |  |  |  |  |  |
| Model 2 | 7.68 | 5.66 | -0.55 | 76.19 | -15.04 | 7.86 |  |  |  |  |  |  | 95.15% |
| (t-stat) | 99.61*** | 66.39*** | -14.77*** | 52.23*** | -14.72*** | 13.06*** |  |  |  |  |  |  |  |
| Model 3 | 7.70 | 5.65 | -0.54 | 76.03 | -15.05 | 7.85 | 0.01 |  |  |  |  |  | 95.12% |
| (t-stat) | 96.47*** | 65.92*** | -14.60*** | 51.80*** | -14.73*** | 13.04*** | 0.97 |  |  |  |  |  |  |
| Model 4 | 7.24 | 6.03 | -0.20 | 72.75 | -21.69 | 7.67 | 0.01 | 0.01 | -21.17 | -0.14 |  |  | 95.26% |
| (t-stat) | 68.86*** | 57.08*** | -3.23*** | 47.61*** | -16.28*** | 12.49*** | 0.48 | -0.09 | -2.75*** | -7.87*** |  |  |  |
| Model 5 | 7.26 | 6.01 | -0.22 | 72.69 | -22.09 | 7.78 | 0.01 | 0.01 | -19.28 | -0.13 | -10.38 | 10.03 | 95.27% |
| (t-stat) | 67.68*** | 55.7.9*** | -3.37*** | 47.18*** | -12.92*** | 12.10*** | 0.51 | 0.04 | -2.14** | -7.73*** | -1.25 | 1.17 |  |
| Model 6 | 7.23 | 6.04 | -0.20 | 72.89 | -21.30 | 7.63 |  |  | -18.83 | -0.14 | -2.21 |  | 95.26% |
| (t-stat) | 76.27*** | 62.26*** | -3.60*** | 47.61*** | -13.69*** | 12.39*** |  |  | -2.10** | -7.92*** | -0.49 |  |  |

In the second model, we add four control variables, as in Bessembinder (2003): logarithm of number of orders, information component, inverse price, and standardized order size. We note three things here: first, after adding these control variables, the effective spread for the NYSE almost remain unchanged, at 7.68 cents. On the other hand, the effective spread for the Electronic Markets increases dramatically, from 4.92 cents to 5.66 cents, causing the difference between the two markets to narrow to 2.02 cents (or 26%). This means that the Electronic Markets received relatively easier orders than did the NYSE, hence controlling for difficulty reduces the cost advantage shown by unconditional results. These results highlight the importance of controlling for the relative difficulty of the orders received by different markets before drawing inferences. Second, the slope coefficients are generally consistent with those reported in prior research (see, e.g., Bessembinder (2003)). The average effective spread decreases with the trading activity as measured by total orders in the stock, increases with average information component, decreases with the inverse share price (or increase with share price), and increases with average order size. Each coefficient estimate is highly significant. Third, the $R^2$ increases to 95.15% from the first regression's 70.45%.

In the third model, we further add *SPEED* to the regression. Though it is considered to be the other important dimension of execution quality, it does not seem to have marginal explanatory power for effective spread. The coefficient for *SPEED* is not significantly different from zero. The coefficients for the two dummy variables and the $R^2$ remain almost unchanged.

In the fourth model we further add *ADV, TURNOVER*, and *MCAP.RANK*, trying to capture effects of illiquidity on effective spreads. Coefficients on *TURNOVER* and *MCAP.RANK* are significant and negative, which is intuitive. High turnover and large market cap securities are more liquid, and therefore should have lower execution costs. The coefficient on *ADV* is not significant. The conditional mean effective spread for the NYSE decreases to 7.24 cents, while that for the Electronic Markets increases to 6.03 cents.

The fifth model is the full specification. We further add two volatility variables *VOLA* and *RR*. Neither of them turns out to be significant. The conditional effective spreads for the NYSE and the Electronic Markets are almost unchanged.

The sixth model is our selected model, chosen mainly based on the statistical significance of different factors in previous models. It includes market condition factors such as number of orders, order size; and information component, security illiquidity proxies such as price, turnover, and market cap rank, and a volatility measure, VOLA (though it is the only insignificant factor). The conditional mean effective spread for the NYSE is 7.23 cents, versus 6.04 cents for the Electronic Markets, which represents a difference of 1.19 cents or 16%. Overall, our OLS regression results show that controlling for the above factors narrows the difference in conditional mean effective spread for the NYSE versus the Electronic Markets. However, the Electronic Markets still outperform the NYSE.

## 4.3. Two-Stage Selection Model

The two-stage procedure to control for selection bias follows the work by Heckman (1979) and Maddala (1983). Effective spreads are modeled for the NYSE ($N$) and the Electronic Markets ($EM$) as:

$$ES_{i,N} = \beta_N{}'X_i + \varepsilon_{i,N},$$
$$ES_{i,EM} = \beta_{EM}{}'X_i + \varepsilon_{i,EM}, \tag{5}$$

where $X_i$ is a vector of conditioning variables for each security $i$, $\beta$ is a vector of parameters to be estimated, and the $\varepsilon$'s are error terms. We assume the difference in effective spreads across the two markets is a factor that determines the market selected by a trader for that stock. The difference in expected effective spreads is

$$\begin{aligned} y_i^* &= E\left[ ES_{i,N} - ES_{i,EM} \mid X_i \right] \\ &= \left(\beta_N{}' - \beta_{EM}{}'\right)X_i + \varepsilon_{i,N} - \varepsilon_{i,EM} \\ &= \gamma' X_i + \zeta_i \end{aligned} \tag{6}$$

In this model, a trader of stock $i$ chooses to trade the order in the NYSE if $y_i^* \leq 0$, i.e., the NYSE trade is expected to be less costly. The order submission rule for a security a traders wishes to trade is

$$\begin{aligned} y_i &= 1, \quad \text{if} \quad y_i^* \leq 0; \\ y_i &= 0, \quad \text{if} \quad y_i^* > 0; \end{aligned} \tag{7}$$

with $y_i = 1$ indicates the NYSE and $y_i = 0$ indicates the Electronic Markets. We will use several independent variables discussed previously to model the choice which market to choose from in a Probit framework. Then, the probability a trader chooses the NYSE is estimated, which is,

$$\Pr(y_i = 1) = \Phi(\gamma' X_i), \tag{8}$$

where $\Phi$ is the cumulative distribution function of the standard normal. The next step is to multiply the parameter estimates from the Probit, $\gamma$, with the complementary set of observations, $X$, to estimate the probability of choosing the NYSE ($\Phi(\gamma'X)$).

In the second stage of this method, the Probit probability estimates are used to control for the selection bias. Because an stock $i$ is traded on the NYSE only when $y_i^* \leq 0$, the error term $\varepsilon_{i,N}$ does not have a zero mean, conditional on being NYSE. The conditional expected execution costs for the NYSE and the Electronic Markets are denoted as:

$$\begin{aligned} E\left[ ES_{i,N} \mid y^* \leq 0 \right] &= \beta_N{}'X_i + \alpha_N \frac{\phi(\gamma'X_i)}{\Phi(\gamma'X_i)}, \\ E\left[ ES_{i,EM} \mid y^* > 0 \right] &= \beta_{EM}{}'X_i + \alpha_{EM} \frac{-\phi(\gamma'X_i)}{1-\Phi(\gamma'X_i)}; \end{aligned} \tag{9}$$

where $\phi(\gamma'X_i)$ and $\Phi(\gamma'X_i)$ are the density and cumulative distribution function of the standard normal evaluated at $\gamma'X_i$, respectively. $\alpha = \text{cov}(\varepsilon_i, \zeta_i)$. In this methodology, estimating the second stage equation by OLS provides consistent estimates of the parameters.

$\lambda_1 = \dfrac{\phi(\gamma'X_i)}{\Phi(\gamma'X_i)}$ is the "Inverse Mills Ratio". It is monotonically decreasing in the probability that an order will be routed to the NYSE. $\lambda_2 = -\dfrac{\phi(\gamma'X_i)}{1-\Phi(\gamma'X_i)}$. The Heckman method can detect the selection bias in a rather straightforward fashion. Potentially, the parameters from the Heckman method can also be used to examine the trade-offs in the market selection strategies.

## 4.4. Selection Model Results

The full specification for the first stage Probit regression is as follows:

$$\Pr(NYSE_{ip} = 1) = g(\beta_0 + \beta_1 \log(MCAP_i) + \beta_2 \log(VOL_i) + \beta_3 \log(ORD.SZ_{ip})$$
$$+ \beta_4 Info_{ip} + \beta_5 AQS_{ip} + \beta_6 SPEED_{ip} + \beta_7 RR_i + \beta_8 VOLA_i + \beta_9 CBMA_i + \beta_{10} I1 \quad (10)$$
$$+ \beta_{11} PSGAMMA + \varepsilon_{ip})$$

In the second stage OLS regression correcting for selection bias, we use the full model and the model selected previously. The specification of the full model is as follows:

$$AES_{ip} = \alpha_1 NYSE_{ip} + \alpha_2 EM_{ip} + \alpha_3 (\lambda_1 NYSE_{ip}) + \alpha_4 (\lambda_2 EM_{ip})$$
$$+ \alpha_5 \log(NUM.ORD_i) + \alpha_6 INFO_{ip} + \alpha_7 \dfrac{1}{PRC_i} + \alpha_8 \dfrac{ORD.SZ_{ip}}{VOL_i} + \alpha_9 SPEED_{ip} \quad (11)$$
$$+ \alpha_{10} ADV_i + \alpha_{11} TURNOVER_i + \alpha_{12} MCAP.RANK_i + \alpha_{13} VOLA_i + \alpha_{14} RR_i + e_{ip}$$

In the literature there appears to be some inconsistency as to whether only $\lambda_1$, or both $\lambda_1$ and $\lambda_2$ should be included in the second stage regression. We did both. To adapt to our specific model where the two parts of sample (the NYSE and the Electronic Markets) are combined into one model, indicated by two dummy variables, we create two new variables $\lambda_1 NYSE$ and $\lambda_2 EM$. Note that these two variables are highly correlated with each other.

Table 4 Panel A presents first stage Probit regression results. We start with a model similar to that in Bessembinder (2003). The independent variables include market capitalization, order volume, order size, information component, and quoted spread. All coefficients are significant at least at the 95% level, confirming the presence of systematic selection biases in order routing. The coefficient on order volume is significantly negative, indicating that actively traded stocks are more likely to be executed in the Electronic Markets. Coefficients on market capitalization, order size, information component, and quoted spread are all significantly positive, suggesting that orders for larger stocks, with larger order sizes, containing more information, and with worse market condition, tend to be executed on the NYSE. We then further add variables including *SPEED, RR, VOLA, CBMA, I1* and *PSGAMMA* to the Probit model. These variables comprise volatility measures and illiquidity measures.

## Table 4. Two-Stage Selection Model

This table presents selection model results. Panel A presents the first stage Probit regressions for the likelihood of an order being executed by the NYSE. Panel B presents the second stage OLS regression of conditional average effective spreads.

### Panel A. First Stage Probit Regressions for the Likelihood of an Order Being Executed by the NYSE

| | Log (MCAP) | Log (VOL) | Log (ORD.SZ) | INFO | AQS | SPEED | RR | VOLA | CBMA | I1 | PSGAMMA | | |
|---|---|---|---|---|---|---|---|---|---|---|---|---|---|
| | $\beta_1$ | $\beta_2$ | $\beta_3$ | $\beta_4$ | $\beta_5$ | $\beta_6$ | $\beta_7$ | $\beta_8$ | $\beta_9$ | $\beta_{10}$ | $\beta_{11}$ | Pseudo $R^2$ | Prob > $\chi^2$ |
| Model 1 | 1.04 | -2.29 | 16.99 | 28.56 | 6.67 | | | | | | | 89.57% | 0.00 |
| (z-stat) | 6.87*** | -10.17*** | 17.45*** | 8.57*** | 2.34** | | | | | | | | |
| Model 2 | 0.90 | -2.32 | 18.94 | 32.03 | 9.82 | -0.10 | -49.07 | 54.19 | -117.63 | 3.58 | -56665.03 | 93.10% | 0.00 |
| (z-stat) | 3.14*** | -6.07*** | 12.79*** | 7.95*** | 2.62*** | -8.23*** | -2.24** | 2.59*** | -2.39*** | 1.59 | -2.01** | | |

### Panel B. Second Stage OLS Regressions of Conditional Average Effective Spreads

| | NYSE | EM | $\lambda_1$NYSE | $\lambda_2$EM | Log(NUM. ORD) | INFO | 1/PRC | ORD.SZ /VOL | SPEED | ADV | TURNOVER | MCAP. RANK | VOLA | RR | $R^2$ |
|---|---|---|---|---|---|---|---|---|---|---|---|---|---|---|---|
| | $\alpha_4$ | $\alpha_2$ | $\alpha_3$ | $\alpha_4$ | $\alpha_5$ | $\alpha_6$ | $\alpha_7$ | $\alpha_8$ | $\alpha_9$ | $\alpha_{10}$ | $\alpha_{11}$ | $\alpha_{12}$ | $\alpha_{13}$ | $\alpha_{14}$ | |
| Model 1 | 7.14 | 4.92 | -0.74 | -0.02 | | | | | | | | | | | 72.42% |
| (t-stat) | 57.42*** | 39.68*** | -1.72* | -0.05 | | | | | | | | | | | |
| Model 2 | 7.75 | 4.92 | -1.32 | | | | | | | | | | | | 70.56% |
| (t-stat) | 57.86*** | 37.32*** | -2.78*** | | | | | | | | | | | | |
| Model 3 | 7.08 | 4.92 | | -0.02 | | | | | | | | | | | 72.38% |
| (t-stat) | 59.22*** | 39.66*** | | -0.05 | | | | | | | | | | | |
| Model 4 | 7.25 | 6.02 | 0.11 | | -0.22 | 72.82 | -22.09 | 7.74 | 0.01 | 0.01 | -19.66 | -0.13 | -10.42 | 10.01 | 95.27% |
| (t-stat) | 65.80*** | 55.71*** | 0.54 | | -3.31*** | 46.75*** | -12.92*** | 11.94*** | 0.53 | 0.01 | -2.18** | -7.74*** | -1.26 | 1.17 | |
| Model 5 | 7.22 | 6.04 | 0.10 | | -0.20 | 73.01 | -21.30 | 7.59 | | | -19.18 | -0.14 | -2.27 | | 95.26% |
| (t-stat) | 74.01*** | 62.21*** | 0.52 | | -3.56*** | 47.16*** | -13.69*** | 12.20*** | | | -2.13** | -7.93*** | -0.50 | | |

## Table 5. OLS Regressions for Two Order Difficulty Sub-Samples

This table presents OLS regression results for the two order difficulty sub-samples. Panels A and B present results for easy and difficult orders respectively, where order difficulty is defined by the fitted value using the model for the whole sample.

### Panel A. Sub-Sample of Easy Orders

|  | NYSE | EM | Log(NUM.ORD) | INFO | 1/PRC | ORD.SZ/VOL | TURNOVER | MCAP.RANK | VOLA | $R^2$ |
|---|---|---|---|---|---|---|---|---|---|---|
|  | $\alpha_2$ | $\alpha_3$ | $\alpha_4$ | $\alpha_5$ | $\alpha_6$ | $\alpha_9$ | $\alpha_{10}$ | $\alpha_{11}$ | | |
| Model 1 | 3.11 | | | | | | | | | 82.74% |
| (t-stat) | 51.08*** | 48.01*** | | | | | | | | |
| Model 2 | 3.01 | −0.18 | 46.87 | −16.35 | 29.34 | 23.96 | −0.04 | −2.60 | | 90.84% |
| (t-stat) | 39.23*** | −3.37*** | 14.55*** | −10.76*** | 10.49*** | 2.83** | −2.00** | −0.63 | | |

Model 1 row: $\alpha_4$ = 3.70

Model 2 row: $\alpha_4$ = 3.82; (t-stat) $\alpha_4$ = 41.56***

### Panel B. Sub-Sample of Difficult Orders

|  | NYSE | EM | Log(NUM.ORD) | INFO | 1/PRC | ORD.SZ/VOL | TURNOVER | MCAP.RANK | VOLA | $R^2$ |
|---|---|---|---|---|---|---|---|---|---|---|
|  | $\alpha_2$ | $\alpha_3$ | $A_4$ | $\alpha_5$ | $\alpha_6$ | $\alpha_9$ | $\alpha_{10}$ | $\alpha_{11}$ | | |
| Model 1 | 7.29 | | | | | | | | | 84.63% |
| (t-stat) | 64.88*** | 39.87*** | | | | | | | | |
| Model 2 | 4.52 | −0.33 | 70.49 | −28.62 | 6.04 | −56.98 | −0.15 | −4.51 | | 96.18% |
| (t-stat) | 19.50*** | −2.94*** | 31.59*** | −9.52*** | 6.89*** | −3.30*** | −5.40*** | −0.54 | | |

Model 1 row: $\alpha_4$ = 10.70

Model 2 row: $\alpha_4$ = 6.59; (t-stat) $\alpha_4$ = 30.02***

# Table 6. Two-Stage Selection Model for Two Order Difficulty Sub-Samples

This table presents selection model results for the two order difficulty sub-samples. Panels A and B present results for easy and difficult orders respectively, where order difficulty is defined by the fitted value using the model for the whole sample.

## Panel A. Sub-Sample of Easy Orders

First Stage Probit Regressions for the Likelihood of an Order Being Executed by the NYSE

|  | Log (MCAP) | Log (VOL) | Log (ORD.SZ) | INFO | AQS | SPEED | RR | VOLA | CBMA | I1 | PSGAMMA | Pseudo R² | Prob > $\chi^2$ |
|---|---|---|---|---|---|---|---|---|---|---|---|---|---|
|  | $\beta_1$ | $\beta_2$ | $\beta_3$ | $\beta_4$ | $\beta_5$ | $\beta_6$ | $\beta_7$ | $\beta_8$ | $\beta_9$ | $\beta_{10}$ | $\beta_{11}$ | 95.82% | 0.00 |
|  | 2.29 | -5.04 | 45.60 | 32.85 | 23.98 | -0.11 | -68.14 | 75.07 | 50.94 | 10.59 | -112142 |  |  |
| (z-stat) | 3.32*** | -4.95*** | 5.70*** | 2.46*** | 1.82* | -3.78*** | -1.35 | 1.64* | 0.46 | 1.25 | -1.01 |  |  |

Second Stage OLS Regressions of Conditional Average Effective Spreads

|  | NYSE | EM | $\lambda_1$NYSE | Log(NUM. ORD) | INFO | 1/PRC | ORD.SZ /VOL | TURNOVER | MCAP. RANK | VOLA | R² |
|---|---|---|---|---|---|---|---|---|---|---|---|
|  | $\alpha_1$ | $\alpha_2$ | $\alpha_3$ | $\alpha_5$ | $\alpha_6$ | $\alpha_7$ | $\alpha_8$ | $\alpha_{11}$ | $\alpha_{12}$ | $\alpha_{13}$ |  |
| Model 1 | 3.69 | 3.10 | 0.02 |  |  |  |  |  |  |  | 82.73% |
| (t-stat) | 49.48*** | 47.83*** | 0.04 |  |  |  |  |  |  |  |  |
| Model 2 | 3.79 | 3.01 | 0.51 | -0.18 | 0.48 | -16.21 | 29.68 | 24.50 | -0.04 | -2.70 | 90.85% |
| (t-stat) | 40.75*** | 39.28*** | 1.48 | -3.29*** | 14.70*** | -10.67*** | 10.60*** | 2.90*** | -1.83* | -0.66 |  |

## Table 6. Continued

### Panel B. Sub-Sample of Difficult Orders

First Stage Probit Regressions for the Likelihood of an Order Being Executed by the NYSE

| | Log (MCAP) | Log (VOL) | Log (ORD.SZ) | INFO | AQS | SPEED | RR | VOLA | CBMA | I1 | PSGAMMA | | Pseudo $R^2$ | Prob > $\chi^2$ |
|---|---|---|---|---|---|---|---|---|---|---|---|---|---|---|
| | $\beta_1$ | $\beta_2$ | $\beta_3$ | $\beta_4$ | $\beta_5$ | $\beta_6$ | $\beta_7$ | $\beta_8$ | $\beta_9$ | $\beta_{10}$ | $\beta_{11}$ | | | |
| | 0.67% | -1.87 | 14.12 | 26.46 | 4.39 | -0.06 | -104.25 | 91.97 | -82.22 | 0.49 | -37041.59 | | 94.40% | 0.00 |
| (z-stat) | 1.06 | -2.14** | 7.05*** | 4.22*** | 0.68 | -4.36*** | -2.38** | 2.20** | -1.30 | 0.18 | -1.24 | | | |

Second Stage OLS Regressions of Conditional Average Effective Spreads

| | NYSE | EM | $\lambda_1$NYSE | Log(NUM. ORD) | INFO | 1/PRC | ORD.SZ /VOL | TURNOVER | MCAP. RANK | VOLA | $R^2$ |
|---|---|---|---|---|---|---|---|---|---|---|---|
| | $\alpha_4$ | $\alpha_2$ | $\alpha_3$ | $\alpha_5$ | $\alpha_6$ | $\alpha_7$ | $\alpha_8$ | $\alpha_{11}$ | $\alpha_{12}$ | $\alpha_{13}$ | |
| Model 1 | 10.71 | 7.29 | -0.31 | | | | | | | | 84.63% |
| (t-stat) | 63.32*** | 37.85*** | -0.30 | | | | | | | | |
| Model 2 | 6.63 | 4.50 | -0.47 | -0.35 | 70.36 | -28.56 | 6.04 | -55.27 | -0.15 | -4.82 | 96.18% |
| (t-stat) | 29.58*** | 19.37*** | -0.90 | -3.03*** | 31.45*** | -9.50*** | 6.88*** | -3.18*** | -5.41*** | -0.58 | |

Out of those new variables, the coefficients on *SPEED, RR, VOLA,* and *CBMA* are all significant at the 99% level, and *PSGAMMA* is significant at the 95% level. Interestingly, many of these same variables have shown little explanatory power in previous OLS regressions on effective spreads. One explanation is that these factors affect order routing decisions rather than execution costs directly.

Table 4 Panel B presents the second stage OLS regressions. When both $\lambda_1 NYSE$ and $\lambda_2 EM$ are added to the model in addition to the two dummy variables, the coefficient on $\lambda_1 NYSE$ is significant only at the 90% level, while the coefficient on $\lambda_2 EM$ is not significant. This could be because the two constructed variables are highly correlated. So we also include $\lambda_1 NYSE$ and $\lambda_2 EM$ separately in second and third model. $\lambda_1 NYSE$ becomes more significant, but $\lambda_2 EM$ is still not significant. In the fourth and fifth models, we include $\lambda_1 NYSE$ (the Probit factor) and other control variables. The Probit factor becomes insignificant. It is probably because that the constructed variable is closely linked to variables that are known to affect execution costs, therefore contain similar information. This is consistent with Bessembinder's (2003) finding that OLS regressions seem to do a good job at controlling for order difficulty, and selection models do not seem add incremental explanatory power.

To summarize results obtained so far, unconditional mean effective spread is higher for the NYSE than the Electronic Markets. Controlling for stock and order characteristics in multivariate OLS regressions decreases this difference, though the NYSE still has significantly higher conditional effective spread than the Electronic Markets. Selection models do not significantly change OLS regression results.

## 5. Difficulty Sub-Sample Analysis

Since the above analysis only examines the execution cost at the in-sample mean points, it is worthwhile to conduct analysis for the two markets at other difficulty levels. One might think that the impact of different dimensions of difficulty may change depending on the levels of difficulties. One might also expect that the selection effect could be stronger among more difficult orders. In order to do this, we calculate the fitted value based on our selected model $\alpha'X$ without intercept. These fitted values are estimates of order difficulty. We then sort our sample according to this order difficulty measure and split our sample to two sub-samples. The OLS analysis and selection model analysis are reproduced for each difficulty sub-sample.

Table 5 presents OLS results for the two difficulty sub-samples. Panel A is for the sub-sample of easy orders, while Panel B is for the sub-sample of difficult orders, according to our difficulty measure $\alpha'X$. We note some interesting results here: (1) More difficult orders show a greater cost decrease in mean effective spreads conditionally (after including various factors in the regression) versus unconditionally. The NYSE conditional mean effective spread dropped 38.41%, from unconditional mean of 10.70 cents to conditional mean of 6.59 cents. The Electronic Markets mean effective spread dropped a similar 38.00%, from unconditional mean of 7.29 cents to conditional mean of 4.52 cents. On the other hand, the conditional means of effective spreads for easy orders do not change as much. (2) For easy orders, the conditional effective spread difference on and off the NYSE is wider than the unconditional means'. It means that including demeaned explanatory variables increases divergence. This result is in contrast to the common conception that easier orders are more often sent to the Electronic Markets. (3) For difficult orders, the conditional effective spread difference on and off the NYSE is narrower, which confirms the NYSE's assertion that they receive more difficult orders. (4) For difficult order sub-sample, turnover has a negative correlation with the effective spread, meaning that high volume orders are charged with lower costs. However, for easy orders, the relationship between turnover and effective spread is significantly reversed. High volume easy orders get higher execution costs. (5) The $R^2$ increases more for the difficult order sub-sample, from unconditional model's 84.63% to the conditional model's 96.18%. The $R^2$ change in the easy order sub-sample is not as big: it increases from 82.74% to 90.84%.

Table 6 presents the Heckman (1979) two stage selection model, correcting for selection bias. Again, Panel A is for the sub-sample of easy orders, Panel B is for the difficult order sub-sample, according to our difficulty measure $\alpha'X$. The second stage OLS regression results are similar to the results of simple OLS regression results shown in Table 5. The coefficients of the Probit regression factor are not significant in both sub-samples.

## 6. What if the NYSE and the Electronic Markets Executed Each Other's Orders?

Like most other studies, our analysis so far has focused on the same model for orders executed both on the NYSE and the Electronic Markets. Implicitly, the underlying assumption is that the "definition" of order difficulty is the same across the two markets. Specifically, in the regression framework, orders executed on the two markets are "pooled" together as observations, and the regression coefficients on independent variables are constrained to be the same for the two markets, even though the intercepts were allowed to differ by using two dummy variables for the two markets. It might be reasonable to think that the same factors may have different impact on execution costs for different market mechanisms. One could interact the dummy variables with the independent variables to allow the coefficients to differ across the two markets, though this has not been done by previous studies, perhaps because this may make the model cumbersome.

We adopt a simple methodology: we model the two markets separately. This allows for maximum freedom to capture the differences across the two markets. This simple method also enables us to answer very interesting questions: what if the NYSE executed the Electronic Markets' orders? And what if the Electronic Markets executed the NYSE' orders? To answer the former question, after we estimate different models for the two markets, we then plug the observations from the Electronic Markets (using the Electronic Markets' independent variable values) into the estimated model for the NYSE (using the NYSE model coefficients). These fitted values ($\alpha_N + \beta_N'X_{EM}$) have a very nice interpretation: these are the expected effective spreads that the Electronic Markets' orders would have received, had they been executed on the NYSE. We can then compare these fitted effective spreads using the NYSE coefficients with the observed (realized) effective spreads of the Electronic Markets' orders.

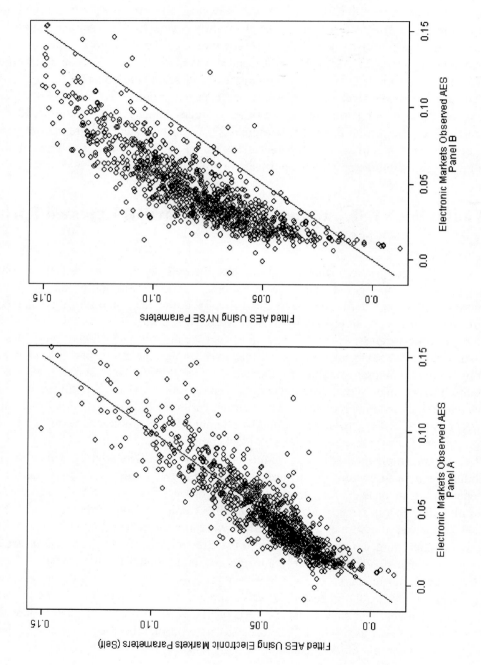

Figure 1. What If the NYSE Executed the Electronic Markets' Orders?

## Table 7. What If the NYSE and the Electronic Markets Executed Each Other's Orders?

This table presents results of the what-if analysis. Panel A reports observed AES and fitted AES for the Electronic Markets' orders, and fitted AES assuming these orders are executed according the NYSE's model parameters (and its difference from observed AES). Panel B reports observed AES and fitted AES for the NYSE' orders, and fitted AES assuming these orders are executed according the Electronic Markets' model parameters (and its difference from observed AES).

### Panel A. What If the NYSE Executed the Electronic Markets' (EM) Orders?

| Decile | EM Observed AES (1) | Fitted AES Using EM Parameters (Self) (2) | Fitted AES using NYSE Parameters (3) | Diff (3) – (1) | t-stat for Diff |
|---|---|---|---|---|---|
| 1 | 1.20 | 1.83 | 3.93 | 2.73 | 10.12*** |
| 2 | 2.24 | 2.68 | 5.45 | 3.21 | 23.78*** |
| 3 | 2.86 | 3.41 | 6.56 | 3.70 | 24.19*** |
| 4 | 3.37 | 3.82 | 7.23 | 3.86 | 30.88*** |
| 5 | 3.97 | 4.16 | 7.77 | 3.80 | 27.24*** |
| 6 | 4.61 | 4.69 | 8.36 | 3.75 | 26.94*** |
| 7 | 5.49 | 5.25 | 9.04 | 3.55 | 26.34*** |
| 8 | 6.43 | 6.13 | 10.18 | 3.76 | 24.96*** |
| 9 | 7.89 | 7.30 | 11.21 | 3.32 | 19.59*** |
| 10 | 11.73 | 10.52 | 14.28 | 2.55 | 10.77*** |
| All | 4.98 | 4.98 | 8.40 | 3.42 | 61.31*** |

## Table 7. Continued

### Panel B. What If the Electronic Markets (EM) Executed the NYSE's Orders?

| Decile | NYSE Observed AES (1) | Fitted AES Using NYSE Parameters (Self) (2) | Fitted AES using EM Parameters (3) | Diff (3) – (1) | t-stat for Diff |
|---|---|---|---|---|---|
| 1 | 1.82 | 1.98 | 1.77 | -0.05 | -0.74 |
| 2 | 2.89 | 3.54 | 2.82 | -0.07 | -1.12 |
| 3 | 3.90 | 4.69 | 3.76 | -0.14 | -0.58 |
| 4 | 4.78 | 5.23 | 4.20 | -0.58 | -3.56*** |
| 5 | 5.80 | 6.09 | 5.00 | -0.80 | -6.15*** |
| 6 | 7.12 | 7.31 | 6.07 | -1.05 | -10.54*** |
| 7 | 8.53 | 8.26 | 7.00 | -1.53 | -11.55*** |
| 8 | 10.32 | 9.97 | 8.66 | -1.66 | -11.59*** |
| 9 | 13.02 | 12.59 | 11.69 | -1.33 | -5.93*** |
| 10 | 18.32 | 16.85 | 16.18 | -2.14 | -6.44*** |
| All | 7.65 | 7.65 | 6.71 | -0.94 | -15.54*** |

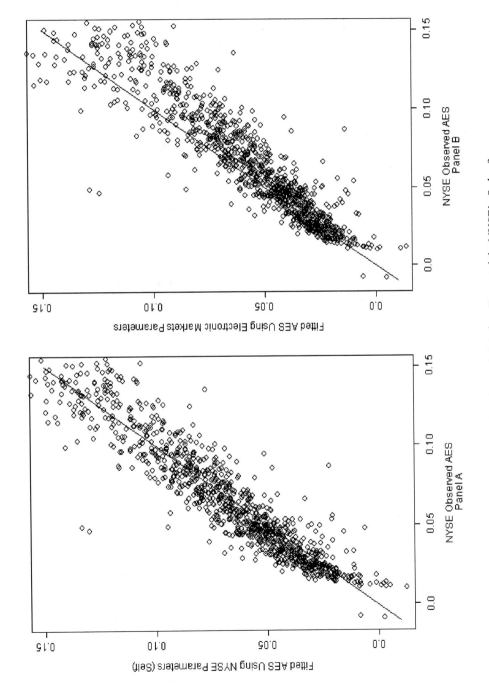

Figure 2. What If the Electronic Markets Executed the NYSE's Orders?

Figure 1 plots the Electronic Markets' observed effective spreads on the horizontal axis. Figure 1 Panel A plots fitted effective spreads using parameters of the model for the Electronic Markets on the vertical axis ($\alpha_{EM} + \beta_{EM}'X_{EM}$). The sample points should be scattered evenly around the 45 degree line, since this is using the Electronic Markets' "self" model. Figure 1 Panel A confirms this. Figure 1 Panel B plots fitted effective spreads using the NYSE model parameters ($\alpha_N + \beta_N'X_{EM}$) on the vertical axis. Figure 1 Panel B clearly shows that the NYSE executions would have been more costly for the Electronic Markets' orders, because most sample points are above the 45 degree line. These results are also presented in Table 7 Panel A. It first sorts the observed effective spreads of the Electronic Markets' orders into 10 deciles. We then calculate the fitted effective spreads using its "self" model, as well as using the NYSE model in each decile. Fitted effective spreads using the NYSE model parameters are significantly larger than the corresponding observed Electronic Markets effective spreads in all 10 deciles. These results confirm that if these the Electronic Markets' orders had been executed on the NYSE, they would have received higher execution costs.

Figure 2 and Table 7 Panel B present results for the "reverse test": what if the Electronic Markets executed the NYSE's orders. In Figure 2 Panel B, most sample points are below the 45 degree line, suggesting that the NYSE's orders would have received lower effective spreads, had they been executed by the Electronic Markets. Similarly in Table 7 Panel B, we see that the fitted effective spreads for the NYSE's orders using the Electronic Markets' model parameters are significantly lower than the observed NYSE effective spreads overall. They are also lower in each of the 10 deciles (statistically significant in 7 deciles). Overall, our what-if analysis in this section suggests that the Electronic Markets' (NYSE's) orders would have been worse (better) off, had they been executed by the NYSE (Electronic Markets).

# 7. Conclusion

In this paper, we conduct a thorough analysis comparing execution costs between the NYSE and the Electronic Markets, adopting a variety of techniques attempting to correct for the selection bias problem. Conventionally, the point comparison of execution costs is conducted at each market's own average, which is widely criticized because of the selection bias problem, i.e., the difficulties of the orders routed to the two markets could be different. Unlike current literature, we find that after controlling for the selection bias problem, the Electronic Markets still offer lower execution costs than the NYSE. We also carry out our analysis at different levels of order difficulty, measured by a vector of control variables, instead of just controlling for selection biases at sample mean level of order difficulty. Our results are robust under different model specifications. In addition, the results of our what-if analysis show that the Electronic Markets' (the NYSE's) orders would have been worse (better) off, had they been executed by the NYSE (Electronic Markets). Overall, our results highlight the superiority of the Electronic Markets' execution quality. In terms of a firm's exchange listing decision, our results are consistent with Chemmanur and Fulghieri's (2006) theoretical analysis: execution costs alone do not drive a firm's listing decision.

# Appendix: Sample Selection and List of Market Centers

### Table A1. Sample Selection

This table describes the selection of the final sample from all securities in the CRSP database. The filters are not mutually exclusive; therefore their ordering is important.

### General Filters

| | |
|---|---|
| All securities on 12/31/2002 | 2557 |
| + Single class | 2355 |
| + Ordinary common stock which need not be further defined | 1329 |
| + not "no price on 12/31/2002" | 1329 |
| + not "no SIC code on 12/31/2002" | 1328 |
| + no "missing daily price during 01/01/2001 and 12/31/2003" | 1218 |
| + no switch | 1204 |
| + mean daily trading volume >=$20,000 | 1192 |
| + no missing daily volume, any day during the fourth quarter of 2002 | 1192 |
| + no daily price during the fourth quarter of 2002<$3.00 | 1111 |
| + no change exchange | 1108 |
| Total symbols | 1116 |

### Further Modifications

| | |
|---|---|
| Top 10% of market capitalization on 2002/12/31 | 19 (out of 343) |
| Top 10% of average daily volume during the fourth quarter of 2002 | 18 (out of 135) |
| Top 10% of average daily dollar volume during the fourth quarter of 2002 | 8 (out of 135) |
| Total final symbols | 1146 |
| For dash 5 data | 1142 (no records for NMG, CCR, PZL, KM) |
| Exclude those without full year's data | 1138 (HI, MIR, PHA, UAL) |

### Table A2. List of Market Centers

This table lists market centers for the NYSE and electronic markets, respectively.

### Panel A. NYSE Specialist firms

| | |
|---|---|
| N0003 | WAGNER STOTT BEAR SPEC. |
| N0034 | LA BRANCHE CO. |
| N0041 | FLEET MEEHAN SPECIALIST |
| N0050 | SUSQUEHANNA SPECIALISTS |
| N0055 | SPEAR LEEDS AND KELLOGG |
| N0061 | VAN DER MOOLEN SPECIALISTS USA |
| N0070 | PERFORMANCE SPECIALIST GROUP LLC |
| N9999 | NYSE ITS |

## Table A2. Continued

### Panel B. Electronic (NASD) Market Centers

| | |
|---|---|
| SCHB | SCHB(US) SCHWAB CAPITAL MARKETS L.P. |
| TACT | TACT(US) AUTOMATED CONFIRMATION TRANSACTION SERVICE |
| TARCA | ARCA(US) ARCHIPELAGO SECURITIES L.L.C. |
| TAUTO | AUTO(US) AUTOMATED TRADING DESK FINANCIAL SERVICES, LLC |
| TBBNT | BBNT (US) SCOTT AND STRINGFELLOW INC. |
| TBRGE | BRGE (US) NEWBRIDGE SECURITIES CORPORATION |
| TBRUT | BRUT(US) BRUT, LLC |
| TCAES | CAES(US) COMPUTER ASSISTED EXECUTED SYSTEM |
| TDIRA | DIRA (US) DIRECT ACCESS BROKERAGE SERVICES |
| TFAHN | FAHN (US) OPPENHEIMER & CO. INC. |
| TFPKI | FPKI (US) FOX-PITT KELTON INC. |
| TFRGP | FRGP (US) FORGE FINANCIAL GROUP, INC. |
| TINET | INET(US) INET ATS, INC. |
| TISLD | ISLD(US) ISLAND CORPORATION |
| TJBOC | JBOC (US) NATIONAL CLEARING CORP. |
| TLQNT | LQNT(US) LIQUID NET INC. |
| TLYON | |
| TMADF | MADF(US) BERNARD L. MADOFF |
| TMAYF | MAYF(US) MAY FINANCIAL CORP |
| TMCBT | MCBT(US) MOORS AND CABOT INC. |
| TMONT | MONT(US) BANC OF AMERICA SECURITIES LLC |
| TNYFX | NYFX(US) NYFIX MILLENIUM, L.L.C. |
| TPRMX | PRMX(US) PRIMEX PRIME ELECTRONIC EXECUTION INC. |
| TSBSH | SBSH (US) CITIGROUP GLOBAL MARKETS INC. |
| TSOAR | |
| TSSBS | SSBS(US) STATE STREET GLOBAL MARKETS, LLC |
| TSWST | SWST(US) SOUTHWEST SECURITIES, INC. |
| TTDCM | TDCM(US) TD WATERHOUSE CAPITAL MARKETS, INC. |
| TTHRD | THRD(US) THE THIRD MARKET CORP. |
| TTRIM | TRIM(US) KNIGHT CAPITAL MARKETS, INC. |
| TUBSW | UBS SECURITIES LLC |
| TVFIN | VFIN (US) VFINANCE INVESTMENTS INC. |
| TWRHC | WRHC (US) WILLIAM R. HOUGH & CO. |
| WATHWATH | WATH(US) TD WATERHOUSE INVESTOR SERVICES, INC. |

# References

Amihud, Y., 2002, Illiquidity and stock returns: cross-section and time-series effects, *Journal of Financial Markets* **5,** 31-56.

Bessembinder, H., 2003, Selection Biases and cross-market trading cost comparisons, working paper.

Blume, M.E., and Goldstein, M.A., 1992, Displayed and effective spreads by market, *Rodney L. White Center for Financial Research* Working Paper 27-92, The Wharton School, December.

Boehmer, E., 2005, Dimensions of execution quality: Recent evidence for U.S. equity markets, *Journal of Financial Economics* **78**, 553-582.

Chemmanur, T. J., and Fulghieri, P., 2006, Competition and co-operation among exchanges: a theory of cross listing and endogenous listing standards, *Journal of Financial Economics* **82**, 455-489.

Christie, W., and Schultz, P., 1994, Why do Nasdaq market makers avoid odd-eighth quotes? *Journal of Finance* **49**, 1813-1840.

Chung, K., Van Ness, B., and Van Ness, R., 2001, Can the treatment of limit orders reconcile the differences in trading costs between NYSE and Nasdaq issues, *Journal of Financial and Quantitative Analysis* **36**, 267-286.

Davis, P.L., Pagano, M.S., and Schwartz, R.A., 2006, Life after the Big Board goes electronic, *Financial Analysts Journal* **62** (5), 14-20.

Goldstein, M., Shkilko, A., Van Ness, B., and Van Ness, R., 2008, Competition in the market for NASDAQ securities, *Journal of Financial Markets* **11** (2), 113-143.

Hasbrouck, J., 2006, Trading costs and returns for US equities: Estimating effective costs from daily data, *Journal of Finance* **64** (3), 1445 - 1477.

Heckman, J., 1979, Sample selection biases as a specification error, *Econometrica* **47**, 153-162.

Kalay, A., and Portniaguina, E., 2001, Swimming against the tides: the case of Aeroflex move from NYSE to Nasdaq, *Journal of Financial Markets* **4**, 261-267.

Lipson, M., 2005, *Competition among market centers*, working paper.

Maddala, G., 1983, *Limited dependent and qualitative variables in econometrics*, Cambridge University Press.

Nguyen, V., Van Ness, B., and Van Ness, R., 2005, Archipelago's move towards exchange status: An analysis of Archipelago trading in NYSE and Nasdaq stocks, *Journal of Economics and Business* **57**, 541-554.

Pagano, M.S., and Schwartz, R.A., 2003, A closing call's impact on market quality at Euronext Paris, *Journal of Financial Economics* **68**, 439-484.

Pastor, L., and Stambaugh, R.F., 2003, Liquidity risk and expected stock returns, *Journal of Political Economy* **111**, 642-685.

Petersen, M.A., and Fialkowski, D., 1994, Posted verses effective spreads: good prices or bad quotes?, *Journal of Financial Economics* **35**, 269-292.

Peterson, M., and Sirri, E., 2002, Order submission strategy and the curious case of marketable limit orders, *Journal of Financial and Quantitative Analysis* **37**, 221–241.

Pruitt, S., Van Ness, B., and Van Ness, R., 2002, The first of many? The microstructure effects of Aeroflex Corporation's move from the NYSE to the Nasdaq, *Journal of Applied Finance* **12**, 46-54.

SEC, 2001, Report on the comparison of order execution across equity market structures, U.S. Securities and Exchange Commission, Washington.

Van Ness, B., Van Ness, R., and Warr, R., 2005, Nasdaq trading and trading costs: 1993-2002, *Financial Review* **40**, 281-304.

In: Liquidity, Interest Rates and Banking
Editors: J. Morrey and A. Guyton, pp. 169-187
ISBN: 978-1-60692-775-5
© 2009 Nova Science Publishers, Inc.

*Chapter 8*

# PAYMENT SYSTEMS AND LIQUIDITY

## *Francisco J. Callado Muñoz[a] and Natalia Utrero González[b]*
University of Girona, Economics Department, Campus de Montilivi
17071 Girona (Spain)

### Abstract

The purpose of this paper is to investigate the links between the concept of liquidity and the role of payment systems in a globalized financial system. The actual characteristics of payment systems' design are analyzed, underlining their features and consequences for market and system liquidity. Then, literature on payment systems is reviewed stressing and deepening the understanding of liquidity in this context. Research results are critically analyzed in terms of their relevance for the study of liquidity in payment systems, and some lines of future work are proposed.

**Journal of Economic Literature classification**: G21, E51, E58.

**Keywords:** Payment Systems, Liquidity, Credit, Financial Crisis, Contagion.

## 1. Introduction

Liquidity can be defined as the ability to fund increases in assets and meet obligations as they come due (BIS (2000)). This is a very important issue not only at a bank level but also for the financial system as a whole. In fact, a good management of liquidity can help in reducing the possibility of meeting serious problems both by the financial system and individual banks. This importance is even greater with the increase in the internationalization and globalization of the economy and of financial markets.

---

[a] E-mail address: franciscojose.callado@udg.edu. Francisco J. Callado Muñoz acknowledges financial support from the Spanish Ministry of Education (SEJ2007-60671/ECON).
[b] E-mail address: natalia.utrero@udg.edu. Natalia Utrero González acknowledges financial support from the Spanish Ministry of Education (SEJ2007-62500 and SEJ2007-67895-C04-02).

Payment systems are part of the infrastructure that defines a financial system and are very related to the concept of liquidity. They are in charge of sending and receiving payments from the various actors in the economy. Therefore they play a crucial role in allowing economic agents to have sufficient funds to be able to meet their obligations at the right moment. The importance of payment systems have grown also in the last years as they have witnessed an important increase both in the volume and value of funds transferred through them. This growth has been fostered by various factors, such as financial innovation, technological improvements and financial markets' globalization as in the case of liquidity. Partly because of this increase in value, changes of the design or of the risk management policies of payment systems have been considered. In accordance with the importance and relevance of payment systems and within them, liquidity, financial authorities have increased their attention to the adequate design and functioning of existing settlement systems.

A major distinction between different interbank payment designs is whether a system is operating on a net or gross basis and whether payments are processed individually or in batches. The most common three pure implementations of these principles are real-time gross settlement, time-designated net settlement and continuous or secured net settlement. A pure real-time gross settlement (RTGS) system is defined as a system in which, for each transaction, delivery of payment information and final settlement in central bank money take place simultaneously and continuously. Transfers are settled individually during the day without netting debits against credits. An RTGS system provides continuous intraday finality for the processed transfers (BIS 1997). In a time-designated net settlement (TDNS) system, the settlement of payments occurs on a net basis at predefined points of time during the day or at the end of the day. The net position, i.e. the sum of payments the bank has received up to the end of the settlement period minus the payments it has sent, can either be calculated on a bilateral or multilateral basis. In continuous net settlement (CNS) systems, payments are credited individually and immediately to receivers' accounts, but final settlements occur periodically or at the end of the day. These systems entail settlement delay, and the amount of risk depends on the total or net value of delayed settlements. As it will be discussed, each kind has different implications and needs with respect to liquidity of individual participants and the system. Generally speaking, RTGS reduce the potential risk that the inability of an institution to meet its obligations affects the rest of participants. However, this systemic risk reduction has a cost: the increase in liquidity needs of banks to face each payment order. Besides these greater needs of participants, the system itself can also provide some mechanisms to help liquidity management. On the contrary, net systems (NS) require less liquidity since the bank should satisfy only the net debit position with the system at the end of the day. In return, they are more vulnerable to systemic risk given that there exists an automatic extension of credit among participants between the processing of the operation and its settlement.

The usual point of departure of comparisons between the different models of payments systems is the balance between the risk of the system and the cost of processing payments through it[1] (Rossi, (1998)). Hence, on one side, previous studies in this field focused mainly on the way in which the payment system design affects systemic risk and how this risk can be avoided or at least mitigated. On the other side, the stress is on the ability of payment system

---

[1] Part of these studies appear in the special number of the Journal of Money Credit and Banking (Vol-28, n° 4, Part 2), such as Greenspan (1996), Berger et al. (1996) etc.

design to reduce the cost of participants and to process in an efficient and rapid way payments orders. Liquidity is always part of this analysis as it is one of the elements that define the functioning and cost of a payment processing. In fact, the liquidity issue, and its costs, becomes even more relevant in financial crises.

The objective of this paper is precisely to investigate the links between the concept of liquidity and the role of payment systems in a globalized financial system. This task is carried out in two steps. First, the nowadays characteristics of payment systems' design and implementation are analyzed, underlining their features and consequences for market and system liquidity, both at times when the financial system works properly and in the event of a crisis. Second, literature on payment systems is critically reviewed stressing and deepening the understanding of liquidity in this context. In this vein, research results are analyzed in terms of their relevance for the study of liquidity in payment systems. Together with this review, some lines of future work are proposed.

The paper is organized as follows: section 2 presents the evolution of the design and implementation of payment systems and analyses these changes in terms of liquidity. Section 3 reviews literature on payment systems relating existing results to liquidity and suggesting lines of future work. Finally, section 4 offers some conclusions.

## 2. Payment System Characteristics and Liquidity

One of the objectives of the recent evolution in payment systems, both theoretical and technical, is the increase in efficiency. The ideal, or the efficiency standard, is the payment with currency (Greenspan, 1996). In this kind of transaction, real payment and at the moment, a legal obligation that origin payments rapidly disappear once the payment process begins. However, liquidity of participants in these payments should be total, having idle balances to face each payment order. When there is a time span between the payment initiation and its conclusion, with its settlement, risks arise in the operation (Berger, Hancock and Marquardt, 1996; Folkerts-Landau et al., 1996; Humphrey, 1997). Quite often, innovations in payment systems mean a movement or displacement in the risks between participants in the system (Greenspan, 1996). A reduction in time between the different operations involved in the process of a payment order, ceteris paribus, would reduce and maybe eliminate the system's risk and the greatest efficiency would be achieved. However, the reduction in this time gap usually means an increase in the cost of processing the payment, an increase that should be taken into account in the efficiency analysis (Greenspan, 1996). One of the main costs in this time reduction will be the liquidity of participants.

### 2.1. Initial Advances in Payment Systems

In the last years and as a consequence of the work carried out at the Bank of International Settlements (Lamfalussy Report, BIS, 1990; *"Core Principles for Systemically Important Payment Systems"*, BIS, 2001) several measures that aim at improving the risk-cost efficiency relationship in each system have been proposed. Usually, in the case of gross settlement systems, the goal is to achieve a reduction in the required level of reserves by means of the design and implementation of policies of intraday liquidity provision by the central bank[2]. This instrument has a positive effect on the functioning of the systems increasing the speed of payment processing, avoiding payment queues and reducing the complexity of liquidity management by participants. In the case of net systems, the improvements have tried to reduce the risk for the financial system.

Within the mechanisms that are nowadays used in existing payment systems two ways of providing liquidity can be distinguished. The first one corresponds to the model of the gross payment system of the Federal Reserve where participants have access to intraday liquidity through overdrafts on their accounts. The main problem with this mechanism is that credit risk, that gross systems usually eliminate, becomes an issue. In this case, it is the corresponding central bank, the one that guarantees intraday overdrafts, which therefore bears the credit risk. One tool used to limit and reduce this credit risk is the establishment of a price for these overdrafts. The goal of this price is to prevent participants from using extensively intraday credit, and therefore to achieve a reduction in their individual debt and the system debt itself. In fact, in 1994 the Federal Reserve established this tariff in the intraday overdrafts of the Fedwire system. The implementation of this tariff has brought about a reduction in the level of overdrafts from the very first moment, both in the average and in the maximum amount (Rochet and Tirole, 1996a; Hancock and Wilcox, 1996; Humphrey, 1997; Rossi, 1998). This decrease in intraday credit means that the tariff has made participants change and improve their liquidity management (Rochet and Tirole, 1996a; Hancock and Wilcox, 1996).

The second way of providing liquidity corresponds to the mechanism established by the European Central Bank (ECB) in the TARGET system. In this case, participants have access to intraday credit with no cost, but this overdraft has to be covered by adequate collateral. In this way credit risk, which appeared in the previous model, is eliminated. In fact, the use of collateral assets to guarantee credit operations is one of the most commonly used mechanisms not only in payment systems but also in monetary policy operations. This way of providing liquidity means a kind of limit to the credit (Rochet and Tirole, 1996a): since banks have a restricted amount of collateral assets in their balances and, then, they can not generate overdrafts unboundedly. Although in this kind of mechanism, intraday credit, that is liquidity, has no explicit cost, the pose of collateral means an implicit cost for participants. Some works have tried to estimate this cost in payment systems. Rochet and Tirole (1996a), consider this cost to be the opportunity cost of investing in this kind of asset and not in others that are less liquid but with a greater return. Rossi (1998) identifies the different components that could have this cost and estimates its amount. However, this calculation takes into account only the difference in return between eligible and non-eligible assets but leaves apart liquidity cost and the cost of not investing in the optimum portfolio. Other studies consider the cost of collateral as the difference in interest rates between collateralized and non-collateralized credit. (Humphrey, 1995; Folkerts-Landau et al., 1996). Again this kind of study does not include all the costs involved in these operations and substitutability of both credits is not straightforward. The calculation of this cost is interesting since in a sense it would be a measure of the cost of liquidity in payment systems. Future works could try to answer this question.

---

[2] For an analysis of the role of central bank money in payment systems and the importance of accession to intraday credit in recent settlement systems see CPSS (BIS, 2003).

A third mechanism has to do with the reduction in credit risk and is usually related to net systems: the establishment of limits to the credit participants extended during the day in the payment system. These credit limits can be bilateral, global or a combination of these two. Bilateral are those limits established between participants bis a bis. Global limits on the contrary are limits established for a participant in the whole system. As an example, in the EURO1, a high-value net payment system operated by the European Banking Association, limits are bilateral negotiated in a decentralized way and at the same time there is a global limit for each participant in the system. The Federal Reserve has also used these credit limits. Since 1986, banks were asked to establish a cap on their overdraft level. The way in which this mechanism has been implemented has evolved till the actual system with a limit on the credit extended in the Fedwire system.

Callado (2008) studies the use of credit limits and intraday credit with a cost in both net and gross systems. It is shown how a gross system with an intraday liquidity facility can improve its initial disadvantage with a net system in terms of liquidity cost: the access to intraday credit reduces the amount of reserves to be maintained by participants. In the case of net systems, although the use of credit limits does not eliminate systemic risk, it achieves a significant reduction maintaining at the same time part of the advantages in terms of cost to its participants. Contrary to previous results of Freixas and Parigi (1998), a gross system is not preferred to a net when liquidity demanded by economic agents is higher. This only happens when liquidity in the payment system increases. An interesting part of this work is the empirical analysis carried out. The main conclusion is that economies with an important cash use and a limited volume of payments seemed to be better off if they relied on net systems. With financial development and the introduction of electronic means of payment this initial preference would change and gross systems would be the model chosen.

Callado (2007) analyses the use of collateral in payment systems. Not only in gross systems, where it is usually used to back up intraday credit, but also in net systems where it has been introduced as an extra measure to reduce the consequences of credit risk. In fact both elements are nowadays present in existing gross (such as TARGET) and net (such as Euro1) payment systems. Results show that net systems will tend to be preferred to gross systems, the lower the failure probability, the lower the consequences of this failure, the greater the expected return on risky assets, the lower their variance and the greater the return on eligible assets. The paper includes a calibration of the model that provides some insights in the comparison of the two models. The preference for a gross system would be justified only if the level of risk aversion is relatively high. However, for lower risk aversion, private banks would have greater benefits using a net system as the main channel for payments. Then, financial authorities and central banks should create the adequate environment for commercial and private banks to have incentives to participate in a gross system and reduce systemic risk. In the end, liquidity, and the way in which it is provided to the system, plays a major role in giving some advantage to any of the two settlement models. The definition and implementation of the intraday credit facility is a key issue in guaranteeing the smooth and efficient functioning of a payment system.

An element that would be interesting to analyze in depth would be the consequences of a critical liquidity crisis in the functioning of these tools. If the financial system faced a great crisis, as the one fostered by the *subprimes*, the efficiency of some of these instruments could be affected. As a first move to this analysis we discuss some of the possible implications. As highlighted above, net systems rely on intraday credit given by participants. If banks did not trust one another, either there would be no credit in the system or the limits established by each participant would not be sufficient to adequately process payments. In the case of a gross system, if intraday credit is not collateralized and has a cost, the risk is borne by the corresponding financial authority. Although central banks are concerned with the sound functioning of the financial system, they could also reduce the limit each participant could have in the system. When collateral is present, as soon as participants have sufficient eligible assets to cover their liquidity needs, the system would not suffer from any delay and operations would be processed normally.

## 2.2. Latest Innovations

There are other references that introduce new changes and innovations in the field of payment system design and implementation. One part of these references deal with what has been called "hybrid" systems, that is, systems that try to include the best characteristics of each of the two models. The other presents and discusses a way of saving liquidity in the processing of payments: Liquidity Saving Mechanisms (LSM).

Beginning with the latter, a LSM can be defined as a way to attempt to reduce liquidity demand in RTGS systems, while maintaining the flexibility to make timely payments (Atalay, et al., 2008)[3]. There are many possibilities of designing a LSM but some features are common to all of them. A LSM is an alternative channel to send payments to the system. These payments enter a queue and are released only when some types of event occur (arrival of funds, offsetting payments of other bank etc.). Some papers have studied these mechanisms. Roberds (1999) introduces this third model (gross system with LSM) in the comparison. He focuses on the incentives participants have to engage in risk-taking behaviour in each of the different systems. Kahn and Roberds (2001) consider the benefits of coordination from an LSM in the case of Continuous Linked Settlement (foreign exchange payment system). Willison (2005) examines the conduct of participants in an LSM. Martin and McAndrews (2007) study two different designs for a LSM. Finally the work of Atalay et. al. (2008) is an interesting reference that centres the analysis in the economic consequences of these liquidity-saving mechanisms. It is a first attempt to quantify the possible welfare effects of alternative designs of large value payment system. Quite appealing is the distinction between the size of liquidity shocks a participant may face. If these shocks are not very large, a central planner chooses the same allocation with and without a LSM. However, Martin and McAndrews (2007) show that higher welfare can be achieved in equilibrium if a LSM is available. When liquidity shocks are large, the planner can improve welfare by making banks with a negative liquidity shock delay their payments. Some of these banks will receive a payment that will offset the liquidity shock and reduce their borrowing cost. The calibration for Fedwire data shows that the size of liquidity shocks are relatively small, suggesting that implementing a LSM would have important welfare benefits. Besides, this calibration helps to describe the change in the timing of settlement that could be expected from implementing an LSM.

The case of *hybrid* systems is mainly driven by the evolution of technology. As Martin (2005) claims, the evolution of payment systems can be seen as an attempt to achieve a better trade-off between liquidity and risk in a changing environment. One factor influencing this

---

[3] McAndrews and Trundle (2001) and BIS (2005) present and review descriptive material on LSMs.

trade-off, at any given time, is the level of technology. Greater computing power and faster processors have allowed payment systems to implement finer measures of risk control. Two types of "hybrid" systems have emerged. The first type has evolved from net settlement systems and aims to provide faster settlement, as "real-time" systems do. As in netting systems, payment participants send their payment messages to the settlement institution throughout the day without having to worry about securing intraday credit. An algorithm searches through the payment messages to see if some set of payments might offset each other. Once such a set of payments is found, they are settled. This type of design can greatly reduce the delay between the time a payment message is sent and the time is settled for large numbers of payments, so that many, or most, end up being settled very rapidly. Unwinding risk is thus substantially reduced while the system keeps most of the advantages of netting from a liquidity standpoint. An example of such a system is newCHIPS, the updated version of CHIPS (private US net system). The other type of system has evolved from RTGS systems. It tries to reduce the need for liquidity by creating a queue to which payments that have not yet been settled are sent. An algorithm searches the queue for offsetting payments. All payments are processed on a gross basis, but the need for intraday credit is reduced since many payments can offset each other at the time they are settled. An example of such a system is RTGSplus, the payment system currently used in Germany. This later example of hybrid systems resembles partly the LSM discussed above.

McAndrews and Trundle (2001) discuss the main changes related to these hybrid systems, the pros and cons of different designs and issues raised by its evolution. They suggest that there are many common elements in this kind of systems and that the combination of lower settlement risk with lower liquidity costs may be possible. However, there will be still a trade-off between those two different objectives. Leinonen and Soramäki (1999) quantify the relationship between liquidity usage and settlement delay in the three different models of settlement net, gross and hybrid systems. Their major findings relate to risk reduction via real-time settlement, to effects of optimization routines in hybrid systems, and to the effects of liquidity costs on banks' choice of settlement speed. A system where settlement takes place continuously in real-time and with queuing features is more efficient, from the perspective of liquidity and risks, than a net settlement system with batch processing.

Willison (2005) contrasts RTGS and hybrid payment systems that are based on payment offset, using a two-period, multi-bank model. The comparison is performed according to two criteria: liquidity needs and speed of settlement in order to capture the exposure of a system to exogenous operational risk. Hybrid payment systems are shown to outperform RTGS when payments are offset in the first period and when they are offset in both periods. This suggests that in a hybrid system, the offsetting facility should be in operation all day, or, at the very least, for some time after the system opens in the morning. A system in which the offsetting facility was only switched on late in the day would not necessarily be preferred to RTGS. These results are shown to be robust to changes in the transparency of the central queue of payments awaiting offset. However, this robustness may not hold with different forms of information asymmetry. Finally, Johnson, McAndrews and Soramäki (2004) propose an alternative way of settling payments submitted to the Fedwire Funds Service with the objective of reducing intraday credit extensions. This is a first examination of this kind of arrangements in the context of Fedwire. They present a novel mechanism: a receipt-reactive gross settlement system. This system bases the settlement of a bank's payments on the value of its receipts over a given time, rather than on the bank's balance. They conclude that this mechanism can clearly reduce intraday credit extensions and that the delay in the time of payment settlement would not be very important. At the same time, the mechanism also provides good incentives for banks to submit payments earlier in the day.

## 3. Literature Review

Traditional studies on payment system focus on two different aspects: there some descriptive[4] papers that make policy recommendations and others that are more formal works that recognise the influence of payment systems in the economic outcome. These latter papers are the starting point to understand relevant settlement features and the role of liquidity in financial markets.

Freeman (1996) presents a model in which consumers themselves issue their own currency to pay for their acquisitions. These notes are settled through the use of authorized money. In this scenario liquidity is one of the main issues if the system is to work properly. Freeman finds a parameterization in which central bank intervention could improve the economy welfare. This intervention should be conveyed through the purchase of notes from customers providing additional liquidity to the system. Green (1999), deepening the design presented by Freeman, obtained the same result but in this case the provision of liquidity to the system is achieved through the intervention of a private agent instead of the monetary authorities. Some other works have focused on the economic aspects of the agreements to carry out payments. McAndrews and Roberds (1995) model the risk of bank payments using the Diamond-Dybvig model of speculative bank runs[5]. They pay attention to the demand of reserves by banks. In fact, they consider a multilateral net system in which liquidation of payment orders is valid only if there is a transfer of reserves to the receiving bank. Again liquidity, in this case as the amount of reserves a bank holds, is present when analysing payment systems. Khan and Roberds (1995) study the role of limited information in the understanding of interbank clearing and settlement agreements that are observed in practice.

Market information is a key element in the existence and provision of liquidity. The same authors in a later work (Khan and Roberds (1996)) raised interesting aspects related to settlement risk in a framework of partial equilibrium. They stress the trade-off between risks and cost, in terms of interest rate, of maintaining reserves at the central bank. Rochet and Tirole (1996(b)) model interbank loans to study the issue of contagion, including for the first time systemic risk in the analysis and the "too big to fail" policy. They discuss the justification of this policy and the possible measures that could guarantee central bank solvency, while preserving liquidity in the interbank market.

Lacker (1997) analyses the cost of maintaining reserves and how this cost is affected by the characteristics of the central bank payment system. In a sense, the paper is relating the cost of liquidity (bank reserves) with the design of the payment system. Rochet and Tirole (1996(a)) study the externalities among the different payment systems distinguishing between complementary and substitute systems. Finally, Berger, Hancock and Marquardt (1996), present a framework based on the risk and cost trade-off that arises in payment systems.

---

[4] For references of this kind of works see Rossi (1998), preface.
[5] For some references on bank runs see Rochet and Tirole (1996(b)), note 3.

Within this framework they analyse the effects of three kinds of efficiency innovations: technologic financial or regulatory.

Although in almost every paper discussed above, liquidity is present either in the analysis or underlining the issues covered it is not deeply studied. The review of research results from the point of view of liquidity could be very interesting. This is so not only in normal times, but also in the event of financial or economic crisis that could increase, even more, the relevance of this kind of analysis.

Following Leinonen and Soramäki (1999) three categories of payment systems' current research can be distinguished: descriptions of current arrangements in different countries, analysis of the risks associated in these systems and central bank policy issues and finally, comparisons of different designs of settlement systems (mainly gross and net). Besides a new category is included to review recent papers that analyze payment systems and liquidity in the event of a financial crisis.

## 3.1. Description of Existing Systems

In this kind of studies, the goal is to describe the design of payment systems that are in use. In some cases, the attempt is to try to find a common structure and the key similarities and differences among these systems. The studies by Borio, Russo and Bergh (1992), the survey by the Committee on Payment and Settlement Systems (CPSS) on large-value funds transfer systems in the G10 countries (BIS 1990) and the report by CPSS on Real-time gross settlement (BIS 1997) are good examples. In this section other papers that analyze the system of a given country and have a stress on liquidity will be reviewed.

Schmitz and Puhr (2006) study the Austrian real time interbank system from the point of view of liquidity, risk concentration and network structure. Their results are very interesting with respect to the concept of liquidity at a system level and for individual participants. They show that, even in the case of sufficient aggregate liquidity in the payment system, individual accounts were sometimes illiquid. This unbalance usually ended up in payment delays. In a disaggregated analysis they note that liquidity usage was very heterogeneous across participants and that the three main banks concentrated the greater amount of payments both in value and number. These results are quite appealing in terms of the policy regarding liquidity. Financial authorities should be careful when analysing liquidity, not only in payment systems but also in the financial system as a whole. Conclusions drawn from aggregate liquidity data do not necessarily apply to individual banks. Then, although liquidity of the financial system can be sufficient, this could end up with individual participants having difficulties in processing their payments. The functioning of the financial system could be clearly affected. These consequences could be stronger in the event of a financial crisis when liquidity, and its management, becomes crucial to restore financial and economic markets.

Also related to liquidity is the work by Grąt-Osińska and Pawliszyn (2007) where they analyze the large volume payment system SORBNET run by the National Bank of Poland. They carry out this research with the payment system simulator BoF-PSS2 developed by the Bank of Finland. They try to determine what level of liquidity is necessary to carry out the settlement and what could be the impact of decreasing this level on the settlement delay. They take the opening balances on banks' current account kept at the central bank and compare them with liquidity needs along the day. They show that banks could maintain much lower levels of liquidity for the purpose of settlement in the payment system. This lower liquidity would not cause operational problems in the payment system and would not affect delay in payments settlement. The idea behind this work could be extended to other systems and could help in improving liquidity management. Carrying out this kind of simulations could allow participants to adjust their liquidity position in central bank money, and therefore improve the cost-efficiency of the corresponding system. However, to better examine this minimum amount of liquidity, simulations should be performed for longer periods of time (in this study they analyze data from April 2006). Given data availability and the advance in computer power, series length should be clearly extended.

Finally, Liu, Wei, Pan, Zhang, Chen (2008) empirically study liquidity in gross payment systems of China. As in the previous paper, the BoF-PSS2 simulator developed by Bank of Finland is used. The paper addresses the different issues related to liquidity: the relationship between reserve ratio and liquidity requirement of payment systems, the effects on liquidity needs and system efficiency when optimization algorithms are introduced in the system, and finally a new framework of managing liquidity risk in payment systems is proposed. Results show that increases in the reserve ratio could potentially increase liquidity pressure of participants in the system. Therefore, monetary policy instruments can affect operations in the payment system. Financial authorities should analyze the overall picture of the financial system when making decisions on liquidity. Finally, they underline that the introduction of optimization algorithms can help in reducing liquidity needs of participants and at the same time enhance system efficiency. These algorithms together with the new framework proposed revealed as effective ways to manage liquidity risk in payment systems[6].

## 3.2. Payment System Risk and Central Bank Policy

The common goal of this research has been on one hand to understand and provide good insights of risk in payments systems. On the other, they try to offer central banks the adequate methodology to be able to ensure the stability and smooth functioning of the payment system. BIS (1989), Borio and Van den Bergh (1993) and Angelini et al. (1996) are good examples of the attempt to shed some light on issues concerning systemic risk in payment systems. With respect to central bank policy, several papers focus on different aspects. Humphrey (1990), and Furfine and Stehm (1998) study intraday credit policy, Shoenmaker (1993) and Angelini (1998) analyze externalities of payment systems and Dale and Rossi (1996) relate them to monetary policy.

Again some references specially related to liquidity will be reviewed. Some studies focus on the role of intraday liquidity cost in the timing of transactions and participants' behavior in the system. Bech and Garratt (2003) analyze the effects of these costs on RTGS's participants. In their model an intraday overdraft fee encourages participants to non-cooperatively coordinate payments either early in the day, or late whenever the cost of this liquidity exceeds the social cost of payment delay. If intraday credit is free there exists an equilibrium concentration early in order to reduce the social cost of payment delay. Mills and Nesmith (2007) build up on the work by Bech and Garratt (2003). They relax the assumption of the existence of a social cost of payment delay and introduce a settlement shock. They

---

[6] Unfortunately this new framework cannot be better explained since the whole paper is only available in Chinese.

model the strategic interaction of participants in both payment and settlement systems to better understand the intraday patterns of settlement. The main innovation of the paper is the inclusion of settlement risk as a significant factor influencing the timing of transactions. Factoring settlement risk into participants' timing decisions implies that late-day coordination in RTGS payment systems may be optimal. If participants limit their risk exposure by delaying payments, the potential for contagion may be smaller ex post than might otherwise be the case. This conclusion is consistent with that of Angelini et al. (1996) for the Italian payment system. Besides, their model provides an interesting starting point for future policy analysis. Evaluation of different payment system arrangements with respect to settlement risk and how participants respond in times of stress are some of the issues that could be addressed. Introducing an emphasis on liquidity when analyzing these aspects of payment system design could be of great interest.

Other reference is the work by Lasaosa and Tudela (2008). Through simulation, this paper quantify by how much tiering affects, on the one hand, concentration and credit risk and on the other, liquidity needs of a payment system. In particular, it focuses on the large-value payment system in the United Kingdom (CHAPS), which is highly tiered: a few settlement banks make payments on behalf of many customer banks. Results show that concentration risk would rise substantially in a highly concentrated system. The likelihood of contagion of credit problems to the broader financial system would be remote in a more tiered system. More importantly, their analysis shows that the increase in credit risk brought to the system by settlement banks leaving CHAPS bears little relationship to the values settled by each individual bank. The key determining factor is the timing of intraday payments of second-tier banks, a variable that central banks do not observe directly. With respect to liquidity, they find that increasing the degree of tiering leads to substantial liquidity savings, although the liquidity saved is only a fraction of the spare liquidity currently posted in the system. Most of the savings are due to liquidity pooling rather than to internalization of payments. There is a strong relationship between changes in values settled and liquidity needs. This relationship can be used to forecast the impact on liquidity needs if more banks were to join the system.

Finally there is an interesting and very promising reference for future work, the paper by Koeppl, Monnet and Temzelides (2007). In their work, by means of a dynamic general equilibrium model, they try to provide a concise and integrated framework that can guide policymakers in the efficient design and implementation of a payment system. They present a modeling of the fundamental reasons why a payment system is necessary and a general welfare analysis. In this framework they conclude first, that efficient use of information requires that agents participating in transactions that do not involve monitoring frictions subsidize those that are subject to such frictions. The paper also suggests that the payment system should explore the trade-off between higher liquidity costs from settlement and the need to provide inter-temporal incentives.

### 3.3. Comparisons of Settlement Systems

Examples of comparison between different payment system arrangements are the following. Schoenmaker (1995) compare pure RTGS systems with net settlement systems with caps and loss sharing rules. Kahn and Roberds (1998) analyze net and gross systems in a framework of bank incentives and moral hazard problems. Kobayakawa (1997) probes whether there is a rationale for gross and net settlement systems to coexist in the same economy.

When comparing RTGS and NS an interesting reference is the work of Freixas and Parigi (1998). They study the trade-off between the two ways of clearing and settlement payment orders. They carry out this task in general equilibrium model based on Diamond and Dybvig (1983) where uncertainty arises from several sources: the time of consumption, the location of consumption, and the return on investment. Payments across locations can be made either by directly transferring liquidity or by transferring claims against the bank in the other location. The results obtained are coherent with the intuition: gross systems do not face the risk of contagion but liquidity needs are greater. Net systems economize on liquidity but expose participants to contagion and systemic risk. Besides they relate liquidity of the financial system with the preference for one of the two models. A gross system would be preferred to a net the greater the liquidity demanded by economic agents. Although interesting, this work analyses gross and net systems in their simplest way. Callado (2007) and (2008) builds up on this work including intraday credit policies and risk control measures. Willison (2004) compares Real-Time Gross Settlement and hybrid payment systems. These last four are reviewed in previous sections. One more reference will be discussed here.

Galos and Soramäki (2005) compare two net settlement arrangements (unsecured and secured) for payments currently settled in TARGET. An unsecured multilateral end-of-day netting does not have any risk controls and payments to and from the failing participant are simply unwound in case of a participant failure. Secured net settlement systems have rules that aim at guaranteeing the settlement of all payments also in the case where one or more participants are unable to deliver their multilateral net dues to the settlement institution. These include limits on intraday credit, collateralization of intraday positions and loss sharing. Results indicate that systemic consequences of a particular type of systemic event, a sudden and unexpected failure of a bank where contagion is contained to the payment system, can be rather low. As regards unsecured netting, the failure of the vast majority of banks did not cause any systemic consequences. If risk management techniques such as legal certainty for multilateral netting, limits on exposures, collateralization of exposures and loss-sharing rules are introduced, such systemic consequences can be mitigated to a high degree. These results are in line with previous evidence: Angelini et al. (1996) for the Italian interbank payment system and Bech et al. (2002) for the Danish one. However some caveats in the interpretation and limitations for the applicability of the results should be kept in mind. These include better measures for bank liquidity, a wider scope by extending analysis to incorporate other sources of systemic risk to the model, and, as in Grąt-Osińska and Pawliszyn (2007), longer time period of analysis to capture rare but high exposures that might manifest under abnormal market situations.

## 3.4. Financial Crisis and Contagion

In this section, some papers that study payment systems and liquidity in the case of stress situations are reviewed. Leitner (2005) deals with the consequences of contagion. The paper shows that a network in which agents are closely interlinked may be optimal both because of and despite the potential for contagion. Further, the paper tries to characterize optimal networks, that is, whether and how agents should be linked to one another. Contrary to previous research papers on the matter (Allen and Gale, 2000; Kiyotaki and Moore, 1997; Lagunoff and Schreft, 2001; and Rochet and Tirole, 1996b) it includes the threat of contagion as part of an optimal network design. This idea can be applied, for example, to the design of payment systems. Net systems induce linkages that create the threat of contagion. This, in turn, can motivate banks to help one another, even in cases in which they could not pre-commit to do so. Besides, it analyzes the role of central bank authorities in private banks' bailouts. Again, contrary to existing literature, bailouts are optimal even from an ex ante point of view. The crucial assumption is the availability of some coordinating device when the threat of contagion arises. The main weakness of the paper is that it ignores other issues that may be important in optimal network design, such as moral hazard, coordination and free-riding problems. However, conclusions from this work are quite appealing. Net systems could have good properties in the case of financial crisis. Given their lower liquidity needs some of the comparisons made with gross systems could be revisited and reinterpreted to better understand the real trade-offs between them.

Bech and Garratt (2006) investigate how a wide-scale disruption is likely to impair the smooth functioning of the interbank payment system. Such a disruption will almost by definition create operational difficulties for the system and its participants in some way or another. However, they address a problem that is perhaps less obvious: the operational difficulties of some participants may induce other participants to change behavior in terms of how they process payments. In particular, this may lead to a break down of coordination. The paper argues that the ability of banks (in Fedwire) to maintain payment coordination following a wide-scale disruption depends critically on a number of different factors. First of all, it depends on the size of the disruption. A disruption that affects a large part of the nation or a disruption that hits a key geographical area is more likely to result in the break down of payment coordination, as more banks will experience operational difficulties. Secondly, it also depends on the relative cost of liquidity and the cost of postponing payments. The cheaper liquidity, the more likely banks will be to maintain coordination by themselves. Thirdly, they argue that banking structure can influence the smooth functioning of the payment system after a wide-scale disruption and that a bank can be considered too big to fail in a new interesting way. The resiliency of a large bank could be important not only in terms of its share of payment flow but also in terms of this bank being pivotal in maintaining coordination. Fourthly, they show that Central Banks can play a critical role in avoiding coordination failures by advocating patience to large banks and encouraging them to continue with timely processing of payments following a disruption to small banks. If large banks can be persuaded to wait for small banks to resume timely processing following a disruption, then more drastic measures, such as reducing the liquidity costs, might not be required to restore coordination. This is an instance where moral suasion can be effective. These results are relevant since they analyze what factors are behind or could potentially foster a systemic failure in the payment system and, as a result, in the financial system. The availability of liquidity is one of these factors and could help in reducing the probability of this event. There are other interesting features not covered in the paper but that could improve the understanding of these coordination's mechanisms. These are the time of the day in which the disruption occurs and how long it persists. These could be good directions for future research on the matter.

Beyeler, Glass, Bech and Soramäki (2006) deal directly with the issue of liquidity. Payment system participants have an economic incentive to minimize funds committed to payment processing because liquidity used for settling payments imposes an opportunity cost on banks. Underfunding can also be costly, especially for bank customers and other banks in the system. Shortfalls of funds can delay a bank's payment processing, and payment systems can even enter gridlock states in which no bank can process a payment. Delayed payments are unavailable to intended recipients: in this way congestion in the payment system can propagate into the economy by restricting money flow among banks, and eventually among their customers. In this paper, they develop a parsimonious model of the interbank payment system to study congestion and the role of liquidity markets in alleviating congestion. In particular, the model tries to explain how congestion is influenced by two control parameters: the global liquidity level and the conductance of a global liquidity market. The model includes an endogenous instruction arrival process, a scale-free topology of payments between banks, a fixed total liquidity used by banks to process arriving instructions, the ability of banks to build and work off queues of instructions they cannot process, and a global market that distributes liquidity among the banks. Banks will not queue, and the system will not become congested, provided banks can respond by either drawing down reserves, or obtaining adequate liquidity from the market. Results suggest that the system can remain uncongested if the time constant for banks to return to a net position of 0 is small compared to the time to exhaust reserves, or large compared to the time to redistribute liquidity through the market. They also find that a global liquidity market, a feature of many modern payment systems, can effectively compensate for the imbalances created by the payment instructions received by banks. The market can substantially attenuate congestion, and only a small fraction of the payment-induced liquidity flow is required to achieve strong beneficial effects.

In the same vein, Bech and Soramäki (2005) analyze the importance and consequences of gridlocks in interbank payment systems and present and evaluate an algorithm to solve this kind of situations. The analysis is carried out for a RTGS system both in normal operating conditions and in the case of stress in the system. Using data from the Danish and Finnish systems they found that the algorithm effectively reduces queuing in the systems at all levels of liquidity, but in particular when intraday liquidity is scarce. It can also alleviate settlement delays caused by the failure of a bank to participate in settlement. Together with this work there are some other references that use simulations to study liquidity and risk in payment systems in Leinonen (2005). Pettersson (2005) discusses efficiency issues of the Swedish payment system. Liquidity needs could be reduced and capacity improved with some changes in the design and throughput rules of the system. McAndrews and Wasilyew (2005) study the performance of payment systems after the failure of one participant in the system. They conclude that the non-execution risk of payment order depends on the number of participants in the settlement system, the variance of the size of payments entered into the system, and the likelihood of interaction among banks in the system. Bedford, Millard and Yang (2005) analyze the consequences of operational incidents in payment systems. They proposed a methodology to study these incidents and apply it to the case of CHAPS. They conclude that the risk of disruption in the system caused by an operational failure is low. This is so because of the contingency arrangements of the system and the level of liquidity. Mazars and Woelfel (2005) carry out a similar analysis for the Paris Net Settlement (PNS). They show that the technical default of a participant in this system has negative consequences on the smooth running of the system. The fact that a major participant is unable to send payment orders could mean congestion in the system and almost 10% of payments rejected. These consequences could be more benign if bilateral limits would be lower and the reaction to the first notice of a technical default was quicker.

# 4. Conclusion

In this paper, payment system literature with an emphasis on liquidity is reviewed. The current characteristics of payment systems' design are satisfactorily covered in the existing literature. Both the first versions of gross and net systems and the consequent improvements have been widely studied and liquidity is an important issue in these analyses. From the initial liquidity advantage of net systems over gross, to the improvement in the latter due to the use of intraday credit facilities, liquidity is the main aspect in the comparison. However, an element that would be interesting to analyze in depth would be the consequences of a financial shock in the different designs of payment systems. If the financial system faced a great crisis, as the one fostered by the *subprimes*, the risk-cost analysis could be affected.

Apart from these initial advances on the design of payment systems, two innovations arose in the last years: *Hybrid* systems and LSM. Reviewing the existing references, the conclusion is that both elements imply liquidity savings and improvements in payment processing. RTGS with some kind of *hybrid* arrangements are shown to be highly efficient. Risk control measures in net systems clearly reduce contagion risk and improve upon purely net designs. In order to complete this kind of study, some elements should be taken into account. These include better measures for bank liquidity, a wider scope, to incorporate other sources of systemic risk, and longer time periods of analysis to capture rare but high exposures that might manifest under abnormal market situations.

The analysis of risks associated with payment systems and central bank policy has mainly focused on the role of central bank monetary policy in providing sufficient liquidity. Temporary increases of this liquidity can improve the functioning of payment systems, especially in stress situations. The timing of payments is also an area of concern. The cost of intraday liquidity and settlement risk can shape participants' behavior with respect to their payment orders. These two factors could foster coordination by banks, ending up with liquidity savings. In the same vein, the degree of concentration of a payment system could increase both liquidity needs and the risk of contagion. A more tiered system would improve those two factors. Finally, a very promising reference presents a dynamic model of payment systems. It could serve as a basic framework to deeply analyze the design and implementation of payment systems, including all the economic aspects involved.

Finally, papers devoted to financial crises and their effects on the payment systems are also reviewed. They provide some clues to help to improve the response of the system to these situations and liquidity needs of participants. The existence of a private liquidity market is one of those measures. Besides, the introduction of some procedures to coordinate payments could potentially reduce liquidity and the possibility of a gridlock. In the end, the ability of central banks to maintain payment coordination and reduce the spread of a failure depends on certain factors: the size of the initial disruption, the relative cost of liquidity, banking structure and the forbearance of large banks to continue to process payments normally. Finally, there is a reference that offers some conclusions that are quite appealing. Net systems could have good properties in the case of financial crisis. Given their lower liquidity needs, some of the comparisons made with gross systems could be revisited and reinterpreted to better understand the real trade-offs between them.

To sum up, the analysis of existing literature reveals that one of the key elements in the smooth and efficient functioning of payment systems is liquidity. In net systems the receivers of a payment extend automatically intraday credit to the sending institution and liquidity needs are fundamentally lower. However, credit risk concern, mainly of financial authorities, has limited the amount of credit of any participant. The adoption of RTGS has resulted from risk concerns. However, in gross systems the provision of intraday liquidity is crucial to the successful operation of the system. The design of the intraday credit facilities is very important for the smoothness of settlement systems in order to ease payment processing, to improve risk controls by central banks, as well as, to incorporate technology innovations that could help the system to be more efficient, in particular in times of stress.

# References

Allen, F. & Gale D. (2000). Financial contagion. *Journal of Political Economy*. **108**, 1-33.

Angelini, P. (1998) An analysis of competitive externalities in gross settlement systems, *Journal of Banking and Finance*, **22**, 1-18.

Angelini, P., Maresca, G. & Russo, D., (1996). Systemic risk in the netting system, *Journal of Banking & Finance*, vol. 20(5), 853-868,

Atalay, E.; Martin, A. & McAndrews, J. (2008). "The Welfare Effects of a Liquidity-Saving Mechanism" Federal Reserve Bank of New York Staff Reports, no. 331

Bech, M. L., Madsen, B., & Natorp, L. (2002). *Systemic Risk in the Danish Interbank Netting System*. Danmarks Nationalbank Working Papers. 2002, 8.

Bech, M. L. & Garratt R. (2003). The intraday liquidity management game. *Journal of Economic Theory*. 109, 2, 198-219.

Bech, M. L. & Garratt R. (2006). *Illiquidity in the Interbank Payment System following Wide-Scale Disruptions*. Federal Reserve Bank of New Cork, Staff Report no. 239

Bedford, P., Millard, S. & Yang, J. (2005) Analysing the impact of operational incidents in large-value payment systems: a simulation approach. In Harry Leinonen, *Liquidity Risks and Speed in Payment and Settlement Systems, a simulation approach* (247-274). Helsinki, Bank of Finland.

Beyeler, W. E., Glass, R. J., Bech, M. L. & Soramaki, K. (2006). *Congestion and cascades in payment systems*. Staff Reports 259, Federal Reserve Bank of New York.

Bech, M. L. & Soramäki, K. (2005) Gridlock resolution and bank failures in interbank payment systems. In Harry Leinonen, *Liquidity Risks and Speed in Payment and Settlement Systems*, a simulation approach (149-176). Helsinki, Bank of Finland.

Berger, A.N., Hancock, D. & Marquardt, J.C. (1996). A framework for analyzing efficiency, risks, costs and innovations in the payment system. *Journal of Money, Credit, and Banking*. Vol-28, nº 4, Part 2, 696-732.

BIS (1989). *Report on Netting Schemes* (Angell report). CPSS.

BIS. (1990). Report of the Committee on interbank *Netting Schemes of the central banks of the Group of Ten countries (Lamfalussy Report)*. CPSS, report 4.

BIS (1997). *Real-time gross settlement systems*. CPSS report 22.

BIS (2000). *Sound Practices for Managing Liquidity in Banking Organizations*. Basel Committee on Banking Supervision.
BIS, CPSS. (2001). *Core Principles for Systemically Important Payment Systems*. BIS, CPSS num. 43.
BIS (2003). *The Role of Central Bank Money in Payment Systems*. CPSS report 55.
BIS (2005). New developments in large-value payment systems. CPSS report 67.
Borio, C., Russo, D. & Van den Bergh, P. (1992). Payment System Arrangements and Related Policy Issues: A Cross Country Comparison. *Papers on Monetary Policy and Financial Systems* 13, Société Universitaire Européenne de Recherches Financiéres, Tilburg.
Borio and Van den Bergh (1993). The nature and management of payment system risks: An international perspective. *Economic Papers* 36. BIS.
Callado, F.J. (2007). The use of Collateral in Gross and Net payment systems, *European Journal of Finance*, 13 (5-6), 459-481 (2007).
Callado F.J. (2008). Risk Control Measures in Payment Systems. *The Quarterly Review of Economics and Finance*, forthcoming.
Dale, S. & Rossi, M. (1996). *A Market for Intraday Funds: Does it have Implications for Monetary Policy?* Bank of England.
Diamond, D.W. & Dybvig, P.H. (1983). Bank runs, deposit insurance, and liquidity. *Journal of Political Economy*. 91, 3, 401-419.
Folkers-Landau, D., Garber, P. & Schoenmaker, D. (1996). The reform of wholesale payment systems and its impact on financial markets. *Group of Thirty Occasional Paper* 51, Washington D.C.
Freeman, S. (1996). The Payments System, Liquidity, and Rediscounting, *American Economic Review*, 86, 5, 1126-1138.
Freixas, X. & Parigi, B.M. (1998). Contagion and Efficiency in Gross and Net Systems. *Journal of Financial Intermediation*. 7, 3-31.
Furfine, C.H. & Stehm J. (1998). Analyzing Alternative Intraday Credit Policies in Real-Time Gross Settlements Systems. *Journal of Money, Credit, and Banking*. 30, 4, 832-848.
Galos, P. & Soramäki, K. (2005). Systemic risk in alternative payment system designs. European Central Bank WP 508.
Grąt-Osińska, A. & Pawliszyn, M. (2007). *Liquidity Levels and Settlement Delays in the SORBNET System – Simulation-based Approach with the Application of the BoF-PSS2 Payment System Simulator*. Bank I Credit. 53-66.
Green E. J. (1999). Money and debt in the structure of payments. *Quarterly Review*, Federal Reserve Bank of Minneapolis. Spring, 13-29
Greenspan A. (1996). Remarks on evolving payment system issues. *Journal of Money, Credit, and Banking*. 28, 4, Part 2, 689,695.
Hancock, D. & Wilcox, J.A. (1996). Intraday management of bank reserves: The effects of caps and fees on daylight overdrafts. *Journal of Money, Credit, and Banking*. 28, 4, Part 2.
Humphrey, D.B. (1990). Pricing intraday overdrafts. In: Haraf, E.S. & Cagan, P. (eds). *Monetary Policy for a Changing Financial Environment* (108-131), AIE Press, Lanham.
Humphrey, D.B. (1995). Payment systems: Principles, practice, and improvements. *Banco Internacional de Reconstrucción y Fomento*. World Bank Technical Papers, 260.

Humphrey, D.B. (1997). Advances in financial market clearing and settlement. The 1987 Crash, Ten Years Later: Evaluating the Health of the Financial Markets. *Brookings-Wharton Papers on Financial Services, First Annual Conference*, Oct-29-30.

Johnson, K., McAndrews, J.J. & Soramäki, K. (2004). Economizing on liquidity with deferred settlement mechanisms," *Economic Policy Review*, Federal Reserve Bank of New York. December, 51-72.

Kahn, C.M. y Roberds, W. (1995). On the efficiency of cash settlement. *Federal Reserve Bank of Atlanta. Working paper,* 95-11.

Kahn, C.M. y Roberds, W. (1996). On the role of bank coalitions in the provisions of liquidity. Federal Reserve Bank of Atlanta. *Working paper*, 96-11.

Kahn, C.M. & Roberds, W. (1998). Payment System Settlement and Bank Incentives. *Review of Financial Studies*. **11**, 4, 845-70.

Kahn, C.M. & Roberds, W., (2001). The CLS bank: a solution to the risks of international payments settlement? *Carnegie-Rochester Conference Series on Public Policy*, Elsevier, 54(1), 191-226.

Kiyotaki, N. & Moore, J. (1997). *Credit chains. Working paper*, University of Minnesota and London School of Economics.

Kobaykawa, S. (1997). The comparative analysis of settlement systems. Centre for Economic Policy Research. *Discussion Paper* nº **1667**.

Koeppl, T. V., Monnet, C. & Temzelides, T. (2007*). A Dynamic Model of the Payment System*. FRB of Philadelphia, Working Paper 07-22.

Lacker, J.M. (1997). Clearing settlement and monetary policy. *The Journal of Monetary Economics*. **40**, 347-381.

Lagunoff, R. & Schreft, S. L. (2001). A model of financial fragility. *Journal of Economic Theory*. **99**, 220-264.

Lasaosa, A. & Tudela, M. (2008). *Risks and efficiency gains of a tiered structure in large-value payments: a simulation approach*. Bank of England WP 337.

Leinonen H. & Soramäki, K. 1999. Optimizing Liquidity Usage and Settlement Speed in Payment Systems. *Bank of Finland Discussion Papers* 16/99

Leinonen, H. (2005). *Liquidity Risks and Speed in Payment and Settlement Systems, a simulation approach*. Helsinki, Bank of Finland.

Leitner, Y. (2005). Financial networks: contagion, commitment, and private sector bailouts. *The Journal of Finance*. **LX**, 6, 2925-2953.

Liu, C., Wei, X., Pan, S., Zhang, M. & Chen, M. (2008). *Liquidity Risk in the Payment Systems of China*. SSRN: http://ssrn.com/abstract=1105336

Martin, A. (2005). *Recent Evolution of Large-Value Payment Systems: Balancing Liquidity and Risk* Federal Reserve Bank Of Kansas City Economic Review, first quarter, 33-57.

Martin, A. & McAndrews, J. (2007). *Liquidity- Saving Mechanisms*. Federal Reserve Bank of New York. Staff report 282.

McAndrews, J., & Roberds, W. (1995). Banks, payments and coordination, *Journal of Financial Intermediation*, vol. 4, 305–327.

McAndrews, J. & Trundle, J. (2001). New Payment System Designs: Causes and Consequences. *Financial Stability Review*, Bank of England, December, 127-36.

McAndrews, J. J. & Wasilyew, G. (2005). Simulations of failure in a payment system. In Harry Leinonen, *Liquidity Risks and Speed in Payment and Settlement Systems, a simulation approach* (227-246). Helsinki, Bank of Finland.

Mazars, E: & Woelfel, G. (2005). Analysis, by simulation, of the impact of a technical default of a payment system participant. In Harry Leinonen, *Liquidity Risks and Speed in Payment and Settlement Systems,* a simulation approach (297-320). Helsinki, Bank of Finland.

Mills, D. C. & Nesmith, T. D. 2007. Risk and Concentration in Payment and Securities Settlement Systems. *Journal of Monetary Economics.* Forthcoming.

Pettersson, J. (2005). Simulation of liquidity levels and delays in the Swedish RIX systems. In Harry Leinonen, *Liquidity Risks and Speed in Payment and Settlement Systems, a simulation approach* (217-226). Helsinki, Bank of Finland.

Roberds, W. (1999). The Incentive Effect of Settlement Systems: A Comparison of Gross Settlement, Net Settlement, and Gross Settlement with Queuing. *IMES Discussion Paper Series,* **99-E-25**, Bank of Japan.

Rochet, J.C. & Tirole, J. (1996a). Controlling risks in payment systems. *Journal of Money, Credit, and Banking.* **28**, 4, Part 2, 832-862.

Rochet, J.C. & Tirole, J. (1996b). Interbank lending and systemic risk. *Journal of Money, Credit, and Banking.* **28**, 4, Part 2, 733-762.

Rossi, M. (1998). *Payment systems in the Financial Markets: real-time gross settlement systems and the provision of intraday liquidity.* London, Macmillan.

Schmitz, S. W. & Puhr, C. (2006). Liquidity, risk concentration and network structure in the Austrian large value payment system. *Working paper series.*

Shoenmaker, D. (1993). Externalities in payment systems: Issues for Europe. *London School of Economics Financial Markets Group Discussion Paper* n. **211**.

Shoenmaker, D. (1995) A comparison of alternative interbank settlement systems, *London School of Economics Financial Markets Group Discussion Paper* n. **204**.

Willison, M. (2005). *Real-Time Gross Settlement and hybrid payment systems: a comparison,* Bank of England WP 252.

In: Liquidity, Interest Rates and Banking
Editors: J. Morrey and A. Guyton, pp. 189-212

ISBN: 978-1-60692-775-5
© 2009 Nova Science Publishers, Inc.

*Chapter 9*

# OPTIMAL PLANNING, SCHEDULING AND BUDGETING WITH ENTERPRISE-WIDE INTEGRATION PRESERVING LIQUIDITY

*Mariana Badell*
Universitat Politècnica de Catalunya, Barcelona, Spain

## Abstract

In industry the concept behind progress in enterprise systems is the optimization of financial decisions considering the enterprise functionality integration as a cohesive entity including supply chain management and corporate financial management. Acquiescent that every supply chain has a value added chain in parallel (Shapiro 2001), then a value added chain can be seen as the value view of the supply chain. Here we analyze enterprise logics, the value added chain, problems and efforts to improve performance preserving liquidity throughout several modelling / simulation frameworks capable to uphold – with flexibility, simplicity and friendly approach – enterprise-wide financial cross-functional co-ordination links with optimal cash flow management and liquidity control. The results obtainable could reach the optimality of financial and production operations besides the optimal plan, budget and decision making. Integrated solutions models also permit fixed asset investment analysis in an altogether scenario of management. Here we show how different are the investment solutions when transactional objective functions are compared with others that cover the whole functionality as maximum corporate value. In industry the concept behind progress in enterprise systems is the optimization of financial decisions considering the enterprise functionality integration as a cohesive entity (Reklaitis 2005) including supply chain management (Varma et al. 2007) and corporate financial management (Badell et al. 2004). Acquiescent that every supply chain has a value added chain in parallel (Shapiro 2001), then a value added chain can be seen as the value view of the supply chain. Here we analyze enterprise logics, problems and efforts to improve performance preserving liquidity throughout several modeling/simulation frameworks capable to uphold – with flexibility, simplicity and friendly approach – enterprise-wide financial cross-functional co-ordination links with optimal cash flow management and liquidity control. The results obtainable could reach the optimality of financial and production operations besides the optimal plan, budget and decision making. Integrated solutions models also permit fixed asset investment analysis in an altogether scenario of management. Here we show how different are the investment solutions when transactional objective functions are compared with others that cover the whole functionality as maximum corporate value.

**Keywords**: liquidity control, supply chain, optimization, scheduling, budgeting

# 1. Introduction

One of the challenges for the new millennium in the chemical industry are the development of new products to achieve value growth, the optimization of the supply chain (SC) to achieve value preservation, and the improvement of the global life cycle to maintain living viability. The overall integration of all the SC decision-making levels through optimized financial links considering firm's liquidity aspects should be the main concept in order to achieve enterprise systems improvements, efficiency and viability.

Among priorities is essential the optimal use of intellectual intangible assets to create a knowledge society. Wealth and growth in today's economy are mainly motivated by deployment of intangible intellectual assets. The admirable rise in value and impact of intangibles continuously creates stem changes in IT covering communication and computing area. Up till now enterprises don't have appropriate services of commercial software or analytic modeling tools neither absolutely defined the theory to provide reliable answers for optimal decision making on so dissimilar enterprise areas as treasury, production or service. The majority of finance software applications are based on commercial off-the-shelf packages that analyze each financial item individually. Consequently the financial tools available today don't take into account the set of interacting logics that every company has in its attempt to obtain the benefit accredited to its virtual value-added chain. It is dangerous not been aware that the available enterprise tools, as ERP, are limited to transactional logic, not capturing intangible values, adding the fact that the knowledge of financial items is restricted by the praxis of individual item analysis. Seamless corporate integrated models considering planning, budgeting, decision making and investment assessments could tear down the functional walls merging facets contained in specialties as CFM, CAPE, PSE, SCM, IT and KM (Romero et al. 2003; Guillen et al. 2006, 2007; Lainez et al. 2007).

Years ago inflation was not as dangerous to social order as now. Higher interest rates, tight money, insolvency and cash management are interdependent problems that people, banks and companies must manage to escape. Today in companies many decision makers use current intuitive reasoning owing to the lack of early warning systems (forward-looking systems). A model looking to the future inserts more difficulties during its validation since users cannot check against the existing accounting structure because accountancy bookkeeping is a backward looking system that covers past and present, but not future. However, the use of rolling horizons when modeling medium and short term planning/scheduling minimizes risk. Another problem is that budgets are today in danger of extinction if 70% of budget designers continue using EXCEL platform or succedaneum (see www.cfo.com). The generalized use of spreadsheet makes budget cycles of ≈93 days, four budgets per year, and this happens when cash officers surely want to see optimal automatic real time budgets to welcome them. Despite being cash the chain of the most expensive resource, the financial chain is the less planned and the less supported by programs. Nowadays, useful tools will be only those that are capable of preserving the firms' liquidity while providing a quick and optimal response to orders, through the optimization of delivery dates and price–time trade-off solutions.

## 2. Problem Statement

In the introduction are described the problems and challenges regarding functionality deficits in the today enterprise. The objectives that demand modification of the traditional way of planning and scheduling include

   (1) New modeling frameworks (fig. 4.1 and Grossmann, 2003)
   (2) Multi-criteria schedulers (fig. 3.2 a bicriteria time-value-added)
   (3) New friendly profile sight of money (fig. 2.1) for user analysis

Models are complex and have limitations by problem size and running time, particularly with combinatorial optimization. Integrated measure-made modeling applications could imply special designs for CEO, CFO or market manager adding more complexity to a system competent to optimize CFM, SCM, resource assignment, investment, plan, schedule, budget, operation and work links to order management systems (OMS). Example of the benefits of integrated models can be shown through the results of a case study (Romero et al. 2003) that uses as objective function 'maximize dividend'. Compared with the traditional sequential model the integrated model generates 9.5% more dividend. Moreover, fig. 2.2 exhibits the results of integrated modeling: less time less debt, less inventory stock and invests more in securities.

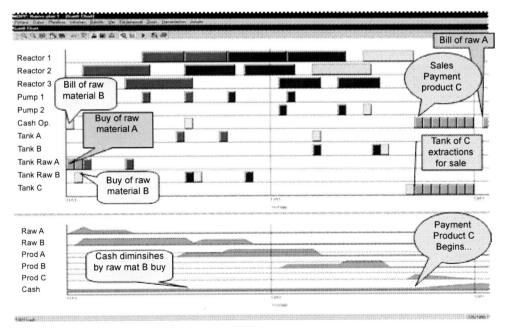

Figure 2.1. Financial-production integration by financial and operative recipes in APS.

Many industries use APS, a system with less precision. Production recipes define equipment and process time. For the integration of financial operations are used virtual recipes for each financial operation. When APS is used to plan finances virtual recipes (Badell et al. 2004), see fig. 2.1, other problems appear. The APS framework cannot give quick response to OMS and needs continuous rescheduling to update the integrated solution. In Section 3 we suggest a bicriteria algorithmic solution to couple schedules in OMS. We draw attention to our proposal through a multi-product plant example with infinite demand. Section 4 compares the power of logics and its necessary computer aid for CFM. Afterwards, in Section 5, the three levels of planning decisions and the rise above of tactical level as an adequate framework to support eagerness of investors with financial information in real time where firms could show its performance through integrated models. In Section 6 are analyzed two case study and next, conclusions and references.

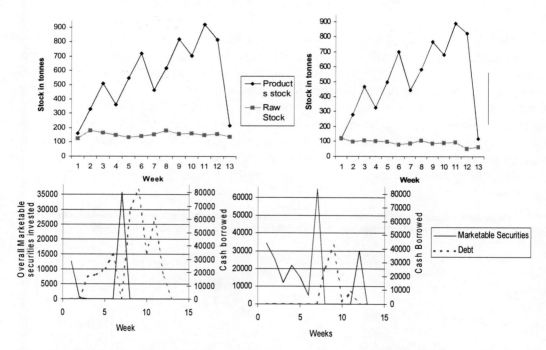

Figure 2.2. Results of sequential (right) and integrated (left) models. The integrated model has less time less debt, less inventory stock and invests more in securities.

## 3. Order Management with a Bicriteria Performance Measure

Today short lifecycles of huge quantities of products and processes require quick sharp and finely tuned integrated management actions as date fulfillment guided by OMS (Badell et al.1998a, 2001). A competitive tool must keep track of orders and money movements. CFOs need more information and consensus about operative plans and decisions.

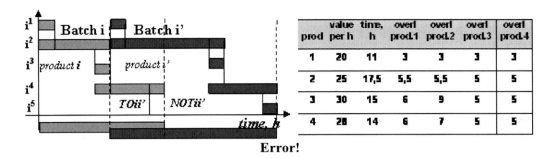

Figure 3.1. Binary schedule overlap TOii', NOTii' and data of products 1 to 4.

**Table 3.1. Ternary sequences of four products ordered by total value**

| label | TOii | Cii' | Dii' |
|---|---|---|---|
| 3-2 | 9 | 23,5 | 37,77 |
| 3-3 | 5 | 25 | 36 |
| 3-4 | 5 | 24 | 35,08 |
| 4-3 | 5 | 24 | 35,08 |
| 4-4 | 5 | 23 | 34,09 |
| 4-2 | 7 | 24,5 | 33,86 |
| 3-1 | 6 | 20 | 33,5 |
| 2-3 | 5 | 27,5 | 32,27 |
| 4-1 | 6 | 19 | 32,21 |
| 2-4 | 5 | 26,5 | 31,3 |
| 2-2 | 5,5 | 29,5 | 29,66 |
| 1-3 | 3 | 23 | 29,13 |
| 2-1 | 5,5 | 23 | 28,59 |
| 1-4 | 3 | 22 | 27,82 |
| 1-2 | 3 | 25,5 | 25,78 |
| 1-1 | 3 | 19 | 23,16 |

| N° | ternary sched | 1st time,h | 2nd time,h | 3rd time,h | time, h | total value | value.h | Overlap |
|---|---|---|---|---|---|---|---|---|
| 1 | 3-3-3 | 15 | 10 | 10 | 35 | 1350 | 38,57 | 5+5 => 10 |
| 2 | 3-2-3 | 15 | 8,5 | 10 | 33,5 | 1337,5 | 39,93 | 9+5 =>14 |
| 3 | 2-3-2 | 17,5 | 10 | 8,5 | 36 | 1325 | 36,81 | 5+9=>14 |
| 4 | 2-2-2 | 17,5 | 12 | 12 | 41,5 | 1312,5 | 31,63 | 5,5+5,5=>11 |
| 5 | 3-4-3 | 15 | 9 | 10 | 34 | 1292,0 | 38,00 | 5+5=>10 |
| 6 | 2-4-2 | 17,5 | 9 | 10,5 | 37 | 1267,0 | 34,24 | 5+7=>12 |
| 7 | 4-3-4 | 14 | 10 | 9 | 33 | 1234 | 37,39 | 5+5=>10 |
| 8 | 4-2-4 | 14 | 10,5 | 9 | 33,5 | 1221,5 | 36,46 | 7+5=>12 |
| 9 | 4-4-4 | 14 | 9 | 9 | 32 | 1176 | 36,75 | 5+5=>10 |
| 10 | 3-1-3 | 15 | 5 | 12 | 32 | 1120,0 | 35,00 | 6+3=> 9 |
| 11 | 2-1-2 | 17,5 | 5,5 | 14,5 | 37,5 | 1095,0 | 29,20 | 5,5+3=> 8,5 |
| 12 | 4-1-4 | 14 | 5 | 11 | 30 | 1004 | 33,47 | 6+3=> 9 |
| 13 | 1-3-1 | 11 | 12 | 5 | 28 | 890,0 | 31,79 | 3+6=> 9 |
| 14 | 1-2-1 | 11 | 14,5 | 5,5 | 31 | 877,5 | 28,31 | 3+5,5=> 8,5 |
| 15 | 1-4-1 | 11 | 9 | 11 | 31 | 832,0 | 26,84 | 3+6=> 9 |
| 16 | 1-1-1 | 11 | 8 | 8 | 27 | 660 | 24,44 | 3+3=> 6 |

The supply chain optimization integrating the finance chain in an altogether focus is performed using as target key performance indicators that consider the business and operation influence in the corporate value. Thus, at the planning-scheduling levels, and in order to directly capture the problematic of both chains, a bicriteria representation, as a time-value aggregate, could be proposed (Badell et al. 2007). This point of view can provide the necessary merge to integrate functionality performance measurement. Under this framework the economical analysis of the due date policy, tardiness and earliness, could be managed dynamically with price-time trade-offs (Badell, Grau et al. 1999). While engineers use powerful tools to optimally manage interactions between batches during production, business managers and financial officer lack a similar tool for finance. The main interaction between batches during process is provoked by overlapping times (fig. 3.1, left). If the overlapping time is override with a value density, the twofold problem can be treated as one. Calculating a priori all possible binary schedules as data (fig.3.1, right), it is calculated the value density per hour of its completion time (table 3.1) The value created by two products forming binary schedules is schedule dependent (Badell et al.1998b). The value density Dii' is the hourly value contribution $HVC_i$ of the binary schedule of product batches multiplied by processing times and divided by the sum of processing times (ti; ti') deducting overlapping TOii' as:

$$Dii' = ( HVCi \cdot ti + HVCi' \cdot ti') / (ti + ti' - TOii')$$

Ternary schedules are created as placing a piece in a puzzle, adding to its binary schedule the needed product to repeat the same ternary sequence, that is the value of binary '3-2' needs the value of '2-3', to form a '3-2-3' ternary sequence, during the completion of 120h week horizon. The best ternary is '3-3-3' but uses only 115h instead of 120h. Here a set of iterations done by a computer program arrives to optimum, which result was validated by a MILP model: 119h & 5350 mu.

sequence **3-2-3-2-3-2-3-2-3-2-3-2**      117h & 5325
sequence **3-2-3-2-3-2-3-2-3-2-3-3**      118h & 5337
sequence 3-3-2-3-3-3-2-3-2-3-2-3      119h & 5350 mu = optimum

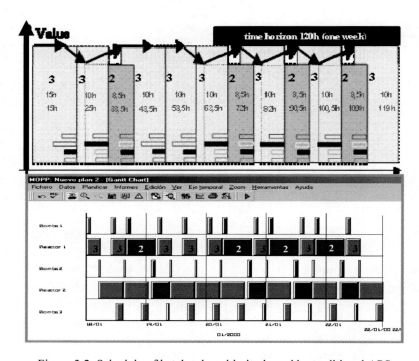

Figure 3.2. Schedule of batches by a bicriteria and by traditional APS.

## 4. Scales of Logics to Balance Management in CFM

The MRP - a system for the exclusive use of the operational planning - is the tool of the material logic that promoted in companies the functional partitioned planning process through the procedure denominated hierarchical production planning (HPP). As a consequence, the production plan was separated from the other functional plans of the company. It is worth mentioning that since the hierarchical planning requires a trial and error loop between

Material Requirements Planning (MRP) and production plan, it cannot offer the necessary uphold to an economy that must respond to a financial logic dynamically. Therefore financial analysis aspects have to be taken into account during the SC operations optimization process. This strategy can generate strong acceptance from the CFO while reducing the probability of enterprise failure.

The MRP, first forward looking system created decades ago and so far, installed the material logic in medium and large plants putting in chains the presence of company finances during planning. This MRP and HPP solution imposed an iteration loop to search a feasible supply of materials to provision one operative plan suggested by the marketing and business staff. Since the 70s and so far, the medium and large companies functioned with good health using MRP and HPP because the previous economic era had an exponential economic growth following the logic of more-capacity-more-earnings.

This old 'philosophy' promotes the separate development of functional plans. As a result this focus obstructed the altogether optimization in an appropriate modeling framework to find optimal schedules, plans and budgets with liquidity control. The partitioned solution still obstructs the optimal enterprise-wide planning of the firm while people are not conscious that this old methodology is far of optimum. With 'historic rights', the plant manager based on MRP an HPP decisions thinks that production is and must be a decentralized function separated from business staff that he must manage without financial control. So in his daily routine he decides the production plan, informs to business staff the changes and sends an invoice to the financial area so they pay in 90 days 120 € of raw materials because he has to produce 700 kg of product B. The financial manager fulfils his order following a master/slave relation and without checking if it is financially feasible. This happens when the core logic is not the material, but the financial.

Being the finance theory funded on a cash flow description of the firm, the obvious center to assume the enterprise-wide decision making is the financial manager. Financial management must calculate the optimal assignment of funds to each function including production. The variables to compile during planning and budgeting are the distribution of funds to each value producer. Today the HPP is an insufficient methodology that opposites the performance of a healthy financial company and could provoke bankruptcies. MRP as a forward looking system related with material logic and inventory control, gave a rich reward to world economy. Similar results could be obtained if a 'FRP' system is designed to control money.

The logic of the backward looking accountancy system is related with book-keeping the historic transactional records of a corporation. While transactional logic knows about information on the past and present through accountancy, financial statements and balance sheet, the analytical models can assess additionally the intangible asset impacts and risk when do future estimates to identify assured decisions through models with rolling horizons. When the task is to find the optimal operative sequence to design a schedule, we are searching a schedule, and it is the 'variable' to find. When applying MRP and HPP the CEO suggests a master plan as data to the MRP in order to find, by trial & error, a feasible inventory plan for the master plan requested. In this case the material plan is the variable to find; that is why material logic is dominant now. Applying the financial logic to the algorithm proposed in Section 3, we can see that to calculate the variable 'optimal schedule' we use time-value data to calculate batch contributions in descendent order lists. The total value of ternary sequence '3-3-3' are 3 batches of product *3* by 15h of process time by the value contribution of 30mu/h which is equal to a total value of 1350 mu. The arithmetical solution avoids the non linear knapsack problem combinatorial optimization. The altogether tradeoff solution can centralize liquidity, finances, marketing, production and logistic areas, sales, R+D and others (see fig. 4.1).

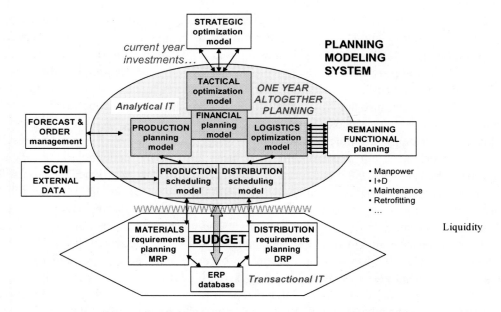

Figure 4.1. Modeling framework for the supply chain optimization.

The definite framework envisaged is a general flexible and systematic normative optimization model with integrated CFM and SCM that lets the deployment of an agent based system. The information is captured from internal sources (as accountancy system, physical inventory status, process control) and from external sources (as sales web site, sales at value market, asset investment analysis, distribution).

Managers can increase their knowledge with each execution of modeling tools. Modeling frameworks designed specifically to SMEs can enlarge their possibilities. The ERP has the historic data, ratios, the ongoing plan, budget and working capital cash of the firm. The results of models can inform about best plan, best budget, best decisions and the future cash profile timed for the plan and budget proposed. The user will know where the money will be, what is going to do with it and when receivables arrive. Once a simultaneous model finds global optimum, this information can compare the proficiency accessing to the historic data of the mini-ERP and could valuate how competitive is the firm's position.

Organizations can sum great benefits if updated logics introduce flexibility and adaptability in the right course letting the creation of KM resources. The key of management is the extraction process from the human experts' qualitative controversy. The contextual knowledge may be a source of updates for the new organization. Tools with KM can trace and add changes to fill visible gaps or oversights. Managers can increase their knowledge with each execution of modeling tools. The financial officer needs an updated view of where the money is, what is going to do with it and when receivables would arrive to their hands.

With this information it can be compared the proficiency accessing to the historic data kept in data bases and could valuate how competitive is the firm's position.

## 5. Tactical Level Perspectives as Real Time Informing Framework

Planning happens at all three levels of decision-making. Getting the right strategic, tactical and operational decisions empowers business forward. The company's driving force is to hit on the top strategic planning to effectively modulate the globalization effects on its market and SC. However, today dynamic's logic conspires against this paradigm. It is not enough to compete in cost, service and corporate value having a static strategic-planning model only reviewed in certain periods. Each day more strategic plans must be shortened in horizon and permanently reviewed by the one-year tactical model. Each day more operative models must treat the integrated influence of firm's investments. The optimal management of funds from capital budget or long term debt to invest in new equipment has to be assessed with the concern and influence of the ongoing tasks at the operative level.

At the bottom floor the operative level must have a priori a realistic cash flow vision of the working capital of short term plans and budgets to avoid the impact if suddenly appears a capital investment. In medium term it will be necessary to maintain an updated systematic perpetual altogether tactical optimization modeling system with links up and down connecting with the top strategic issues and the bottom operative schedules in progress. Hence it is convenient a modeling approach based on an altogether-one-year-tactical-model with optimal plan, budget and decision making showing which financial decisions are best within a rolling horizon. An integrated tactical model with financial logic dominance could be a premise to design the absent tools that must govern firm's financial information in real time. The maximum corporate value as target and the altogether tactical model as general manager of enterprise-wide decision making could be a step forward towards an ongoing report of financial results. Computer systems capable of exposing core data to financial investors in the value market will necessary require a holistic approach as shown here. Such system can avoid the disappointing privileged information today obtainable by the executive staff of firms. A country with such failures cannot measure intangible assets, financial vision and therefore cannot define tax policy with impartiality.

The maximum corporate value as the target and the holistic model itself constitute a first step forward in creating this ongoing planning system. To the best of our knowledge, a system based on an integrated normative model has not been implemented so far. A mathematical model could be a premise to find the absent paradigm of this economic era. Further work can focus on taking into account uncertainty and risk analysis into the aforementioned integrated models. Without a shred of doubt, how to integrate financial function into the brains of firms requires huge academic and practical efforts.

## 6. Gap to Overcome by PSE and CAPE Communities

The gap that PSE and CAPE communities must eliminate is to find the overall enterprise-wide-objective-function able to optimize its integrated-functionality as value-producer while teaches, with the aid of a global mathematical programming model, which are the optimal decisions of schedules, plans, budgets and investments. The multidisciplinary know-how contained in this review increases the scientific nature of PSE creating a new challenge to the computer and process engineering developers from PSE, CAPE and IT.

Next in subsections 6.1 and 6.2 are analyzed the results obtained by two models already published: Guillen, M. Badell et al., 'Simultaneous optimization of process and financial decisions to enhance the integrated planning/scheduling of chemical supply chains' published in *Comp. & Chem. Eng.*, 30 (2006) 421-436 and Lainez, Guillen, Badell et al., 'Enhancing corporate value in the optimal design of chemical supply chains', *Ind. Eng. Chem. Res.*, 46, 23, (2007) 7739-7757.

## 6.1. Results of Integrating SCM Model in Multi-site Chemical Plant

This Guillen et al. 2006 case study modeled the integration of planning, scheduling and budgeting in a chemical SC with embedded multi-purpose batch chemical plants using a CPLEX 7.0 MIP solver. The impact of this article in the literature (see Comp. & Chem. Eng. TOP25 2006 1st half year) justifies its importance and our interest in evoking it.

**Error!**

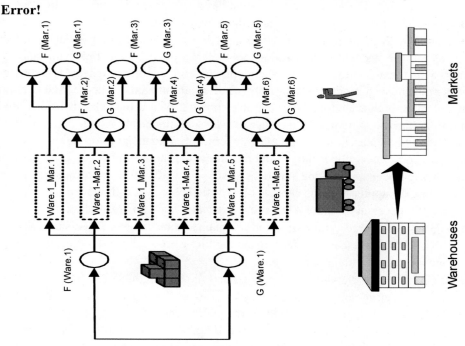

Figure 6.1.1. SC structure of the multipurpose batch plants.

Today the independent modeling of operations, isolated from finances as well as from the other areas of the firm and SC, continues as the typical working routine. The current policy of 'first-decide-operations-and-afterwards-try-to-fit-finances' is not the only risky procedure of operative management. The operative models today use partial objective functions as maximum profit that only captures the transactional part of the value created by the enterprise and its financial sources. Here we used a financial objective function: [MAX] Δ Equity or maximize the increment of equity. This objective function permits elitist accumulation of capital sacrificing the promotion of fixed asset investments or obliges to make a full use of debt when paying investments, preserving equity. Hence you must be aware that a [MAX] Δ Equity model is acceptable only for short term horizons. That is why the strategic long term case study detailed in the next subsection 6.2. uses [MAX] CV (maximize corporate value) as objective function.

The case under analysis has two batch multipurpose plants *F* and *G* that produce two products *P1* and *P2* and three warehouses for six markets *Ware* and *Mar*. Such structure of multipurpose batch plants is depicted in fig. 6.1.1. The formulation considers a time horizon of 13 weeks (90 days). A detailed schedule is obtained during the first week by dividing the week into 60 discrete intervals H2 of length 2 hours. The planning results are obtained in the remaining 12 week periods of length H1 given in fig. 6.1.2.

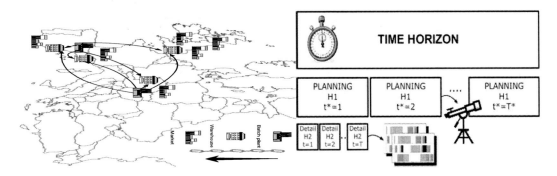

Figure 6.1.2. Structure of the model.

Production is planned using known or estimated demands provided by forecasting tools. The first planning period is a detailed scheduling. The following future planning periods include estimated decisions. The rolling horizon model only applies a subset of periods. When the first planning order of length H1 (one week) is fulfilled, the model is rerun. Therefore, the results of the planning horizon beyond the first period H1 will never be executed. Besides the operative schedule, one can also schedule the necessary materials for the following periods. So the reschedule reruns each H1 period providing more updated and reliable information, aiding afterwards a more realistic development of decision making able to uphold the fulfillment of the optimal short term production schedule and budget taking all facts into account. This is an evolving continuous flow of short and medium-term plans with the corresponding global budget. Both plans promote a very important body of knowledge: the opportunity of having a quantitative tool looking to the future letting to learn more about how to adjust the production rate that ensure the logistic steps of producing quantities of products at the planned time. This happens together with the flows of materials stored and transported to other nodes of the network as well as the flows of cash entering and going out from the virtual value-added chain.

To highlight the advantages of the optimization with the integrated model, a two-step sequential scheduling-planning and budgeting model was applied. The first stage of the model contains the detailed scheduling of the different sites of the SC as well as the transport decisions throughout the nodes. The second stage of production planning is estimated by an aggregated graph State Task Network, STN, (Kondili et al. 1993) which is limited by an upper bound: the number of batches that can be carried out in any feasible solution not exceeds the length of each planning interval H1. Three modeling constraints embody the process flexibility and plant capacity management: (1) assignment; (2) batch size; (3) mass balance. The fig. 6.1.3 shows the different process solutions for the multipurpose batch plants embedded in the network.

On the other hand the budget model and cash management applied considers cash transactions by accounts receivable as exogenous receipts of sales of products or marketable securities, as well as accounts payable, prompt payment discount, delayed payment, advanced payment, repayment, credit line, funds from short-term financing sources, pledging, dividends, taxes and *others*, that include the overall funds of enterprise-wide functions not yet modeled as manpower, R&D and asset investments.

The all-together optimization model uses a financial objective function coming from the accountancy equation $\Delta E = \Delta CA + \Delta FA - \Delta CL - \Delta L$ as maximum increment in equity achieved by the enterprise for a given time horizon. The term can be computed as the net difference between the change in assets, which include both, current assets ($CA$) and fixed assets ($FA$), and change in liabilities, comprising the current liabilities ($CL$) and long-term debts ($L$). To achieve the integration between operative and financial decisions, the production liabilities and exogenous cash inputs at every week-period are calculated as a function of production planning variables. The inflows of cash were the sales of products assuming a known delay between the purchase execution and its payment, while the amount of raw materials and utilities bought to suppliers were calculated by operative variables.

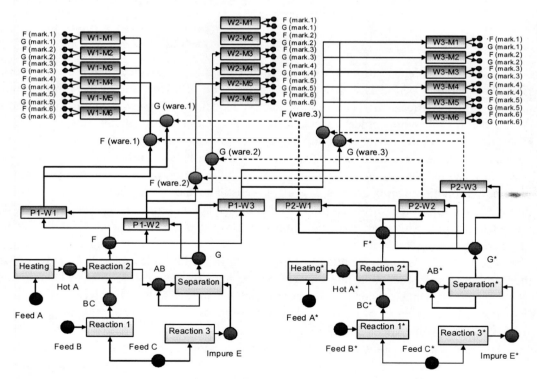

Figure 6.1.3. STN representation of the planning and scheduling operative model.

This industrial sample had a specific but common situation in practice: one product had higher profitability than the other. Such product has a high price and consumes an expensive raw material. Given this data, the planning-scheduling model decides to fulfill the demand of the expensive product as much as possible, as it contributes highly to the objective function value that was maximize the increment in equity. By the traditional modeling approach the sequential production model expresses first its optimal plan and afterwards the financial model tries to fit to this plan but it provokes an inevitable insolvency that forces to pledge the accounts receivable striking the working capital. In fig. 6.1.4 the schedules in Gantt charts show the different production results obtained by the two types of models.

The first part of fig. 6.1.5 shows that the sequential approach is producing and storing a high amount of expensive product at early periods with low demand in order to enlarge sales and profit in later periods in which the demand increases. In order to provide the financial resources to carry out the SC decisions computed by the planning model, the budget model is forced to pledge receivables mainly in periods 7 and 8 in which many raw materials purchased must be paid.

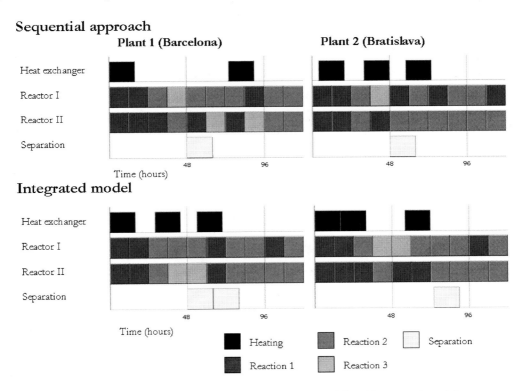

Figure 6.1.4. Production Gantt charts for the sequential and integrated model.

On the other hand, the integrated approach leads to a lower product P2 production rate and inventory of G that avoids pledging such quantity of receivables. In the integrated model the increment of equity was achieved at the end of the horizon time. Comparing the traditional method with the integrated one, it can be observed that the increment in equity achieved by the company improves substantially, a 13.7% higher in the integrated approach than in the sequential. The integrated model had 4,876,560 m.u of equity and the sequential

4,208,530 m.u. The finances, expressed in thousands of m.u., associated with the operation of the SC and securities investments are shown in Gantt chart in fig. 6.1.5. It can be observed how the sequential solution pledges more receivables than the integrated with a very high cost to the firm. The sequential model pledged around 12,628,217 m.u., with a cost of around 2,525,643 mu to the firm. The integrated solution pledges 3,105,391 with a cost of 621,078 m.u. In fig. 6.1.6 are shown the inventories and sales of sequential and integrated models. The sequential GAMS planning model had 340681 equations, 38204 continuous variables and 23066 discrete variables (1079 CPU sec to reach solution with a 0% integrality gap on AMD

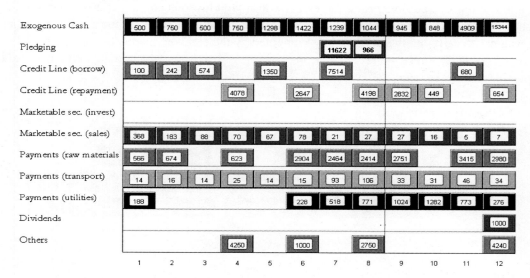

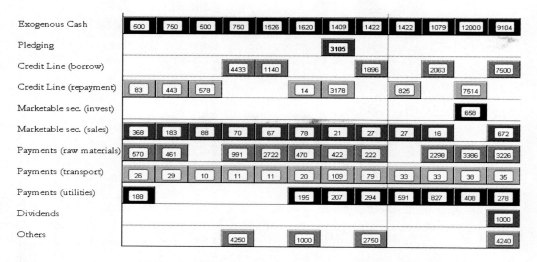

Figure 6.1.5. Gantt charts of the financial-operative actions.

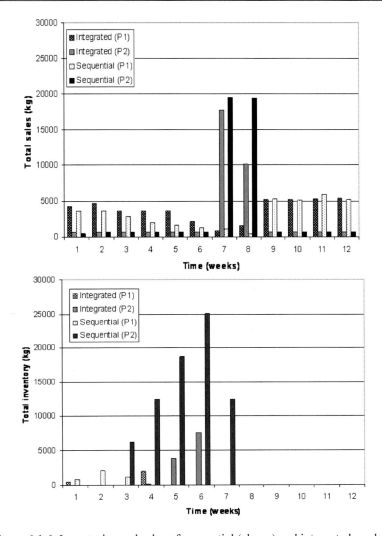

Figure 6.1.6. Inventories and sales of sequential (above) and integrated models.

Athlon 3000 computer using MIP solver of CPLEX 7.0). The financial model has 448 single equations and 664 continuous variables. The model is solved in 0.015 CPU sec. In opposition, the integrated model had 341157 equations, 55093 continuous variables and 23066 discrete variables that were solved in 2257 CPU sec to reach a solution with a 0% integrality gap on the same computer. The benefit of optimizing the financial management jointly with operation management achieved an annual increase in earnings of around a 14%, 668030 m.u.

It would be extremely useful to be able to manage operations simultaneously with transparent and forward looking information because if so, the areas receiving the assignment of firm's limited resources would know previously what contributions to shareholders' value are going to be produced by them. The synergy between corporate financial management and supply chain management has not been exploited up to now. Even though the advantages of joint functional integration have not been evaluated, there is a positive consensus in literature regarding this advance.

## 6.2. Integrated Modeling Results to Optimally Design Supply Chains

The Lainez et al. 2007 case study describes the design and retrofit of a SC using an operative and financial integration in an enterprise-wide model including, besides the medium term operative plan, the strategic decision-making level with the novelty that the same framework could solve the financial sustainability of short term operative schedules.

As mentioned in subsection 6.1, here we will use CV as objective function due to the fact that we plan capital investments in a 5 years' horizon. The market value of a company is a function of four factors: investments, cash flows, capital cost and economic life. The SHV and CV of the firm is incremented when produces cash and when investors buy stocks. However, the objective function CV, as so, will not promote directly all the necessary advancements as enterprise growth or R&D intensification. It is necessary to force growth and intensification including more objectives or constraints or extending the horizon time to cover the impact in value added given by hypothetical investments. The erratic creation of objective functions could provoke partial plans that can affect the tasks of other functional areas without prevention.

A disappointing management based on defective models not including liquidity control or cross-functional links with its functionality, can mislay opportunities or provoke sudden arrivals of unexpected insolvencies. Only the design of an integrated model, developed with the correct objective function and suitable constraints and covering the full activities of value producers, can achieve in whichever firm the maximum performance and hence the maximum value added for its conditions.

SC planning model could link the financial model with the decision making process in its three levels. The optimal assignment of limited funds to enterprise operation, design and retrofitting implies the consideration of money as the universal quantitative variable that assigns funds to the three operative, tactical and strategic levels. Now guided by a myopic hierarchically sequenced procedure, are firstly decided the enterprise functional decisions and plans, and afterwards in second place a budget is fitted to cover the sum of 'best plans' prepared by operative managers.

In this case study the financial funding to each functional area is the variable to optimize, fitting the optimal size of functional plans in a global optimal plan and budget. Our procedure gives the advantage to the firm-as-a-whole instead of giving the advantage to the segmented 'best plan' of the operative manager. Today managers decide plans first and afterwards budget changing petitions of areas' proposals. Indeed, the most important decisions of the firm are decided without any global optimal analysis of cash management. The master-slave relation acts in detriment of financial management. If financial budgets are fitted considering subjective reasons in that master/slaver relation, far from optimum are governed the firms.

Being the focus of this modeling framework a software able to find a feasible optimal solution, then this modeling framework could be a prototype of management system if and only if the terms that model, the constraints that bound and the objective functions that target, are always kept updated or renewed and validated.

In order to validate the global involvement of firm's functionality by an optimal objective function, were modeled and studied their Pareto curves to compare the following pairs: (1) corporate value vs. profit; (2) net present value vs. profit and (3) corporate value vs. net present value. Here the CV of the firm was selected as the objective to fulfill.

In order to reduce model complexity, the case study under analysis is solved using a mixed-integer deterministic model although the problem has five years of horizon with 61 intervals or periods. The model assumes initially a plant site having one technology (equipment), a distribution centre and an assigned market (in fig. 6.2.1 are encircled by discontinuous line). The design/planning model tries to determine the optimal assignment of processing sites and distribution centre for markets. The first constraint of the design/planning model is the mass balance that is made in the nodes integrating the network. The second is a balance of product sales that must be less/equal than demand.

**Error!**

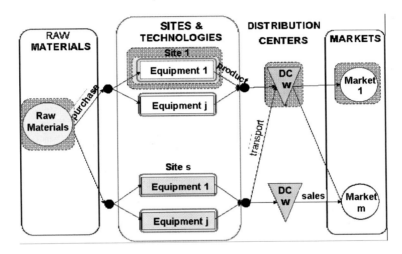

Figure 6.2.1. General structure of the SC.

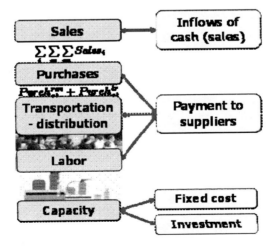

Figure 6.2.2. Integration scheme of operative and financial models.

The operative capacity constraint automatically enlarges the capacity if more capacity is needed. If even more capacity is needed than the available by node site, it is decided the construction of a new site in the SC network. Binary variables control the decision of creating more capacity. The model uses continuous variables to express the ongoing total capacity of the SC. The raw material purchases, production rates, labor cost, transportation-distribution flows and the amount of sales and inventory are included in the sales equation. The cash balance and the equation of payments links the quantity of products produced with the incoming flows of cash from sales. The integration is summarized in fig. 6.2.2.

To manage inflows and outflows of cash, a financial balance is built-in covering the cash left by the previous period, the sales of products or marketable securities, credit lines, purchases, payments, prompt payment, loan/debt, pledging, taxes, fixed assets and fixed costs. The purchase to providers of raw material, labor cost, utilities and transport services is positioned in the financial equation of payments.

The financial variable fixed asset considers the capital invested to expand the capacity installed in the SC. The financial side of the problem includes a set of constraints that fine-tune the previously mentioned facts. A constraint limiting a minimum safety stock of cash is incorporated in the cash balance to avoid unexpected insolvencies. A minimum stock of cash is pre-coordinated by a committed agreement with credit banks.

The discounted-free-cash-flow DFCF method was applied to assess the investment decisions undertaken by the firm. The enterprise market value of a firm is given by the difference between the discounted stream of future cash flows during the planning horizon and the total net debt at the end of its life time, taking into account the capital cost during the time horizon. The net debt is the total debt of the firm at the end of the planning horizon. The CV is calculated by subtracting the net debt from the DFCF through planning horizon. Consequently, if the assessment of a business is determined by the discounted free cash flow over its lifetime, the objective demands a continuous creation of capacity when it is needed in order to increase the free cash flow generation.

The case study illustrates a specific situation where a production manager discovers that there is available the market M2. The manager decides to expand the SC and produces as more as possible to satisfy the whole demand of M2 at once. However, the model and the manager fail to notice that M2 buyers cannot buy all at once. Investing in more capacity and making an expensive production campaign provokes an important and unexpected immobilization of funds at the firm. Not measuring the impact of investments on its limited financial resources could result "as to die of success", a very common cause of firms' failure. To avoid this it is necessary to use a normative financial management tool with the adequate objective function.

If maximum profit or NPV are the objectives in the model, CV will fall as Pareto curves reveal in fig. 6.2.3. With profit or NPV as objectives, models fail to detect if the buyers delay payments in market M2. Using CV as objective function the income benefits are greater. In fact, the value computed when maximizing profit corresponds to a 25% of the maximum CV obtained and when maximizing NPV, a 27%. Benefits could be expanded, but expending a dramatic diminution of CV reducing firm's equity. In 6.2.4 the NPV model discards technology TB. Conversely CV model finds opportunities in site1 with technology TB. The integrated focus with CV maximizes value to 145.023.155,58 m.u.

In fig. 6.2.5, for a matter of space, the planning periods have been compacted from months to quarters making 25 condensed periods. With the traditional objective functions the model of a new supply chain makes the sale all at once. The model with myopic objectives fails to notice that in market M2 the accounts receivable are extremely delayed by the buyers. As a result to face important payments the budgeting model is forced to pledge receivables during several months reducing the firm's capacity of creating value. While this happens to the transactional objective functions, the integrated model with the correct objective function satisfies market M2 demand with a slower production rate favoring a better liquidity position. The robustness of integrated CV model is demonstrated in the Gantt charts of the cases under analysis. in fig. 6.2.5.

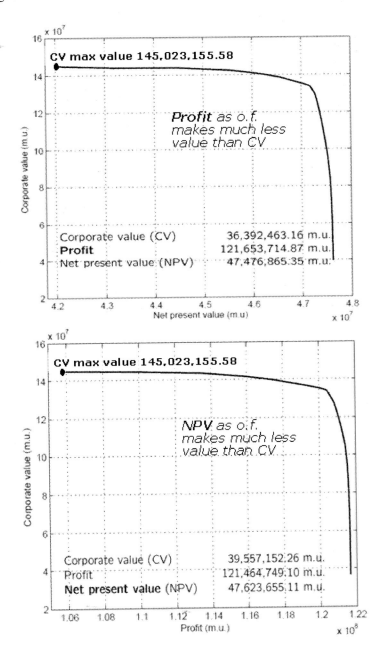

Figure 6.2.3. Pareto curve of CV – PROFIT and CV – NPV.

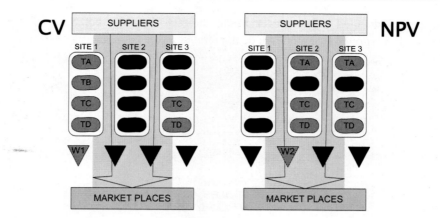

Figure 6.2.4. Final 5 years' allocation by design and retrofit, black sites disappeared.

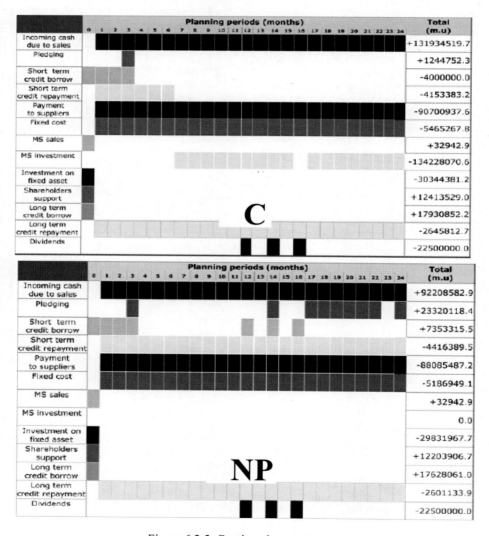

Figure 6.2.5. Continued on next page.

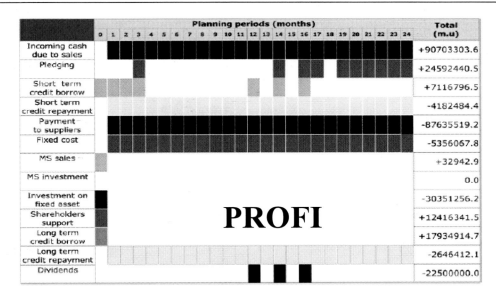

Figure 6.2.5. CV, NPV and profit optimal financial report in Gantt Charts.

## 7. Conclusions

Wrong financial management is the first cause of business failure and this happens when the worldwide financial officers work without appropriate financial tools to make budgets. The 70% of them use Excel to calculate budgets (www.cfo.com). They don't use any integrated tool because they are not in the market. They use classical budget design that decouples the planning and scheduling decisions from budgeting considerations and decide first on planning and scheduling and after that it simply performs the financial computations for budgeting following a master/ slave management relation. Neither budget nor the cash management has software with enterprise-wide integration when the integrated management makes an invaluable difference.

Due to the lack of software capable to link corporate databases and optimization modeling systems, the material logic of the pioneer MRP system still remains as the kernel of most of the current commercial ERPs. The transactional structure of ERP gives inflexibility to changes and only solves the transactional part of the problem. They don't have multi-functional analytical models integrated in their managerial systems to optimize the combined effects of the different variables involved in a company.

It is not strange that the leading cause of failures of companies is financial mismanagements and of course will remain so, as long as the managers of cash don't have computational robust tools to help determine the optimal investment in production and in other business functions. That tool should report the inventory of money in the near future. Cash managers also have insolvable uncertainties, as when will collect the revenues.

Being possible since the 60s the MRP systems that give a detailed inventory of current and future resources such as raw materials and finished product in storage or in transit, for money is most important and still we lack such tool. The logic now is to create first operative plans and then cash manager pays. CFO authorizes such payment blindly and in a subordinate form. Indeed the CFO should make a budget first to determine optimal global solutions. It is appropriate to know previously the amount of money invested and determine if such opportunity deserves the funds requested.

Cash is the most expensive resource and the less planned. MRP shows the future inventory of materials in a minute, but there is not something like that for money. Money must be the variable. Under his government must determine optimal plans and budgets to optimize production or services with transparent information about the cash inventory planned in the near future. It is important to know how much money the firm will have by looking at its profile to be able to respond at a minute their exigencies.

It is a fact that if all the models of operative planning, design of SC, including also the massive independent partial analysis of investments, don't verify their global financial viability with overall joint models, the results could be unfeasible, incorrect besides not optimum. One can obtain significant earnings if plans and budgets are solved simultaneously, while cash maintains its level of safety stock. When are used partial analysis of NPV or maximum profit to evaluate investments, the designed plants are different in comparison with those analyzed in altogether models with maximum corporate value as objective. Which is the optimal?

Not only about theory exits disagreement. Besides the scientific formal logic of management, among the personnel in the routine practice exist informal logic. It happens among personnel of plant, marketing, business and so on. Operative and marketing management are often in conflict. Market managers want production variety and quick delivery but plant managers want less variety and less change to avoid capacity mistreatment and extra costs. True solutions for these problems need enterprise-wide integration into adequate modeling frameworks including knowledge management. When the informal logic is positively organized and optimal plan, budget and decision making are obtained, other issues never considered could be focused by the staff, as new solutions to dynamic prices, inventory levels, products in process, capacities, bottlenecks, the reliability of schedules in due dates, minimal lead time in delivery and transport or quicker OMS. The tradeoff solution of opposite logics is also part of the challenge related with integration of SCM and CFM. The formalism of the informal logic in management is a reserve of management power and productivity that today escapes by the windows of corporate buildings in the form of endless discussions.

Even though today's dynamics, companies are still based on a functional organizational structure with separate departments for the different areas, where most planning is done sequentially by areas according to a hierarchy. The interactions between functions of a firm can be solved only if the multiple functional plans are simultaneously considered taking into account all constraints in unison as in enterprise-wide optimization or real EWO systems. Business and academic environment are making more conscientious to financial officers, specifically about the financial dimension of decision making, to progressively have more officers driven by the goal of enhancing corporate value by analytic software.

Indeed, the business is increasingly being more boundary less, meaning that internal and external functional barriers are somewhat removed in favour of horizontal process management as in SCM. This indicates that externally the gaps between vendors, distributors, customers and firms are gradually changing. SCM aims to integrate plants with their suppliers and customers so that they can be managed as a single entity, synchronizing all input/output flows so that acceptable financial returns and desired costumer satisfaction levels are achieved.

Numerical results show that the integrated solution not only guarantees the feasibility of assessing strategic decisions from financial viewpoint. An integrated solution also leads to superior economic positions given its higher visibility to create value for the firm. Thus the executives of big, small and medium enterprises will have to achieve the learning of how to work with software that contains tailor made models inside to integrate the financial function with the remaining functionality of the company. These tools can automatically generate the optimal operative plan or service, the optimal global budget and the optimal decision making, analyzing all the areas that produce value in the business including its supply chain.

Improving the management of SMEs with tailor made tools is an important pathway towards the improvement of world economy. SMEs produce the 80% of USA richness and so on in Europa and many other developed countries. SMEs can achieve the advance of having a higher productivity fostering growth. If SMEs gave that richness to the world working with blindness and hence top stress, living with minimums, working many hours without achieving growth or innovation, what richness uplift would conquer SMEs with 1$^{rst}$ class tools to optimize management?

When the enterprise is endowed with up to the minute information about the overall budget status, demands, costs, schedules, allocation of resources, reschedules and cost of capital, then the enterprise is ready to respond efficiently to events as they arise, with full knowledge of where are the optimal decisions and the less expenditures. However, besides the reduction of costs or increment of revenues and the benefits of balancing firm's financial liquidity in integrated models, there is an internal benefit in companies that rarely is possible to be measured with something else than intuitive reasoning. It is the opportunity cost ignored by not optimizing the quality of management decisions, and very especially in the resource assignment to functional areas that create value to enterprise.

# References

M. Badell et al., 'Integrated on line production and financial scheduling provided with intelligent autonomous agent-based information system', *Computers & Chem. Eng.*, **22S**, (1998a) 271- 278.

M. Badell et al., A new conceptual approach in ERM systems, *AIChE Series* **94** (320) (1998b) 217–223.

M. Badell, R. Grau et al., 'Scheduling with economic evaluation of the due date policy', *PRES 99 2$^{nd}$ Conference on Process Integration, Modeling and Optimization.* Budapest, May 31-June 2, 1999.

M. Badell, L. Puigjaner, "Advanced ERM systems for the batch industry. The TicTac Toe Algorithm", *Comp. & Chem. Eng.*, **25** (2001) 517-538.

M. Badell, J. Romero, et al. 'Planning, Scheduling and Budgeting Value Added Chains', *Comp. & Chem. Eng.*, **28** (2004) 45-61.

M. Badell, J. Romero et al., 'Optimal budget and cash flows during retrofitting periods in chemical process industries', *Intrntl. J. Prod. Econ.*, **95** (2005) 359-372.

M. Badell, G. Guillen et al. 'Empowering financial trade-off in joint financial and Supply chain Scheduling and Planning Modeling', *Mathematical & Computer Modeling,* **46** (2007) 12-23.

G. Guillen, M. Badell et al., 'Simultaneous optimization of process and financial decisions to enhance the integrated planning/ scheduling of chemical supply chains', *Comp. & Chem. Eng.,* **30** (2006) 421-436.

G. Guillen, M. Badell et al., 'A holistic framework for short-term supply chain management integrating production and corporate financial planning', *Intrntl. J. Prod. Econ.,* **106** (2007) 288-306.

I.E. Grossman, 'Challenge in the new millennium: Product discovery and design, enterprise and supply chain optimization, global life cycle assessment', *Comp. & Chem. Eng.,* **29** (2003) 29–39.

Kondili, E., C. C. Pantelides and R. Sargent, 'A General Algorithm for Short-Term Scheduling of Batch Operations I. MILP Formulation'. *Comp. & Chem. Eng.* **17** (1993), 211-228.

J.M. Lainez, et al., 'Enhancing corporate value in the optimal design of chemical supply chains', *Ind. Eng. Chem. Res.,* **46**, 23, (2007) 7739-7757.

G.V.Reklaitis, ESCAPE 15, Keynote in Plenary of. Barcelona (2005).

J. Romero, M.Badell et al., 'Integrating Budgeting Models into Scheduling and Planning Models for Chemical Batch Industry', *Ind. Eng.Chem.Res.,* **42** (2003) 6125-6134.

J.F. Shapiro, *Modeling the Supply Chain,* Ed. Duxbury Press (2001).

V.A. Varma, G.V. Reklaitis et al., 'Enterprise-wide modeling and optimization. An overview of emerging research challenges and opportunities' *Computers & Chem. Eng.,* **31** (2007) 692-711.

In: Liquidity, Interest Rates and Banking
Editors: J. Morrey and A. Guyton, pp. 213-232

ISBN 978-1-60692-775-5
© 2009 Nova Science Publishers, Inc.

Chapter 10

# LIQUIDITY, FUTURES PRICE DYNAMICS, AND RISK MANAGEMENT

*Kit Pong Wong*[*]
University of Hong Kong

### Abstract

This paper examines the optimal design of a futures hedge program by a competitive firm under output price uncertainty. Due to a capital constraint and the marking-to-market procedure of futures contracts, the firm faces endogenous liquidity risk. If the futures prices are sufficiently positively correlated, we show that the capital constraint is non-binding in that the optimal amount of capital earmarked to the futures hedge program is less than the firm's capital endowment. Otherwise, we show that the capital constraint becomes binding in that the firm optimally puts aside all of its capital stock for the futures hedge program. In the case of non-binding capital constraint, we show that the firm's optimal futures position is likely to be an over-hedge for reasonable preferences. In the case of binding capital constraint, the firm's optimal futures position is an under-hedge or an over-hedge, depending on whether the autocorrelation coefficient of the futures price dynamics is below or above a critical positive value, respectively.

**JEL classification:** D21; D81; G13

**Keywords:** Endogenous liquidation; Futures price dynamics; Marking to market; Prudence

## 1. Introduction

According to the Committee on Payment and Settlement Systems (1998), firms should take liquidity risk seriously when devising their risk management strategies. Failure to do so is

---
[*]E-mail address: kpwong@econ.hku.hk (K. P. Wong). Tel.: 852-2859-1044, fax: 852-2548-1152, Correspondence to: Kit Pong Wong, School of Economics and Finance, University of Hong Kong, Pokfulam Road, Hong Kong

likely to result in fatal consequences for even technically solvent firms. An apposite example of this sort is the disaster at Metallgesellschaft A. G. (MG), the 14th largest industrial firm in Germany.[1]

In 1993, MG Refining and Marketing, Inc. (MGRM), the U.S. subsidiary of MG, offered long-term contracts for oil and refined oil products that allow its customers to lock in fixed prices up to 10 years into the future. To hedge its exposure to the oil price risk, MGRM took on large positions in energy derivatives, primarily in oil futures. When oil prices plummeted in December 1993, MGRM was unable to meet its variation margin payments due to the denial of credit from its banks.[2] This debacle resulted in a $2.4 billion rescue package coupled with a premature liquidation of its futures positions *en masse* so as to keep MG from going bankrupt (Culp and Miller, 1995).

While basis risk in oil futures would certainly imply that MG's hedge did not successfully lock in value (Ross, 1997; Hilliard, 1999; Neuberger, 1999), Mello and Parsons (1995, 2000) identify the funding requirements of MG's hedging strategy as one of the central causes of the problem. Indeed, Mello and Parsons (1995, 2000) show that a perfect hedge does not create its own liquidity, and that the inability to fund a hedging strategy to its end is a serious defect in the design of many popular hedging strategies. In light of these findings, the purpose of this paper is to examine whether there is any role of liquidity constraints in the optimal design of a futures hedge program that allows an endogenously determined provision for terminating the program.

This paper develops a two-period model of the competitive firm under output price uncertainty (Sandmo, 1971). Specifically, the firm produces a single commodity that is sold at the end of the planning horizon. Since the subsequent spot output price is not known ex ante, the firm trades unbiased futures contracts for hedging purposes. All of the unbiased futures contracts are marked to market in that they require cash settlements of gains and losses at the end of each period. The futures price dynamics is assumed to follow a first-order autoregression that includes a random walk as a special case.[3]

The firm devises its futures hedge program by choosing a futures position and an amount of capital earmarked for the program. According to its futures hedge program, the firm commits to premature liquidation of its futures position on which the interim loss incurred exhausts the earmarked capital. The capital commitment as such constitutes an endogenous liquidity constraint, where the choice of the former dictates the severity of the latter. The firm is subject to a capital constraint in that the earmarked capital cannot exceed the firm's capital endowment. We show that the liquidity risk arising from the capital constraint and the marking-to-market procedure of the futures contracts truncates the firm's payoff profile, which plays a pivotal role in shaping the optimal design of the firm's futures hedge program.

---

[1] Another example is the debacle of Long-Term Capital Management (Jorion, 2001).

[2] Culp and Hanke (1994) report that "four major European banks called in their outstanding loans to MGRM when its problems became public in December 1993. Those loans, which the banks had previously rolled-over each month, denied MGRM much needed cash to finance its variation margin payments and exacerbated its liquidity problems."

[3] Using a unique data set of 280 different commodities, Andersson (2007) does not reject a unit root (random walk) except for some 15% of the commodity price series. He attributes these findings to the low power of statistical unit root tests. As an alternative to statistical tests, he proposes using the hedging error in option prices as an economic test of mean reversion. For the 162 series, the mean reverting process provides a mean absolute error of 3.8% compared to 7.5% for the geometric Brownian motion (random walk).

Given that the futures prices are autocorrelated, the resulting intertemporal linkage is likely to induce the firm to consider a provision for premature termination of its futures hedge program.

In the benchmark case that the firm is not liquidity constrained, the celebrated separation and full-hedging theorems of Danthine (1978), Holthausen (1979), and Feder, Just, and Schmitz (1980) apply. The separation theorem states that the firm's production decision depends neither on its risk attitude nor on the underlying output price uncertainty. The full-hedging theorem states that the firm should completely eliminate its output price risk exposure by adopting a full-hedge via the unbiased futures contracts.

When the choice of the capital commitment, i.e., the severity of the liquidity constraint, is endogenously determined by the firm, we show that the firm voluntarily chooses to limit the amount of capital earmarked for its futures hedge program should the futures prices be positively autocorrelated. The autoregressive specification of the futures price dynamics renders predictability, of which the firm has incentives to take advantage. Specifically, a positive autoregression implies that a loss from a futures position tends to be followed by another loss from the same position. The firm as such finds premature liquidation of its futures position to be ex-post optimal. The amount of capital earmarked to the futures hedge program is thus chosen to strike a balance between ex-ante and ex-post efficient risk sharing. If the futures prices are sufficiently positively correlated, we show that the capital constraint is non-binding in that the optimal capital commitment is less than the firm's capital endowment. Otherwise, we show that the capital constraint becomes binding in that the firm optimally puts aside all of its capital stock for the futures hedge program. In the case of non-binding capital constraint, we show that the firm's optimal futures position is likely to be an over-hedge for reasonable preferences. In the case of binding capital constraint, the firm's optimal futures position is an under-hedge or an over-hedge, depending on whether the autocorrelation coefficient of the futures price dynamics is below or above a critical positive value, respectively. Finally, if the futures prices are uncorrelated or negatively autocorrelated, premature liquidation of the futures position is never ex-post optimal, thereby making the firm prefer not to be liquidity constrained and the separation and full-hedging theorems follow.

In a similar model in which the competitive firm faces an exogenous liquidity constraint and the futures price dynamics follows a random walk, Lien (2003) shows the optimality of an under-hedge. Wong (2004a, 2004b) and Wong and Xu (2006) further show that the liquidity constrained firm optimally cuts down its production. These results are in line with those of Paroush and Wolf (1989) in that the presence of residual unhedgeable risk would adversely affect the hedging and production decisions of the competitive firm under output price uncertainty. In contrast, we follow Wong (2008) to allow not only an endogenous liquidity constraint but also a first-order autocorrelation of the futures price dynamics. The latter renders the futures prices predictability of which the firm has incentives to take advantage. This explains why an over-hedge, coupled with a commitment to premature liquidation, is optimal when the futures prices are positively autocorrelated. When the futures prices are uncorrelated or negatively autocorrelated, premature liquidation is suboptimal and thus the firm adopts a full-hedge. In the case of an exogenously liquidity constraint, premature liquidation is inevitable so that an under-hedge is called for to limit the potential loss due to a lack of liquidity. The disparate results thus identify factors such as the predictability of futures prices, the severity of liquidity constraints, and the attitude of risk preferences to be crucial for the optimal design of a futures hedge program.

The rest of this paper is organized as follows. Section 2 develops a two-period model of the optimal design of a futures hedge program by a competitive firm under output price uncertainty. Due to a capital constraint and the marking-to-market procedure of futures contracts, the firm faces endogenous liquidity risk. Section 3 examines a benchmark case in which the firm is not subject to any liquidity constraints. Section 4 derives the firm's optimal futures hedge program when the firm is endowed with an infinite amount of capital. Section 5 goes on to derive the firm's optimal futures hedge program when the firm is endowed with a finite amount of capital. Section 6 constructs numerical examples to shed light on the theoretical findings. The final section concludes.

## 2. The Model

Consider a dynamic variant model of the competitive firm under output price uncertainty à la Sandmo (1971). There are two periods with three dates, indexed by $t = 0$, 1, and 2. Interest rates in both periods are known with certainty at $t = 0$. To simplify notation, we suppress the known interest factors by compounding all cash flows to their futures values at $t = 2$.

To begin, the firm is endowed with a fixed amount of capital, $\overline{k} > 0$. The firm produces a single commodity according to a deterministic cost function, $c(q)$, where $q \geq 0$ is the level of output chosen by the firm at $t = 0$. We assume that $c(q)$ satisfies that $c(0) = c'(0) = 0$, and that $c'(q) > 0$ and $c''(q) > 0$ for all $q > 0$. The firm sells its entire output, $q$, at $t = 2$ at the then prevailing spot price, $p_2$, that is not known ex ante.

To hedge its exposure to the output price uncertainty, the firm can trade infinitely divisible futures contracts at $t = 0$. Each of the futures contracts calls for delivery of one unit of output at $t = 2$, and is marked to market at $t = 1$. Let $f_t$ be the futures price at date $t$ ($t = 0$, 1, and 2). While the initial futures price, $f_0$, is predetermined at $t = 0$, the other futures prices, $f_1$ and $f_2$, are regarded as positive random variables. In the absence of basis risk, the futures price at $t = 2$ must be set equal to the spot price at that time by convergence. Thus, we have $f_2 = p_2$.

We model the futures price dynamics by assuming that $f_t = f_{t-1} + \varepsilon_t$ for $t = 1$ and 2, where $\varepsilon_2 = \rho\varepsilon_1 + \delta$, $\rho$ is a scalar, and $\varepsilon_1$ and $\delta$ are two random variables independent of each other. To focus on the firm's hedging motive, vis-à-vis its speculative motive, we further assume that $\varepsilon_1$ and $\delta$ have means of zero so that the initial futures price, $f_0$, is unbiased and set equal to the unconditional expected value of the random spot price at $t = 2$, $p_2$. The futures price dynamics as such is a first-order positive or negative autoregression, depending on whether $\rho$ is positive or negative, respectively. If $\rho = 0$, the futures price dynamics becomes a random walk.

We delineate the firm's futures hedge program by a pair, $(h, k)$, where $h > 0$ is the number of the futures contracts sold by the firm at $t = 0$, and $k \in [0, \overline{k}]$ is the fixed amount of capital earmarked for the futures hedge program.[4] Due to marking to market at

---

[4]In the appendix, we show that it is never optimal for the firm to opt for a long futures position, i.e., $h < 0$. Hence, we can restrict our attention to the case that the firm always chooses a short futures position.

$t = 1$, the firm suffers a loss (or enjoys a gain if negative) of $(f_1 - f_0)h$ at $t = 1$ from its short futures position, $h$. The firm's futures hedge program, $(h, k)$, dictates the firm to prematurely liquidate its short futures position at $t = 1$ if the interim loss exhausts the earmarked capital, i.e., if $(f_1 - f_0)h > k$. Thus, the firm's random profit at $t = 2$ in this liquidation case, $\pi_\ell$, is given by

$$\pi_\ell = p_2 q + (f_0 - f_1)h - c(q) = f_0 q + \varepsilon_1[(1+\rho)q - h] + \delta q - c(q), \qquad (1)$$

where the second equality follows from the assumed futures price dynamics. On the other hand, if $(f_1 - f_0)h \leq k$, the firm holds its short futures position until $t = 2$. Thus, the firm's random profit at $t = 2$ in this continuation case, $\pi_c$, is given by

$$\pi_c = p_2 q + (f_0 - f_2)h - c(q) = f_0 q + [(1+\rho)\varepsilon_1 + \delta](q - h) - c(q), \qquad (2)$$

where the second equality follows from the assumed futures price dynamics.

The firm is risk averse and possesses a von Neumann-Morgenstern utility function, $u(\pi)$, defined over its profit at $t = 2$, $\pi$, where $u'(\pi) > 0$ and $u''(\pi) < 0$.[5] Anticipating the endogenous liquidity constraint at $t = 1$, the firm chooses its output level, $q \geq 0$, and devises its futures hedge program, $(h, k)$, so as to maximize the expected utility of its random profit at $t = 2$:

$$\max_{q \geq 0, h > 0, 0 \leq k \leq \bar{k}} \int_{-\infty}^{k/h} \mathrm{E}[u(\pi_c)] g(\varepsilon_1) \, \mathrm{d}\varepsilon_1 + \int_{k/h}^{\infty} \mathrm{E}[u(\pi_\ell)] g(\varepsilon_1) \, \mathrm{d}\varepsilon_1, \qquad (3)$$

where $\mathrm{E}(\cdot)$ is the expectation operator with respect to the probability density function of $\delta$, $g(\varepsilon_1)$ is the probability density function of $\varepsilon_1$, and $\pi_\ell$ and $\pi_c$ are defined in Eqs. (1) and (2), respectively. We refer to the short futures position, $h$, as an under-hedge, a full-hedge, or an over-hedge if $h$ is less than, equal to, or greater than $q$, respectively.

The Kuhn-Tucker conditions for program (3) are given by[6]

$$\int_{-\infty}^{k^*/h^*} \mathrm{E}\{u'(\pi_c^*)[f_0 + (1+\rho)\varepsilon_1 + \delta - c'(q^*)]\} g(\varepsilon_1) \, \mathrm{d}\varepsilon_1$$

$$+ \int_{k^*/h^*}^{\infty} \mathrm{E}\{u'(\pi_\ell^*)[f_0 + (1+\rho)\varepsilon_1 + \delta - c'(q^*)]\} g(\varepsilon_1) \, \mathrm{d}\varepsilon_1 = 0, \qquad (4)$$

$$- \int_{-\infty}^{k^*/h^*} \mathrm{E}\{u'(\pi_c^*)[(1+\rho)\varepsilon_1 + \delta]\} g(\varepsilon_1) \, \mathrm{d}\varepsilon_1 - \int_{k^*/h^*}^{\infty} \mathrm{E}[u'(\pi_\ell^*)] \varepsilon_1 g(\varepsilon_1) \, \mathrm{d}\varepsilon_1$$

$$- \mathrm{E}[u(\pi_{c0}^*) - u(\pi_{\ell 0}^*)] g(k^*/h^*) k^*/h^{*2} = 0, \qquad (5)$$

$$\mathrm{E}[u(\pi_{c0}^*) - u(\pi_{\ell 0}^*)] g(k^*/h^*)/h^* - \lambda^* \leq 0, \qquad (6)$$

---

[5] The risk-averse behavior of the firm can be motivated by managerial risk aversion (Stulz, 1984), corporate taxes (Smith and Stulz, 1985), costs of financial distress (Smith and Stulz, 1985), and capital market imperfections (Stulz, 1990; Froot, Scharfstein, and Stein, 1993). See Tufano (1996) for evidence that managerial risk aversion is a rationale for corporate risk management in the gold mining industry.

[6] The second-order conditions for program (3) are satisfied given risk aversion and the strictly convexity of $c(q)$.

and
$$\overline{k} - k^* \geq 0, \tag{7}$$

where conditions (5) and (6) follow from using Leibniz's rule, $\lambda^*$ is the Lagrange multiplier, $\pi^*_{c0} = f_0 q^* + [(1+\rho)k^*/h^* + \delta](q^* - h^*) - c(q^*)$, $\pi^*_{\ell 0} = [f_0 + (1+\rho)k^*/h^* + \delta]q^* - k^* - c(q^*)$, and an asterisk (*) signifies an optimal level. Should $k^* > 0$, condition (6) holds with equality. Likewise, should $\lambda^* > 0$, condition (7) holds with equality.

## 3. Benchmark Case with no Liquidity Constraints

As a benchmark, we consider in this section the case that the firm is not liquidity constrained, which is tantamount to setting $k = \infty$. In this benchmark case, Program (3) becomes

$$\max_{q \geq 0, h > 0} \int_{-\infty}^{\infty} \mathrm{E}[u(\pi_c)] g(\varepsilon_1) \, \mathrm{d}\varepsilon_1. \tag{8}$$

The first-order conditions for program (8) are given by

$$\int_{-\infty}^{\infty} \mathrm{E}\{u'(\pi_c^0)[f_0 + (1+\rho)\varepsilon_1 + \delta - c'(q^0)]\} g(\varepsilon_1) \, \mathrm{d}\varepsilon_1 = 0, \tag{9}$$

and

$$-\int_{-\infty}^{\infty} \mathrm{E}\{u'(\pi_c^0)[(1+\rho)\varepsilon_1 + \delta]\} g(\varepsilon_1) \, \mathrm{d}\varepsilon_1 = 0, \tag{10}$$

where a nought ($^0$) indicates an optimal level.

Solving Eqs. (9) and (10) yields the following proposition, where all proofs of propositions are given in Appendix B.

**Proposition 1.** *Given that the competitive firm is not liquidity constrained, i.e., $k = \infty$, the firm's optimal output level, $q^0$, solves*

$$c'(q^0) = f_0, \tag{11}$$

*and its optimal futures position, $h^0$, is a full-hedge, i.e., $h^0 = q^0$.*

The intuition of Proposition 1 is as follows. If the firm is not liquidity constrained, its random profit at $t = 2$ is given by Eq. (2) only. The firm could have completely eliminated all the price risk had it chosen $h = q$ within its own discretion. Alternatively put, the degree of price risk exposure to be assumed by the firm should be totally unrelated to its production decision. The optimal output level is then chosen to maximize $f_0 q - c(q)$, thereby yielding $q^0$ that solves Eq. (11). Since the futures contracts are unbiased, they offers actuarially fair "insurance" to the firm. Being risk averse, the firm finds it optimal to opt for full insurance via a full-hedge, i.e., $h^0 = q^0$. These results are simply the well-known separation and full-hedging theorems of Danthine (1978), Holthausen (1979), and Feder, Just, and Schmitz (1980).

## 4. The Case of Infinite Capital Endowments

In this section, we consider the case that the firm is endowed with an infinite amount of capital, $\bar{k} = \infty$, and optimally chooses the liquidity threshold, $k$, at $t = 0$. This is also the case analyzed by Wong (2008).

The following proposition characterizes the firm's optimal liquidation threshold, $k^*$, as a function of the autocorrelation coefficient, $\rho$.

**Proposition 2.** *Given that the competitive firm is endowed with an infinite amount of capital, $\bar{k} = \infty$, and optimally devises its futures hedge program, $(h^*, k^*)$, the firm commits to the optimal liquidation threshold, $k^*$, that is positive and finite (infinite) if the autocorrelation coefficient, $\rho$, is positive (non-positive).*

The intuition of Proposition 2 is as follows. If the firm chooses $k = \infty$, risk sharing is ex-ante efficient because the firm can completely eliminate all the price risk. However, this is not ex-post efficient, especially when $\rho > 0$. To see this, note that for any given $k < \infty$ the firm prematurely liquidates its futures position at $t = 1$ for all $\varepsilon_1 \in [k/h, \infty)$. Conditioned on premature liquidation, the expected value of $f_2$ is equal to $f_1 + \rho \varepsilon_1$, which is greater (not greater) than $f_1$ when $\rho > (\leq) 0$. Thus, it is ex-post optimal for the firm to liquidate its futures position prematurely to limit further losses if $\rho > 0$. In this case, the firm chooses the optimal threshold level, $k^*$, to be finite so as to strike a balance between ex-ante and ex-post efficient risk sharing. If $\rho \leq 0$, premature liquidation is never ex-post optimal and thus the firm chooses $k^* = \infty$.

The following proposition is an immediate consequence of Propositions 1 and 2.

**Proposition 3.** *Given that the competitive firm is endowed with an infinite amount of capital, $\bar{k} = \infty$, and optimally devises its futures hedge program, $(h^*, k^*)$, the firm's optimal output level, $q^*$, equals the benchmark level, $q^0$, and its optimal futures position, $h^*$, is a full-hedge, i.e., $h^* = q^*$, if the autocorrelation coefficient, $\rho$, is non-positive.*

When $\rho > 0$, Proposition 2 implies that the firm voluntarily chooses to be liquidity constrained, i.e., $k^* < \infty$. Hence, in this case, condition (6) holds with equality and the solution, $(q^*, h^*, k^*)$, solves Eqs. (4), (5), and (6) simultaneously. The following proposition characterizes the liquidity constrained firm's optimal futures position, $h^*$.

**Proposition 4.** *Given that the competitive firm is endowed with an infinite amount of capital, $\bar{k} = \infty$, and optimally devises its futures hedge program, $(h^*, k^*)$, the firm's optimal futures position, $h^*$, is an over-hedge, i.e., $h^* > q^*$, if the autocorrelation coefficient, $\rho$, is positive and the firm's utility function, $u(\pi)$, satisfies either constant or increasing absolute risk aversion.*

To see the intuition of Proposition 4, we refer to Eqs. (1) and (2). If the firm adopts a full-hedge, i.e., $h = q$, its profit at $t = 2$ remains stochastic due to the residual price risk, $(\rho \varepsilon_1 + \delta)q$, that arises from the premature closure of its hedge program at $t = 1$. This creates an income effect because the presence of the liquidity risk reduces the attainable expected utility under risk aversion. To attain the former expected utility level (with no risk), the firm has to be compensated with additional income. Taking away this compensation gives rise to the income effect (see Wong, 1997). Under IARA (DARA), the firm becomes less (more) risk averse and thus is willing (unwilling) to take on the liquidity risk. The firm as such shorts more (less) of the futures contracts so as to enlarge (shrink) the interval, $[k/h, \infty)$, over which the premature liquidation of the futures position at $t = 1$ prevails. Since $\rho > 0$, inspection of Eqs. (1) and (2) reveals that the high (low) realizations of the firm's random profit at $t = 2$ occur when the futures position is (is not) prematurely liquidated at $t = 1$. Being risk averse, the firm would like to shift profits from the high-profit states to the low-profit states. This goal can be achieved by shorting more of the futures contracts, i.e., $h > q$, as is evident from Eqs. (1) and (2). Such an over-hedging incentive is reinforced (alleviated) under IARA (DARA). Thus, the firm optimally opts for an over-hedge, i.e., $h^* > q^*$, under either CARA or IARA.

## 5. The Case of Finite Capital Endowments

In this section, we consider the case that the firm is endowed with a finite amount of capital, $0 < \bar{k} < \infty$, and optimally chooses the liquidity threshold, $k$, at $t = 0$.

Suppose that the capital constraint is strictly binding, i.e., $\lambda^* > 0$ so that $k^* = \bar{k}$.[7] The Kuhn-Tucker conditions for program (3) under the binding capital constraint become

$$\int_{-\infty}^{\bar{k}/h^*} \mathrm{E}\{u'(\pi_c^*)[f_0 + (1+\rho)\varepsilon_1 + \delta - c'(q^*)]\}g(\varepsilon_1)\,\mathrm{d}\varepsilon_1$$

$$+ \int_{\bar{k}/h^*}^{\infty} \mathrm{E}\{u'(\pi_\ell^*)[f_0 + (1+\rho)\varepsilon_1 + \delta - c'(q^*)]\}g(\varepsilon_1)\,\mathrm{d}\varepsilon_1 = 0, \qquad (12)$$

$$- \int_{-\infty}^{\bar{k}/h^*} \mathrm{E}\{u'(\pi_c^*)[(1+\rho)\varepsilon_1 + \delta]\}g(\varepsilon_1)\,\mathrm{d}\varepsilon_1 - \int_{\bar{k}/h^*}^{\infty} \mathrm{E}[u'(\pi_\ell^*)]\varepsilon_1 g(\varepsilon_1)\,\mathrm{d}\varepsilon_1$$

$$-\mathrm{E}[u(\pi_{c0}^*) - u(\pi_{\ell 0}^*)]g(\bar{k}/h^*)\bar{k}/h^{*2} = 0, \qquad (13)$$

and

$$\mathrm{E}[u(\pi_{c0}^*) - u(\pi_{\ell 0}^*)] > 0, \qquad (14)$$

where $\pi_{c0}^* = f_0 q^* + [(1+\rho)\bar{k}/h^* + \delta](q - h^*) - c(q^*)$ and $\pi_{\ell 0}^* = [f_0 + (1+\rho)\bar{k}/h^* + \delta]q^* - \bar{k} - c(q^*)$.

To examine the firm's optimal futures position, $h^*$, under the binding capital constraint, we let $L(\rho)$ be the left-hand side of Eq. (13) evaluated at $h^* = q^*$:

$$L(\rho) = -(1+\rho)u'[f_0 q^* - c(q^*)] \int_{-\infty}^{\bar{k}/q^*} \varepsilon_1 g(\varepsilon_1)\,\mathrm{d}\varepsilon_1$$

$$- \int_{\bar{k}/q^*}^{\infty} \mathrm{E}\{u'[(f_0 + \rho\varepsilon_1 + \delta)q^* - c(q^*)]\}\varepsilon_1 g(\varepsilon_1)\,\mathrm{d}\varepsilon_1$$

---

[7] This is the case analyzed by Lien (2003) and Wong (2004a, 2004b), and Wong and Xu (2006) who restrict the correlation coefficient, $\rho$, to be zero, i.e., the futures price dynamics follows a random walk.

$$+\left\{\mathrm{E}\{u[(f_0+\delta)q^*+\rho\bar{k}-c(q^*)]\}-u[f_0q^*-c(q^*)]\right\}g(\bar{k}/q^*)\bar{k}/q^{*2}. \tag{15}$$

Since $\varepsilon_1$ has a mean of zero, we can write Eq. (15) as

$$L(\rho)=\int_{\bar{k}/q^*}^{\infty}\left\{(1+\rho)u'[f_0q^*-c(q^*)]-\mathrm{E}\{u'[(f_0+\rho\varepsilon_1+\delta)q^*-c(q^*)]\}\right\}\varepsilon_1 g(\varepsilon_1)\,\mathrm{d}\varepsilon_1$$

$$+\left\{\mathrm{E}\{u[(f_0+\delta)q^*+\rho\bar{k}-c(q^*)]\}-u[f_0q^*-c(q^*)]\right\}g(\bar{k}/q^*)\bar{k}/q^{*2}. \tag{16}$$

If $L(\rho) < (>) 0$, it follows from Eq. (13) and the second-order condition for program (3) that $h^* < (>) q^*$.

When there are multiple sources of uncertainty, it is well-known that the Arrow-Pratt theory of risk aversion is usually too weak to yield intuitively appealing results (Gollier, 2001). Kimball (1990, 1993) defines $u'''(\pi) \geq 0$ as prudence, which measures the propensity to prepare and forearm oneself under uncertainty, vis-à-vis risk aversion that is how much one dislikes uncertainty and would turn away from it if one could. As shown by Leland (1968), Drèze and Modigliani (1972), and Kimball (1990), prudence is both necessary and sufficient to induce precautionary saving. Moreover, prudence is implied by decreasing absolute risk aversion, which is instrumental in yielding many intuitive comparative statics under uncertainty (Gollier, 2001).

The following proposition characterizes the firm's optimal futures position, $h^*$, under the binding capital constraint, $k^* = \bar{k}$.

**Proposition 5.** *Given that the competitive firm is endowed with a finite amount of capital, $0 < \bar{k} < \infty$, and optimally devises its futures hedge program, $(h^*, k^*)$, such that $k^* = \bar{k}$, the firm's optimal futures position, $h^*$, is an under-hedge, a full-hedge, or an over-hedge, depending on whether the autocorrelation coefficient, $\rho$, is less than, equal to, or greater than $\rho^*$, respectively, where $\rho^* > 0$ uniquely solves $L(\rho^*) = 0$, if the firm is prudent.*

To see the intuition of Proposition 5, we refer to Eqs. (1) and (2). If the firm adopts a full-hedge, i.e., $h = q^*$, its random profit at $t = 2$ becomes

$$\pi = \begin{cases} f_0 q^* - c(q^*) & \text{if } \varepsilon_1 \leq \bar{k}/q^*, \\ (f_0 + \rho\varepsilon_1 + \delta)q^* - c(q^*) & \text{if } \varepsilon_1 > \bar{k}/q^*. \end{cases} \tag{17}$$

Eq. (17) implies that a full-hedge is not optimal due to the residual output price risk, $(\rho\varepsilon_1 + \delta)q^*$, that arises from the premature liquidation of the futures position at $t = 1$. According to Kimball (1990, 1993), the prudent firm is more sensitive to low realizations of its random profit at $t = 2$ than to high ones. If $\rho$ is not too (is sufficiently) positive, i.e., $\rho < (>) \rho^*$, it is evident from Eq. (17) that the low realizations of the firm's random profit at $t = 2$ occur when the futures position is (is not) prematurely liquidated at $t = 1$. Thus, to avoid these realizations the prudent firm has incentives to short less (more) of the futures contracts, i.e., $h < (>) q^*$, so as to shrink (enlarge) the interval, $[\bar{k}/h, \infty)$, over which the premature liquidation of the futures position prevails at $t = 1$. The prudent firm as such optimally opts for an under-hedge (over-hedge), i.e., $h^* < (>) q^*$, when $\rho < (>) \rho^*$.

Proposition 5 characterizes the firm's optimal futures position only when the capital constraint is indeed binding, which is the case when condition (14) holds. The following proposition characterizes sufficient conditions under which condition (14) holds.

**Proposition 6.** *Given that the competitive firm is endowed with a finite amount of capital, $0 < \bar{k} < \infty$, and is prudent, the firm finds it optimal to put aside all of its capital stock, $\bar{k}$, for the futures hedge program, $(h^*, k^*)$, if the autocorrelation coefficient, $\rho$, is non-positive.*

If the firm were endowed with an infinite amount of capital, we know from Proposition 2 that the firm would have chosen $k^* = \infty$ for all $\rho \leq 0$. Since $\bar{k}$ is in fact finite, it follows that the firm optimally chooses $k^* = \bar{k}$ for all $\rho \leq 0$, as is shown in Proposition 6.

We now consider the case that the capital constraint is non-binding or just binding, i.e., $\lambda^* = 0$. From Proposition 6, we know that a necessary condition for this case is that $\rho > 0$. The Kuhn-Tucker conditions for program (3) under the non-binding or just-binding capital constraint become

$$\int_{-\infty}^{k^*/h^*} \mathrm{E}\{u'(\pi_c^*)[f_0 + (1+\rho)\varepsilon_1 + \delta - c'(q^*)]\}g(\varepsilon_1)\,\mathrm{d}\varepsilon_1$$

$$+ \int_{k^*/h^*}^{\infty} \mathrm{E}\{u'(\pi_\ell^*)[f_0 + (1+\rho)\varepsilon_1 + \delta - c'(q^*)]\}g(\varepsilon_1)\,\mathrm{d}\varepsilon_1 = 0, \tag{18}$$

$$-\int_{-\infty}^{k^*/h^*} \mathrm{E}\{u'(\pi_c^*)[(1+\rho)\varepsilon_1 + \delta]\}g(\varepsilon_1)\,\mathrm{d}\varepsilon_1 - \int_{k^*/h^*}^{\infty} \mathrm{E}[u'(\pi_\ell^*)]\varepsilon_1 g(\varepsilon_1)\,\mathrm{d}\varepsilon_1 = 0, \tag{19}$$

and

$$\mathrm{E}[u(\pi_{c0}^*) - u(\pi_{\ell 0}^*)] = 0, \tag{20}$$

where $\pi_{c0}^* = f_0 q^* + [(1+\rho)k^*/h^* + \delta](q^* - h^*) - c(q^*)$ and $\pi_{\ell 0}^* = [f_0 + (1+\rho)k^*/h^* + \delta]q^* - k^* - c(q^*)$. We derive the solution in the case that the firm's preferences exhibit constant absolute risk aversion in the following proposition.[8]

The following proposition characterizes the firm's optimal futures position, $h^*$, under the non-binding capital constraint, i.e., $k^* < \bar{k}$, or the just binding capital constraint, i.e., $k^* = \bar{k}$.

**Proposition 7.** *Given that the competitive firm is endowed with a finite amount of capital, $0 < \bar{k} < \infty$, and has constant absolute risk aversion, the firm's optimal futures position, $h^*$, is an over-hedge, i.e., $h^* > q$, and the autocorrelation coefficient, $\rho$, is greater than $\rho^*$, if the capital constraint is either non-binding or just binding.*

The intuition of Proposition 7 is similar to that of Proposition 4 and thus is omitted.

## 6. Numerical Examples

To gain more insights into the theoretical findings, we construct numerical examples to quantify the severity of the endogenous liquidity constraint, which is inversely gauged by

---
[8] We do not consider increasing absolute risk aversion (IARA) because IARA is inconsistent with prudence.

the optimal liquidation threshold, $k^*$. We assume that the firm has a negative exponential utility function: $u(\pi) = -e^{-\gamma\pi}$, where $\gamma > 0$ is the constant Arrow-Pratt measure of absolute risk aversion. We further assume that $\varepsilon_1$ and $\delta$ are normally distributed with means of zero and variances of 0.01. For normalization, we set $q = f_0 = 1$ and $c(q) = 0$.

Table 1 report the firm's optimal futures position, $h^*$, for the case that the liquidation threshold, $k$, is exogenously set equal to the fixed capital endowment, $\bar{k}$. Setting $\gamma = 2$, we document the firm's optimal futures position, $h^*$, and the critical autocorrelation coefficient, $\rho^*$, for different values of $k$ and $\rho$.

### Table 1. Optimal futures positions under exogenous liquidity constraints

|  | $\bar{k} = 0.05$ |  | $\bar{k} = 0.1$ |  | $\bar{k} = 0.15$ |  | $\bar{k} = 0.2$ |  |
| --- | --- | --- | --- | --- | --- | --- | --- | --- |
|  | $\rho^*$ | $h^*$ | $\rho^*$ | $h^*$ | $\rho^*$ | $h^*$ | $\rho^*$ | $h^*$ |
| $\rho = 0.01$ |  | 0.9381 |  | 0.9337 |  | 0.9566 |  | 0.9787 |
| $\rho = 0.03$ |  | 0.9728 |  | 0.9659 |  | 0.9801 |  | 0.9906 |
|  | 0.0460 | 1.0000 | 0.0514 | 1.0000 | 0.0462 | 1.0000 | 0.0395 | 1.0000 |
| $\rho = 0.07$ |  | 1.0391 |  | 1.0286 |  | 1.0287 |  | 1.0225 |
| $\rho = 0.09$ |  | 1.0707 |  | 1.0592 |  | 1.0538 |  | 1.0383 |

**Notes:** The competitive firm has a negative exponential utility function: $u(\pi) = -e^{-2\pi}$. The underlying random variables, $\varepsilon_1$ and $\delta$, are normally distributed with means of zero and variances of 0.01. Both the level of output, $q$, and the initial futures price, $f_0$, are normalized to unity. The liquidation threshold, $k$, is exogenously set equal to the firm's fixed amount of capital, $\bar{k}$. This table reports the optimal futures position, $h^*$, and the critical autocorrelation coefficient, $\rho^*$, for different values of the exogenous liquidity constraint, $\bar{k}$, and the autocorrelation coefficient, $\rho$.

As is evident from Table 1, $h^* < (>) 1$ when $\rho < (>) \rho^*$, in accord with Proposition 5. Table 1 also reveals that $h^*$ moves further away from a full-hedge as $\bar{k}$ decreases. That is, when the exogenous liquidity constraint becomes more severe, the firm has to deviate more from full-hedging so as to better cope with the output price uncertainty and the liquidity risk simultaneously.

Table 2 reports the firm's optimal futures position, $h^*$, and the optimal liquidation threshold, $k^*$, when the capital constraint is not binding, i.e., $k^* < \bar{k}$. We document the firm's optimal futures hedge program, $(h^*, k^*)$, for different values of $\gamma$ and $\rho$.

Table 2 shows that a full-hedge is optimal if $\rho$ is small, or else an over-hedge is optimal, implying that an under-hedge is never used. It is also evident from Table 2 that $k^*$ decreases as either $\rho$ increases or $\gamma$ decreases. That is, the firm is willing to commit itself to a more aggressive (i.e., severe) liquidity constraint provided that premature liquidation is indeed ex-post profitable or that the firm is less risk averse and thus does not mind to take on excessive risk.

Table 3 reports the firm's optimal futures position, $h^*$, and the optimal liquidation threshold, $k^*$, when the capital constraint can be binding, i.e., $k^* = \bar{k}$. Setting $\gamma = 2$

**Table 2. Optimal futures hedge programs under non-binding capital constraints**

|  | $\gamma = 1$ |  | $\gamma = 2$ |  | $\gamma = 3$ |  | $\gamma = 4$ |  |
|---|---|---|---|---|---|---|---|---|
|  | $h^*$ | $k^*$ | $h^*$ | $k^*$ | $h^*$ | $k^*$ | $h^*$ | $k^*$ |
| $\rho = 0.01$ | 1.0000 | 0.5000 | 1.0000 | 0.9884 | 1.0000 | 1.4852 | 1.0000 | 1.4998 |
| $\rho = 0.02$ | 1.0000 | 0.2494 | 1.0000 | 0.5000 | 1.0000 | 0.7481 | 1.0000 | 0.9901 |
| $\rho = 0.05$ | 1.0726 | 0.1000 | 1.0070 | 0.1999 | 1.0000 | 0.2970 | 1.0000 | 0.3990 |
| $\rho = 0.1$ | 1.2313 | 0.0473 | 1.0738 | 0.0997 | 1.0188 | 0.1485 | 1.0073 | 0.2000 |
| $\rho = 0.2$ | 1.5103 | 0.0185 | 1.2385 | 0.0472 | 1.1349 | 0.0737 | 1.1031 | 0.0990 |
| $\rho = 0.5$ | 2.1670 | 0.0036 | 1.6292 | 0.0121 | 1.4354 | 0.0243 | 1.3294 | 0.0357 |

**Notes:** The competitive firm has a negative exponential utility function: $u(\pi) = -e^{-\gamma\pi}$, where $\gamma$ is a positive constant. The underlying random variables, $\varepsilon_1$ and $\delta$, are normally distributed with means of zero and variances of 0.01. Both the level of output, $q$, and the initial futures price, $f_0$, are normalized to unity. The capital constraint is assumed to be non-binding, i.e., $k^* < \bar{k}$. This table reports the optimal futures position, $h^*$, and the optimal liquidation threshold, $k^*$, for different values of the risk aversion coefficient, $\gamma$, and the autocorrelation coefficient, $\rho$.

and $\bar{k} = 0.2$, we document the firm's optimal futures hedge program, $(h^*, k^*)$, for different values of $\rho$.

**Table 3. Optimal futures hedge programs**

| $\rho$ | 0.01 | 0.03 | 0.0395 | 0.05 | 0.1 | 0.2 | 0.5 |
|---|---|---|---|---|---|---|---|
| $h^*$ | 0.9787 | 0.9906 | 1.0000 | 1.0070 | 1.0738 | 1.2385 | 1.6292 |
| $k^*$ | 0.2 | 0.2 | 0.2 | 0.1999 | 0.0997 | 0.0472 | 0.0121 |

**Notes:** The competitive firm has a negative exponential utility function: $u(\pi) = -e^{-2\pi}$ and is endowed with a fixed amount of capital, $\bar{k}$, set equal to 0.2. The underlying random variables, $\varepsilon_1$ and $\delta$, are normally distributed with means of zero and variances of 0.01. Both the level of output, $q$, and the initial futures price, $f_0$, are normalized to unity. The critical value, $\rho^*$, as defined in Proposition 5 is 0.0395. This table reports the optimal futures position, $h^*$, and the optimal liquidation threshold, $k^*$, for different values of the autocorrelation coefficient, $\rho$.

It is evident from Table 3 that the capital constraint is binding, i.e., $k^* = \bar{k}$, for all $\rho < 0.05$, and is non-binding, i.e., $k^* < \bar{k}$, for all $\rho \geq 0.05$. Furthermore, in the case of non-binding capital constraint, the firm's optimal futures position, $h^*$, is an over-hedge, i.e., $h^* > q$, and the autocorrelation coefficient, $\rho$, exceeds the critical level, $\rho^*$, that is defined

# 7. Conclusion

In this paper, we have examined the optimal design of a futures hedge program by the competitive firm under output price uncertainty (Sandmo, 1971). The firm's futures hedge program consists of a futures position and an amount of capital earmarked for the program. The firm is subject to a capital constraint in that the earmarked capital cannot exceed the firm's capital endowment. Due to the capital constraint and the marking-to-market procedure of futures contracts, the firm faces endogenous liquidity risk. The futures price dynamics follows a first-order autoregression that includes a random walk as a special case.

When the futures prices are sufficiently positively correlated, we have shown that the capital constraint is non-binding. In this case, the optimal amount of capital earmarked to the futures hedge program is less than the firm's capital endowment. Furthermore, the firm's optimal futures position is likely to be an over-hedge for reasonable preferences. When the futures prices are not too positively correlated, we have shown that the capital constraint is binding. In this case, the firm optimally puts aside all of its capital stock for the futures hedge program. Furthermore, the firm's optimal futures position is an under-hedge or an over-hedge, depending on whether the autocorrelation coefficient of the futures price dynamics is below or above a critical positive value, respectively.

# Appendix A

The firm's ex-ante decision problem is to choose a futures position, $h$, so as to maximize the expected utility of its random profit at $t = 2$, $EU$:

$$\int_{-\infty}^{k/h} \mathrm{E}\Big\{u\{f_0 q + [(1+\rho)\varepsilon_1 + \delta](q-h) - c(q)\}\Big\} g(\varepsilon_1)\,\mathrm{d}\varepsilon_1$$

$$+ \int_{k/h}^{\infty} \mathrm{E}\Big\{u\{f_0 q + \varepsilon_1[(1+\rho)q - h] + \delta q - c(q)\}\Big\} g(\varepsilon_1)\,\mathrm{d}\varepsilon_1 \qquad (\mathrm{A}.1)$$

if $h > 0$, and

$$\int_{-\infty}^{k/h} \mathrm{E}\Big\{u\{f_0 q + \varepsilon_1[(1+\rho)q - h] + \delta q - c(q)\}\Big\} g(\varepsilon_1)\,\mathrm{d}\varepsilon_1$$

$$+ \int_{k/h}^{\infty} \mathrm{E}\Big\{u\{f_0 q + [(1+\rho)\varepsilon_1 + \delta](q-h) - c(q)\}\Big\} g(\varepsilon_1)\,\mathrm{d}\varepsilon_1 \qquad (\mathrm{A}.2)$$

if $h < 0$. In order to solve the firm's optimal futures position, $h^*$, we need to know which equation, Eq. (A.1) or Eq. (A.2), contains the solution.

Consider first the case that $h > 0$. Using Leibniz's rule to partially differentiate $EU$ as defined in Eq. (A.1) with respect to $h$ and evaluating the resulting derivative at $h \to 0^+$ yields

$$\lim_{h \to 0^+} \frac{\partial EU}{\partial h} = -\int_{-\infty}^{\infty} \mathrm{E}\Big\{u'\{[f_0 + (1+\rho)\varepsilon_1 + \delta]q - c(q)\}[(1+\rho)\varepsilon_1 + \delta]\Big\} g(\varepsilon_1)\,\mathrm{d}\varepsilon_1. \qquad (\mathrm{A}.3)$$

Since $\varepsilon_1$ and $\delta$ has means of zero, the right-hand side of Eq. (A.3) is simply the negative of the covariance between $u'\{[f_0 + (1+\rho)\varepsilon_1 + \delta]q - c(q)\}$ and $(1+\rho)\varepsilon_1 + \delta$ with respect to the joint probability density function of $\varepsilon_1$ and $\delta$. Since $u''(\pi) < 0$, we have $\lim_{h \to 0^+} \partial EU/\partial h > 0$.

Now, consider the case that $h < 0$. Using Leibniz's rule to partially differentiate $EU$ as defined in Eq. (A.2) with respect to $h$ and evaluating the resulting derivative at $h \to 0^-$ yields

$$\lim_{h \to 0^-} \frac{\partial EU}{\partial h} = -\int_{-\infty}^{\infty} \mathrm{E}\Big\{u'\{[f_0 + (1+\rho)\varepsilon_1 + \delta]q - c(q)\}[(1+\rho)\varepsilon_1 + \delta]\Big\} g(\varepsilon_1)\, \mathrm{d}\varepsilon_1. \quad \text{(A.4)}$$

Inspection of Eqs. (A.3) and (A.4) reveals that $\lim_{h \to 0^+} \partial EU/\partial h = \lim_{h \to 0^-} \partial EU/\partial h > 0$. Since $EU$ as defined in either Eq. (A.1) or Eq. (A.2) is strictly concave, the firm's optimal futures position, $h^*$, must be a short position, i.e., $h^* > 0$.

## Appendix B

*Proof of Proposition 1.* Adding Eq. (10) to Eq. (9) yields

$$[f_0 - c'(q^0)] \int_{-\infty}^{\infty} \mathrm{E}[u'(\pi_c^0)] g(\varepsilon_1)\, \mathrm{d}\varepsilon_1 = 0. \quad \text{(B.1)}$$

Since $u'(\pi) > 0$, Eq. (B.1) reduces to Eq. (11). If $h^0 = q^0$, the left-hand side of Eq. (10) becomes

$$-(1+\rho) u'[f_0 q^0 - c(q^0)] \int_{-\infty}^{\infty} \varepsilon_1 g(\varepsilon_1)\, \mathrm{d}\varepsilon_1 = 0, \quad \text{(B.2)}$$

since $\varepsilon_1$ and $\delta$ have means of zero. Inspection of Eqs. (10) and (B.2) reveals that $h^0 = q^0$ is indeed the optimal futures position.

*Proof of Proposition 2.* To facilitate the proof, we fix $h = q = q^0$ in program (3) to yield

$$\max_{k \geq 0} u[f_0 q^0 - c(q^0)] \int_{-\infty}^{k/q^0} g(\varepsilon_1)\, \mathrm{d}\varepsilon_1$$

$$+ \int_{k/q^0}^{\infty} \mathrm{E}\{u[(f_0 + \rho\varepsilon_1 + \delta)q^0 - c(q^0)]\} g(\varepsilon_1)\, \mathrm{d}\varepsilon_1. \quad \text{(B.3)}$$

The Kuhn-Tucker condition for program (B.3) is given by

$$\Big\{u[f_0 q^0 - c(q^0)] - \mathrm{E}\{u[(f_0 + \delta)q^0 + \rho k^0 - c(q^0)]\}\Big\} g(k^0/q^0)/q^0 \geq 0, \quad \text{(B.4)}$$

where $k^0$ is the optimal liquidity threshold when $h = q = q^0$. Should $k^0 < \infty$, condition (B.4) holds with equality.

If $\rho \leq 0$, it follows from $u''(\pi) < 0$, $\mathrm{E}(\delta) = 0$, and Jensen's inequality that $u[f_0 q^0 - c(q^0)] \geq u[f_0 q^0 + \rho k^0 - c(q^0)] > \mathrm{E}\{u[(f_0 + \delta)q^0 + \rho k^0 - c(q^0)]\}$, and thus $k^0 = \infty$ by condition (B.4). Since Proposition 1 implies that $h^* = q^* = q^0$ if $k^* = \infty$, it must be the case that $h^* = q^* = q^0$ and $k^* = \infty$ if $k^0 = \infty$. On the other hand, if $\rho > 0$, it is evident that $\mathrm{E}\{u[(f_0+\delta)q^0+\rho k - c(q^0)]\}$ is increasing in $k$. When $k = 0$, it follows from $u''(\pi) < 0$, $\mathrm{E}(\delta) = 0$, and Jensen's inequality that $\mathrm{E}\{u[(f_0 + \delta)q^0 - c(q^0)]\} < u[f_0 q^0 - c(q^0)]$. Also, for $k$ sufficiently large, it must be the case that $\mathrm{E}\{u[(f_0 + \delta)q^0 + \rho k - c(q^0)]\} > u[f_0 q^0 - c(q^0)]$. Thus, there exists a unique point, $k^0 \in (0, \infty)$, such that condition (B.4) holds with equality. Suppose that $k^* = \infty$ but $k^0 < \infty$. It then follows from Proposition 1 that $h^* = q^* = q^0$, which would imply that $k^0 = k^* = \infty$, a contradiction to $k^0 < \infty$.

*Proof of Proposition 3.* When $\rho \leq 0$, Proposition 2 implies that $k^* = \infty$. It then follows from Proposition 1 that $h^* = q^* = q^0$.

*Proof of Proposition 4.* To facilitate the proof, we reformulate the firm's ex-ante decision problem as a two-stage optimization problem with $q$ fixed at $q^*$. In the first stage, the firm chooses its optimal liquidation threshold, $k(h)$, for a given futures position, $h$:

$$k(h) = \arg\max_{k \geq 0} \int_{-\infty}^{k/h} \mathrm{E}[u(\pi_c)]g(\varepsilon_1)\,\mathrm{d}\varepsilon_1 + \int_{k/h}^{\infty} \mathrm{E}[u(\pi_\ell)]g(\varepsilon_1)\,\mathrm{d}\varepsilon_1, \quad (\text{B.5})$$

where $\pi_\ell$ and $\pi_c$ are given in Eqs. (1) and (2) with $q = q^*$, respectively. In the second stage, the firm chooses its optimal futures position, $h^*$, taking the liquidation threshold, $k(h)$, as given by Eq. (B.5):

$$\max_h F(h) = \int_{-\infty}^{k(h)/h} \mathrm{E}[u(\pi_c)]g(\varepsilon_1)\,\mathrm{d}\varepsilon_1 + \int_{k(h)/h}^{\infty} \mathrm{E}[u(\pi_\ell)]g(\varepsilon_1)\,\mathrm{d}\varepsilon_1, \quad (\text{B.6})$$

where $\pi_\ell$ and $\pi_c$ are given in Eqs. (1) and (2) with $q = q^*$ and $k = k(h)$, respectively. The complete solution is thus given by $h^*$ and $k^* = k(h^*)$.

Differentiating $F(h)$ in Eq. (B.6) with respect to $h$, using the envelope theorem, and evaluating the resulting derivative at $h = q^*$ yields

$$F'(q^*) = -(1+\rho)u'[f_0 q^* - c(q^*)] \int_{-\infty}^{k(q^*)/q^*} \varepsilon_1 g(\varepsilon_1)\,\mathrm{d}\varepsilon_1$$

$$- \int_{k(q^*)/q^*}^{\infty} \mathrm{E}\{u'[(f_0 + \rho\varepsilon_1 + \delta)q^* - c(q^*)]\}\varepsilon_1 g(\varepsilon_1)\,\mathrm{d}\varepsilon_1, \quad (\text{B.7})$$

where $k(q^*)$ solves

$$u[f_0 q^* - c(q^*)] = \mathrm{E}\{u[(f_0 + \delta)q^* + \rho k(q^*) - c(q^*)]\}. \quad (\text{B.8})$$

It is evident from Eq. (B.8) that $\rho k(q^*)$ is equal to the risk premium of the zero-mean risk, $\delta q^*$, in the usual Arrow-Pratt sense.

Rewrite Eq. (B.8) as

$$u[f_0 q^* - c(q^*) + m] = \mathrm{E}\{u[(f_0 + \delta)q^* + \rho k(q^*) - c(q^*) + m]\}, \quad (\text{B.9})$$

where $m$ can be interpreted as endowed wealth that takes on an initial value of zero. Differentiating Eq. (B.9) with respect to $m$ and evaluating the resulting derivative at $m = 0$ yields

$$\left.\frac{\partial \rho k(q^*)}{\partial m}\right|_{m=0} = \frac{u'[f_0 q^* - c(q^*)] - \mathrm{E}\{u'[(f_0 + \delta)q^* + \rho k(q^*) - c(q^*)]\}}{\mathrm{E}\{u'[(f_0 + \delta)q^* + \rho k(q^*) - c(q^*)]\}}. \quad (\text{B.10})$$

If $u(\pi)$ satisfies decreasing, constant, or increasing absolute risk aversion (DARA, CARA, or IARA), $\partial \rho k(q^*)/\partial m$ is negative, zero, or positive, respectively. Using the fact that $\varepsilon_1$ has a mean of zero, Eq. (B.7) can be written as

$$F'(q^*) = \int_{k(q^*)/q^*}^{\infty} \left\{ (1+\rho)u'[f_0 q^* - c(q^*)] \right.$$
$$\left. - \mathrm{E}\{u'[(f_0 + \rho\varepsilon_1 + \delta)q^* - c(q^*)]\} \right\} \varepsilon_1 g(\varepsilon_1) \, d\varepsilon_1. \tag{B.11}$$

If $u(\pi)$ satisfies CARA (IARA), Eq. (B.10) implies that

$$u'[f_0 q^* - c(q^*)] = (>) \mathrm{E}\{u'[(f_0 + \delta)q^* + \rho k(q^*) - c(q^*)]\}. \tag{B.12}$$

Since $\rho > 0$, Eq. (B.22) and risk aversion imply that $(1+\rho)u'[f_0 q^* - c(q^*)] > \mathrm{E}\{u'[(f_0 + \delta)q^* + \rho k(q^*) - c(q^*)]\} > \mathrm{E}\{u'[(f_0 + \rho\varepsilon_1 + \delta)q^* - c(q^*)]\}$ for all $\varepsilon_1 > k(q^*)/q^*$. It then follows from Eq. (B.11) that $F'(q^*) > 0$ and thus $h^* > q^*$ if $u(\pi)$ satisfies either CARA or IARA.

*Proof of Proposition 5.* Differentiating $L(\rho)$ with respect to $\rho$ yields

$$L'(\rho) = \int_{\bar{k}/q^*}^{\infty} \left\{ u'[f_0 q^* - c(q^*)] - \mathrm{E}\{u''[(f_0 + \rho\varepsilon_1 + \delta)q^* - c(q^*)]\}\varepsilon_1 q \right\} \varepsilon_1 g(\varepsilon_1) \, d\varepsilon_1$$
$$+ \mathrm{E}\{u'[(f_0 + \delta)q^* + \rho\bar{k} - c(q^*)]\} g(\bar{k}/q^*)\bar{k}^2/q^{*2}. \tag{B.13}$$

Since $u'(\pi) > 0$ and $u''(\pi) < 0$, Eq. (B.13) implies that $L'(\rho) > 0$. Evaluating Eq. (16) at $\rho = 0$ yields

$$L(0) = \left\{ u'[f_0 q^* - c(q^*)] - \mathrm{E}\{u'[(f_0 + \delta)q^* - c(q^*)]\} \right\} \int_{\bar{k}/q^*}^{\infty} \varepsilon_1 g(\varepsilon_1) \, d\varepsilon_1$$
$$+ \left\{ \mathrm{E}\{u[(f_0 + \delta)q^* - c(q^*)]\} - u[f_0 q^* - c(q^*)] \right\} g(\bar{k}/q^*)\bar{k}/q^{*2}. \tag{B.14}$$

Since $u''(\pi) < 0$ and $\mathrm{E}(\delta) = 0$, Jensen's inequality implies that $\mathrm{E}\{u[(f_0+\delta)q^* - c(q^*)]\} < u[f_0 q^* - c(q^*)]$. The second term on the right-hand side of Eq. (B.14) is negative. Since $u'''(\pi) \geq 0$, it follows from $\mathrm{E}(\delta) = 0$ and Jensen's inequality that $\mathrm{E}\{u'[(f_0 + \delta)q^* - c(q^*)]\} \geq u'[f_0 q^* - c(q^*)]$. The first term on the right-hand side of Eq. (B.14) is non-positive and thus $L(0) < 0$. Now, consider the case that $\rho$ is sufficiently large such that $(1+\rho)u'[f_0 q^* - c(q^*)] > \mathrm{E}\{u'[(f_0+\rho\varepsilon_1+\delta)q^*-c(q^*)]\}$ for all $\varepsilon_1 > 0$ and $u[f_0 q^* - c(q^*)] < \mathrm{E}\{u[(f_0 + \delta)q^* + \rho\bar{k} - c(q^*)]\}$. Thus, for $\rho$ sufficiently large, it follows from Eq. (16) that $L(\rho) > 0$. Since $L(0) < 0$, $L(\rho) > 0$ for $\rho$ sufficiently large, and $L'(\rho) > 0$, there must exist a unique point, $\rho^* > 0$, that solves $L(\rho^*) = 0$. Thus, for all $\rho < (>) \rho^*$, we have $L(\rho) < (>) 0$. It then follows from Eq. (13) and the second-order condition for program (3) that $h^* < (>) q^*$ for all $\rho < (>) \rho^*$.

*Proof of Proposition 6.* Let $\Phi(\pi_{\ell 0}^*)$ and $\Psi(\pi_{c 0}^*)$ be the cumulative distribution functions (CDFs) of $\pi_{\ell 0}^*$ and $\pi_{c 0}^*$ defined in condition (14), respectively, and let

$$T(x) = \int_{-\infty}^{x} [\Phi(y) - \Psi(y)] \, dy. \tag{B.15}$$

Using Eq. (B.15), we can write the left-hand side of condition (14) as

$$\mathrm{E}[u(\pi_{\ell 0}^*)] - \mathrm{E}[u(\pi_{c0}^*)] = \int_{-\infty}^{\infty} u(x)\,\mathrm{d}[\Phi(x) - \Psi(x)] = \int_{-\infty}^{\infty} u''(x) T(x)\,\mathrm{d}x, \quad (\text{B.16})$$

where the second equality follows from $u'(\infty) = 0$ and integration by parts. In light of Eq. (B.16), condition (14) holds if $\Phi(x)$ is either a second-order stochastic dominance shift or a mean-preserving-spread shift of $\Psi(x)$.

Note that $T(-\infty) = 0$ and

$$T(\infty) = \int_{-\infty}^{\infty} [\Phi(x) - \Psi(x)]\,\mathrm{d}x = \int_{-\infty}^{\infty} x\,\mathrm{d}\Psi(x) - \int_{-\infty}^{\infty} x\,\mathrm{d}\Phi(x) = -\rho \bar{k}, \quad (\text{B.17})$$

where the second equality follows from integration by parts. Since $\rho \leq 0$, Eq. (B.17) implies that $T(\infty) \geq 0$, where the equality holds only when $\rho = 0$. We can write

$$\pi_{\ell 0}^* = \pi_{c0}^* + \rho \bar{k} + \delta h^*$$

$$= \pi_{c0}^* + \left[\pi_{c0}^* - f_0 q^* - \bar{k}\left(\frac{q^* - h^*}{h^*}\right) + c(q^*)\right]\left(\frac{h^*}{q^* - h^*}\right). \quad (\text{B.18})$$

Using the change-of-variable technique (Hogg and Craig, 1989) and Eq. (B.18), we have $\Psi(\pi_{c0}^*) = \Phi\{\pi_{c0}^* + [\pi_{c0}^* - f_0 q^* - \bar{k}(q^* - h^*)/h^* + c(q^*)]h^*/(q^* - h^*)\}$. Differentiating $T(x)$ in Eq. (B.15) with respect to $x$ and using Leibniz's rule yields $T'(x) = \Phi(x) - \Psi(x)$. It follows from $\Psi(x) = \Phi\{x + [x - f_0 q^* - \bar{k}(q^* - h^*)/h^* + c(q^*)]h^*/(q^* - h^*)\}$ and $h^* < q^*$ that $\Phi(x) - \Psi(x) > (<) 0$ if $x < (>) f_0 q^* + \bar{k}(q^* - h^*)/h^* - c(q^*)$. Hence, $T(x)$ is strictly increasing for all $x < f_0 q^* + \bar{k}(q^* - h^*)/h^* - c(q^*)$ and strictly decreasing for all $x > f_0 q^* + \bar{k}(q^* - h^*)/h^* - c(q^*)$. Since $T(-\infty) = 0$, $T(\infty) \geq 0$, and $T(x)$ is first increasing and then decreasing in $x$, we have $T(x) > 0$ for all $x$. In other words, $\Phi(x)$ is a second-order stochastic dominance shift of $\Psi(x)$ for all $\rho < 0$ and is a mean-preserving-spread shift of $\Psi(x)$ when $\rho = 0$. Thus, for all $\rho \leq 0$, Eq. (B.16) implies that $\mathrm{E}[u(\pi_{c0}^*)] > \mathrm{E}[u(\pi_{\ell 0}^*)]$ given risk aversion.

*Proof of Proposition 7.* To facilitate the proof, the firm's ex-ante decision problem is formulated as a two-stage optimization problem. In the first stage, the firm chooses its optimal liquidation threshold, $k(h)$, for a given short futures position, $h$:

$$k(h) = \arg\max_{k \geq 0} \int_{-\infty}^{k/h} \mathrm{E}[u(\pi_c)] g(\varepsilon_1)\,\mathrm{d}\varepsilon_1 + \int_{k/h}^{\infty} \mathrm{E}[u(\pi_\ell)] g(\varepsilon_1)\,\mathrm{d}\varepsilon_1, \quad (\text{B.19})$$

where $\pi_\ell$ and $\pi_c$ are given in Eqs. (1) and (2) with $q = q^*$, respectively. In the second stage, the firm chooses its optimal futures position, $h^*$, taking the liquidation threshold, $k(h)$, as given by Eq. (B.19):

$$\max_h G(h) = \int_{-\infty}^{k(h)/h} \mathrm{E}[u(\pi_c)] g(\varepsilon_1)\,\mathrm{d}\varepsilon_1 + \int_{k(h)/h}^{\infty} \mathrm{E}[u(\pi_\ell)] g(\varepsilon_1)\,\mathrm{d}\varepsilon_1, \quad (\text{B.20})$$

where $\pi_\ell$ and $\pi_c$ are given in Eqs. (1) and (2) with $q = q^*$ and $k = k(h)$, respectively. The complete solution is thus given by $h^*$ and $k^* = k(h^*)$, which also solves Eqs. (19) and (20).

Differentiating $G(h)$ in Eq. (B.20) with respect to $h$, using the envelope theorem, and evaluating the resulting derivative at $h = q^*$ yields

$$G'(q^*) = -(1+\rho)u'[f_0 q^* - c(q^*)] \int_{-\infty}^{k(q^*)/q^*} \varepsilon_1 g(\varepsilon_1)\,\mathrm{d}\varepsilon_1$$

$$- \int_{k(q^*)/q^*}^{\infty} \mathrm{E}\{u'[(f_0 + \rho\varepsilon_1 + \delta)q^* - c(q^*)]\}\varepsilon_1 g(\varepsilon_1)\,\mathrm{d}\varepsilon_1, \tag{B.21}$$

where $k(q^*)$ solves

$$u[f_0 q^* - c(q^*)] = \mathrm{E}\{u[(f_0 + \delta)q^* + \rho k(q^*) - c(q^*)]\}. \tag{B.22}$$

It is evident from Eq. (B.22) that $\rho k(q^*)$ is equal to the risk premium of the zero-mean risk, $\delta q^*$, in the usual Arrow-Pratt sense.

Rewrite Eq. (B.22) as

$$u[f_0 q^* - c(q^*) + m] = \mathrm{E}\{u[(f_0 + \delta)q^* + \rho k(q^*) - c(q^*) + m]\}, \tag{B.23}$$

where $m$ can be interpreted as endowed wealth that takes on an initial value of zero. Differentiating Eq. (B.23) with respect to $m$ and evaluating the resulting derivative at $m = 0$ yields

$$\left.\frac{\partial \rho k(q^*)}{\partial m}\right|_{m=0} = \frac{u'[f_0 q^* - c(q^*)] - \mathrm{E}\{u'[(f_0 + \delta)q^* + \rho k(q^*) - c(q^*)]\}}{\mathrm{E}\{u'[(f_0 + \delta)q^* + \rho k(q^*) - c(q^*)]\}}. \tag{B.24}$$

Since $u(\pi)$ satisfies CARA, Eq. (B.24) implies that

$$u'[f_0 q^* - c(q^*)] = \mathrm{E}\{u'[(f_0 + \delta)q^* + \rho k(q^*) - c(q^*)]\}. \tag{B.25}$$

Using the fact that $\varepsilon_1$ has a mean of zero, we can write Eq. (B.21) as

$$G'(q^*) = \int_{k(q^*)/q^*}^{\infty} \Big\{(1+\rho)u'[f_0 q^* - c(q^*)]$$

$$- \mathrm{E}\{u'[(f_0 + \rho\varepsilon_1 + \delta)q^* - c(q^*)]\}\Big\}\varepsilon_1 g(\varepsilon_1)\,\mathrm{d}\varepsilon_1. \tag{B.26}$$

Since $\rho > 0$, Eq. (B.25) and risk aversion imply that $(1+\rho)u'[f_0 q^* - c(q^*)] > \mathrm{E}\{u'[(f_0 + \delta)q^* + \rho k(q^*) - c(q^*)]\} > \mathrm{E}\{u'[(f_0 + \rho\varepsilon_1 + \delta)q^* - c(q^*)]\}$ for all $\varepsilon_1 > k(q^*)/q^*$. It then follows from Eq. (B.26) that $G'(q^*) > 0$ and thus $h^* > q^*$ if $u(\pi)$ satisfies CARA.

Suppose that there is a point, $\rho_1 \in (0, \rho^*]$, at which the capital constraint is either non-binding or just binding. Since $k^* = \bar{k}$ for all $\rho \leq 0$ according to Proposition 2, continuity implies that there must exist a point, $\rho_2 \in (0, \rho_1]$, such that the capital constraint is just binding, i.e., $k^* = \bar{k}$. Since $\rho_2 \leq \rho^*$, Proposition 1 implies that $h^* \leq q$ at $\rho_2$, a contradiction to our conclusion that $h^* > q$ if the capital constraint is either non-binding or just binding. Hence, our supposition is wrong so that $\rho > \rho^*$ whenever the capital constraint is either non-binding or just binding.

# References

Andersson, H. (2007). Are commodity prices mean reverting? *Applied Financial Economics*, **17**, 769–783.

Committee on Payment and Settlement Systems (1998). *OTC derivatives: Settlement procedures and counterparty risk management*. Basel, Switzerland: Bank for International Settlements.

Culp, C. L., & Hanke, S. H. (1994). Derivative dingbats. *The International Economy*, **8**, 12.

Culp, C. L., & Miller, M. H. (1995). Metallgesellschaft and the economics of synthetic storage. *Journal of Applied Corporate Finance*, **7**, 62–76.

Danthine, J.-P. (1978). Information, futures prices, and stabilizing speculation. *Journal of Economic Theory*, **17**, 79–98.

Drèze, J. H., & Modigliani, F. (1972). Consumption decisions under uncertainty. *Journal of Economic Theory*, **5**, 308–335.

Feder, G., Just, R. E., & Schmitz, A. (1980). Futures markets and the theory of the firm under price uncertainty. *Quarterly Journal of Economics*, **95**, 317–328.

Froot, K. A., Scharfstein, D. S., & Stein, J. C. (1993). Risk management: Coordinating corporate investment and financing policies. *Journal of Finance*, **48**, 1629–1658.

Gollier, C. (2001). *The Economics of Risk and Time*. Cambridge, MA: MIT Press.

Hilliard, J. E. (1999). Analytics underlying the Metallgesellschaft hedge: Short term futures in a multi-period environment. *Review of Quantitative Finance and Accounting*, **12**, 195–219.

Hogg, R. V., & Craig, A. T. (1989). *Introduction to Mathematical Statistics* (4th ed.). New York, NY: Macmillan Publishing Company.

Holthausen, D. M. (1979). Hedging and the competitive firm under price uncertainty. *American Economic Review*, **69**, 989–995.

Jorion, P. (2001). *Value at Risk: The New Benchmark for Managing Financial Risk* (2nd ed.). New York, NY: McGraw-Hill.

Kimball, M. S. (1990). Precautionary saving in the small and in the large. *Econometrica*, **58**, 53–73.

Kimball, M. S. (1993). Standard risk aversion. *Econometrica*, **61**, 589–611.

Leland, H. E. (1968). Saving and uncertainty: The precautionary demand for saving. *Quarterly Journal of Economics*, **82**, 465–473.

Lien, D. (2003). The effect of liquidity constraints on futures hedging. *Journal of Futures Markets*, **23**, 603–613.

Mello, A. S., & Parsons, J. E. (1995). Maturity structure of a hedge matters: Lessons from the Metallgesellschaft debacle. *Journal of Applied Corporate Finance*, **8**, 106–120.

Mello, A. S., & Parsons, J. E. (2000). Hedging and liquidity. *Review of Financial Studies*, **13**, 127–153.

Neuberger, A. (1999). Hedging long-term exposures with multiple short-term futures contracts. *Review of Financial Studies*, **12**, 429–459.

Paroush, J., & Wolf, A. (1989). Production and hedging decisions in the presence of basis risk. *Journal of Futures Markets*, **9**, 547–563.

Ross, S. A. (1997). Hedging long run commitments: Exercises in incomplete market pricing. *Economic Notes*, **26**, 99–132.

Sandmo, A. (1971). On the theory of the competitive firm under price uncertainty. *American Economic Review*, **61**, 65–73.

Smith, C. W., & Stulz, R. M. (1985). The determinants of firms' hedging policies. *Journal of Financial and Quantitative Analysis*, **20**, 391–405.

Stulz, R. M. (1984). Optimal hedging policies. *Journal of Financial and Quantitative Analysis*, **19**, 127–140.

Stulz, R. M. (1990). Managerial discretion and optimal financial policies. *Journal of Financial Economics*, **26**, 3–27.

Tufano, P. (1996). Who manages risk? An empirical examination of risk management practices in the gold mining industry. *Journal of Finance*, **51**, 1097–1137.

Wong, K. P. (1997). On the determinants of bank interest margins under credit and interest rate risks. *Journal of Banking and Finance*, **21**, 251–271.

Wong, K. P. (2004a). Hedging, liquidity, and the competitive firm under price uncertainty. *Journal of Futures Markets*, **24**, 697–706.

Wong, K. P. (2004b). Liquidity constraints and the hedging role of futures spreads. *Journal of Futures Markets*, **24**, 909–921.

Wong, K. P. (2008). Production, liquidity, and futures price dynamics. *Journal of Futures Markets*, **28**, 1–14.

Wong, K. P., & Xu, J. (2006). Liquidity risk and the hedging role of options. *Journal of Futures Markets*, **26**, 789–808.

# SHORT COMMUNICATION

In: Liquidity, Interest Rates and Banking
Editors: J. Morrey and A. Guyton, pp. 235-247

ISBN: 978-1-60692-775-5
© 2009 Nova Science Publishers, Inc.

# SEMIPARAMETRIC ESTIMATION OF THE FRACTIONAL DIFFERENCING PARAMETER IN THE US INTEREST RATE

*Luis A. Gil-Alana*[*]

University of Navarre, Department of Economics, Pamplona, Spain

## Abstract

The monthly structure of the US interest rate (Federal Funds) is examined in this article by means of fractionally integrated techniques. Using several semiparametric methods, we show that the order of integration of the series is smaller than one but close to it, implying that it is nonstationary but with a mean reverting behaviour.

**Keywords**: Interest rates; Fractional integration; Long memory.

**JEL Classification**: C22.

## 1. Introduction

This paper deals with the estimation and testing of the fractional differencing parameter in the US interest rate. This is important since it can give us an indication of the degree of persistence of the series. Furthermore, it has strong implications in terms of economic policy. Thus, for example, if this parameter is equal to or greater than one, any shock in the series will have permanent effects, so a policy action will be required to bring the variable back to its original level. On the other hand, if the differencing parameter is smaller than one, the

---

[*] E-mail address: alana@unav.es .Phone: 00 34 948 425 625. Fax: 00 34 948 425 626
The author gratefully acknowledges financial support from the Spanish Ministry of Science and Technology (SEJ2005-07657/ECON). Correspondence author: Luis A. Gil-Alana, University of Navarra, Faculty of Economics, Edificio Biblioteca, Entrada Este, E-31080 Pamplona, Spain

series will be mean-reverting, with the effect of the shocks dying away in the long run, so that there is less need for policy action since the series will in any case return to its original level.

For the purpose of the present paper, we define an I(0) process $\{u_t, t = 0, \pm 1, ...\}$ as a covariance stationary process, with spectral density function that is positive and finite at the zero frequency. In this context, we say that $x_t$ is I(d) if

$$(1 - L)^d x_t = u_t, \qquad t = 1, 2, ..., \qquad (1)$$

$$x_t = 0, \qquad t \leq 0, \qquad (2)$$

where L is the lag-operator, $(Lx_t = x_{t-1})$ and where d can be any real number. Note that the polynomial in (1) can be expanded in terms of its Binomial expansion, such that for all real d,

$$(1 - L)^d = 1 - dL + \frac{d(d-1)}{2!}L^2 - \frac{d(d-1)(d-2)}{3!}L^3 + ...,$$

implying that higher d is, higher will be the level of association between the observations. If d > 0 in (1), the process is said to be a long memory process, (which includes the unit root model in case of d equal to 1). This type of processes was introduced by Granger and Joyeux (1980), Granger (1980, 1981) and Hosking (1981), (though earlier work by Adenstedt, 1974, and Taqqu, 1975, show an awareness of its representation) and was theoretically justified in terms of aggregation of ARMA series by Granger (1980), Robinson (1978). In another paper, Parke (1999) also justifies this model in terms of the duration of shocks. Empirical studies based on fractionally integrated models are amongst others Diebold and Rudebusch (1989), Baillie and Bollerslev (1994) and Gil-Alana and Robinson (1997), and surveys of long memory processes can be found in Beran (1994), Baillie (1996), Robinson (2003), Doukham et al. (2003), and more recently, Gil-Alana and Hualde (2008).

The fact that the US interest rate might be fractionally integrated has been suggested by many authors. Shea (1991) was one of the first papers investigating the consequences of long memory in interest rates for tests of the expectations hypothesis of the term structure. He found that allowing for long memory significantly improves the performance of the model, even though the expectations hypothesis cannot be fully resurrected. In a related work, Backus and Zin (1993) observed that the volatility of bond yields does not decline exponentially when the maturity of the bond increases; in fact, they noticed that the decline was hyperbolically slow, which is consistent with the fractionally integrated specification. Tsay (2000) employs a parametric AutoRegressive Fractionally Integrated Moving Average (ARFIMA) model to provide evidence that the US real interest rate can be described as an $I(d)$ process. In another paper, Gil-Alana (2004a) comes to the conclusion that US interest rates may be well described in terms of an I(0.79) process. He uses a version of the tests of Robinson (1994a) that permits us to test I(d) statistical models also in a fully parametric way. Further evidence can be found in Barkoulas and Baum (1997), Meade and Maier (2003) and Gil-Alana (2004b, c). Couchman, Gounder and Su (2006) estimated ARFIMA models to ex-post and ex-ante interest rates for sixteen countries. Their results suggest that, for the majority of countries, the fractional differencing parameter lies between 0 and 1, and it seems to be considerably smaller for the ex-post real rates than for the ex-ante rates. However, on estimating with parametric approaches, the correct choice of the model is important: if it is misspecified, the estimates of d are liable to be inconsistent. In fact, misspecification of the short run component of the series can invalidate the estimation of its long run parameter. Thus, there might be some advantages in estimating d on the basis of semiparametric approaches.[1] We propose in this article the use of several semiparametric procedures proposed by P.M. Robinson in a number of papers. These procedures will be briefly described in Section 2. In Section 3, they will be applied to the US interest rate (Federal Funds) while Section 4 contains some concluding comments.

## 2. Testing the Order of Integration in Univariate Time Series

We briefly describe in this section a "local" Whittle estimate of d (Robinson, 1995a); a log-periodogram regression estimate (LPE), initially proposed by Porter-Hudak (1983) and modified later by Künsch (1986) and Robinson (1995b); and an averaged periodogram estimate (APE, Robinson, 1994b). All the methods presented below require that d must belong to the stationary region, (i.e., $d \in (-0.5, 0.5)$), so that if the time series is nonstationary, then an appropriate number of differences have to be taken before proceeding to the estimation.[2]

The estimate in Robinson (1995a) is basically a "local Whittle estimate" in the frequency domain, considering a band of frequencies that degenerates to zero. The estimate is implicitly defined by:

$$d_1 = \arg\min_d \left( \log \overline{C(d)} - 2d \frac{1}{m}\sum_{j=1}^{m} \log \lambda_j \right), \qquad (3)$$

$$\text{for } d \in (-1/2, 1/2); \quad \overline{C(d)} = \frac{1}{m}\sum_{j=1}^{m} I(\lambda_j) \lambda_j^{2d}, \quad \lambda_j = \frac{2\pi j}{T}, \quad \frac{m}{T} \to 0.$$

Under finiteness of the fourth moment and other conditions, Robinson (1995a) proves the asymptotic normality of this estimate, while Lobato (1999) extended it to the multivariate case.[3]

The log-periodogram regression estimate (LPE) was initially proposed by Geweke and Porter-Hudak (1983) and modified later by Künsch (1986) and Robinson (1995b). It is based on the regression model

$$\log I(\lambda_j) = c - 2d \log \lambda_j + \varepsilon_j \qquad (4)$$

---

[1] Lai (1997) and Phillips (1998) provided evidence based on semiparametric methods that ex-ante and ex-post US real interest rates are fractionally integrated.
[2] Velasco (1999a, b) shows however that the fractional differencing parameter d can be consistently semiparametrically estimated even for nonstationary series by means of tapering.
[3] Extension and further refinements of this procedure can be found in Phillips and Shimotsu (2004, 2005).

where $I(\lambda_j) = (2\pi T)^{-1/2} \left| \sum_{t=1}^{T} x_t e^{i\lambda_j t} \right|^2$; $\lambda_j = \dfrac{2\pi j}{T}$, $j = 1,...m$, $\dfrac{m}{T} \to 0$,

$$C \sim \log\left(\frac{\sigma^2}{2\pi} f(0)\right), \quad \varepsilon_j = \log\left(\frac{I(\lambda_j)}{f(\lambda_j)}\right),$$

and the estimate is just the OLS estimate of d in (4). Unfortunately, it has not been proved that this estimate is consistent for d, but Robinson (1995b) modifies the former regression introducing two alterations: the use of a pooled periodogram instead of the raw periodogram, and introducing a trimming number q, so that frequencies $\lambda_j$, j = 1,2,....q, are excluded from the regression, where q tends to infinity slower than J, so that q/J tends to zero. Thus, the final regression model is

$$Y_K^{(J)} = C^{(J)} - 2d \log \lambda_K + U_K^{(J)}, \quad \text{with} \quad Y_K^{(J)} = \log\left(\sum_{j=1}^{J} I(\lambda_{k+j-J})\right),$$

with k = q+J, q+2J, ..., m, where J controls the pooling and q controls the trimming. The estimate of d is

$$d_2 = -\frac{1}{2} \frac{\sum_{j=q+1}^{J}\left(\log \lambda_j - J^{-1}\sum_{j=q+1}^{J}\log \lambda_j\right)\log I(\lambda_j)}{\sum_{j=q+1}^{J}\left(\log \lambda_j - J^{-1}\sum_{j=q+1}^{J}\log \lambda_j\right)^2}, \qquad (5)$$

and assuming Gaussianity, he proves the consistency and asymptotic normality of $d_2$ in a multivariate framework.

The averaged periodogram estimate of Robinson (1994b) is based on the average of the periodogram near zero frequency,

$$\overline{F(\lambda_m)} = \frac{2\pi}{T}\sum_{j=1}^{m} I(\lambda_j),$$

suggesting the estimator

$$d_3 = \frac{1}{2} - \log\left(\frac{\overline{F(q\lambda_m)}}{\overline{F(\lambda_m)}}\right)\bigg/2\log q, \qquad (6)$$

where $\lambda_m = \frac{2\pi m}{T}$, $\frac{m}{T} \to 0$, for any constant $q \in (0,1)$. He proves the consistency of this estimate under very mild conditions, and Lobato and Robinson (1996) shows the asymptotic normality for $0 < d < 1/4$, and the non-normal limiting distribution for $1/4 < d_3 < 1/2$.

Finally, in the empirical application carried out in the following section, we also present a testing procedure due to Robinson (1994a) that permits us to test I(d) statistical models like (1), with a non-parametric approach for the I(0) disturbances $u_t$, which is due to Bloomfield (1973). This approach assumes that $u_t$ has a spectral density function given by

$$f(\lambda;\tau) = \frac{\sigma^2}{2\pi} \exp\left(2\sum_{l=0}^{k} \tau_l \cos(\lambda l)\right). \tag{7}$$

Bloomfield (1973) showed that the logarithm of the spectral density function of an ARMA (p, q) process is a fairly well-behaved function and can thus be approximated by a truncated Fourier series. He showed that the log of (7) approximates well the log of the spectrum of ARMA processes where p and q are of small values, which usually happens in economics. Like the stationary AR(p) case, this model has exponentially decaying autocorrelations and thus, using this specification, we do not need to rely on so many parameters as in the ARMA processes, which always result tedious in terms of estimation, testing and model specification.

Robinson (1994a) proposed a Lagrange Multiplier (LM) test of the null hypothesis:

$$H_o : d = d_o, \tag{8}$$

in (1) and (2) for any real value $d_o$. Specifically, the test statistic is given by

$$\hat{r} = \left(\frac{T}{\hat{A}}\right)^{1/2} \frac{\hat{a}}{\hat{\sigma}^2}, \tag{9}$$

where T is the sample size, and

$$\hat{a} = \frac{-2\pi}{T} \sum_{j=1}^{T-1} \psi(\lambda_j) g(\lambda_j;\hat{\tau})^{-1} I(\lambda_j); \quad \hat{\sigma}^2 = \frac{2\pi}{T} \sum_{j=1}^{T-1} g(\lambda_j;\hat{\tau})^{-1} I(\lambda_j);$$

$$\hat{A} = \frac{2}{T}\left(\sum_{j=1}^{T-1} \psi(\lambda_j)^2 - \sum_{j=1}^{T-1} \psi(\lambda_j)\hat{\varepsilon}(\lambda_j)' \times \left(\sum_{j=1}^{T-1} \hat{\varepsilon}(\lambda_j)\hat{\varepsilon}(\lambda_j)'\right)^{-1} \times \sum_{j=1}^{T-1} \hat{\varepsilon}(\lambda_j)\psi(\lambda_j)\right)$$

$$\psi(\lambda_j) = \log\left|2\sin\frac{\lambda_j}{2}\right|; \quad \hat{\varepsilon}(\lambda_j) = \frac{\partial}{\partial \tau}\log g(\lambda_j;\hat{\tau}); \quad \lambda_j = \frac{2\pi j}{T}.$$

$I(\lambda_j)$ is the periodogram of $\hat{u}_t$, where $\hat{u}_t = (1-L)^{d_o} y_t$, and the function g above is a known function coming from the spectral density function of $u_t$, which in case of (7) becomes:

$$g(\lambda; \tau) = \exp\left( 2 \sum_{l=0}^{k} \tau_l \cos(\lambda l) \right)$$

with $\hat{\tau}$ obtained by minimising $\sigma^2(\tau)$.

Robinson (1994a) established that under certain regularity conditions:

$$\hat{r} \to_d N(0,1) \quad as \quad T \to \infty. \tag{10}$$

Thus, an approximated one-sided test of $H_o$ (8) against the alternative: $H_a$: $d > d_o$, will reject $H_o$ if $\hat{r} > z_\alpha$, where the probability that a standard normal variate exceeds $z_\alpha$ is $\alpha$, and conversely, a one-sided test of $H_o$ (8) against $H_a$: $d < d_o$, will reject $H_o$ if $\hat{r} < -z_\alpha$. As these rules indicate, we are in a classical large-sample testing situation by reasons described in Robinson (1994a), who also showed that the above tests are efficient in the Pitman sense against local departures from the null. This version of the tests of Robinson (1994a) was used in an empirical application in Gil-Alana (2001a) and other versions of his tests based on purely parametric models are Gil-Alana and Robinson (1997) and Gil-Alana (2000).[4]

## 3. Testing the Order of Integration in the US Interest Rate

The time series data analysed in this section corresponds to the monthly, (seasonally unadjusted), structure of the US interest rate (Federal Funds), for the time period 1954m7 – 2001m3, obtained from the St. Louis Reserve Federal Bank database.

We start now presenting the results based on the semiparametric procedures described in Section 2. In all cases, the estimates are based on the first differenced series, so that in order to obtain the proper estimates of d we need to add 1 to the values obtained throughout the procedures.

We start with the Whittle estimate of Robinson (1995a). The results for the whole range of values of m in (3) are given in the upper part of Figure 1. We see that they are very sensitive to the choice of m, and the most stable behaviour appears to be when m ranges between 25 and 150. Thus, in the lower part of the figure, we display the estimates of d for this range of values. We observe that practically all them are below 0, implying that the order of integration of the original series may be below 1. In fact, the most stable behaviour is obtained when m is between 100 and 135, with $d_1$ oscillating around –0.05 and thus, suggesting an order of integration of around 0.95.

---

[4] The tests of Robinson (1994a) can also be extended to allow for seasonal (quarterly and monthly) and cyclical models, and empirical applications of these procedures can be found respectively in Gil-Alana and Robinson (2001) and Gil-Alana (1999, 2001b).

# Semiparametric Estimation of the Fractional Differencing Parameter... 241

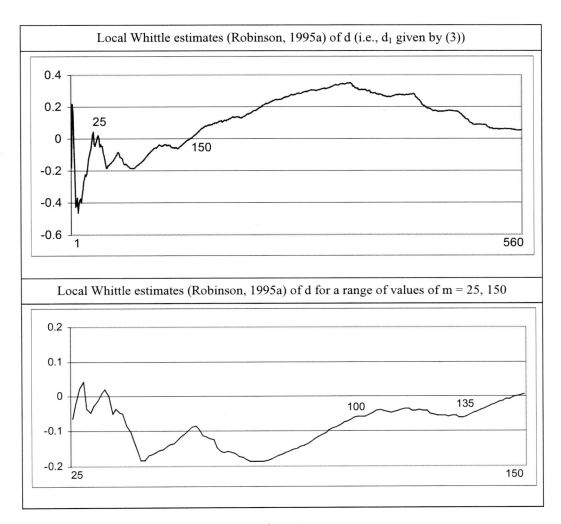

Figure 1.

Figure 2 displays the results of the log–periodogram regression estimate (LPE) of Robinson (1995b), i.e., $d_2$ given by (4). The results displayed in this figure correspond to $d_2$ for values $q = 0$, 1 and 5 of the trimming number and J initially (in the upper part of the figure) for its whole range. We see that if J is smaller than 50, the values are very sensitive to the choice of q. The second plot in the figure gives the results when J is between 50 and 150. Once more the values are sensitive to q, especially if J is smaller than 90, so that in the last plot of the figure, we present the estimates of d, based on J in the interval [90, 130]. Similarly to the previous case, the estimates are practically all slightly below 0, and the most stable behaviour is obtained here when J is between 100 and 120, with $d_2$ around −0.03. That means that, according to the LPE, the order of integration of the US interest rate is below 1 though slightly higher than the value obtained throughout the Whittle procedure above.

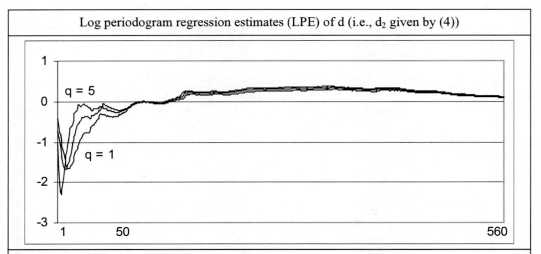
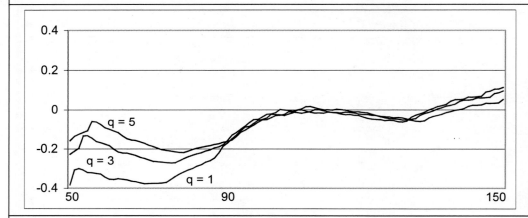
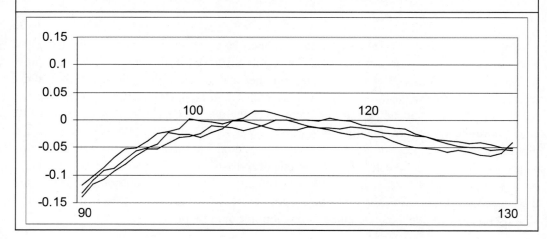

Figure 2.

# Semiparametric Estimation of the Fractional Differencing Parameter... 243

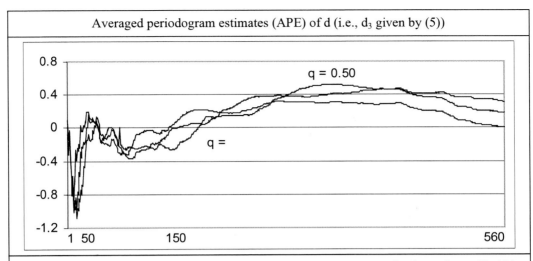
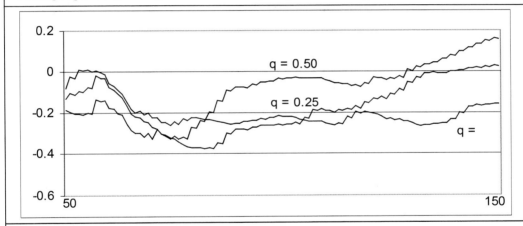
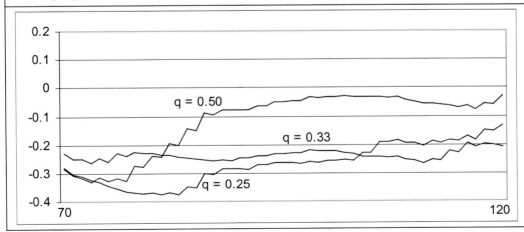

Figure 3.

The averaged periodogram estimate of Robinson, (APE, 1994b), i.e., $d_3$ in (5) was next computed for values q equal to 0.25, 0.33 and 0.50. The upper part of Figure 3 displays the results of $d_3$ for the whole range of values of m. Similarly to the previous cases, the values are very sensitive to the choice of q is m is small. The second plot of the figure displays the results based on m ∈ [50, 150]. We see here that the values oscillate between 0 and −0.4, implying once more orders of integration smaller than 1. If we further reduce the interval, we see in the lower plot of the figure (where m is between 70 and 120), that $d_3$ appears to be around −0.05 if q = 0.50, but much smaller for the other choices of q. Thus, if q = 0.25 or 0.33, the estimated values of d are around −0.25, implying orders of integration of around 0.75. Thus, the results based on this procedure are only consistent with the previous ones if q = 0.50, while for the remaining values of q, the orders of integration appear smaller.

Finally, we have also performed the tests of Robinson (1994a) based on the Bloomfield (1973) exponential disturbances. Denoting the time series $x_t$, we have employed throughout model (1) and (2), testing $H_o$ (8) for values $d_o$ equal to 0.50 (0.10), 1.50. Thus, we test for stationarity (i.e., d = 0.5); for unit roots (i.e., d = 1); as well as other fractionally integrated possibilities.

**Table 1. Testing the order of integration with the tests of Robinson and Bloomfield (m) disturbances**

| m / $d_o$ | 0.50 | 0.60 | 0.70 | 0.80 | 0.90 | 1.00 | 1.10 | 1.20 | 1.30 | 1.40 | 1.50 |
|---|---|---|---|---|---|---|---|---|---|---|---|
| 1 | 8.26 | 4.66 | 2.25 | 0.05' | −1.39' | −2.84 | −3.61 | −4.32 | −5.02 | −5.34 | −5.74 |
| 2 | 6.93 | 5.17 | 1.33' | 0.93' | −0.08' | −0.81' | −1.83 | −4.70 | −4.85 | −5.08 | −5.30 |
| 3 | 7.00 | 4.99 | 2.01 | 1.15' | −0.14' | −1.45' | −2.14 | −4.14 | −4.59 | −5.13 | −5.59 |

' and in bold: Non-rejection values at the 95% significance level.

The test statistic reported across Table 1 is the one-sided statistic $\hat{r}$ given by (9), so that significantly positive values of this are consistent with orders of integration higher than the one hypothesized under the null, whereas significantly negative ones are consistent with values smaller than $d_o$. A notable feature observed across Table 1 is the fact that $\hat{r}$ monotonically decreases with $d_o$. This is something to be expected in view of the fact that it is a one-sided statistic. Thus, for example, if $H_o$ (8) is rejected with $d_o$ = 1 against the alternative: $H_a$: d > 1, an even more significant result in this direction should be expected when $d_o$ = 0.75 or $d_o$ = 0.50 are tested. We see in this table that if m = 1, the unit root null hypothesis is rejected in favour of smaller orders of integration, which is consistent with the results obtained above with the semiparametric estimation procedures. We also observe that in this case, the non-rejection values of d occur when d is equal to 0.80 or 0.90. If m = 2, $H_o$ (8) cannot be rejected in this two cases along with d = 0.70 and d = 1. Finally, if m = 3, the non-rejection values of d take place when d is between 0.80 and 1.

In view of all these results, we may conclude by saying that the US interest rate may follow an I(d) process with d smaller than or equal to 1. The semiparametric procedures of Robinson (1994b, 1995a,b) seem to indicate that d is smaller than one, thus implying that the series possesses mean reverting behaviour. However, the fact that d is in many cases close to 1, (and also the fact that it cannot be rejected in some cases with the tests of Robinson, 1994a) suggests that the unit root model may also be plausible, and thus it may not invalidate the inference of a unit root in case of testing cointegration with this series.

## 4. Concluding Comments

The monthly structure of the US interest rate (Federal Funds) has been examined in this article by means of fractionally integrated techniques. Using several semiparametric methods proposed by Robinson in a number of papers along with a testing procedure for testing I(d) statistical models, we show that the series may be specified in terms of an I(d) process with d smaller than 1. The results obtained in this article are consistent with those in Gil-Alana (2004a). In that paper, he showed that the US interest rate may be well described in terms of an I(0.79) process with AR(2) disturbances. He used a version of the tests of Robinson (1994a) that permits us to specify the time series in a fully parametric way. However, on estimating with parametric approaches, the model must be correctly specified. Otherwise, the estimates are liable to be inconsistent. Thus, there are some advantages on estimating d with semiparametric procedures. The results obtained in this paper seem to indicate that d is smaller than 1 (though the value obtained is slightly higher than the one obtained in Gil-Alana, 2004a), suggesting, similarly to that paper, that the series has mean reverting behaviour. However, modelling the disturbances in terms of the Bloomfield (1973) exponential spectral model, the unit root case was not rejected in some cases. This may suggest that though the true value of d is smaller than 1, the inference about a unit root may also be plausible and thus, the standard approach of assuming I(1) in the interest rate when testing cointegration may still be appropriate.

The frequency domain approach used in this article seems to be unpopular with many econometricians. There also exist procedures based on the time domain (e.g., the minimum distance estimate, (MDE, Robinson, 1994c) and the log autocovariance estimate (LAE, Robinson, 1994c), however, several empirical applications carried out with these procedures, (e.g., Gil-Alana, 2002) showed that the frequency domain procedures performed better than those based on the time domain. A diskette containing the FORTRAN codes for the programmes is available from the author upon request.

## References

Adenstedt, R.K., 1974, On large-sample estimation for the mean of a stationary random sequence, *Annals of Statistics* **2**, 259-272.

Backus, D. and S. Zin, 1993, Long memory inflation uncertainty. Evidence from the term structure of interest rates. *Journal of Money, Credit and Banking* **25**, 681-700.

Baillie, R.T., 1996, Long memory and fractional integration in econometrics, *Journal of Econometrics* **73**, 5-59.

Baillie, R.T. and T. Bollerslev, 1994, Cointegration, fractional cointegration and exchange rate dynamics, *Journal of Finance* **49**, 737-745.

Barkoulas, J.T. and C.F. Baum, 1997, Fractional differencing modeling and forecasting of eurocurrency deposit rates. *The Journal of Financial Research* **20**, 355-372.

Beran, J., 1994, *Statistics for long memory processes, Monographs on statistics and applied probability* **61**, Chapman and Hall, New York, NY.

Bloomfield, P., 1973, An exponential model for the spectrum of a scalar time series, *Biometrika* **60**, 217-226.

Couchman, J., R. Gounder and J.J. Su, 2006, Long memory properties of real interest rates for 16 countries. *Applied Financial Economics Letters* **2**, 25-30.

Diebold, F.X. and G.P. Rudebusch, 1989, Long memory and persistence in aggregate output, *Journal of Monetary Economics* **24**, 189-209.

Doukhan, P., G. Oppenheim and M.S. Taqqu, 2003, *Theory and applications of long range dependence,* Birkhäuser, Basel.

Geweke, J. and S. Porter-Hudak, 1983, The estimation and application of long memory time series models, *Journal of Time Series Analysis* **4**, 221-238.

Gil-Alana, L.A., 1999, Testing fractional integration with monthly data, *Economic Modelling* **16**, 613-629.

Gil-Alana, L.A., 2000, Mean reversion in the real exchange rates, *Economics Letters* **69**, 285-288.

Gil-Alana, L.A., 2001a, A fractionally integrated exponential spectral model for the UK unemployment, *Journal of Forecasting* **20**, 329-340.

Gil-Alana, L.A., 2001b, Testing stochastic cycles in macroeconomic time series, *Journal of Time Series Analysis* **22**, 411-430.

Gil-Alana, L.A., 2002, Semiparametric estimation of the fractional differencing parameter in the UK unemployment, *Computational Economics* **19**, 323-339.

Gil-Alana, L.A., 2004a, Modelling the US interest rate in terms of I(d) statistical models, *Quarterly Review of Economics and Finance* **44**, 475-486.

Gil-Alana, L.A., 2004b, Long memory in the interest rates in some Asian countries. *International Advances in Economic Research* **9**, 257-267.

Gil-Alana, L.A., 2004c, Long memory in the US interest rate. *International Review of Financial Analysis* **13**, 265-276.

Gil-Alana, L.A. and J. Hualde, 2008, Fractional integration and cointegration. A review and an empirical application, *Palgrave Handbook of Applied Econometrics*, Volume 2, forthcoming.

Gil-Alana, L.A. and P.M. Robinson, 1997, Testing of unit and fractional roots in macroeconomic time series, *Journal of Econometrics* **80**, 247-268.

Gil-Alana, L.A. and P.M. Robinson, 2001, Testing seasonal fractional integration in the UK and Japanese consumption and income, *Journal of Applied Econometrics* **16**, 95-114.

Granger, C.W.J., 1980, Long memory relationships and the aggregation of dynamic models, *Journal of Econometrics* **14**, 227-238.

Granger, C.W.J., 1981, Some properties of time series data and their use in econometric model specification, *Journal of Econometrics* **16**, 121-130.

Granger, C.W.J. and R. Joyeux, 1980, An introduction to long range time series models and fractional differencing, *Journal of Time Series Analysis* **1**, 15-30.

Hosking, J.R.M., 1981, Fractional differencing, *Biometrika* **68**, 165-176.

Künsch, H., 1986, Discrimination between monotonic trends and long-range dependence, *Journal of Applied Probability* **23**, 1025-1030.

Lai, K.S., 1997, Long term persistence in real interest rate. Some evidence of a fractional unit root. International *Journal of Finance and Economics* **2**, 225-235.

Lobato, I., 1999, A semiparametric two-step estimator for a multivariate long memory process, Jour*nal of Econometrics* **73**, 303-324.

Lobato, I. and P.M. Robinson, 1996, Averaged periodogram estimation of long memory, *Journal of Econometrics* **73**, 303-324.

Meade, N. and M.R. Maier, 2003, Evidence of long memory is short term interest rates. *Journal of Forecasting* **22**, 553-568.

Parke, W.R., 1999, What is fractional integration?, *The Review of Economics and Statistics* **81**, 632-638.

Phillips, P.C.B., 1998, Econometric analysis of Fisher's equation, Yale University, *Cowles Foundation Discussion Paper* **1180**.

Phillips, P.C.B. and K. Shimotsu, 2004, Local Whittle estimation in nonstationary and unit root cases. *Annals of Statistics* **32**, 656-692.

Phillips, P.C.B. and K. Shimotsu, 2005, Exact local Whittle estimation of fractional integration. *Annals of Statistics* **33**, 4, 1890-1933.

Robinson, P.M., 1978, Statistical inference for a random coefficient autoregressive model, *Scandinavian Journal of Statistics* **5**, 163-168.

Robinson, P.M., 1994a, Efficient tests of nonstationary hypotheses, *Journal of the American Statistical Association* **84**, 1420-1437.

Robinson, P.M., 1994b, Semiparametric analysis of long memory time series, *Annals of Statistics* **22**, 515-539.

Robinson, P.M., 1994c, Time series with strong dependence, In C.A. Sims ed., *Advances in Econometrics:* Sixth World Congress, Vol 1, 47-95, Cambridge University Press.

Robinson, P.M., 1995a, Gaussian semiparametric estimation of long range dependence, *Annals of Statistics* **23**, 1630-1661.

Robinson, P.M., 1995b, Log-periodogram regression of time series with long range dependence, *Annals of Statistics* **23**, 1048-1072.

Robinson, P.M., 2003, Long memory time series, Time Series with Long Memory, (P.M. Robinson, ed.), Oxford University Press, Oxford, 1-48.

Shea, G., 1991, Uncertainty and implied variance bounds in long memory models of the interest rate term structure. *Empirical Economics* **16**, 287-312.

Taqqu, M.S., 1975, Weak convergence to fractional Brownian to Rosenblatt processes, *Z. Wahrsch. Verw. Geb.* **31**, 287-3

Velasco, C., 1999a, Nonstationary log-periodogram regression, *Journal of Econometrics* **91**, 299-323.

Velasco, C., 1999b,. Gaussian semiparametric estimation of nonstationary time series, *Journal of Time Series Analysis* **20**, 87-127.

# INDEX

## A

academic, 137, 142, 197, 210
accelerator, 79
access, 115, 172, 173
accommodation, 10, 11, 21, 26
accounting, 11, 13, 26, 96, 97, 146, 190
accuracy, 48, 82, 96
acquisitions, 176
actuarial, 96, 97, 98, 110
acute, 113
ad hoc, 60
adaptability, 196
adjustment, 4, 5, 17, 23, 105, 143
age, 98, 103, 105
agent, 78, 82, 90, 91, 92, 114, 176, 196
agents, vii, 3, 4, 5, 17, 91, 92, 148, 170, 173, 179, 180
aggregates, 10, 21, 25, 143
aggregation, 24, 65, 236, 246
agricultural, 61, 65, 70
aid, 192, 198
aiding, 199
Alaska, 70
algorithm, 48, 62, 72, 73, 175, 182, 195
alternative, 7, 8, 15, 24, 25, 43, 113, 174, 175, 185, 187, 214, 240, 244
ambiguity, 21
American Academy of Actuaries, 109
AMEX, 127
Amsterdam, 30, 51, 55
analytical models, 195, 209
annual rate, 81
annuities, 100, 101, 103, 106
appendix, 63, 216
application, 21, 47, 97, 104, 105, 106, 117, 127, 239, 240, 246
aptitude, 96
arbitrage, ix, 41, 48, 95
argument, 4, 59
ARS, 145
Asian, 54, 246

Asian countries, 246
assessment, ix, 48, 95, 110, 206, 212
assets, 61, 70, 96, 97, 98, 99, 169, 172, 173, 174, 190, 197, 200, 206
assignment, 191, 195, 200, 203, 204, 205, 211
assumptions, ix, 5, 8, 10, 11, 24, 25, 60, 95, 96, 97, 100, 149
asymmetric information, ix, 111, 131, 136, 142
asymmetry, 43, 138, 175
asymptotic, 237, 238, 239
ATM, 71
attitudes, 23
Australia, 38, 39
authority, 37, 38, 42, 174
autocorrelation, xi, 46, 213, 215, 219, 221, 222, 223, 224, 225
automation, ix, 111, 112, 114, 115, 116, 117, 118, 119, 124, 127, 129, 131, 132, 133, 134, 135, 136, 138
autoregressive model, 247
availability, 65, 114, 129, 181
average costs, viii, 58, 59, 63, 70
aversion, 173, 217
awareness, 236

## B

balance sheet, 96
bank failure, 68, 69, 184
Bank of England, 50, 185, 186, 187
Bank of Japan, 187
bankers, 59, 71
banking, viii, 4, 10, 15, 26, 57, 58, 59, 60, 65, 67, 68, 69, 70, 71, 181, 183
banks, viii, 5, 11, 14, 16, 26, 28, 57, 58, 59, 60, 64, 65, 68, 69, 70, 71, 169, 170, 172, 173, 174, 175, 176, 177, 178, 179, 180, 181, 182, 183, 184, 190, 206, 214
barriers, 210
basis points, 92
Bayesian, 13, 27, 38, 46, 85

behavior, viii, 4, 43, 58, 59, 60, 65, 68, 70, 71, 77, 106, 112, 114, 117, 118, 121, 128, 140, 178, 181, 183, 217
Belgium, 39, 40, 45
benchmark, 142, 215, 216, 218, 219
beneficial effect, 182
benefits, 58, 59, 61, 112, 128, 173, 174, 191, 196, 206, 211
benign, 183
Bernanke, Ben, 29
bias, ix, 7, 9, 16, 21, 28, 65, 139, 141, 146, 151, 152, 153, 159, 164
binding, x, 213, 215, 220, 221, 222, 223, 224, 225, 230
BIS, 169, 170, 171, 172, 174, 177, 178, 184, 185
blindness, 211
Board of Governors, 16, 56
bondholders, 82
bonds, vii, 3, 4, 37, 45, 105
bootstrap, 13, 27
borrowing, 13, 15, 21, 22, 79, 101, 174
Boston, 50, 139
bottlenecks, 210
bounds, 247
branching, 70
breakdown, 42
Bretton Woods, 41, 42
Britain, 68
broad money, 10, 25
Brownian motion, 104, 214
Btus, 58
Bubbles, 54
budget cuts, 91
budget deficit, viii, 77, 78, 79, 80, 81, 82, 85, 90, 91, 92
buildings, 210
business cycle, vii, 3, 4, 5, 23, 24, 35, 36, 41, 46, 47, 79, 85
bust, 69
buyer, 117, 148

## C

calculus, 104
calibration, 105, 173, 174
Canada, 37, 38, 39, 40, 43, 45, 46, 51, 57, 78, 92
capacity, 79, 182, 200, 205, 206, 210
capital cost, 204, 206
capital expenditure, 78
caps, 179, 185
case study, 137, 191, 192, 198, 199, 204, 205, 206
cash flow, x, 98, 189, 195, 197, 204, 206, 211, 216
causality, 47, 48
CCR, 165
Central Bank, 4, 38, 52, 137, 170, 172, 173, 174, 176, 177, 178, 179, 181, 183, 184, 185
CEO, 191, 195
changing environment, 174

chemical industry, 190
China, 178, 186
Christmas, 116
classes, 62, 80, 85, 143
classical, 12, 104, 209, 240
classification, 96, 169, 213
closure, 219
clustering, ix, 111, 112, 116, 118, 121, 122, 123, 124, 127, 128, 129, 136, 137
CNS, 170
coalitions, 186
Cochrane, vii, 3, 6, 7, 18, 23, 30
codes, 77, 245
cohort, 98
collateral, 172, 173, 174
collusion, 114, 129, 140
Colorado, 70
*Columbia*, 54
Columbia University, 54
commercial bank, viii, 57, 59, 65, 68, 69, 70, 71
commodity, 14, 19, 27, 214, 216, 231
Common Market, 50
communication, 190
communities, 197
compensation, 220
competition, 71, 137, 140, 142
competitive advantage, 138
competitiveness, 115
complexity, 172, 191, 205
components, ix, 14, 16, 17, 27, 28, 98, 100, 111, 117, 131, 136, 172
computation, 143
computing, 175, 190
concentration, ix, 111, 113, 128, 131, 136, 177, 178, 179, 183, 187
conception, 158
conditional mean, 141, 149, 151, 158
conditioning, 152
conductance, 182
confidence, 13, 27, 79, 121, 122, 125, 126, 127, 129, 130
confidence interval, 13, 27, 121, 122, 125, 126, 127, 129, 130
confidence intervals, 13, 27, 122, 126, 127, 129
Confidence intervals, 121
conflict, 210
Congestion, 184
Congress, 247
Congressional Budget Office, 82
conjecture, 116, 117, 118, 129, 131
consensus, 24, 114, 192, 203
constraints, 5, 60, 200, 204, 206, 210, 214, 216, 223, 224, 231, 232
construction, 129, 205
consumer price index, 10, 17, 25, 28
consumers, 35, 37, 176
consumption, 6, 14, 17, 35, 36, 37, 38, 40, 45, 180, 246
contingency, 182

continuity, 230
contracts, x, 11, 26, 96, 97, 99, 100, 112, 116, 136, 137, 138, 213, 214, 215, 216, 218, 220, 221, 225, 231
control, ix, x, 22, 23, 65, 132, 139, 141, 143, 148, 149, 151, 152, 158, 164, 175, 180, 182, 183, 189, 190, 195, 204, 205
convergence, 96, 216, 247
conversion, 115, 116
conviction, 21
coordination, x, 174, 179, 181, 183, 186
corporations, 61, 70
correlation, 7, 38, 78, 81, 134, 159, 220
correlation coefficient, 81, 220
correlations, 11, 26
costs, vii, viii, ix, 48, 58, 59, 60, 61, 63, 64, 70, 71, 112, 113, 114, 115, 116, 117, 118, 138, 139, 140, 141, 142, 143, 144, 147, 148, 149, 151, 152, 158, 159, 164, 167, 171, 172, 175, 178, 179, 181, 184, 206, 210, 211, 217
coupling, 117
covering, 106, 190, 204, 206
CPI, 10, 11, 14, 17, 19, 25, 28, 82
CPU, 202, 203
credit, 14, 20, 21, 27, 170, 172, 173, 174, 175, 176, 178, 179, 180, 183, 184, 200, 206, 214, 232
critical value, 224
criticism, 58
cross-country, 36
cross-sectional, 58, 65, 141, 149
crowding out, 78
cumulative distribution function, 44, 152, 228
currency, 10, 16, 25, 28, 171, 176
current account, 177
customers, 11, 26, 117, 176, 182, 210, 214
cycles, 190, 246

# D

danger, 190
data availability, 178
data set, 64, 214
database, 80, 82, 142, 143, 145, 165, 196, 240
dating, 65
death, 105
death rate, 105
debt, 82, 97, 172, 185, 191, 192, 197, 199, 206
debts, 200
decision makers, 190
decision making, x, 142, 189, 190, 195, 197, 199, 204, 210, 211
decisions, x, 36, 142, 148, 158, 178, 179, 189, 192, 195, 196, 197, 198, 199, 200, 201, 204, 206, 209, 211, 212, 215, 231
deficit, 78, 79, 80, 82, 83, 84, 85, 90
deficits, viii, 77, 78, 79, 80, 81, 83, 90, 91, 92, 191
definition, 14, 72, 96, 148, 159, 173, 181
deflation, 78

deflator, 14, 17, 27, 64, 80
degrees of freedom, 62, 126, 133
delivery, 115, 116, 170, 191, 210, 216
demand, vii, 3, 4, 5, 7, 8, 9, 10, 11, 12, 14, 15, 16, 21, 22, 24, 25, 26, 27, 28, 37, 70, 79, 80, 174, 176, 191, 192, 201, 205, 206, 207
demand curve, 15
denial, 214
Denmark, 40
density, 152, 193, 236, 239, 240
dependent variable, 45, 49, 150
deposits, 11, 16, 19, 26, 28, 59, 61, 62, 70
deregulation, 22, 40, 58, 70
derivatives, 112, 214, 231
designers, 190
desire, 22, 23, 117
developed countries, 41, 43, 211
deviation, 119, 132, 133, 141
Diamond, 180, 185
diffusion, 104
directives, 21
disaster, 214
disclosure, 96
discounting, ix, 95, 96, 99
discounts, 117
discrete variable, 202, 203
discreteness, 137
dispersion, 127, 129
displacement, 171
dissatisfaction, 22, 23
distribution, 44, 116, 118, 122, 123, 125, 129, 131, 152, 195, 196, 205, 228, 239
divergence, 158
dividends, 200
division, 85
dominance, 115, 197, 229
dominant strategy, 114
duration, 5, 24, 97, 98, 99, 100, 103, 236

# E

early warning, 190
earnings, 203, 210
econometrics, 137, 167, 245
economic activity, vii, viii, 16, 28, 35, 36, 37, 38, 40, 41, 42, 43, 46, 79, 80
economic crisis, 177
economic growth, 40, 44, 47, 195
economic growth rate, 44
economic policy, 235
economic reform, 81
economic reforms, 81
economics, 58, 59, 69, 231, 239
election, 90
electronic systems, ix, 111, 113, 127, 136
electronic trade, 113
employees, 61
employment, 79

EMU, 44
encapsulated, 128
endogeneity, 10, 11, 12, 14, 16, 25, 28
energy, 70, 214
enterprise, x, 189, 190, 191, 195, 197, 198, 200, 204, 206, 211, 212
environment, 41, 48, 58, 109, 113, 116, 142, 173, 210, 231
equality, 41, 72, 217, 218, 219, 226, 227, 229
equilibrium, 5, 17, 37, 97, 128, 174, 176, 178, 179, 180
equilibrium price, 97
equipment, 78, 192, 197, 205
equities, 167
equity, 136, 140, 167, 199, 200, 201, 206
equity market, 167
ERPs, 209
estimating, viii, 6, 7, 44, 57, 59, 63, 65, 85, 104, 141, 152, 237, 245
estimator, 68, 72, 73, 238, 246
Euro, viii, 35, 44, 47, 51, 52, 55
Eurocurrency, 56
Europe, 52, 55, 187
European Central Bank, 52, 172, 185
European Union, 40
evening, 112, 119, 131, 135
evolution, 20, 60, 62, 70, 171, 174, 175
exchange rate, 19, 20, 29, 246
exchange rates, 20, 29, 246
execution, vii, ix, 112, 113, 137, 138, 139, 140, 141, 142, 143, 144, 147, 149, 151, 152, 158, 159, 164, 167, 196, 200
exercise, 49
exogeneity, 9, 12
expansions, 37, 46, 69, 79
expenditures, 58, 78, 79, 83, 90, 211
exposure, 109, 110, 175, 179, 214, 215, 216, 218
externalities, 176, 178, 184
extinction, 190
extraction, 196
extraction process, 196

# F

failure, vii, 3, 6, 8, 11, 24, 26, 69, 70, 117, 173, 180, 181, 182, 183, 186, 195, 206, 209
fax, 213
February, 29, 30, 51, 81
federal budget, 79, 91, 92
Federal Deposit Insurance Corporation, viii, 57, 59, 64, 65, 68, 69, 71, 74, 75
federal funds, 4, 10, 11, 13, 14, 15, 16, 17, 25, 26, 27, 28, 46, 48, 49
federal government, 80
Federal Open Market Committee, 4, 13, 21, 22
Federal Reserve, 4, 7, 10, 11, 12, 13, 14, 15, 20, 21, 22, 23, 25, 26, 27, 29, 31, 32, 33, 41, 42, 49, 50, 51, 52, 53, 54, 55, 56, 68, 74, 78, 81, 82, 91, 172, 173, 184, 186
Federal Reserve Bank, 4, 29, 31, 32, 49, 50, 51, 52, 53, 54, 55, 74, 82, 184, 186
Federal Reserve Board, 56
fee, 178
feedback, 7, 9
fees, 140, 142, 185
filters, 165
finance, 37, 190, 193, 195, 214
financial crises, 171, 183
financial crisis, 177, 181, 183
financial development, 173
financial distress, 217
financial fragility, 186
financial loss, 147
financial markets, 112, 169, 170, 176, 185
financial planning, 212
financial resources, 206
financial support, 169, 235
financial system, vii, viii, x, 57, 59, 70, 169, 170, 171, 172, 173, 174, 177, 179, 181, 183
financing, 61, 200, 231
Finland, 177, 178, 184, 186, 187
firms, 58, 59, 65, 71, 114, 140, 142, 143, 148, 165, 190, 192, 197, 204, 206, 210, 213, 214, 232
fixed costs, 113
flexibility, x, 174, 189, 196, 200
flooring, 140
flow, x, 98, 101, 103, 141, 143, 148, 181, 182, 189, 195, 197, 199, 206
fluctuations, 7, 14, 22, 38, 101
focusing, 4, 14, 115
forecasting, viii, 15, 16, 35, 36, 38, 39, 40, 41, 42, 44, 45, 47, 48, 77, 96, 110, 199, 245
foreign exchange, 127, 174
Fourier, 239
fragility, 68
France, 39, 40, 45, 46, 47, 78, 112
freedom, 62, 126, 133, 159
Friedman, Milton, 31
fulfillment, 192, 199
full employment, 79
funding, 204, 214
funds, 10, 15, 16, 20, 21, 23, 25, 28, 48, 61, 70, 79, 80, 82, 170, 174, 177, 181, 182, 195, 197, 200, 204, 206, 210
futures, ix, x, xi, 111, 112, 114, 115, 116, 117, 128, 135, 136, 137, 138, 213, 214, 215, 216, 217, 218, 219, 220, 221, 222, 223, 224, 225, 226, 227, 229, 231, 232
futures markets, 112, 117

# G

Gaussian, 247
GDP deflator, 80, 81, 82, 85, 92
generation, 206

Germany, 39, 40, 45, 46, 47, 48, 50, 51, 53, 55, 78, 175, 214
Gibbs, 148
globalization, 47, 169, 170, 197
GNP, 39, 64, 90
gold, 38, 41, 42, 68, 127, 217, 232
gold standard, 38, 42, 68
government, 45, 61, 68, 78, 80, 81, 82, 83, 91, 92, 112, 210
government budget, 78, 80
government revenues, 82
government securities, 68
graph, 199
Great Depression, 68, 69
Gross Domestic Product, 14, 17, 19, 27, 35, 36, 38, 39, 40, 41, 45, 46, 49, 50, 56, 80, 81, 82, 83, 85, 86, 87, 92
groups, 147
growth, viii, 4, 5, 6, 7, 10, 11, 13, 20, 21, 22, 23, 26, 27, 35, 36, 37, 38, 39, 40, 41, 42, 43, 44, 45, 46, 47, 49, 68, 70, 78, 170, 190, 195, 204, 211
growth rate, 4, 6, 7, 11, 13, 23, 27, 36, 38, 39, 43, 47
guidance, 96
guidelines, ix, 95, 104

# H

handling, 142
hands, 196
health, 195
hedging, 214, 215, 216, 218, 231, 232
hegemony, 90
heterogeneous, 177
heteroscedasticity, 134
heteroskedasticity, viii, 77, 84
holistic, 197, 212
holistic approach, 197
Holland, 55
homogeneity, 61, 62
Hong Kong, 137, 213
horizon, 8, 11, 26, 42, 45, 100, 194, 197, 199, 200, 201, 204, 205, 206, 214
household, 79
human, 196
hybrid, 174, 175, 180, 183, 187
Hybrid systems, 183
hypothesis, viii, 36, 77, 78, 83, 90, 91, 92, 116, 118, 121, 122, 124, 126, 127, 128, 129, 131, 133, 134, 236, 239, 244

# I

ice, 97, 104, 142
identification, viii, 3, 8, 11, 12, 14, 24, 25, 27, 28
identification problem, 14
identity, 10
Illinois, 70

imbalances, 182
IMF, 51, 54
imitation, 137
immobilization, 206
implementation, ix, 21, 96, 170, 171, 172, 173, 174, 179, 183
inauguration, 91
incentive, ix, 13, 111, 131, 136, 181, 220
incentives, 173, 174, 176, 179, 180, 215, 221
incidence, 69
inclusion, 42, 45, 47, 179
income, 37, 61, 79, 82, 90, 97, 206, 219, 220, 246
independent variable, 83, 85, 90, 152, 153, 159
indication, 68, 235
indicators, 45, 47, 48, 141, 144
indirect measure, 119
industrial, 10, 14, 17, 25, 28, 35, 45, 61, 65, 78, 201, 214
industrial production, 10, 17, 25, 28, 35, 45
industrialized countries, 78, 105
industry, x, 59, 65, 74, 96, 189, 190, 211, 217, 232
inelastic, vii, 3, 4, 11, 14, 26, 27
inequality, 226, 227, 228
inferences, 151
infinite, 192, 216, 219, 222
inflation, 5, 6, 7, 17, 21, 23, 35, 36, 37, 38, 39, 42, 43, 45, 46, 49, 50, 77, 78, 80, 81, 82, 83, 84, 85, 90, 91, 92, 190, 245
information asymmetry, 138, 175
information technology, 71
infrastructure, 170
initial state, 72
initiation, 171
innovation, 12, 16, 28, 58, 65, 110, 170, 179, 211
inspection, 129, 220, 226
instability, 44
institutionalization, 68
institutions, 59, 61, 69
instruction, 182
instruments, 13, 37, 173
insurance, viii, ix, 95, 96, 97, 103, 110, 185, 218
intangible, 190, 195, 197
integration, x, xi, 138, 189, 190, 191, 192, 198, 200, 203, 204, 206, 209, 210, 229, 235, 240, 241, 244, 245, 246, 247
intensity, 99
interaction, 22, 113, 179, 182, 193
interactions, 193, 210
interbank market, 176
interest margins, 232
interest rates, vii, viii, 3, 4, 5, 6, 7, 8, 10, 11, 12, 13, 14, 17, 21, 22, 23, 26, 27, 35, 36, 40, 43, 45, 47, 48, 77, 78, 79, 80, 81, 83, 85, 90, 91, 92, 96, 97, 98, 99, 100, 101, 105, 106, 110, 172, 190, 236, 237, 245, 246, 247
internalization, 179
International Financial Reporting Standard, 96, 110
internationalization, 169
interpretation, 37, 129, 159, 180

interval, 73, 81, 117, 119, 122, 133, 135, 200, 220, 221, 241, 244
intervention, 176
intuition, 59, 180, 218, 219, 221, 222
inventories, 202
investment, viii, x, 14, 17, 40, 45, 57, 70, 71, 78, 79, 180, 189, 190, 191, 196, 197, 206, 209, 231
investment spending, 79
investors, 35, 112, 140, 142, 192, 197, 204
ions, 21, 23, 96, 113, 147, 172, 176, 180, 183, 190, 191
IPO, 140
Ireland, 113, 138
IS-LM, 31, 36
IS-LM model, 36
Italian population, 105
Italy, 39, 45, 46, 47, 51, 95, 106
iteration, 195

## J

January, 30, 32, 40, 81, 91, 106, 110, 116, 143
Japan, 39, 40, 45, 46, 54, 55, 78, 187
Japanese, 246
judgment, 20, 97
Jun, 55
justification, 176

## K

Kalman filter, viii, 48, 57, 58, 59, 66, 71
Kazakhstan, 77
kernel, 209
King, 5, 23, 31
Korean, 68

## L

labor, 61, 205, 206
Lamfalussy, 171, 184
large banks, 14, 70, 181, 183
lead, 4, 8, 10, 12, 24, 58, 96, 113, 117, 118, 181, 210
learning, 60, 63, 211
learning process, 60, 63
legislative, 69
Leibniz, 218, 225, 226, 229
lending, 187
LIFE, 95
life cycle, 190, 212
lifetime, 102, 206
likelihood, 63, 65, 66, 129, 134, 135, 154, 179, 182
limitations, 24, 58, 59, 80, 81, 90, 180, 191
linear, 10, 17, 26, 37, 39, 43, 44, 71, 105, 196
linear model, 39, 43, 44
linear regression, 39, 44, 105
linkage, 49, 215

links, vii, x, 169, 171, 189, 190, 191, 197, 204, 206
liquidate, 217, 219
liquidation, 176, 213, 214, 215, 217, 219, 220, 221, 223, 224, 227, 229
liquidity, vii, viii, ix, x, 3, 4, 5, 6, 7, 8, 9, 10, 11, 12, 13, 14, 15, 16, 17, 18, 20, 21, 23, 24, 25, 26, 27, 28, 29, 111, 112, 113, 114, 116, 119, 129, 131, 135, 136, 137, 138, 139, 140, 144, 147, 148, 169, 170, 171, 172, 173, 174, 175, 176, 177, 178, 179, 180, 181, 182, 183, 184, 185, 186, 187, 189, 190, 195, 196, 204, 207, 211, 213, 214, 215, 216, 217, 218, 219, 220, 222, 223, 225, 226, 231, 232
living standard, 78
living standards, 78
loans, 61, 62, 69, 176, 214
location, 180
London, 110, 111, 112, 127, 136, 137, 138, 140, 186, 187
long period, 65
longevity, 105
long-term, vii, viii, 7, 35, 36, 37, 39, 49, 58, 59, 70, 77, 78, 79, 80, 81, 85, 90, 91, 92, 200, 214, 231
losses, 61, 214, 219
Louisiana, 70
low power, 214
LSM, 174, 175, 183
lying, 37

## M

machines, 58, 71
macroeconomic, vii, viii, 3, 4, 5, 41, 45, 49, 50, 77, 81, 91, 246
macroeconomists, 5, 36
maintenance, 15, 196
management, x, 5, 20, 23, 60, 70, 110, 169, 170, 172, 177, 178, 180, 184, 185, 189, 190, 191, 192, 195, 196, 197, 198, 200, 203, 204, 206, 209, 210, 211, 212, 213, 217, 231, 232
mandates, 142
manipulation, 4
manpower, 200
mapping, ix, 95
market, vii, ix, x, 4, 10, 11, 14, 15, 16, 17, 20, 21, 22, 23, 26, 28, 40, 68, 70, 78, 81, 90, 91, 92, 95, 96, 97, 101, 102, 104, 111, 112, 113, 114, 115, 116, 117, 118, 127, 128, 129, 131, 132, 134, 135, 136, 137, 138, 139, 140, 141, 142, 143, 144, 146, 147, 148, 149, 151, 152, 153, 159, 164, 165, 166, 167, 169, 171, 176, 180, 182, 183, 186, 191, 196, 197, 204, 205, 206, 207, 209, 213, 214, 216, 217, 232
market capitalization, 148, 153, 165
market prices, 144, 147
market share, 115
market structure, 113, 138
market value, ix, 95, 97, 204, 206
marketing, 195, 196, 210

markets, vii, ix, 7, 65, 69, 112, 113, 114, 116, 117, 127, 136, 137, 138, 139, 140, 141, 142, 143, 144, 146, 147, 148, 149, 151, 152, 158, 159, 164, 165, 167, 177, 182, 199, 205, 231
Markov, viii, 35, 44, 46, 49
Massachusetts, 57, 70, 137
mathematical programming, 198
matrix, 72
Maximum Likelihood, 48, 52
meanings, 105
measurement, 8, 24, 58, 59, 60, 65, 96, 99, 193
measures, viii, 7, 11, 12, 13, 14, 17, 20, 25, 26, 27, 28, 29, 35, 38, 57, 59, 60, 64, 65, 68, 69, 82, 83, 84, 85, 90, 91, 116, 122, 142, 144, 147, 148, 153, 171, 175, 176, 180, 181, 183, 221
meat, 65
median, 80, 82, 85, 90, 92, 115, 144
memory, 235, 236, 245, 246, 247
memory processes, 236, 245
mergers, 59, 65
messages, 175
metric, 116, 127
Mexican, 53
Mexico, 39
microeconomics, 5
microstructure, 112, 137, 147, 167
migration, 112
military, 91
Milton Friedman, 4
minimum price, 115
mining, 217, 232
Ministry of Education, 169
Minnesota, 186
MIP, 198, 203
mirror, 147
misleading, 8, 24, 41
misunderstanding, 97
MIT, 30, 51, 231
model specification, ix, 46, 48, 139, 141, 164, 239, 246
modeling, x, 48, 58, 59, 60, 65, 71, 179, 189, 190, 191, 195, 196, 197, 198, 200, 201, 204, 209, 210, 212, 245
models, vii, viii, x, 3, 4, 5, 7, 8, 10, 12, 13, 15, 17, 23, 24, 25, 29, 35, 36, 37, 38, 39, 41, 42, 43, 44, 45, 46, 49, 59, 60, 77, 79, 80, 85, 86, 90, 91, 92, 97, 113, 134, 135, 151, 158, 159, 170, 173, 174, 175, 180, 189, 190, 191, 192, 195, 196, 197, 198, 201, 202, 203, 204, 205, 206, 209, 210, 211, 236, 239, 240, 245, 246, 247
modernization, 140
monetary aggregates, 8, 10, 25, 45
monetary policy, vii, 3, 4, 5, 8, 10, 11, 12, 14, 15, 17, 20, 21, 24, 25, 26, 27, 28, 29, 36, 37, 38, 42, 43, 48, 49, 172, 178, 183, 186
monetary policy instruments, 178
money, vii, 3, 4, 5, 6, 7, 8, 9, 10, 11, 12, 13, 14, 16, 20, 21, 22, 23, 24, 25, 26, 27, 28, 29, 44, 170, 172, 176, 178, 182, 190, 191, 192, 195, 196, 204, 209, 210
money markets, 4
money supply, vii, 3, 4, 6, 7, 8, 9, 10, 11, 12, 25, 44
moral hazard, 180, 181
morning, 4, 175
mortality, 96, 97, 98, 99, 101, 105, 110
mortality rate, 97
motion, 104, 214
motivation, 21, 65
movement, 9, 115, 171
multidisciplinary, 198
multilateral, 170, 176, 180
multiples, 122, 129
multiplier, 218
multivariate, 7, 46, 146, 158, 237, 238, 246
myopic, 204, 206

# N

NASDAQ, 140, 147, 167
nation, 90, 181
*national*, 69, 79, 82, 90
National Association of Insurance Commissioners, 96
national debt, 82
national income, 79, 82
natural, 65, 147
Nebraska, 3, 35, 70
negative consequences, 182
negative relation, 5, 134
negotiating, 128
negotiation, 116, 118, 128, 129
net income, 97
net present value, 97, 204
Netherlands, 30, 39, 45, 46
network, 43, 46, 177, 180, 181, 187, 199, 200, 205
neural network, 43, 46
New England, 50
New Jersey, 137
New York, 4, 21, 29, 32, 52, 54, 55, 70, 138, 184, 186, 231, 245
New Zealand, 37, 114, 137
Nielsen, 49, 55
nodes, 199, 205
noise, 60, 71, 72
non-binding, x, 213, 215, 222, 224, 225, 230
nonlinear, 43, 44, 46, 47, 49
nonlinearities, 43, 44
nonparametric, 46
normal, 44, 83, 112, 113, 122, 152, 177, 182, 240
normalization, 223
North Carolina, 74
Northeast, 70
novelty, 204
null hypothesis, 121, 126, 127, 239
NYSE, ix, 127, 139, 140, 141, 142, 143, 144, 145, 146, 147, 148, 149, 150, 151, 152, 153, 154, 155,

156, 157, 158, 159, 160, 161, 162, 163, 164, 165, 167

## O

obligation, 115, 171
obligations, 105, 169, 170
observations, 15, 62, 69, 81, 116, 117, 121, 129, 130, 132, 133, 152, 159, 236
obsolete, 70
OECD, 46, 47
off-the-shelf, 190
oil, 78, 91, 214
Oklahoma, 70
omission, 116
one-sided test, 240
open market operations, 4, 15, 16
operator, 217
opposition, 203
optimization, x, 60, 175, 178, 189, 190, 191, 193, 195, 196, 197, 198, 199, 200, 209, 210, 212, 227, 229
organization, 65, 196
OTC, 231
outliers, 143
output gap, 41, 48, 82

## P

Pacific, 136
paper, vii, 3, 4, 6, 7, 12, 19, 23, 31, 32, 50, 51, 54, 55, 56, 57, 58, 59, 60, 70, 73, 93, 95, 97, 105, 137, 138, 140, 142, 164, 166, 167, 169, 171, 173, 176, 177, 178, 179, 180, 181, 182, 183, 185, 186, 187, 213, 214, 216, 225, 235, 236, 245, 247
parameter, viii, 35, 38, 49, 62, 63, 65, 66, 85, 104, 105, 106, 152, 235, 236, 237, 246
parameter estimates, 62, 63, 65, 66, 85, 152
parameter estimation, 104
Pareto, 204, 206, 207
Paris, 115, 138, 140, 167, 182
partnerships, 61
pears, 48
Pennsylvania, 70
pension, vii, viii, 95
performance, viii, x, 12, 27, 42, 45, 57, 58, 59, 64, 65, 71, 97, 114, 182, 189, 192, 193, 195, 204, 236
performance indicator, 193
permit, x, 41, 189
personal, 61, 90, 114
Philadelphia, 186
Philippines, 65
Phillips curve, 37
philosophy, 195
planning, 190, 191, 192, 194, 195, 196, 197, 198, 199, 200, 201, 202, 204, 205, 206, 209, 210, 212, 214

planning decisions, 192
plants, 195, 198, 199, 200, 210
play, 170, 181
Poland, 177
polarity, 119
policy makers, 114
policy rate, 101
policymakers, 35, 43, 58, 179
polynomial, 39, 236
poor, 6, 7
population, 68, 105
portfolio, ix, 96, 97, 98, 99, 100, 101, 102, 103, 106, 107, 108, 109, 172
portfolios, 70, 100, 106
positive correlation, 40
positive relation, 147
positive relationship, 147
posture, 91, 92
power, 8, 11, 26, 36, 38, 39, 40, 41, 42, 43, 45, 46, 47, 151, 158, 175, 178, 192, 210, 214
praxis, 190
precautionary demand, 231
predictability, 40, 42, 46, 48, 49, 55, 56, 215, 216
prediction, 46, 48, 49, 72, 116
predictive accuracy, 44
predictors, 45
preference, 173, 180
premium, 36, 38, 41, 103, 104, 106, 148, 227, 230
premiums, 98, 100
present value, 97, 99, 106, 204
president, 90
pressure, 5, 140, 178
prevention, 204
price deflator, 19
price index, 14, 19
prices, ix, x, 4, 5, 8, 13, 14, 17, 24, 27, 39, 60, 68, 70, 78, 105, 111, 113, 114, 117, 118, 119, 121, 122, 127, 128, 129, 132, 133, 134, 135, 136, 138, 142, 144, 147, 149, 167, 210, 213, 214, 215, 216, 225, 231
priorities, 190
private, 79, 117, 148, 173, 175, 176, 181, 183, 186
private banks, 173, 181
private sector, 186
probability, 45, 46, 99, 101, 102, 152, 153, 173, 181, 195, 217, 226, 240, 245
probability density function, 217, 226
probit models, 44, 45
process control, 196
producers, 204
production, viii, x, 11, 14, 17, 19, 25, 28, 35, 37, 45, 57, 58, 59, 60, 61, 62, 71, 189, 190, 193, 194, 195, 196, 199, 200, 201, 205, 206, 207, 209, 210, 211, 212, 215, 218
production function, 60
productivity, 68, 210, 211
profit, viii, 57, 60, 96, 198, 201, 204, 206, 209, 210, 217, 218, 219, 220, 221, 225
profitability, 70, 201

profits, 220
program, x, 194, 213, 214, 215, 216, 217, 218, 219, 220, 221, 222, 223, 224, 225, 226, 228
promote, 199, 204
proposition, 218, 219, 221, 222
prototype, 204
proxy, vii, ix, 6, 58, 59, 139, 148
prudence, 221, 222
public, 21, 36, 214
punishment, 114

## Q

Quebec, 57

## R

random, 9, 37, 43, 58, 60, 62, 71, 72, 101, 105, 214, 215, 216, 217, 218, 220, 221, 223, 224, 225, 245, 247
random walk, 37, 43, 60, 214, 215, 216, 220, 225
randomness, 101
range, 7, 10, 24, 66, 123, 127, 128, 130, 141, 146, 147, 149, 240, 241, 242, 243, 244, 246, 247
rate of return, 78, 98
rational expectations, 36
raw material, 195, 200, 201, 205, 206, 209
raw material purchases, 205
raw materials, 195, 200, 201, 209
Reagan Administration, 91
real estate, 61
real time, 177, 190, 192, 197
reality, 80
reasoning, 190, 211
recall, 104, 105
recession, 36, 37, 42, 44, 45, 46, 47, 49, 70
recessions, viii, 35, 36, 39, 40, 44, 45, 46, 47, 48, 49, 69, 79
reciprocity, 114
recognition, 96
reconcile, 167
recovery, 90
reduction, ix, 70, 111, 117, 133, 134, 136, 170, 171, 172, 173, 175, 211
regional, 69
regression, viii, 9, 35, 39, 41, 44, 45, 46, 49, 60, 79, 80, 83, 85, 90, 105, 141, 149, 150, 151, 153, 154, 155, 158, 159, 237, 238, 241, 242, 243, 247
regression analysis, viii, 35, 80, 141, 149
regression equation, 49, 79
regression method, 149
regressions, 6, 7, 40, 42, 45, 79, 154, 158
regular, 142
regulation, 40, 70, 96
regulations, 71
regulators, 112, 113, 114
rejection, 23, 129

relationship, vii, ix, 3, 5, 6, 7, 10, 11, 15, 16, 25, 26, 28, 36, 37, 38, 39, 40, 41, 42, 43, 44, 46, 48, 63, 90, 91, 111, 114, 117, 119, 134, 136, 147, 159, 171, 175, 178, 179
relationships, ix, 4, 5, 49, 72, 111, 114, 136, 246
relevance, x, 169, 170, 171, 177
reliability, 210
reputation, 142
research, viii, 7, 35, 40, 41, 77, 78, 79, 80, 85, 91, 139, 142, 151, 171, 177, 178, 181, 212
researchers, 20, 29, 42, 58, 65, 140
reserves, 4, 8, 10, 11, 12, 14, 15, 16, 19, 20, 21, 22, 23, 25, 26, 27, 28, 29, 101, 171, 173, 176, 182, 185
residuals, 60, 134
resolution, 128, 184
resources, 60, 69, 196, 201, 203, 206, 209, 211
responsiveness, 6
returns, 79, 149, 166, 167, 211
risk, vii, viii, ix, x, 69, 95, 96, 97, 98, 99, 100, 101, 104, 105, 110, 119, 144, 167, 170, 171, 172, 173, 174, 175, 176, 177, 178, 179, 180, 182, 183, 184, 185, 187, 190, 195, 197, 213, 214, 215, 216, 217, 218, 219, 220, 221, 222, 223, 224, 225, 227, 228, 229, 230, 231, 232
risk aversion, 173, 217, 219, 220, 221, 222, 223, 224, 228, 229, 230, 231
risk factors, 110
risk management, 170, 180, 213, 217, 231, 232
risk sharing, 219
risks, 71, 96, 148, 171, 175, 176, 177, 183, 184, 185, 186, 187, 232
risk-taking, 69, 174
robustness, 12, 27, 141, 175, 207
rolling, 42, 190, 195, 197, 199
routines, 175
routing, 153, 158

## S

safety, 206, 210
sales, 196, 200, 201, 202, 203, 205, 206
sample, viii, ix, 10, 12, 13, 15, 16, 20, 24, 25, 27, 46, 48, 64, 71, 77, 81, 85, 91, 116, 118, 121, 122, 131, 139, 141, 142, 143, 148, 149, 153, 155, 156, 158, 159, 164, 165, 201, 239
sample mean, 141, 164
satisfaction, 211
savings, ix, 70, 111, 136, 179, 183
scalar, 216, 245
scale economies, 63, 72
scheduling, 190, 191, 196, 198, 199, 200, 209, 211, 212
search, 8, 36, 195
searches, 175
searching, 195
Second World, 68
Second World War, 68

securities, 35, 39, 40, 45, 143, 145, 148, 151, 165, 167, 191, 192, 200, 202, 206
Securities and Exchange Commission, 167
security, vii, 92, 142, 147, 148, 151, 152
selecting, 20
Self, 161, 162
sensitivity, ix, 92, 96, 97, 100, 105, 111, 119, 132, 134, 135, 136, 148
separation, 215, 218
series, viii, xi, 13, 27, 60, 77, 80, 81, 82, 84, 91, 92, 106, 140, 178, 187, 214, 235, 236, 237, 239, 240, 244, 245, 246, 247
services, 59, 70, 190, 206, 210
settlements, 170, 214
severity, 214, 215, 216, 222
shape, 183
shaping, 214
shareholders, 203
shares, 140, 142, 143, 145, 146, 147, 148
sharing, 179, 180, 215, 219
shock, 4, 5, 6, 9, 10, 14, 15, 16, 17, 22, 23, 24, 25, 26, 27, 28, 37, 78, 174, 178, 183, 235
shocks, vii, 3, 4, 5, 8, 9, 10, 11, 12, 14, 16, 21, 22, 23, 24, 25, 26, 27, 37, 43, 91, 174, 236
short period, 70
short run, 5, 23, 237
short-term, viii, 7, 32, 33, 35, 36, 37, 38, 40, 41, 42, 43, 46, 49, 77, 78, 80, 81, 85, 90, 92, 200, 212, 231
short-term interest rate, viii, 35, 36, 37, 40, 41, 42, 43, 46, 49, 77, 78, 80, 85, 90
SIC, 165
sign, 49, 80, 99
signals, 15, 48
significance level, 134, 244
signs, 44, 90, 119
silver, 128
simulation, x, 46, 179, 184, 186, 187, 189
simulations, 178, 182
Singapore, 114, 138
sites, 199, 205, 208
small banks, 181
SMEs, 196, 211
smoothing, 23, 37, 43
smoothness, 184
social order, 190
software, 190, 204, 209, 210, 211
solutions, x, 189, 190, 191, 200, 210
solvency, 96, 110, 176
solvent, 214
Southampton, 111
Soviet Union, 81, 90
Spain, 169, 235
spectrum, 8, 44, 239, 245
speculation, 231
speculative motive, 216
speed, 17, 105, 143, 144, 145, 147, 172, 175
SPF, 48
St. Louis, 29, 31, 32, 33, 52, 55, 82, 240

stability, 23, 40, 43, 78, 178
stabilization, 23
stabilize, 21
standard deviation, 118, 119, 123, 132, 133, 134, 135, 149
standard error, 121
standards, 37, 96, 110, 142, 167
statistics, 64, 72, 106, 132, 143, 144, 145, 146, 245
STD, 64
steel, 65, 74
steel industry, 65, 74
stochastic, ix, 17, 37, 38, 71, 72, 74, 95, 97, 101, 104, 105, 109, 219, 229, 246
stock, x, 6, 8, 9, 11, 22, 24, 40, 45, 82, 114, 115, 128, 136, 137, 140, 142, 143, 147, 148, 151, 152, 158, 165, 166, 167, 191, 192, 206, 210, 213, 215, 222, 225
stock exchange, 137, 140
stock markets, 140
stock price, 40, 45
storage, 209, 231
strategic, 179, 197, 199, 204, 211
strategic planning, 197
strategies, 48, 153, 213, 214
strength, 6
stress, 170, 176, 177, 179, 180, 182, 183, 184, 211
structural changes, viii, 35, 49
students, 83
subjective, 204
substitution, 63
superiority, ix, 139, 141, 164
suppliers, 200, 210
supply, x, 4, 6, 9, 10, 11, 14, 15, 16, 24, 25, 26, 79, 80, 114, 189, 190, 193, 195, 196, 198, 203, 206, 211, 212
supply chain, x, 189, 190, 193, 196, 198, 203, 206, 211, 212
supply shock, 9, 10, 11, 15, 16, 24, 25
surplus, 79
survival, 100, 105
surviving, 99
survivors, 98, 99
sustainability, 204
Sweden, 37
Switzerland, 231
symbols, 98, 146, 165
symmetry, 61, 62
systemic risk, 170, 173, 176, 178, 180, 183, 187
systems, vii, ix, x, 12, 20, 25, 27, 29, 111, 112, 113, 114, 119, 124, 129, 133, 134, 136, 137, 138, 169, 170, 171, 172, 173, 174, 175, 176, 177, 178, 179, 180, 181, 182, 183, 184, 185, 186, 187, 189, 190, 191, 197, 209, 210, 211

# T

targets, 21, 22, 42
tariff, 172

# Index

tax policy, 197
taxes, 4, 23, 200, 206, 217
technical change, 63
technological progress, 58
technology, 58, 65, 70, 71, 114, 138, 174, 175, 184, 205, 206
temporal, 24, 59
term plans, 197
test statistic, 132, 239, 244
Texas, 70
The Economist, 70, 74
theory, vii, 3, 4, 5, 6, 8, 36, 110, 114, 144, 167, 190, 195, 210, 221, 231, 232
threat, 181
threshold, 43, 44, 49, 219, 220, 223, 224, 226, 227, 229
threshold level, 219
thresholds, 44
ticks, 119, 129, 130
tides, 167
time, viii, 4, 5, 12, 17, 20, 22, 23, 25, 35, 39, 40, 41, 42, 44, 49, 57, 58, 59, 60, 62, 63, 65, 66, 67, 68, 70, 71, 72, 77, 78, 81, 84, 91, 96, 97, 101, 102, 103, 105, 106, 115, 116, 117, 130, 132, 133, 140, 142, 143, 144, 146, 147, 149, 170, 171, 173, 175, 176, 178, 180, 181, 182, 183, 191, 192, 193, 195, 199, 200, 201, 204, 206, 210, 216, 237, 240, 244, 245, 246, 247
time periods, 12, 25, 39, 41, 66, 183
time series, viii, 77, 81, 84, 91, 106, 237, 240, 244, 245, 246, 247
timing, 44, 65, 174, 178, 179, 183
topology, 182
total costs, 60
total factor productivity, 68
trade, ix, 111, 112, 114, 116, 117, 118, 119, 121, 128, 129, 130, 131, 132, 133, 136, 137, 139, 140, 142, 144, 147, 148, 152, 216
trade-off, 62, 118, 147, 174, 175, 176, 179, 180, 191, 212
trading, vii, ix, 4, 48, 101, 111, 112, 113, 114, 115, 116, 117, 118, 119, 120, 121, 122, 124, 127, 128, 129, 131, 132, 133, 134, 135, 136, 137, 138, 140, 143, 144, 147, 148, 151, 165, 166, 167
traditional model, 201
transaction costs, 112, 114
transactions, ix, 5, 69, 70, 111, 117, 118, 119, 133, 136, 178, 179, 200
transactions demand, 5
transfer, 82, 136, 176, 177
transformations, 13, 27
transition, vii, ix, 43, 111, 115, 136
transmission, 10, 17, 26, 138
transparency, 114, 138, 175
transparent, 113, 203, 210
transport, 199, 206, 210
transpose, 72
Treasury, 15, 19, 35, 39, 40, 45, 68, 80, 81

trend, 17, 58, 59, 67, 68, 69, 70, 82, 101, 105, 112, 114, 127, 140
trial, 194, 195
trial and error, 194
trust, 82, 174
trust fund, 82
turnover, 151, 159
two-way, 48

## U

U.S. economy, 68
U.S. Treasury, 39
Ukraine, 29
uncertainty, x, 96, 180, 197, 213, 214, 215, 216, 221, 223, 225, 231, 232, 245
unemployment, 19, 246
United Kingdom, 37, 38, 39, 40, 43, 45, 46, 47, 48, 51, 78, 84, 92, 111, 179, 238, 246
United States, viii, 31, 35, 38, 39, 40, 41, 42, 43, 45, 46, 52, 53, 55, 74, 77, 90, 92, 140, 142
univariate, 141, 142
updating, 60

## V

validation, 190
validity, 12, 38, 117, 134
values, 43, 44, 63, 66, 70, 85, 96, 97, 98, 100, 101, 102, 103, 106, 116, 117, 123, 127, 128, 129, 130, 131, 132, 133, 134, 135, 141, 158, 159, 179, 190, 216, 223, 224, 239, 240, 241, 242, 243, 244
VaR, 110
VAR models, 8, 12, 13, 15, 24, 25
VAR system, 12, 25
variability, 71, 97, 114, 134
variable, viii, ix, 10, 11, 16, 17, 20, 22, 25, 26, 28, 29, 40, 41, 42, 44, 45, 46, 49, 57, 58, 59, 79, 80, 82, 83, 85, 86, 90, 95, 97, 119, 135, 146, 147, 149, 150, 158, 159, 179, 195, 204, 206, 210, 235
variables, ix, 10, 11, 13, 15, 24, 25, 26, 27, 40, 41, 44, 45, 46, 47, 49, 64, 80, 83, 85, 90, 91, 97, 118, 119, 134, 139, 141, 143, 145, 146, 147, 149, 151, 152, 153, 158, 159, 164, 167, 195, 200, 202, 203, 205, 209, 216, 223, 224
variance, 8, 10, 11, 26, 60, 105, 173, 182, 247
variance-covariance matrix, 72
variation, 45, 46, 58, 106, 214
veal, 149
vector, ix, 10, 38, 45, 46, 60, 63, 71, 72, 104, 105, 139, 141, 149, 152, 164
vein, ix, 111, 112, 136, 171, 182, 183
Vietnam, 68, 91
Vietnam War, 68, 91
visible, 196
vision, 197

volatility, viii, ix, 21, 22, 23, 38, 43, 44, 57, 100, 111, 112, 113, 114, 116, 118, 119, 132, 133, 134, 135, 136, 138, 144, 147, 149, 151, 153, 236

## W

wages, 5, 24
Wales, 111
Wall Street Journal, 70, 75
warning systems, 190
watches, 10
weakness, 181
wealth, 82, 227, 230
web, 69, 196
welfare, 174, 176, 179
wholesale, 185
windows, 42, 210
wisdom, 49
World Bank, 185
World War, 38, 41, 42, 78
World War I, 38, 41, 42, 78
World War II, 38, 41, 78
worry, 175
Wyoming, 70

## Y

yield, 5, 13, 17, 27, 28, 36, 37, 38, 39, 40, 41, 42, 43, 44, 45, 46, 47, 48, 49, 77, 78, 79, 81, 87, 91, 92, 221, 226
yield curve, 36, 37, 38, 39, 42, 46, 47, 48, 49, 77, 78, 79, 91, 92